CU00687330

Veloce *Classic Reprint* Series

The *Daily Mirror* 1970

World Cup Rally

4

Other great books from Veloce –

Those Were The Days ... Series
Alpine Trials & Rallies 1910-1973 (Pfundner)
American 'Independent' Automakers – AMC to Willys 1945 to 1960 (Mort)
American Station Wagons – The Golden Era 1950-1975 (Mort)
American Trucks of the 1950s (Mort)
American Trucks of the 1960s (Mort)
American Woodies 1928-1953 (Mort)
Anglo-American Cars from the 1930s to the 1970s (Mort)
Austerity Motoring (Bobbitt)
Austins, The last real (Peck)
Brighton National Speed Trials (Gardiner)
British and European Trucks of the 1970s (Peck)
British Drag Racing – The early years (Pettitt)
British Lorries of the 1950s (Bobbitt)
British Lorries of the 1960s (Bobbitt)
British Touring Car Racing (Collins)
British Police Cars (Walker)
British Woodies (Peck)
Café Racer Phenomenon, The (Walker)
Don Hayter's MGB Story – The birth of the MGB in MG's Abingdon Design & Development Office (Hayter)
Drag Bike Racing in Britain – From the mid '60s to the mid '80s (Lee)
Dune Buggy Phenomenon, The (Hale)
Dune Buggy Phenomenon Volume 2, The (Hale)
Endurance Racing at Silverstone in the 1970s & 1980s (Parker)
Hot Rod & Stock Car Racing in Britain in the 1980s (Neil)
Last Real Austins 1946-1959, The (Peck)
Mercedes-Benz Trucks (Peck)
MG's Abingdon Factory (Moylan)
Motor Racing at Brands Hatch in the Seventies (Parker)
Motor Racing at Brands Hatch in the Eighties (Parker)
Motor Racing at Crystal Palace (Collins)
Motor Racing at Goodwood in the Sixties (Gardiner)
Motor Racing at Nassau in the 1950s & 1960s (O'Neil)
Motor Racing at Oulton Park in the 1960s (McFadyen)
Motor Racing at Oulton Park in the 1970s (McFadyen)
Motor Racing at Thruxton in the 1970s (Grant-Braham)
Motor Racing at Thruxton in the 1980s (Grant-Braham)
Superprix – The Story of Birmingham Motor Race (Page & Collins)
Three Wheelers (Bobbitt)

Great Cars
Austin-Healey – A celebration of the fabulous 'Big' Healey (Piggott)
Jaguar E-type (Thorley)
Jaguar Mark 1 & 2 (Thorley)
Triumph TR – TR2 to 6: The last of the traditional sports cars (Piggott)

Auto-Graphics Series
Fiat-based Abarths (Sparrow)
Jaguar MKI & II Saloons (Sparrow)
Lambretta Li Series Scooters (Sparrow)

Rally Giants Series
Audi Quattro (Robson)
Austin Healey 100-6 & 3000 (Robson)
Fiat 131 Abarth (Robson)
Ford Escort MkI (Robson)
Ford Escort RS Cosworth & World Rally Car (Robson)
Ford Escort RS1800 (Robson)
Lancia Delta 4WD/Integrale (Robson)
Lancia Stratos (Robson)
Mini Cooper/Mini Cooper S (Robson)
Peugeot 205 T16 (Robson)
Saab 96 & V4 (Robson)
Subaru Impreza (Robson)
Toyota Celica GT4 (Robson)

WSC Giants
Audi R8 (Wagstaff)
Ferrari 312P & 312PB (Collins & McDonough)
Gulf-Mirage 1967 to 1982 (McDonough)
Matra Sports Cars – MS620, 630, 650, 660 & 670 – 1966 to 1974 (McDonough)

Biographies
A Chequered Life – Graham Warner and the Chequered Flag (Hesletine)
A Life Awheel – The 'auto' biography of W de Forte (Skelton)
Amédée Gordini ... a true racing legend (Smith)
André Lefebvre, and the cars he created at Voisin and Citroën (Beck)
Chris Carter at Large – Stories from a lifetime in motorcycle racing (Carter & Skelton)
Cliff Allison, The Official Biography of – From the Fells to Ferrari (Gauld)
Edward Turner – The Man Behind the Motorcycles (Clew)
Driven by Desire – The Desiré Wilson Story
First Principles – The Official Biography of Keith Duckworth (Burr)
Inspired to Design – F1 cars, Indycars & racing tyres: the autobiography of Nigel Bennett (Bennett)
Jack Sears, The Official Biography of – Gentleman Jack (Gauld)
Jim Redman – 6 Times World Motorcycle Champion: The Autobiography (Redman)
John Chatham – 'Mr Big Healey' – The Official Biography (Burr)
The Lee Noble Story (Wilkins)
Mason's Motoring Mayhem – Tony Mason's hectic life in motorsport and television (Mason)
Raymond Mays' Magnificent Obsession (Apps)
Pat Moss Carlsson Story, The – Harnessing Horsepower (Turner)
'Sox' – Gary Hocking – the forgotten World Motorcycle Champion (Hughes)
Tony Robinson – The biography of a race mechanic (Wagstaff)
Virgil Exner – Visioneer: The Official Biography of Virgil M Exner Designer Extraordinaire (Grist)

General
1½-litre GP Racing 1961-1965 (Whitelock)
AC Two-litre Saloons & Buckland Sportscars (Archibald)
Alfa Romeo 155/156/147 Competition Touring Cars (Collins)
Alfa Romeo Giulia Coupé GT & GTA (Tipler)
Alfa Romeo Montreal – The dream car that came true (Taylor)
Alfa Romeo Montreal – The Essential Companion (Classic Reprint of 500 copies) (Taylor)
Alfa Tipo 33 (McDonough & Collins)
Alpine & Renault – The Development of the Revolutionary Turbo F1 Car 1968 to 1979 (Smith)
Alpine & Renault – The Sports Prototypes 1963 to 1969 (Smith)
Alpine & Renault – The Sports Prototypes 1973 to 1978 (Smith)
An Incredible Journey (Falls & Reisch)
Anatomy of the Classic Mini (Huthert & Ely)
Anatomy of the Works Minis (Moylan)
Armstrong-Siddeley (Smith)
Art Deco and British Car Design (Down)
Autodrome (Collins & Ireland)
Automotive A-Z, Lane's Dictionary of Automotive Terms (Lane)
Automotive Mascots (Kay & Springate)
Bahamas Speed Weeks, The (O'Neil)
Bentley Continental, Corniche and Azure (Bennett)
Bentley MkVI, Rolls-Royce Silver Wraith, Dawn & Cloud/Bentley R & S-Series (Nutland)
Bluebird CN7 (Stevens)
BMC Competitions Department Secrets (Turner, Chambers & Browning)
BMW 5-Series (Cranswick)
BMW Z-Cars (Taylor)
BMW Boxer Twins 1970-1995 Bible, The (Falloon)
BMW Cafe Racers (Cloesen)
BMW Classic 5 Series 1972 to 2003 (Cranswick)
BMW Custom Motorcycles – Choppers, Cruisers, Bobbers, Trikes & Quads (Cloesen)
BMW – The Power of M (Vivian)
Bonjour – Is this Italy? (Turner)
British 250cc Racing Motorcycles (Pereira)
British at Indianapolis, The (Wagstaff)
British Café Racers (Cloesen)
British Cars, The Complete Catalogue of, 1895-1975 (Culshaw & Horrobin)
British Custom Motorcycles – The Brit Chop – choppers, cruisers, bobbers & trikes (Cloesen)
BRM – A Mechanic's Tale (Salmon)
BRM V16 (Ludvigsen)
BSA Bantam Bible, The (Henshaw)
BSA Motorcycles – the final evolution (Jones)
Bugatti – The 8-cylinder Touring Cars 1920-34 (Price & Arbey)
Bugatti Type 40 (Price)
Bugatti 46/50 Updated Edition (Price & Arbey)
Bugatti T44 & T49 (Price & Arbey)
Bugatti 57 2nd Edition (Price)
Bugatti Type 57 Grand Prix – A Celebration (Tomlinson)
Caravan, Improve & Modify Your (Porter)
Caravans, The Illustrated History 1919-1959 (Jenkinson)
Caravans, The Illustrated History From 1960 (Jenkinson)
Carrera Panamericana, La (Tipler)
Car-tastrophes – 80 automotive atrocities from the past 20 years (Honest John, Fowler)
Chrysler 300 – America's Most Powerful Car 2nd Edition (Ackerson)
Chrysler PT Cruiser (Ackerson)
Citroën DS (Bobbitt)
Classic British Car Electrical Systems (Astley)
Cobra – The Real Thing! (Legate)
Competition Car Aerodynamics 3rd Edition (McBeath)
Competition Car Composites A Practical Handbook (Revised 2nd Edition) (McBeath)
Concept Cars, How to illustrate and design – New 2nd Edition (Dewey)
Cortina – Ford's Bestseller (Robson)
Cosworth – The Search for Power (6th edition) (Robson)
Coventry Climax Racing Engines (Hammill)
Daily Mirror 1970 World Cup Rally 40, The (Robson)
Daimler SP250 New Edition (Long)
Datsun Fairlady Roadster to 280ZX – The Z-Car Story (Long)
Dino – The V6 Ferrari (Long)
Dodge Challenger & Plymouth Barracuda (Grist)
Dodge Charger – Enduring Thunder (Ackerson)
Dodge Dynamite! (Grist)
Dorset from the Sea – The Jurassic Coast from Lyme Regis to Old Harry Rocks photographed from its best viewpoint (also Souvenir Edition) (Belasco)
Draw & Paint Cars – How to (Gardiner)
Drive on the Wild Side, A – 20 Extreme Driving Adventures From Around the World (Weaver)
Ducati 750 Bible, The (Falloon)
Ducati 750 SS 'round-case' 1974, The Book of the (Falloon)
Ducati 860, 900 and Mille Bible, The (Falloon)
Ducati Monster Bible (New Updated & Revised Edition), The (Falloon)
Ducati Story, The - 6th Edition (Falloon)
Ducati 916 (updated edition) (Falloon)
Dune Buggy, Building A – The Essential Manual (Shakespeare)
Dune Buggy Files (Hale)
Dune Buggy Handbook (Hale)
East German Motor Vehicles in Pictures (Suhr/Weinreich)
Fast Ladies – Female Racing Drivers 1888 to 1970 (Bouzanquet)
Fate of the Sleeping Beauties, The (op de Weegh/Hottendorff/op de Weegh)
Ferrari 288 GTO, The Book of the (Sackey)
Ferrari 333 SP (O'Neil)
Fiat & Abarth 124 Spider & Coupé (Tipler)
Fiat & Abarth 500 & 600 – 2nd Edition (Bobbitt)
Fiats, Great Small (Ward)
Fine Art of the Motorcycle Engine, The (Peirce)
Ford Cleveland 335-Series V8 engine 1970 to 1982 – The Essential Source Book (Hammill)
Ford F100/F150 Pick-up 1948-1996 (Ackerson)
Ford F150 Pick-up 1997-2005 (Ackerson)
Ford Focus WRC (Robson)
Ford GT – Then, and Now (Streather)
Ford GT40 (Legate)
Ford Midsize Muscle – Fairlane, Torino & Ranchero (Cranswick)
Ford Model Y (Roberts)
Ford Small Block V8 Racing Engines 1962-1970 – The Essential Source Book (Hammill)
Ford Thunderbird From 1954, The Book of the (Long)
Formula One - The Real Score? (Harvey)
Formula 5000 Motor Racing, Back then ... and back now (Lawson)
Forza Minardi! (Vigar)
France: the essential guide for car enthusiasts – 200 things for the car enthusiast to see and do (Parish)
From Crystal Palace to Red Square – A Hapless Biker's Road to Russia (Turner)
Funky Mopeds (Skelton)
Grand Prix Ferrari – The Years of Enzo Ferrari's Power, 1948-1980 (Pritchard)
Grand Prix Ford – DFV-powered Formula 1 Cars (Robson)
GT – The World's Best GT Cars 1953-73 (Dawson)
Hillclimbing & Sprinting – The Essential Manual (Short & Wilkinson)
Honda NSX (Long)
How to Restore & Improve Classic Car Suspension, Steering & Wheels (Parish, translator)
Immortal Austin Seven (Morgan)
Inside the Rolls-Royce & Bentley Styling Department – 1971 to 2001 (Hull)
Intermeccanica – The Story of the Prancing Bull (McCredie & Reisner)
Italian Cafe Racers (Cloesen)
Italian Custom Motorcycles (Cloesen)
Jaguar, The Rise of (Price)
Jaguar XJ 220 – The Inside Story (Moreton)
Jaguar XJ-S, The Book of the (Long)
Japanese Custom Motorcycles – The Nippon Chop – Chopper, Cruiser, Bobber, Trikes and Quads (Cloesen)
Jeep CJ (Ackerson)
Jeep Wrangler (Ackerson)
The Jowett Jupiter – The car that leaped to fame (Nankivell)
Karmann-Ghia Coupé & Convertible (Bobbitt)
Kawasaki Triples Bible, The (Walker)
Kawasaki Z1 Story, The (Sheehan)
Kris Meeke – Intercontinental Rally Challenge Champion (McBride)
Lamborghini Miura Bible, The (Sackey)
Lamborghini Urraco, The Book of the (Landsem)
Lambretta Bible, The (Davies)
Lancia 037 (Collins)
Lancia Delta HF Integrale (Blaettel & Wagner)
Lancia Delta Integrale (Collins)
Land Rover Series III Reborn (Porter)
Land Rover, The Half-ton Military (Cook)
Laverda Twins & Triples Bible 1968-1986 (Falloon)
Lea-Francis Story, The (Price)
Le Mans Panoramic (Ireland)
Lexus Story, The (Long)
Little book of microcars, the (Quellin)
Little book of smart, the – New Edition (Jackson)
Little book of trikes, the (Quellin)
Lola – The Illustrated History (1957-1977) (Starkey)
Lola – All the Sports Racing & Single-seater Racing Cars 1978-1997 (Starkey)
Lola T70 – The Racing History & Individual Chassis Record – 4th Edition (Starkey)
Lotus 18 Colin Chapman's U-turn (Whitelock)
Lotus 49 (Oliver)
Marketingmobiles, The Wonderful Wacky World of (Hale)
Maserati 250F In Focus (Pritchard)
Mazda MX-5/Miata 1.6 Enthusiast's Workshop Manual (Grainger & Shoemark)
Mazda MX-5/Miata 1.8 Enthusiast's Workshop Manual (Grainger & Shoemark)
Mazda MX-5 Miata, The book of the – The 'Mk1' NA-series 1988 to 1997 (Long)
Mazda MX-5 Miata Roadster (Long)
Mazda Rotary-engined Cars (Cranswick)
Maximum Mini (Booij)
Meet the English (Bowie)
Mercedes-Benz SL – R230 series 2001 to 2011 (Long)
Mercedes-Benz SL – W113-series 1963-1971 (Long)
Mercedes-Benz SL & SLC – 107-series 1971-1989 (Long)
Mercedes-Benz SLK – R170 series 1996-2004 (Long)
Mercedes-Benz SLK – R171 series 2004-2011 (Long)
Mercedes-Benz W123-series – All models 1976 to 1986 (Long)
Mercedes G-Wagen (Long)
MGA (Price Williams)
MGB & MGB GT– Expert Guide (Auto-doc Series) (Williams)
MGB Electrical Systems Updated & Revised Edition (Astley)
Micro Caravans (Jenkinson)
Micro Trucks (Mort)
Microcars at Large! (Quellin)
Mini Cooper – The Real Thing! (Tipler)
Mini Minor to Asia Minor (West)
Mitsubishi Lancer Evo, The Road Car & WRC Story (Long)
Montlhéry, The Story of the Paris Autodrome (Boddy)
Morgan Maverick (Lawrence)
Morgan 3 Wheeler – back to the future!, The (Dron)
Morris Minor, 60 Years on the Road (Newell)
Moto Guzzi Sport & Le Mans Bible, The (Falloon)
The Moto Guzzi Story - 3rd Edition (Falloon)
Motor Movies – The Posters! (Veysey)
Motor Racing – Reflections of a Lost Era (Carter)
Motor Racing – The Pursuit of Victory 1930-1962 (Carter)
Motor Racing – The Pursuit of Victory 1963-1972 (Wyatt/Sears)
Motor Racing Heroes – The Stories of 100 Greats (Newman)
Motorcycle Apprentice (Cakebread)
Motorcycle GP Racing in the 1960s (Pereira)
Motorcycle Road & Racing Chassis Designs (Noakes)
Motorcycling in the '50s (Clew)
Motorhomes, The Illustrated History (Jenkinson)
Motorsport In colour, 1950s (Wainwright)
MV Agusta Fours, The book of the classic (Falloon)
N.A.R.T. – A concise history of the North American Racing Team 1957 to 1983 (O'Neil)
Nissan 300ZX & 350Z – The Z-Car Story (Long)
Nissan GT-R Supercar: Born to race (Gorodji)
Northeast American Sports Car Races 1950-1959 (O'Neil)
Norton Commando Bible – All models 1968 to 1978 (Henshaw)
Nothing Runs – Misadventures in the Classic, Collectable & Exotic Car Biz (Slutsky)
Off-Road Giants! (Volume 1) – Heroes of 1960s Motorcycle Sport (Westlake)
Off-Road Giants! (Volume 2) – Heroes of 1960s Motorcycle Sport (Westlake)
Off-Road Giants! (volume 3) – Heroes of 1960s Motorcycle Sport (Westlake)
Pass the Theory and Practical Driving Tests (Gibson & Hoole)
Peking to Paris 2007 (Young)
Pontiac Firebird – New 3rd Edition (Cranswick)
Porsche 356 (2nd Edition) (Long)
Porsche 908 (Födisch, Neßhöver, Roßbach, Schwarz & Roßbach)
Porsche 911 Carrera – The Last of the Evolution (Corlett)
Porsche 911R, RS & RSR, 4th Edition (Starkey)
Porsche 911, The Book of the (Long)
Porsche 911 – The Definitive History 2004-2012 (Long)
Porsche – The Racing 914s (Smith)
Porsche 911SC 'Super Carrera' – The Essential Companion (Streather)
Porsche 914 & 914-6: The Definitive History of the Road & Competition Cars (Long)
Porsche 924 (Long)
The Porsche 924 Carreras – evolution to excellence (Smith)
Porsche 928 (Long)
Porsche 944 (Long)
Porsche 964, 993 & 996 Data Plate Code Breaker (Streather)
Porsche 993 'King Of Porsche' – The Essential Companion (Streather)
Porsche 996 'Supreme Porsche' – The Essential Companion (Streather)
Porsche 997 2004-2012 – Porsche Excellence (Streather)
Porsche Boxster – The 986 series 1996-2004 (Long)
Porsche Boxster & Cayman – The 987 series (2004-2013) (Long)
Porsche Racing Cars – 1953 to 1975 (Long)
Porsche Racing Cars – 1976 to 2005 (Long)
Porsche – The Rally Story (Meredith)
Porsche: Three Generations of Genius (Meredith)
Powered by Porsche (Smith)
Preston Tucker & Others (Linde)
RAC Rally Action! (Gardiner)
Racing Colours – Motor Racing Compositions 1908-2009 (Newman)
Racing Line – British motorcycle racing in the golden age of the big single (Guntrip)
Rallye Sport Fords: The Inside Story (Moreton)
Renewable Energy Home Handbook, The (Porter)
Roads with a View – England's greatest views and how to find them by road (Corfield)
Rolls-Royce Silver Shadow/Bentley T Series Corniche & Camargue – Revised & Enlarged Edition (Bobbitt)
Rolls-Royce Silver Spirit, Silver Spur & Bentley Mulsanne 2nd Edition (Bobbitt)
Rootes Cars of the 50s, 60s & 70s – Hillman, Humber, Singer, Sunbeam & Talbot (Rowe)
Rover P4 (Bobbitt)
Runways & Racers (O'Neil)
Russian Motor Vehicles – Soviet Limousines 1930-2003 (Kelly)
Russian Motor Vehicles – The Czarist Period 1784 to 1917 (Kelly)
RX-7 – Mazda's Rotary Engine Sportscar (Updated & Revised New Edition) (Long)
Scooters & Microcars, The A-Z of Popular (Dan)
Scooter Lifestyle (Grainger)
Scooter Mania! – Recollections of the Isle of Man International Scooter Rally (Jackson)
Singer Story: Cars, Commercial Vehicles, Bicycles & Motorcycle (Atkinson)
Sleeping Beauties USA – abandoned classic cars & trucks (Marek)
SM – Citroën's Maserati-engined Supercar (Long & Claverol)
Speedway – Auto racing's ghost tracks (Collins & Ireland)
Sprite Caravans, The Story of (Jenkinson)
Standard Motor Company, The Book of the (Robson)
Steve Hole's Kit Car Cornucopia – Cars, Companies, Stories, Facts & Figures: the UK's kit car scene since 1949 (Hole)
Subaru Impreza: The Road Car And WRC Story (Long)
Supercar, How to Build your own (Thompson)
Tales from the Toolbox (Oliver)
Tatra – The Legacy of Hans Ledwinka, Updated & Enlarged Collector's Edition of 1500 copies (Margolius & Henry)
Taxi! The Story of the 'London' Taxicab (Bobbitt)
This Day in Automotive History (Corey)
To Boldly Go – twenty six vehicle designs that dared to be different (Hull)
Toleman Story, The (Hilton)
Toyota Celica & Supra, The Book of Toyota's Sports Coupés (Long)
Toyota MR2 Coupés & Spyders (Long)
Triumph & Standard Cars 1945 to 1984 (Warrington)
Triumph Bonneville Bible (59-83) (Henshaw)
Triumph Bonneville!, Save the – The inside story of the Meriden Workers' Co-op (Rosamond)
Triumph Motorcycles & the Meriden Factory (Hancox)
Triumph Speed Twin & Thunderbird Bible (Woolridge)
Triumph Tiger Cub Bible (Estall)
Triumph Trophy Bible (Woolridge)
Triumph TR6 (Kimberley)
TT Talking – The TT's most exciting era – As seen by Manx Radio TT's lead commentator 2004-2012 (Lambert)
Two Summers – The Mercedes-Benz W196R Racing Car (Ackerson)
TWR Story, The – Group A (Hughes & Scott)
Unraced (Collins)
Velocette Motorcycles – MSS to Thruxton – New Third Edition (Burris)
Vespa – The Story of a Cult Classic in Pictures (Uhlig)
Vincent Motorcycles: The Untold Story since 1946 (Guyony & Parker)
Volkswagen Bus Book, The (Bobbitt)
Volkswagen Bus or Van to Camper, How to Convert (Porter)
Volkswagens of the World (Glen)
VW Beetle Cabriolet – The full story of the convertible Beetle (Bobbitt)
VW Beetle – The Car of the 20th Century (Copping)
VW Bus – 40 Years of Splitties, Bays & Wedges (Copping)
VW Bus Book, The (Bobbitt)
VW Golf: Five Generations of Fun (Copping & Cservenka)
VW – The Air-cooled Era (Copping)
VW T5 Camper Conversion Manual (Porter)
VW Campers (Copping)
Volkswagen Type 3, The book of the – Concept, Design, International Production Models & Development (Glen)
Volvo Estate, The (Hollebone)
You & Your Jaguar XK8/XKR – Buying, Enjoying, Maintaining, Modifying – New Edition (Thorley)
Which Oil? – Choosing the right oils & greases for your antique, vintage, veteran, classic or collector car (Michell)
Wolseley Cars 1948 to 1975 (Rowe)
Works Minis, The Last (Purves & Brenchley)
Works Rally Mechanic (Moylan)

Veloce's other imprints:
Hubble & Hattie Belvedere

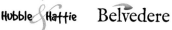

www.veloce.co.uk

First published in March 2010 by Veloce Publishing Limited, Veloce House, Parkway Farm Business Park, Middle Farm Way, Poundbury, Dorchester DT1 3AR, England. Fax 01305 250479 / e-mail info@veloce.co.uk / web www.veloce.co.uk or www.velocebooks.com. Reprinted September 2017. ISBN: 978-1-787112-28-5; UPC: 6-36847-01228-1.

© 2010 and 2017 Graham Robson and Veloce Publishing. All rights reserved. With the exception of quoting brief passages for the purpose of review, no part of this publication may be recorded, reproduced or transmitted by any means, including photocopying, without the written permission of Veloce Publishing Ltd. Throughout this book logos, model names and designations, etc, have been used for the purposes of identification, illustration and decoration. Such names are the property of the trademark holder as this is not an official publication. Readers with ideas for automotive books, or books on other transport or related hobby subjects, are invited to write to the editorial director of Veloce Publishing at the above address.

British Library Cataloguing in Publication Data – A catalogue record for this book is available from the British Library. Typesetting, design and page make-up all by Veloce Publishing Ltd on Apple Mac. Printed and bound by CPI Group (UK) Ltd, Croydon, CR0 4YY.

Veloce *Classic Reprint* Series

The *Daily Mirror*

World Cup Rally

40

THE WORLD'S TOUGHEST RALLY IN RETROSPECT

Graham Robson

VELOCE PUBLISHING
THE PUBLISHER OF FINE AUTOMOTIVE BOOKS

Contents

Introduction & acknowledgements

Sunday, 19 April 1970, Wembley Stadium, London. That date and that location deserve to be even more famous than they are today. It was the occasion when the world's most demanding rally got under way, and when all previous rallies were made to look second-rate. As will become clear as this book unfolds, I am totally fixated by the event which dominated my life in 1970, and has been unforgettable ever since.

To repeat the full and official title – the *Daily Mirror* World Cup Rally – here was the longest, the toughest, and the most ambitious rally that the world had ever known. Linking London to Mexico City, by way of Europe, South and Central America, this would occupy nearly six weeks, more than 16,000 miles (25,750km), 17 of the longest, fastest, highest and most demanding special stages ever laid out, and the promise of making every participant more tired, yet more exhilarated, more downcast and yet more satisfied, than any other event that they had ever tackled.

Since then, no other rally has ever come close to the aura and reputation surrounding this 'World Cup' – and probably never will. This wasn't the first ever transcontinental event, and eventually it wasn't even the longest of all – but no other motoring event has ever included so many big names, so many excellent cars, so much ultra-professional competition, and so many stupendous performances, achievements, and incidents.

Forty years on, make no mistake, we know that no modern organising body would ever allow such a tiring schedule to be set – during the 15 day South American section there were only four official overnight rest halts – and we doubt the 'official' average speeds set on some open-road sections in South America would ever again be nodded through by the authorities.

The miracle, too, was not merely that this event could be held at all, but that it could sweep aside such bureaucratic nightmares as Customs procedures and border delays without a second thought. Not only that (and we only discovered this after the event had passed through) but the mere idea of an international World Cup Rally crossing their borders had actually encouraged some nations to speak to their neighbours, and to appear friendly, in a way that was quite unlike their usual behaviour.

To my joy, I was invited to be a travelling controller on the original event, stayed with it from day one to the end, and came away convinced that I would never again experience such highs (and the occasional low!) again. Whenever I saw the sometimes laughable attempts which were made to replicate this wonderful challenge, I would smile secretly, sure in the knowledge that it was never going to be possible.

All of which explains why I wanted to write this book, as a 40th Anniversary homage to a unique event. I knew that a trawl through all the cuttings would not do it justice – so instead I approached many of the characters that made the World Cup so special.

Any researcher, I concluded, could perhaps dig up the bald facts of what, when, how fast and how many were involved between the two World Cup stadiums – Wembley at the start, and Mexico City's Aztec Stadium at the end, but I set out to visit and interview as many of the important personalities as would see me. Amazingly, only one or two refused to give me any of their time, and those who did were still enthusiastic about an event that had enthralled them so much.

This, then, is not merely a book about a rally, and much more than a passionless list of Prime (stage) times and finishing orders. It is a book which, I hope, reminds everyone of how the World Cup Rally came to be organised at all, why it was difficult to get established, why some of the professional drivers gave over much of their time in the months leading up to the start, and why there are new stories to be told even decades afterwards.

No logical business reason was ever needed for a team, a company or an individual driver to enter this World Cup. I recall some hero once being asked why he set out to climb Mount Everest. His response, quite simply was: "Because it's there ..."

For myself, and for many of the friends and colleagues involved in the running of the event, this book also brings back memories of unlikely events, which we may never experience again. Sharing the oxygen tube in the back of British Leyland's unpressurised Cessna with mechanic Brian

Moylan, for example; standing up to my ankles in warm storm water on the Panama Canal dockside; sitting in a hot car for more than 12 hours at the end of the Argentinian Prime, with no other building within 400 yards; linking arms with Prince Michael to hold back the crowds at the Fortin Control; being fed with ice cream through the chain-link fencing of the Santiago Parc Fermé while policing the action; watching Tony Fall's Escort arriving at a Control on three wheels and a brake disc; harassing a police motorcycle outrider in Buenos Aires, until he suddenly fell off; and being one of the stop-watch-clicking fanatics at the take-off of the overladen Boeing 707 in Lisbon ...

Acknowledgements

The only way to put together a big book like this, I decided, was to find and interview as many of the surviving personalities involved as possible. Not only that, I thought, but I should try to dig deep and source images that would illustrate a stunning story.

Unhappily, some of the characters who would surely have added spice to this story – Tony Ambrose, Peter Ashcroft, Bill Bengry, Jean Denton, Tony Fall, Henry Liddon, Donald Morley, Gilbert Staepelaere and René Trautmann among them – have left us, but I still found it fascinating to talk to many others.

John Sprinzel, the inspiration behind much of the event, not only provided me with hours of razor-sharp reminiscence of the event, but loaned me an invaluable pile of paperwork connected with the planning and running of the event. Without him, I am sure, it might not even have been worth starting on the task.

In recent months, too, I have been able to talk to all these personalities, who were pivotal in one way or another:

Rauno Aaltonen
Peter Browning
Brian Culcheth
Jim Gavin
Paddy Hopkirk
Rob Lyall
Tony Mason
Hannu Mikkola
Bill Price
Michael Scarlett
Stuart Turner
Patrick Vanson
Patrick Walker

– and in previous discussions and meetings, personalities as diverse as Bill Barnett, Gunnar Palm, HRH Prince Michael of Kent, Timo Makinen, Mike Broad, David Sutton, Dave Watkins, John Brown and Rosemary Smith all added to my knowledge of the event. I made sure that I was not just star gazing, either, for it was only by a miracle that some of the experiences quoted had a happy ending.

Mechanics and engineers, among them Bill Meade and Mick Jones of Ford, Den Green, Brian Moylan and Doug Watts of British Leyland, Des O'Dell (Team Manager) and Gerry Spencer (both of Rootes/Chrysler).

Images and research material came from a number of invaluable sources. Apart from those borrowed from personalities already mentioned, I would also like to mention Dave Hill of the Ford Photographic Archive, Reinhard Klein of McKlein, Bob Redhead, David Scribbs of Mirror Group Newspapers, Alan Zafer, Jon Pressnell, Jason Chinn, Julian Nowill, Dave Richards, Ted Taylor, and Mike Wood.

So, is this a complete and colourful record of the world's most famous rally? I sincerely hope so.

Graham Robson

Foreword

After many years of splendid work by my psychologist, I thought I'd finally got the World Cup Rally out of my system. But I reckoned without Graham Robson's obsession with the event, because along he comes with this book which rekindles so many memories of my own, and of Ford's involvement ... memories of the sheer scale of the event; of the debates over whether the cars should go 2 or 3 up; of whether oxygen or Diet Coke fed intravenously would be needed for the crews; of whether Jimmy Greaves should be playing football in Mexico rather than driving there; of ... well, of so many things, all of which gelled to make it not just the longest, but probably the greatest rally ever held.

Certainly the longest rally held – to put it into perspective, if you've got a calculator handy, add up the stage times of *all* the rounds in a modern World Rally Championship and you'll find that more than one individual stage, or Prime as they were called on the World Cup, was longer. It was so long that there was even some time for service crews to take a tourist trip to Lake Titicaca before the rally arrived. On the other hand, the crews didn't have the modern luxury of time-out for massages at regular intervals (at least none they told their team managers about).

The fact that the many people Graham has interviewed still clearly remember the event as if it were yesterday rather than 40 years ago, illustrates just what an impact the World Cup Rally made on people. It also makes for a totally absorbing book – a worthy addition to the many the author has written on the sport.

But enough. I still think I need to go and lie down in a darkened room.

Stuart Turner
Ex-Competitions Manager, Ford-of-Britain, later Director of
Motorsport, Ford-of-Europe

1

Why don't we ... ?

Although John Sprinzel gets much of the credit for running the World Cup, he freely admits that he did not invent it:

"Soon after the London-Sydney Marathon, it was Paddy Hopkirk and Wylton Dickson who were at a party somewhere early in 1969, and they dreamed up this crazy idea.

"The idea was: Why not unite football and motorsport? Because they were both astute business-minded people, they could see that the advertising spin-off could be enormous."

Although Paddy had finished second in his BMC (British Motor Corporation) 1800 on the London-Sydney Marathon – a close second to Andrew Cowan's Hillman Hunter – Wylton Dickson, who was an independent publicist, had no previous links with rallying.

Paddy recalls that it was in the first few weeks of 1969, at a party:

"My wife Jenny was working for a big advertising agency at that time, and we went to the boss' house in Chelsea for drinks one evening. Wylton Dickson was there, and I had just come back from the London-Sydney Marathon, and I met him for the very first time.

"He wanted to know what I did, so I told him I was a professional rally driver and he, I promise you, then said: 'What's a rally?' He knew nothing about motorsport at all, but on the other hand he was a very successful promoter of events and campaigns. By this time various clients had asked him what he could do, in connection with the World Cup.

"So I told him basically what rallying was all about, he suddenly said: 'Why don't I organise a World Cup Rally?', so I invited him to have another drink, and he promptly forgot all about it. At the time he was as uninformed about rallying as that. Shortly afterwards, though, he rang me about this, and I promptly passed him across to Stuart Turner!"

Dickson, who was Australian, was an archetypal promoter who frankly knew nothing about rallying when the original scheme was dreamed up, but who soon realised what an amazing escapade it could be – for competitors and for sponsors alike. He had a fantastic office in London, just round the corner from where Stirling Moss lived, and from the Hilton Hotel and the Playboy Club, and was a publicist and consummate wheeler/dealer/fixer. He immediately pricked up his ears at the idea of promoting such an escapade, and began making phone calls around the media industry. Sponsorship, and official support, were going to be all-important.

"It wasn't long," John recalls, "before he sold the idea to the *Daily Mirror*. I wasn't involved at all at that time – not for months, as it happened – but he and Paddy also got the RAC (Royal Automobile Club) Motorsport Division involved as well."

Why the *Daily Mirror*? Probably because it was all a matter of pride for one of Britain's largest daily newspapers to get involved. Not only was the *Mirror's* readership fanatically interested in football, but in 1968 the paper had been extremely jealous of the extensive coverage its major rival, the *Daily Express*, had gleaned from sponsorship of the London-Sydney Marathon. If it could get all that out of a pure motorsport event, the *Mirror's* management reasoned, think how much the *Mirror* could gain from a similar event which also had a football connection?

Why the World Cup?

A link with football's World Cup came purely by chance, but the fact that England had won the event as recently as 1966 must have been significant. The football World Cup is held every four years, the location and the choice of hosting nation being in the form of a gift from the sport's governing body FIFA (Fédération Internationale de Football Association). For 1970 this body had decreed that it would be held at various stadiums in Mexico, with the grand final in the Aztec Stadium in Mexico City in June.

For all the obvious publicity-related reasons, Wylton Dickson could see that an intercontinental World Cup Rally should reach its climax just before the football World Cup started – but not much in advance, so that the publicity links would always be obvious. If the route should happen to link historic stadiums – Wembley Stadium in London (where the World Cup final had taken place in 1966) was an obvious starting point, and the Aztec Stadium could host the finish – so much the better.

LONDON TO SYDNEY 1968 – FAR TOO EASY

It wasn't meant to be, of course, but the original Intercontinental Marathon of 1968 – London-Sydney, Australia by way of Bombay and a ship transit to Fremantle in Australia – was neither as rough, as tough, or as demanding as feared.

It seemed enormously long, at the time, but at 10,070 miles (16,206km) it would be totally overshadowed by the 16,000-plus mileage of the World Cup Rally which was to follow. Although there were no overnight halts at all – London-Bombay took 10 days, but Controls were widely spaced – many professional crews spent a lot of time in bed before having to clock in. Before Bombay, only two sections had impossible time schedules, which meant that the rally leader (Roger Clark – Ford Lotus-Cortina) lost only 11 minutes. No fewer than 72 rally cars made it on to the SS Chusan for the long sea trip.

Perth (just inland of Fremantle) to Sydney took four days, and was both faster and more gruelling, Roger Clark led until his Lotus-Cortina engine broke a valve, Bianchi's Citroën DS21 should then have won if it had not been hit by a non-competing Mini on the final morning, which meant that victory was handed over to Andrew Cowan's extremely reliable Hillman Hunter.

Overall, the Hunter lost just 50 minutes – 23 of those minutes in Australia – while even the sixth place man lost only 71 minutes. The rally timing was set to positively encourage stragglers to keep going, which explains why no fewer than 56 crews (of 98 starters) finally reached Sydney.

Rootes/Chrysler, who had not really expected to win, were quite unprepared for this famous victory, made little of it, and shortly closed down the department which had developed the car itself. Except for supplying specifications, and some pieces to the cars which competed in the World Cup, Chrysler took no part in the later event at all.

It was the relative failure of this event to be an exhausting, damaging, or even an ultimate motoring challenge, as forecast, which caused Paddy Hopkirk and Wylton Dickson to have their 'Why don't we ... ?' conversation a few months later.

The fact that for the very first time the football World Cup was to be held in Central America was wonderful happenstance – if the chosen route for an intercontinental rally ended up in Mexico, it could approach Central America through all the football-mad countries of South America, such as Brazil and Argentina. Think what an awful dilemma the rally promoters would have faced if the finish was in North America (where serious high-speed rallying was unknown), or elsewhere in Europe, which would have been far too close to London for such a major motorsport event ...

It was a once-in-a-generation opportunity, for which Hopkirk and Dickson should take all the credit. How unique? Consider the difficulties Dickson had in trying to repeat the dose in 1974, and the fact that no-one, but no-one, ever ran a serious World Cup Rally ever again.

Getting started

Even so, there was a long way to go. The 'big idea' was one thing, but making it all happen was quite another. Neither Paddy Hopkirk nor Wylton Dickson were themselves rally organisers, and even when they took the scheme to Dean Delamont, who was the manager of the RAC Competitions Department in London, they could rely on nothing but official support: neither money nor experienced personnel were available.

At this juncture, John Sprinzel had not yet become involved. Although he had been a top rally driver in the late 1950s/early 1960s, and had competed in the London-Sydney Marathon of 1968, he had virtually ceased to drive in rallies, and was actively involved in the motor trade, and hoped to build up a small chain of retail car-sales outlets. The approach, therefore, came as a real surprise:

"I had already heard of the World Cup proposal, but was not yet involved. Dean called me one day," John Sprinzel recalls, "and asked me if I could spare the time to go and check whether the proposed route was possible, this being a year ahead. The route was there, on paper, and I

guess they had thought about it, but no-one had actually been anywhere! No-one had been anywhere in South America, no-one had talked to any embassies, nothing. Had anyone canvassed the manufacturers to see if they would be interested? I have no idea."

The dates of this event were already almost settled – the cars had to reach Mexico City before the end of May 1970, because the football World Cup would be just about ready to begin. Having looked at the 'paper' route, Sprinzel then suggested that no-one could possibly be certain about the possibilities until the route had actually been surveyed on the ground, and was astonished to be asked to carry this out, all expenses paid, and cars provided.

"I thought I really needed to take someone along with me, a navigator for sure, so decided that this should be John Brown ..."

John was not only a well-respected rally navigator (he had already won the RAC Rally of 1961, alongside Erik Carlsson in a 'works' Saab 96), but his 'day job' was as a promotional and tourism officer in the Midlands. Like all such co-drivers, he tended to read and study maps as a pastime, too – so that combination of skills would obviously be useful in a complex trek around South and Central America.

Purely by chance, John had already been to Ford to talk about the possibilities of the event (originally as a potential competitor, for he was already wondering if a car could be made available), and had talked to its public affairs supremo, Walter Hayes. Realising that this event, if actually held, might be ideal for his company's products, Hayes had offered to help in any way possible, including loaning cars to carry out route surveys.

"The result was that we went along to the Brazilian embassy, decided to go over there, and we got a Ford-owned Willys Jeep on loan from Ford over there. Ford wouldn't let us drive the thing, it was big and black and luxuriously equipped, so they provided a chauffeur as well ..."

And that was how it all began ...

2

Preparation, organisation & practice

First impressions were not favourable. Even Sprinzel and Brown, both experienced in the rallying business, found it difficult to come to terms with the sheer scale of the challenge:

"We went over there, but we couldn't do much. Brazil, as you know, is huge. We managed to complete what became the Brazilian section, but the problem was that the chauffeur didn't want to go on the sort of roads we were after. It was a little bit fraught – but we managed to plan the route OK.

"Then we went to Argentina. That was much better, for they gave us a car – and I do mean that, they gave it to us, and it ended up somewhere in the Andes, quite un-driveable. When that happened, we just took off the number plates and the engine details, and posted them back to Ford-Argentina! That was a sort of early-1960s Falcon, a big car, years out of date, but Ford was still building it in that country.

"That's when we learned all about the altitude problem. When we were high up there, at about 16,000 feet (4877m), we had a puncture, got out of the car, and spent a lot of time just laughing about it! We couldn't do anything, because our brains weren't working too well up there.

"This, at this stage, was just myself, John Brown, and the *Daily Mirror* man – we were the rally at that point. Well, I still wasn't officially involved at that point, but because John Brown and I were old pros, we didn't just go for a drive round the continent. As we carried on, we planned the whole route, the special stages (we called them Primes, but that was later), where the Controls should be, we chatted to all the local motor clubs – so that when we came back we could supply the *Daily Mirror* with a complete rally package.

"John Brown and the *Mirror* man did the last bit, for I had to give in after Chile, where we were finding the road, such as it was, was blocked. The locals north of Santiago guaranteed that they would get bulldozers up there – would that be the Agua Negra pass, which was 15,650 feet (4770m) at the top?"

(Except for using the Pan-American Highway along the coast at this point, which was neither a 'rallying' road, nor demanding enough for Sprinzel's liking, there was really no alternative. The Agua Negra, incidentally, was basically a drover's road from Chile to Argentina on which herds of cattle would be driven, but it was a seasonally-open track, as the winters – and the altitude – were very severe.)

John even found time at this juncture to fly to Miami, to the Conference of the Americas, where he addressed all the chairmen of all the motor clubs in South America, for this was a speedy way of telling them all what was provisionally planned, and to make a plea for help:

"And I remember getting some real criticism from Paraguay and from Venezuela, for we were not planning on going there. Paraguay, well, it didn't quite fit in with what Brown and I wanted to do, but Venezuela, which is a very big country, wanted us to go there – and to take a ship from its Atlantic Coast to Panama. But that just didn't work. The only way we thought the timing would work was if we went down to the Pacific coast in Colombia, to Buenaventura."

It is worth noting that before the intrepid trio made their first trip to South America in April/May, no-one – no-one at all in the organisation – had driven any part of a proposed route.

The very first route existed only on paper – and in the mind of Wylton Dickson – so when John Sprinzel and John Brown settled down to study it carefully, all manner of changes had to be made. Even the original brochure, which was circulated in the spring of 1969, showed a fascinating mixture of 'Dickson' and Sprinzel' ideas.

Because Sprinzel was already beginning to see the potential of the World Cup as a rough, tough endurance event – the 'son of the Liège Marathon' – it was his original idea to send the European section through the city of Liège, and to turn it round in Sofia, where the classic Liège-Sofia-Liège events of the 1960s had all congregated.

Dickson the publicist would have loved to take the rally cars all the

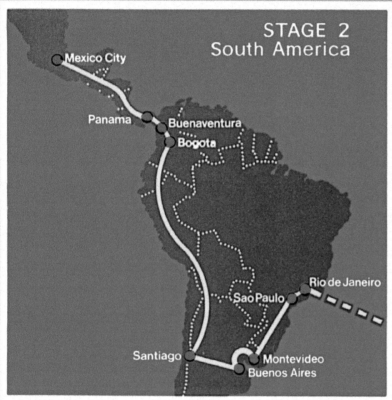

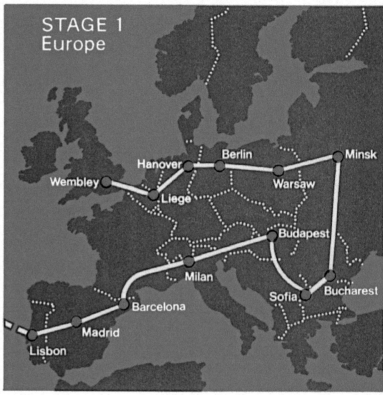

STAGE 2
South America

STAGE 1
Europe

This was the original brochure put together by Wylton Dickson, John Sprinzel, and the Daily Mirror publicists. Note that in the original scheme, the European section was meant to go as far east as Minsk, in the Soviet Union, while the South American section was planned to reach its climax at Bogota in Colombia.

way into the Soviet Union, at Minsk, before routeing them south through Bucharest to Sofia, then visiting Budapest on their way to Milan, and on to France, Spain and Portugal. Apart from the obvious reason for passing through Italy, France and Spain, one object, which 'ticked all the boxes' as far as the football-plus-rallying links were concerned, was that other countries like West Germany, Poland, the Soviet Union, Romania and Hungary could all be swept into the same exercise.

In South America, first ideas about the route were carried through almost without change, with a clockwise circuit of that vast continent starting from Rio de Janeiro in Brazil, and ending at the port of Buenaventura in Colombia. Unhappily, time constraints meant that Dickson's idea of visiting the national capital of Colombia, at Bogota, along the way (where England's football team was due to play a warm-up game in the same weekend that the rally might pass), had to be abandoned.

John Wilson, the *Daily Mirror* staff reporter who accompanied Sprinzel and Brown on much of their epic trip in South America, had this to say in the first brochure to be published:

With top rally drivers John Sprinzel, 38, and John Brown, 30, I have been blazing a trail through 15 South American countries.
Our mission:
To find the toughest roads in the world. We are confident that we have mapped out the most gruelling and spectacular rally ever.
It will be the longest, toughest and highest rally ever held. So high that drivers may have to carry oxygen.
The competitors will:

- *Drive through the vast upland ranches and coffee plantation country of Brazil – and over swaying wooden bridges above bubbling rapids.*
- *Speed at 100mph (160.9kph) over the endless straight dirt roads of the flat Argentine pampas.*
- *Fight their way over the incredibly rough, dusty roads in the Andes Mountains for hundreds of miles – at altitudes never before encountered on an international rally. Sometimes at up to three miles (4.8km) above sea level.*
- *Follow the legendary Inca roads beside Lake Titicaca, the world's highest navigable lake where Indian reed boats still ply the deep blue waters.*
- *Stream in vast dust clouds through desert terrain where colourful Indian folk live, and where only giant cacti grow.*
- *Press on over the Equator in Ecuador and on through Colombia, Panama and Central America en route to the Aztec Stadium in Mexico City.*

Sprinzel and Brown have so far driven me across thousands of miles planning the route.
Helped by friendly Gauchos – Argentine cowboys – we have struggled to push our car out of knee-deep mud on to the pampas.
We have splashed through mountain rivers and gasped for breath changing wheels in the thin air of high snow-covered mountain passes.
We have been stranded, panting for lack of oxygen, on a Chilean mountain road over two-and-a-half miles (4km) above sea level – and 60 miles (96.6km) from civilisation.
We have crept along a narrow mountain road so tiny and dangerous that only one-way traffic is allowed. We have had to swerve violently to miss llamas and goats which have raced into our path. And escaped injury as a speeding Peruvian cab-driver cannoned into us on a lonely road.
Everywhere, officials have been enthusiastic, and are promising every help.
In Argentina, a car club official said: "This will be the most tremendous car rally of all time. Only the adventurous English would think of anything like it ...

Unhappily, almost at once the route envisaged in the Dickson 'Master Plan' had to be simplified a little for, in political terms, it was too

HOW MANY COUNTRIES?

The World Cup Rally started from Wembley Stadium, in London, and ended at the Aztec Stadium in Mexico City. On the way the route led through these countries:

England
France
West Germany
Austria
Hungary
Yugoslavia (which is now split into several countries – the route therefore going through Serbia, Kosovo, Montenegro, Bosnia, Croatia and Slovenia ...)
Italy
France
Spain
Portugal

– then by sea, and on to:

Brazil
Uruguay
Argentina
Chile
Bolivia
Peru
Ecuador
Colombia

– then by a further sea voyage, and on to:

Panama
Costa Rica
Nicaragua
Honduras
El Salvador
Guatemala
Mexico

That made ten in Europe, eight in South America, and seven more in Central America. All this, and four water crossings too ...

ambitious. To run the original Eastern loop, through Berlin, Warsaw and Minsk, would have added two or three extra days to the schedule – and it was by no means certain that the cars could easily have been given access into and out of the Soviet Union. Initial approaches made through British embassies in various Eastern Bloc countries all produced stern resistance, and a series of refusals, so this was quickly abandoned.

13

SEA VOYAGES

Naturally, it was not possible to reach Mexico City from London without sending the cars on several sea trips.

DOVER-BOULOGNE

Since those were the days when the Channel Tunnel still only existed as a drawing in engineers' sketchbooks, and it would have taken a positive fleet of car-ferry aircraft to get all the competitors across the English Channel, the only way to get from England with France was by way of the Dover-Boulogne ferry. This crossing took a mere 1hr 30 minutes, gave crews time for a bit of lunch on the very first day of the event, and was then followed by the long drag for them, across West and Central Europe towards Sofia in Bulgaria.

LISBON TO RIO DE JANIERO

The entire shape of the event could not be settled until an economic way could be found to transport the rally cars across the South Atlantic. By the time that intercontinental classic rallies were reinvented in the 1990s, just two massive jet-powered Antonov freight planes could have done the job, but in 1970 there were no such alternatives.

Instead, the 71 surviving rally cars were stowed in the holds of the SS Derwent ship, and carried across to Brazil on one of its scheduled trips. The entire contingent – but no drivers, service crews, spares, or the organising team – was uplifted in one single voyage.

Could this have been achieved by a different route? Maybe, but the destination had to be to South America, of course, for any football connection would have disappeared under a cloud of indifference if North America had been chosen instead – and the attraction of sending a football-related event through soccer-mad nations like Brazil and Argentina was obvious.

Maybe, just, maybe, there had been momentary thoughts about routeing the event across the Straits of Gibraltar and down the western coast of Africa as far as – say – Dakar – but these were almost immediately abandoned.

The total sea voyage involved was 4220 nautical miles (approx 4800 statute miles), which means that the dear old Derwent was plodding along at about 15 knots (Nautical miles/hour) for day after day ...

COLONIA (URUGUAY) TO BUENOS AIRES

Although it would have been possible to make the connection from Montevideo (Uruguay) to Buenos Aires (Argentina) by road, it would have involved a long and tedious trip north-west to the first road bridge over the River Plate, then returning south-west towards Argentina's capital city. Oddly enough, this would have involved going through a provincial town in Uruguay called Mercedes, then through the town of Fray Bentos (whose corned beef trademark is no doubt familiar to millions).

Instead, it made more sense for the organisers to block book one of the regular ferries which plied their trade across the famous estuary – a journey which took no more than three hours, starting from Colonia (upriver from Montevideo), and which disgorged the rally cars into the vibrant maelstrom of Buenos Aires itself.

All the surviving rally cars were transported on the single ferry. Having left Montevideo in the morning, they could then restart the first of the Argentinian Primes in the evening.

[Forty years on, incidentally, there is now a modern hydrofoil service between the two terminals, which has cut the journey time to 50 minutes ...]

BUENAVENTURA (COLOMBIA) TO CRISTOBAL (PANAMA)

Routeing the World Cup Rally from South America into Central America was always going to be a nightmare, and to reach what was (and still is) called the Darien Gap, meant chartering space in a ship that could carry 'the rally' from Ecuador to Panama.

To do this, the organisers did a deal with the owners of the Italian Lines, to take over most of the space in the MS Verdi, which was a modern ship at the time (it had been launched as recently as 1963), on regular route across the corner of the Pacific Ocean and through the Panama Canal itself, to dock at the port of Cristobal (which was an offshoot of Colon).

For the organisers, when chartering space in the ship, the problem was that the Verdi could only carry 35 cars, but John Sprinzel's team were in luck, as only 26 cars made it that far, so there was also some space for a dozen or so of the recently-retired, 'walking wounded' or for any hangers-on who had made it to the quayside. As pictures show, the cars were all carried on deck, but since the weather was calm, and the journey short, none seem to have suffered the effect of salt winds.

The scheduled two-and-a-half day passage was completed absolutely to schedule, and the event restarted from the quayside at Cristobal.

The fourth and last sea voyage of the World Cup Rally involved a trip through the Panama Canal in the MS Verdi. As can be seen, the 26 rally cars were positioned on deck for this particular voyage.

One of the Triumph 2.5PIs being hoisted aboard the Derwent, prior to that ship setting off for Rio de Janeiro.

15

Even so, before any member of the organising team travelled into Europe to meet up with local motor clubs and officials, they were already expert enough, and familiar with, all the Primes which had been chosen. On one rally or another, Sprinzel himself had covered almost every mile of the route, on several occasions, and he remembers that Tony Ambrose later revisited Portugal to make sure it was still as hoped!

In any case, the schedule of the European section was constrained by the availability of Wembley Stadium, and by the unalterable schedule of cargo ships across the South Atlantic. Dickson and the *Daily Mirror* were determined to start the event on a Sunday, and the only available ship would leave Lisbon seven days later, at midnight on a Saturday.

Building a team

After John Sprinzel returned, he handed over all his findings to Dean Delamont at the Competitions Department of the RAC, told him it was going to be, at once, a great challenge, and great fun – and prepared to withdraw. His idea of actually competing over the route which he had devised was swiftly kicked into touch by the fair-minded Delamont.

THE LIST OF MAJOR OFFICIALS AND CONTROLLERS

John Sprinzel	(ex-international race/rally driver for BMC, Triumph, Ford – who was not only the king-pin, but visited every Main Control)

– aided by:

Tony Ambrose	(ex-international co-driver, for BMC)
Chris Belton	(RAC Competitions Department)
Mike Broad	(travel specialist by profession, later an international co-driver, later CEO of Irmscher UK)
John Brown	(co-driver of Erik Carlsson, to win 1961 RAC Rally)
Jim Gavin	(rally organiser in Britain, and widely travelled overseas)
Peter Harper	(RAC Rally winner 1958, long-time Rootes/Sunbeam driver)
Richard Harper	(British rallies, co-driver and organiser)
Eric Judge	(British rallying stalwart at this time)
'Tiny' Lewis	(ex-Triumph, then Rootes/Sunbeam, rally driver)
Tony Mason	(became Roger Clark's co-driver, including 1972 RAC Rally victory, then broadcaster and commentator)
Donald Morley	(a 'Morley Twin' rally driver – twice won the French Alpine Rallies)
Erle Morley	(the co-driving 'Morley twin')
Val Morley	(was Val Domleo, international co-driver, married Donald)
Logan Morrison	(international 'works' driver for BMC)
Mike Preston	(British Rally personality, and high official of the Morecambe Car Club)
Peter Riley	(international 'works' driver for BMC)
Graham Robson	(ex-international co-driver/Triumph team manager/later motoring historian – the author of this book)
Gerry Ryan	(one-time international co-driver)
David Seigle-Morris	(international 'works' driver for Triumph, BMC and Ford)
Mike Sutcliffe	(ex-works driver for Ford, then Triumph)
Dr John Teall	(established 'rally doctor', great rallying enthusiast)

– and not forgetting:

Dean Delamont	(Clerk of the Course, and supremo of the Competitions Department of the RAC in the UK)
Jack Sears	(distinguished race driver, motorsport administrator, who visited many countries, and embassies, in advance, to smooth over final commercial and diplomatic wrinkles)
John Lewsey	(one-time major organiser of Gulf London Rallies, and runner of the results nerve centre in the Daily Mirror offices in London)

Incidentally, it was Mike Broad who takes much of the credit for arranging the 'cat's cradle' of flights, hire car reservations, and hotel beds which kept all the organising team sane, in the right place, and not totally exhausted. Then, and in later years, Mike had the sort of boundless energy which saw him running where everyone else would walk – which explains why his rally nickname was 'Speedy' (for 'Speedy Gonzales').

Forty years on John Sprinzel (right) talked to the author about the World Cup Rally of 1970. His famous number plate – PMO200 – lives on in a classic Austin-Healey Sprite, at his home in Hawaii.

Organisers and competitors often got together – John Sprinzel, kingpin of the event, John Brown to his left, Gilbert Staepelaere (in rally jacket), and a tired-looking Colin Taylor (competing in the Saab).

Decisions, decisions – John Sprinzel announcing changes to the crews, while Dean Delamont looks placidly on.

One of the most critical points in the event came in Santiago, when the organising team heard of landslides and wintry blockages high in the Andes, which lay ahead. Left to right: John Sprinzel, Tony Ambrose and Dean Delamont.

At which point Dean, who had already been nominated as Clerk of the Course, then astonished Sprinzel by saying: "No, no – in fact we want you to run it for us!" This came as a pleasant shock, for John already had a business to run, so he resisted for a time in rather a coy, motor-trader's, manner:

"Tommy Atkins of the *Mirror* (it was his last job before he retired), and Dean then took me out to lunch at this rather fancy club in Belgrave Square, asked me once again if I would run it for them, to which my reply was: 'Well, maybe, but I want a new Porsche!' They kind of swallowed, looked hard at each other, and eventually said OK, at which point I also said: 'Oh, and by the way, I want First Class travel everywhere, because in South America there's going to be nowhere to sleep, except on aeroplanes, because we're going to have to be everywhere, and go everywhere. My wife [Pam – John's first wife] will be running the PR (public relations) side of the event, just as she does on the Safari, and she will want the same deal.'"

Even 40 years on John recalled with glee that the two men swallowed these demands with good grace, and that the only thing they really argued about was the kennelling of his two pet dogs ...

Then, as soon as the deal was done, John had to put some people together to build an organising team, because no infrastructure existed at all at that moment, and it was also clear that he could not rely, too much, on help from the various motor clubs in South America, particularly in terms of personnel to run every Control, every Prime, every border liaison, and every overnight halt.

There was also the question of setting up a 'Ground Base' in London for the entire six weeks of the event, where results would flow in, Prime times would be assembled, and where stories could be distributed to the world's media. These were the days, of course, when fax machines,

Months before the event, sometimes the official route was found to be impassable when survey cars arrived. This was a section in South America, where the bridge had, quite literally, fallen into the river.

SEVENTEEN PRIMES – THE LONGEST IN HISTORY

No fewer than 17 high-speed, flat-out, Primes were held in the 1970 World Cup. None of these were over closed roads. These are the astonishing statistics.

PRIME	NAME (COUNTRY)	LENGTH (MILES/KM)	TARGET AVERAGE SPEED (MPH)
Prime 1	Montenegro (Yugoslavia)	50/80.5	46.2
Prime 2	Serbian (Yugoslavia)	119/191.5	42.4
Prime 3	San Remo (Italy)	72/115.9	36.0
Prime 4	Alpine (France)	67/107.8	44.7
Prime 5	Portuguese (Portugal)	45/72.4	41.5
European subtotal		353/568.1	
Prime 6	Parana (Brazil)	125/201.2	83.3
Prime 7	Rio Grande (Brazil)	120/193.1	72.0
Prime 8	Uruguayan (Uruguay)	125/201.2	83.3
Prime 9	Pampas (Argentina)	200/321.9	57.1
Prime 10	Trans-Argentine (Argentina)	380/611.6	63.3
Prime 11	Chilean (Chile)	121/194.7	80.7
Prime 12	Gran Premio (Argentina)	510/820.8	63.8
Prime 13	Bolivian Coffee (Bolivia)	270/434.5	54.0
Prime 14	Incas (Peru)	560/901.2	50.9
Prime 15	Ecuador (Ecuador)	250/402.3	83.5
South American subtotal		2661/4282	
Prime 16	Costa Rica Coffee (Costa Rica)	220/354.1	88.0
Prime 17	Aztec (Mexico)	106/170.6	70.0
Central American subtotal		326/524.7	
Grand Total	3340/5375		

you don't believe me, ask Jim Gavin, who worked miracles in organising an aircraft to get him to Potosi in Bolivia, John Brown, who had to re-route the event in Chile after avalanches, and many more ..."

It was at this point that the two Johns, plus Dean Delamont, realised that if Sprinzel was going to spend so much of his time away from London – en route to embassies and even other countries ("I got to know all about the brand-new Boeing 747s, which were a great novelty in those days ..."), then there was a need for more bodies in the rally office, which became established in a basement office of the RAC Motorsport Division, in London's Belgrave Square. It was at this point, therefore, that Tony Ambrose (who had been Rauno Aaltonen's co-driver in the BMC Rally Team, and had to arrange for his own business to be managed in his absence) came on board, and effectively became secretary of the meeting.

("I think Dean actually employed Tony to keep a eye on John and I," Sprinzel chortled, "because we seemed to be far too enthusiastic about the whole thing, and Dean thought we needed to be kept in check. Fortunately, Tony was as enthusiastic as we were, and I don't think anything got toned down ...")

Setting up the schedule took time. On the one hand Sprinzel, a great lover of the Liège-Sofia-Liège philosophy (as arch-organiser Maurice Garot once said: "The ideal Liège would have just one finisher ...") was tempted to set impossibly demanding target times, especially on the Primes, with ruthlessly applied cut-off points for lateness, but the majority view was that it would be better for publicity purposes, and for the feeling of teams who were to spend a fortune on the event, if a fair proportion made it to the end.

Although open road average speed targets sometimes exceeded those of the legal speed limit in some nations, and the average speed target on some Primes looked quite insane when first studied (Prime no 6 in Brazil and Prime 8 in Uruguay were set at 83.3mph/134.1kph too), some of the roads proved to be astonishingly fast.

Although Sprinzel's team was not to know it until it actually arrived at some of the locations on the event itself, local authorities had apparently been ashamed of the condition of some of the unmade tracks chosen for the Primes, and had made haste to smooth out and re-grade them, at some expense, before the rally arrived. In Argentina, therefore, Prime 9 was completed without penalty ('cleaned') by no fewer than 19 crews, while 13 crews then went on to clean Prime 10. Nevertheless, before the event started, many competitors must have been startled to read that Primes might be: " ... between 100km (62.1miles) and 1000km (621.4 miles) in length"!

In the second half of 1969, when the organisation was still finding its feet, the proposed route gradually settled down, and Sprinzel now admits that both British Leyland – Brian Culcheth, Paddy Hopkirk and Andrew Cowan in particular – and Ford (Henry Liddon and Gunnar Palm), reported back with their findings about the practicality of the proposed route, and actually made some recommendations for change, which were accepted.

Brian Culcheth, in particular, emerges as the unsung (unknown, even) hero of this phase of the rally. In mid-1969, and along with Paddy Hopkirk, he was one of the only drivers still to have a motorsport contract with British Leyland. Not only did he have no family commitments at this time

the internet and e-mail had all yet to be invented, when transcontinental telephone calls could still be extremely expensive (and had to be booked hours in advance), and when the ubiquitous Telex (which was beloved by all journalists) was state-of-the-art as far as communications were concerned.

"Then I had to go out and get the best twenty or so British Rally personalities that I knew," Sprinzel recalled. "I had to persuade many such people [see the list in the panel on page 16], who would need to organise time away from work or their professions – reliable people who knew what international rallying was all about. I knew, full well, that there would be times when a controller would find him or herself many miles from anywhere, and would have to make changes and decisions on the hoof. If

Although snow was not expected in South America, the practice crews encountered plenty of it, especially at altitude.

(which gave him much spare time which was made available to the rally team), but he was probably the first rally driver to go into South America and begin a mile-by-mile survey of the proposed route.

Not only did those teams suggest changes to the time schedules – in most cases to tighten them up, so that penalties were sure to follow – but they also reported local gossip about the likelihood of some little used roads and tracks being blocked in May (usually because they were at high altitude, little used, and subject to snow drifting), when the rally was due to pass. In most cases (and this, of course, came to pass at least once, in Chile and Argentina) the possibility of alternative routes was also investigated – Sprinzel gives full credit to John Brown for this.

Maybe he should have expected it, but the truly professional teams – Ford and British Leyland in particular – committed big funds to the event at a very early stage, and started to organise very detailed route surveys, so that they would know exactly what they were meant to be doing at all times. In the early months, for sure, they probably knew more about the route than did the organising team – for the professionals already mentioned spent months in the vast continent of South America.

Eligibility

No sooner had planning begun than the team took a most important decision – that any four-wheeled vehicle which was road-legal would be allowed to compete. There would be no nonsense connected with homologation, which meant that manufacturers could pick and choose what they entered, and what they prepared. Endurance and high performance, therefore, took precedence over the FIA (Fédération Internationale de l'Automobile) Rule Book.

Crossing a piranha-infested river, South American style. There were many of these bridges in the undeveloped parts of South America.

When the regulations were issued, the organising team held nothing back. Entrants surely knew what sort of an event they were facing ...

Another innovation which not only worked well, but created a great deal of hilarity along the way, was that there was to be a 'Parc Fermé/ Service Park' system at major Controls, where the crews would be allowed a considerable amount of time to work on their cars, but mechanics would be strictly barred. Clearly this was meant to make it as easy for private owners to repair their battered machines, as the 'works' crews – and probably for the first time in history, it meant that there were sights of superstars getting their hands dirty.

Even so, crafty and experienced 'works' teams soon worked out how they could make this work – almost. The trick was that cars would be parked close to the barriers, or fences, specialist mechanics could position themselves close by, and advice could then be exchanged – tutorials, even, could be made – without any physical contact taking place. One of the most hilarious vignettes in the Ford film, *Five for the Fiesta*, shows work being done on Escorts behind chain-link fences in Santiago, with Boreham's ace mechanic Mick Jones and Competitions Manager Stuart Turner offering advice from the outside. In the meantime, the author, acting as a rally official, is seeing fair play – and at one point a relay of ice cream cones is passed through the wire mesh to keep everyone happy!

With all this in mind, Sprinzel and Brown were also very careful to write their regulations, rather like those of the Liège-Sofia-Liège – and took them to further extremes – so as to encourage 'specials' to turn up. The factories did not need to go over the horizon to build their best cars – Ford had Escorts with oversized and much-modified engines, British Leyland's Triumph had bodies made from exotic materials, and the Rootes/Chrysler Hunters all used Rapier H120 engines – for it was individuals who really made the headlines.

On what other rally, therefore, was one ever likely to see a 13-year-old Rolls-Royce Silver Cloud which had never before done a rally; an Escort converted to a motor caravan; a rare Trident Venturer sports coupé; a massive four-wheel-drive Jeep Wagoneer; a plastic-bodied VW-based Beach Buggy; a Rolls-Royce Silver Shadow; and a lengthened-wheelbase four-door Mini-Cooper S all taking part?

This very liberal approach to eligibility, therefore, gave serious manufacturers every chance to hone their chosen cars to a peak of performance, and both Ford and British Leyland put in thousands of hours in testing before they began the actual building of the rally cars themselves. Working backwards from the immutable start date of 19 April, it seems that physical building and preparation of their cars did not begin until January/February 1970 – though testing and reconnaissance began in the summer of 1969.

The European section – setting the tone

It would have been easy enough to route the World Cup cars more or less directly from London-Lisbon (this would actually be done when the event was re-enacted in 1995, by the moneyed classic rally car fraternity), but this would have been as boring as the London-Teheran section of the London-Sydney Marathon had been. Even though the original Dickson 'Master Plan' (to send the cars to Minsk) had been abandoned, and the cars would initially be channelled on main roads to Sofia, on the return

In the regulations, the words that succinctly defined eligibility were: "All four-wheeled passenger motor vehicles of any specification." In almost every way, therefore, this was a 'Run what you brung ...' type of challenge.

On the other hand, on the event the rules did not allow major repairs to be made. However, this was worded on the basis that major items like engines, transmissions and axles could be removed, their internals repaired, then reinstalled in the cars, but the casings had to be retained. Special radioactive markings were placed on these casings. Was this rule ever abused? Some competitors think it was ...

leg Sprinzel then intended to run at least one speed section in each of the traditional rally regions.

The original intention was to make the special stages (Sprinzel and Brown called them 'Primes' from a very early stage, an obeisance to the earlier Tour de France, so that is what I must now do ...) not only difficult but very long. Because of the remoteness of much of the countryside in South America, in general these could be made much longer than was usually possible in European events, and wherever possible Sprinzel hoped to set impossible-to-achieve target averages. However, to quote the imperturbable Sprinzel:

"We made Europe hard enough to get rid of the no-hopers, and holiday makers – especially those with unsuitable cars – and we reckoned that all those who reached South America would be up for a real challenge."

This was done, quite simply, to set a precedent – for no-one had ever before set special stages/Primes of such a length, and no-one would ever do so again. The Liège had already died away, the Safari never set special stages at all, and no-where else in the world was there the space to replicate such an exercise. This immediately made the World Cup hugely more demanding than the London-Sydney Marathon had ever been, for there had been no specially-timed stages of any nature on that event.

The 'real rally' – as almost everyone connected with the event was saying – would not start before the cars turned back from Sofia, after which five Primes were to be set, each of them paying homage to an already famous European rally. First there would be the 'Liège' Primes, where not one but two challenges would be run in the rough, tough and barely-civilised mountains of Yugoslavia. Next would be a Prime in the mountains behind San Remo in Northern Italy, fourth would be a serpentine but all-tarmac Prime close to the French Riviera which would use famous French Alpine Rally roads, and finally there would be a Prime close to Lisbon, just to remind everyone that the TAP Rally of Portugal was also an important event.

Sprinzel, who had enjoyed all the events already mentioned, wanted their organisers to know how much he appreciated their territory, and wanted the World Cup competitors to do the same. Thinking that he deserved, if not a holiday, then a trip down memory lane, he personally surveyed these Primes in a borrowed Triumph 2000. The time schedule planned would allow crews to build up quite a lot of time for rest (if, that is, their cars did not give trouble), and each Prime would normally be tackled in full daylight.

South America: politics, customs and soothing words

After the choice of restart point in South America had been made – the decision to use Rio de Janeiro was almost a no-brainer, on reflection – the political dramas then began.

At times, the prospect of getting an entire cavalcade of cars – not just one or two cars – but more than 70 at first – across borders, or getting into and out of countries, seemed almost insuperable. Not only did some nations

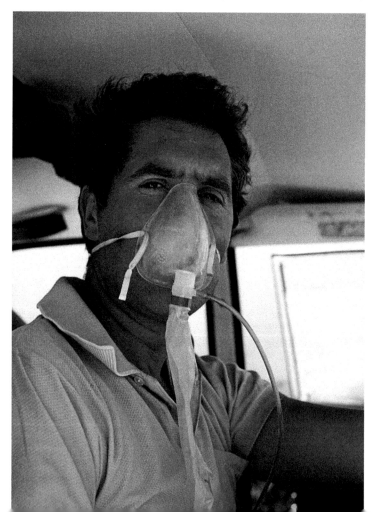

Brian Culcheth trying out the lightweight oxygen supply that was available to all British Leyland crews for the high altitude sections.

DIPLOMACY, AND CUTTING CORNERS
Early in the planning process, it became clear that getting more than 70 cars into Brazil, over the dockside in Rio de Janeiro, could be tricky. When John Sprinzel visited the Brazilian ambassador in London to plead for special facilities ("I need to get all the cars off the ship, and on to the road in Rio, within 48 hours"), the ambassador said that it was impossible – it would take at least a month to get his own car through all the Customs formalities – and he was an ambassador!

So the two Johns flew to Rio, saw the Minister of Transport, the Minister of Ports, the Minister of Labour and the Minister of Tourism, none of whom (for reasons of protocol) would speak to them personally, but sent secretaries, or attaches, to listen to the problems. On each occasion, it seemed, the secretary would eventually tell them how much all this was going to cost ... but the end result was that enough money changed hands for this to be made possible, the cars were unloaded from the SS Derwent in less than 24 hours, all under military guard.

TO TAKE OXYGEN – OR NOT?

No soon had the draft route for the World Cup Rally been published than participants began to worry about 'the oxygen problem'. Problem? Quite simply, in Argentina, Bolivia and Peru the route included the passage of several extremely high passes – at times up to 5000 metres (16,400ft).

At this altitude, it was suggested, the air would be dangerously thin. Although many South American people lived and worked at such altitudes, it was widely agreed that their bodies had been conditioned to the thin air by many generations of breeding.

Could rally drivers, mechanics and organisers, who almost all normally lived at or near sea level, and might never before have experienced such conditions, even cope? Expert medical opinion was that if they did not get involved in physical over-exertion, then everything would be fine, but otherwise ... And what might happen then? Headaches, nausea and light-headedness were apparently the obvious results, but in the extreme they might pass out altogether, and be unable to function.

Most teams took advice, and in almost every case that advice was that they should take oxygen bottles, masks and delivery tubes with them on the high sections. Although this was generally done, the fact is oxygen seems not to have been used regularly, if at all, by the truly professional teams. The top drivers – Hannu Mikkola, Brian Culcheth and Rauno Aaltonen – all confirm this. Some drivers were affected more than others – with Ford team driver Sobieslaw Zasada known to have passed out at the end of one of the Primes.

Drawing on their links with the RAF Red Arrows team (Terry Kingsley and Peter Evans, in a 'works' Maxi, were Red Arrows pilots), the British Leyland team carried out tests in a decompression chamber at RAE Farnborough, where – as predicted – they found that their mental facilities and reactions were adversely affected. As Paddy Hopkirk told me: "We were cocky about this, but they would ask us what 2 + 2 was, and we would answer 15, or something like that ... I hadn't realised just how much it would affect us."

Paddy admits to having used oxygen at times, but not persistently.

Although, as a travelling controller on the event, I did not have to work strenuously at high altitude, I recall feeling groggy, with a bad headache, when officiating at the La Paz Control in Bolivia; this was at an altitude of 4060 metres (13,300ft), close to the International airport. I also recall the need to keep taking breaths from a temporary oxygen supply installed in the Cessna aircraft which British Leyland had hired to get from Salta (in Argentina) to La Paz itself.

The last word, predictably, should go to Ford team boss Stuart Turner, who tells this wonderful (but quite fictitious!) story about driver Roger Clark on his recce of those altitudes:

"'Roger,' I am alleged to have said, 'we need to know the effects of lack of oxygen at height in the Andes. Find a local girl, at 14,000 feet (4267m), make love, and report back ...'

"Roger (equally allegedly) sent back a cable reading: 'Unable to find a girl at 14,000 feet (4267m), but don't recommend oxygen, because no problems when I did it 14 times at 1000 feet (304.8m) ...'"

have border and Customs formalities which seemed archaic to European eyes, but were sometimes – yes, we must be honest about this – corrupt into the bargain. In the survey and recce period, a car's paperwork, the lack of it, or a study of it, could take several hours – yet there seemed to be no hang-ups that a few gifts of alcohol, or even American 'greenback' dollars, could not solve in minutes.

Political problems were less common, but could potentially be more serious. Chile, it seemed, was permanently at loggerheads with Argentina and Bolivia, Bolivia and Chile were not really speaking either, while in Central America it was Guatemala, Honduras and El Salvador which seemed to on the verge of fighting with each other at this time. Happily for international sport in general, and the World Cup Rally in particular, all such hostilities were put firmly away when the cars came to cross the appropriate borders, and there were no incidents:

"The secret," John Sprinzel insists, "was that our event was connected with football – at least the name of it was – and this made all the difference."

Right from the start, the route linking Santiago to La Paz, and then on to Lima (Chile into Argentina, then into Bolivia, and on into Peru), was seen as being the most challenging of all. Not only the organisers, but those professional crews who went out to survey the stages in advance, all came to the same conclusion. The rally, they suggested, would be won and lost in that six day period.

Not only was the event to be run over territory which was still very wild – untamed might be a kinder word – where private cars were still little known, where the most common vehicle was either a tractor or a smoke-belching truck (or maybe an asthmatic bus), but where there was also the problem of altitude. By the time the rally cars had reached 13,000 to 15,000 feet/3962 to 4572m (at which level they were to stay for hours, if not days, at a time) their engines would be delivering no more than half of their sea-level performance. An Escort with no more than 70bhp, therefore, or a Triumph 2.5PI with no more than 75bhp was going to feel slow in the extreme.

Any car that survived the incredibly arduous South American Primes – take one look at the length of them (see the sidebar on page 19) merely to get a feel for that challenge – deserved recognition. Accordingly, the

Team Manager René Cotton actually surveyed much of the South American sections for his Citroën private entries, which meant that driver Patrick Vanson was at least forewarned about some of the awful conditions.

organisers decreed that any car that got to the Pacific Colombian port of Buenaventura (and, by definition, could therefore be loaded on to the MS Verdi to Panama), should qualify as a finisher. This explains why 26 cars were eventually listed as official finishers, despite only 23 ever actually reaching Mexico City, as there were three further retirements in Central America.

Practice makes (nearly) perfect

Although Sprinzel and Brown were convinced that no one individual would find the time to survey and practise the entire 16,000 miles (25,750km) route (and they were right), both the British Leyland and Ford teams collectively managed it.

Over a period of months, which involved Ford loan cars, hire cars, practice cars – and even, on one occasion, the purchase of an ancient machine to survey one particular country – Henry Liddon reconnoitered every inch of the South and Central American route from Rio de Janeiro to Mexico City for Ford, after which he was quoted as saying that:

"Anyone who gets to Mexico City deserves a gold medal, and any private entry who gets to Mexico deserves several gold medals." Liddon, however, did not always find it easy to do his job. There was one point,

reputedly in Guatemala or one such Central American country, where he could not secure a hire car, called Boreham in some distress, and was told that, if all else failed, he should buy a car:

"I'm glad you said that," Liddon replied, "for I just did ..."

Henry, need I say, was a motor trader by profession, so such deals were meat and drink to him ...

Gunnar Palm, too, spent much time – up to four months, including taking time out to win the 1969 Rally of the Incas, with Tony Fall, in an Escort practice car – while Timo Makinen and Hannu Mikkola both spent time looking carefully at the critical sections in Chile and Peru.

If British Leyland's Brian Culcheth had not been foiled by the weather in Yugoslavia, and by road-building operations in Mexico, he might actually have done even more. The serious teams, then, pooled their resources, and made sure that other members, somehow, of their team had seen almost every inch of the roads and tracks chosen for the event.

Not that Sprinzel was too worried about this:

"Some of the Primes in South America were so long that it was really impossible to write real pace notes. Can you really see a co-driver – even a professional co-driver – reading detail notes for 10 and 12 hours at a time, at altitude, in the dust, and after weeks already spent on the road?"

For some of the professional crews, surveying the route, and practising the Primes, often proved to be a very frustrating business, particularly if local bureaucracy and what we might call 'Spanish Customs' were involved. These days, of course, borders and customs barriers have vanished in many parts of Europe, and are much eased elsewhere. In 1969 and 1970, in South America they could be a real barrier. Many countries, it seemed, were always suspicious of their neighbours – and it was always difficult, for example, to exchange one country's currency for that of its neighbouring territory.

Brian Culcheth, who was the pioneer in so many ways on this event, experienced all the truly enervating lows in getting himself, and his car, through national borders. Apart from the six-day hold up in Buenos Aires, he also noted that it took him more than three hours to get across the border from Argentina into Bolivia – this at a point where there was virtually no other traffic to get in his way.

It is in hearing extracts from Brian Culcheth's reminiscences, that one realises how cleverly the organising team had pitched the pace of the event – and it also emphasises just how much effort he, and his much-respected rivals, put in to the job:

"In the nine months between starting work on this event, and the start, I only did one other event – which was the RAC Rally in November 1969. That was when we used Triumph 2.5PI Mk Is, and it was the heavier Mk IIs we were going to use on the World Cup.

"I went out to South America three times, and went into Europe twice. I don't think anyone did as much. I recced all except the very last Prime, which was altered after the route had been fixed."

Brian's first recce was in Argentina, in a standard Triumph 2000 loaned by Leyland Argentina, with Tony Nash and Lacco Ossio. This took five weeks, on rough roads and tracks which would be improved and graded before the event itself arrived) after which they flew back to Britain on Christmas Eve.

"By that time we had decided that we did not want to go three-up on this rally. Having done London-Sydney, along with Tony Fall and Mike Wood, I realised that it was a mistake. I think there was a crucial section where this decision really mattered – which was from Santiago to La Paz. It was 57 hours, with those incredibly

JUST GUESSING

In the months leading up to the start, not only the organisers, but the media, tried to guess just how many rally cars would make it to certain points, and on to the finish.

** For the transatlantic voyage from Lisbon to Rio de Janeiro, the owners of the SS Derwent guaranteed space for just 70 cars. In the event, 71 cars were squeezed tightly on board ...

** For the journey between Buenaventura (Colombia) and Colon (Panama), the MS Verdi guaranteed space for 35 rally cars. In the end, only 26 rally cars were still running at that point, but several other 'walking wounded', and a few stray service cars, also managed to squeeze on board.

** Well before the event, and when seasoned rally veterans had completed their route surveys, the general opinion was that only 10 crews might eventually make it to the end in Mexico City. In the end, no fewer than 23 cars completed the entire route – and a number of those which had been excluded were repaired sufficiently to tag along behind, into Mexico City.

Most factory teams practised for weeks before the event. This is the British Leyland team in South America, using two of the old-shape 2.5PIs which had competed in the 1969 RAC Rally. Paddy Hopkirk, at the front of the cars, is clearly setting off to walk ahead, without his team-mates ...

long Primes. Having recced it twice, I thought there was enough time to get some rest after the long 500-miler (804.7km): the road schedule was relaxed enough to do that.

"I think that what was also favourable to the two-man crew was the weather – as it happened, the World Cup was run in fantastic weather. On the recce we sometimes had floods, and we were stuck more than once in them. There were times when we could hardly move because of the mud ..."

(A Citroën-produced DVD of the event also shows Team Manager René Cotton surveying the route, in South America, and also needing tractor assistance to get his DS21 through floods at one point. The sight of the usually-dignified Cotton wading through flood water, his trousers rolled up to his knees, is worth the price of the DVD on its own ...)

"Once or twice," Culcheth says, "the enormity of it all hit home. There was one time on the recce when we had our third puncture (with only two spare wheels) at a height of 12,000 feet/3658m (north of Santiago). We had spare tubes with us, but no oxygen, and we were really quite woozy and couldn't strip the tyres. We were there, stuck, for 14 hours, and then along came this road grader: the driver put the edge of his grader on the edge of the tyres to break the seal, and we changed the tubes ... In fact we took oxygen with us on the event, but didn't use it: I think the adrenalin kept us going."

In a note sent back to John Sprinzel's office Brian wrote:

"Prime 14. Time taken, 12 hours to Ayacucho (in a Toyota Corona). Some of the drops are a bit hairy ... I think a private owner would take as long as 20 hours on this section. Have you made any arrangements about petrol, on this Prime ...?

"We would recommend that you split into La Paz-Ayacucho, then overnight there, then Ayacucho-Lima ..."

For every professional crew, whether Ford, British Leyland or Citroën, the problem was in getting cars which would not break up under the strain. Culcheth's locally-provided Triumph 2000 soon devoured its exhaust system, and a new, much stronger, component, had to be fabricated. Hire cars were definitely fragile, and could not be driven from one country into another, and in some cases it was very difficult to import their own brand of practice cars from Europe. As John Sprinzel had already discovered, when he talked to the Brazilian Ambassador in London, it seemed to be quite impossible to get cars into Brazil.

Paddy Hopkirk confirms this:

"I must have had months in South America," Paddy Hopkirk recalls. "I remember being in Argentina, with Andrew Cowan and Brian Culcheth, waiting for Customs to release the 2.5PI recce cars into Buenos Aires – we couldn't get them in Brazil at any price, and it took six days' wait. It looked like being a lengthy stand-off, but I had met Juan Manuel Fangio (after my Monte victory in 1964), he was 'God' in Argentina, I rang his offices, told them we needed help, and could he help ...?

'Mr Fangio, he will help you', they said ... In the meantime, because of all the delays, we had seen every film that was in the cinemas in Buenos Aires. They were all American, with Spanish sub-titles, so we were laughing at times when the locals didn't know what we were laughing at.

Practice, practice and more practice – with two of the ex-RAC Rally Triumph 2.5PIs out in South America. Brian Culcheth, Brian Coyle and Andrew Cowan are all identifiable in this shot.

"Anyway, a big man arrived from Fangio's office, found us, asked us if we had any money, and when we said, rather cautiously, 'How much money?' he said 'Enough for a case of whisky!' We bought the whisky in a local shop, our contact marched into the Customs Offices, and five minutes later he re-emerged, with all the release documents for the cars ..."

It was this sort of anecdote which typifies the problems which this fledgling event, and its still-inexperienced characters, had to suffer in the first few months.

For every entrant – whether factory supported, or strictly private and on his own, fuel supplies were going to be a problem. In certain parts of South America, not only would petrol stations be few and far between, but the quality of much of the petrol might also be poor. Although the local authorities tried their best to rectify this situation (once again, national pride had much to do with it), this explains why all the serious entrants carried a lot more fuel than they normally would do so.

Ford and British Leyland, however, also came to bless their oil company sponsor, Castrol, for the way in which that concern set up dumps around the route for its users. Although British Leyland was convinced that, on its recce, some of the road-side supplies had been as low as 66 Octane (a figure not seen in Europe since the 1920s), the fuel supplied by Castrol on the event was of a much higher quality.

Surviving documents show that Castrol set up dumps, or recommended fuel stations, on more than 40 occasions in South America. The remarks made in some cases are fascinating:

"The fuel in Brazil will be a mixture of 50 per cent normal Premium gasoline, and 50 per cent PN100/130 Avgas, giving an approximate octane number of 92 ... the fuel in Argentina will be straight gasoline of approximately 96/97 octane ... the fuel in Peru will be 93/95 octane straight

Right: When surveyed in the winter of 1969/1970, Primes through the Andes were very high, on dirt surfaces, and often threatened with closure due to snow storms. Roger Clark was driving this Escort practice car, with Henry Liddon taking the picture.

Bottom right: Staged? Let's hope so, for Roger Clark was at the wheel in this practice shot, which was taken in Argentina. By South American standards, that was a well-surfaced road.

Below: Although bridges such as this were quite safe, there was no protection in case the car slid to one side. It was important to reach the start of the crossing when well under control!

gasoline, and in all probability will be dispensed by means of 5 gallon (22.7L) cans and funnels ... the fuel in Ecuador will be a mixture of 50 per cent Premium gasoline and 50 per cent PN100/130 Avgas ..."

– which shows just how carefully the big sponsors were prepared to keep their precious charges going.

Telling the world

The *Daily Mirror*, no question, set out to ensure that the whole world knew about 'its' rally, and about the super-professional way that it intended to disseminate updates. Sprinzel's master-stroke was to hire John Lewsey of the London Motor Club, who had evolved Britain's best results service while the Gulf London Rally was at its height in the mid-1960s, and had also done so much to make the London-Sydney Marathon results service

THE REWARDS. MONEY, MONEY, MONEY ...

I must start, of course, by pointing out that in 1970 the value of currency was very different from today. To get a feel for it, I merely note that a new Mini 1000 cost £675, that a Triumph TR6 retailed for £1401, and that a Rolls-Royce Silver Shadow sold for a hefty £8671. These prices, therefore, put into perspective what I now quote. As part of its sponsorship deal, the Daily Mirror and the International Coffee Organisation had been persuaded to back much of the following Prize Fund:

First Overall	£10,000 (say – £150,000 or £200,000 in 2010 currency ...)
Second	£3000
Third	£2000
Fourth	£1500
Fifth	£1000
First Overall at Lisbon	£2000
First Private Entrant at Lisbon	£500
First Ladies' Crew at Lisbon	£200

Private Entrants:

First	£2000
Second	£1000
Third	£500

Ladies' Prizes:

First	£1000
Second	£500
Third	£250

Awards for each and every Prime:

Fastest Time	£250
Fastest Time by a Private Owner	£50
Fastest Private Owner over the longest South American Prime	£100

In addition to this, there were class awards, manufacturers awards, national and club team awards. Not only that, but there was a £500 for the leader at Milan, £500 (from the Bank of London & Montreal) for the winner of the Lima-Cali stage, and any number of cash prizes from trade sponsors to private owners, to female crews, and to those using particular products.

Castrol was the most generous oil company/supplier for their users, offering:

First	£1000
Second	£700
Third	£400
Fourth	£300
Fifth	£200
Best Private Owner	£300
Ladies' Prize	£150

For the victors, and for the best privately-entered crews, it looked as if it could be a very valuable event. Nothing, of course, could quite balance the cost of preparation, and of participation, but it certainly came close. In many ways, winnings were cumulative. Complicated? For sure. When writing his preview of the event in Autosport magazine, Quentin Spurring summed up succinctly like this: "For example, if a privately entered crew existed of Scottish ladies driving a British car of either Ford or British Leyland manufacture, lubricated by Castrol, and they were to lead at all the points qualifying for stage awards, then set best times on all the Primes, and finally win the event outright, they would win the very grand total of £27,407 ..." Well, yes, but ...

into a professional operation. Urged along by the enthusiastic *Mirror* staff, he helped lay out a first-class results and information centre in the foyer of that newspaper's main building in Holborn Circus, in London.

Telephones, tele-printers, visual displays and even a crude (by later standards) computer were all in place, and on view. We must not forget, of course, that in 1970 there was no such-thing as the internet, or e-mail, or satellite telephone transmissions – the ubiquitous Telex being state-of-the art for that moment. Even so, the organisers tried to arrange telephone or private radio contact between Primes and the nearest known tele-printer office, while a huge scoreboard was build up at Holborn Circus to keep track of every competitor's progress.

As the event progressed, this ambitious service paid off, in many ways. As a travelling controller, I recall occasions in South America where the best way to get a message from a Prime to the next Main Control was actually to call London, and ask them to patch it through. Invariably this worked, and as a consequence the event never got out of control.

Even so, Sprinzel, Brown and their colleagues knew that 'Murphy's Law' could hit them just as surely as it could hit everyone else ('If anything can go wrong ... it will!'). The theory of this great enterprise was fine, but would it work out in practice?

The rally timetable: April and May 1970

Sunday, 19 April: Start from Wembley Stadium, London. First car left at 10.00hr.

Time Control at Dover

(Crossing by Sea Link to Boulogne)

Time Control at Boulogne

Monday, 20 April:
Passage Control in Vienna

Monday, 20 April:
Passage Control at Budapest

Tuesday, 21 April:
Passage Control at Sofia, Bulgaria

Wednesday, 22 April:
Arrival Control at Monza, near Milan. Cars in Parc Fermé overnight.

Thursday, 23 April: Departure from Monza

Saturday, 25 April:
Cars arrived at Lisbon docks in Portugal, ready for loading on to the SS Derwent for shipment to Rio de Janeiro in Brazil

– cars then in transit across the South Atlantic Ocean

Friday, 8 May:
Cars unloaded from the SS Derwent at the docks in Rio de Janeiro
Evening: Official restart from outside the Museum of Art, in Rio de Janeiro

Sunday, 10 May:
Arrival Control in Montevideo, Uruguay. Cars in Parc Fermé overnight.

Monday, 11 May:
Restart from Montevideo, ferry to Buenos Aires (Argentina), before beginning the long South American sections

Tuesday night, 12 May/Wednesday, 13 May:
Arrival Control in Santiago, Chile. Cars in Parc Fermé overnight.

Thursday, 14 May:
Restart from Santiago

Saturday, 16 May:
Arrival Control at La Paz, Bolivia. Cars then in Parc Fermé overnight.

Sunday, 17 May:
Restart from La Paz, Bolivia

Monday, 18 May:
Arrival Control at Lima, Peru. Cars then in Parc Fermé overnight.

Tuesday, 19 May:
Restart from Lima, Peru

Thursday, 21 May:
Arrival Control at Cali, Colombia

Friday, 22 May:
Boarding the ship MS Verdi, prior to sea voyage departure to Cristobal

Saturday night/Sunday morning, 23/24 May:
Arrival at Cristobal, in the state of Panama in the MS Verdi. Crews then slept on board.

Sunday, 24 May:
Free day for crews, then cars and crews left the port of Cristobal, for Panama City, and the restart from Panama

Tuesday, 26 May:
Arrival at Fortin, the last competitive Time Control, in Mexico

Wednesday, 27 May:
Arrival at the Aztec Stadium, Mexico City for the end of the London-Mexico Rally

3

Runners and riders

Right from the start, there was enormous interest in the World Cup Rally. Even so, without the immediate support of a major national newspaper, the *Daily Mirror*, it would have been difficult to generate such a head of steam, and it was all to the credit of the publicity-conscious genius of Wylton Dickson that this happened, at once. The fact that the London-Sydney Marathon, run off so recently, had also been a great success, had much to do with it.

But who, or what, would enter an event which was going to be even longer, tougher, and with faster target time schedules, than London-Sydney had ever been? Who would take up the challenge of tackling two continents, in six weeks? And who was about to pay for it all?

What sort of cars, and how many in each car?

There was no doubt that several major motor manufacturers would want to get involved, but for all of them the first decision was to be about the sort of cars to use, and how to crew them. Because this was to be no 'ordinary' rally, the usual ban on four-wheel-drive cars need not apply, and the organisers also made it clear that they would accept non-standard machinery, just as long as it gained the approval of the eagle-eyed scrutineers. Even so, they must have been surprised to see that cars as weird as a soft-top GP Beach Buggy, a long-wheelbase four-door Mini-Cooper S, and a Ford Escort-based motor caravan all stepped up to the plate.

For almost every crew, the other big decision which would have to be made was – three-up or two-up, and whether to carry copious (and heavy) supplies of oxygen to deal with the very high altitudes promised for the Andes sections? Those opting for three-person crews did it so that they could never be accused of running, zombie-like, on the ultra-long sections – especially in South America – while those who opted for two-person crews did so because this meant that they would be saving weight and space in the car, and would therefore liberate more volume for spares, petrol and other equipment to be carried.

As will eventually become clear, the two-up or three-up policy was to be debated among individuals and even at top 'works' team level until a very late stage. No consensus of opinion would ever be reached.

Straight away, too, it is worth looking back at the London-Sydney Marathon of 1968, and to analyse what various major manufacturers had learned from it. It was from these surveys that their own choice of cars, and the recommendations they made to private owners, could be made:

**British Leyland: Although the team had put up an excellent performance in London-Sydney, using front-wheel-drive BMC 1800s (Paddy Hopkirk took second place), these cars were already considered too slow and too ponderous for future use. The whole team, led by Peter Browning, thought they would need more performance to be competitive with the Fords.

A diligent search was made through all the brands now embraced by British Leyland, and it was provisionally decided that the new Triumph 2.5PI saloons, or even the still-secret Range Rovers, might be ideal.

British Leyland's biggest problem was that its top management, led by Lord Stokes, was finance-orientated, and really only wanted to go into the event knowing that it ought to win – an assumption that no rallying realist could understand. Stokes was often described as a consummate salesman, but I know no-one who ever rated him as a motorsport enthusiast who understood the sport. Team Manager Peter Browning realised this at an early stage, and had to come to terms with the corporate expectations throughout the months involved in the project.

**Citroën: By 1969 the French team had virtually come to the end of the competition road with development of the sleek DS19/DS21 pedigree, for although the cars handled better than most other brands, and coped extremely well with rough terrain, they were hampered both by a lack of performance, and by a lack of finance.

Over the years, team boss René Cotton (already, if only we had known it, mortally ill, but refusing to give in to it) had delivered a series of startling performances, including outright victories in Monte Carlo (disputed, but that story has been related, ad nauseum, many times before), Morocco, and Liège-Sofia-Liège.

The DS21, it was thought, had been ideal for London-Sydney, and in fact came very close to winning it. Robert Neyret, Lucien Bianchi and Patrick Vanson had performed well, with Bianchi leading on the last morning until rammed out of the event by a non-competing car, and with Neyret finishing in ninth place.

By 1969, however, the 'works' team's activities had been wound down considerably (Citroën concluded, correctly, that it could no longer prevail in Europe, against the likes of Ford-UK, Lancia, and Porsche). Even though a new fuel-injected version of the DS21 looked promising, there seemed to be no way that a budget, and big enough organisation, could be assembled to tackle the London-Mexico World Cup Rally.

**Ford-UK: Beaten, not to say completely humiliated, by the events of London-Sydney, the Essex-based team had to rethink its entire strategy. New Competitions Manager Stuart Turner took office in June 1969, and approval of the project came in the same period. Money and resources would certainly be made available. But with what cars and what drivers? Turner drove the entire strategy behind the project, his deputy Bill Barnett did most of the day-to-day donkey work, and once a budget (of £40,000 – which looked very small, even in 1969 terms) was agreed, Boreham was left to get on with it.

On the upside, the team was likely to attracted the strongest driver line-up of all, and especially in South America it would have a vitally important 'on-the-ground' umbrella of importing companies, local dealerships, and entrepreneurs to help underpin the mobile effort.

On the downside, the team was rapidly losing faith in the longevity of the 8-valve twin-cam Lotus-Ford engine which powered the most suitable cars. It was these engines which foiled Roger Clark's mission in Australia, Soderstrom's in Europe, and had also inflicted problems in other events before 1969: with fuel supplies in South America likely to be of a very questionable quality, there was a real problem here.

According to the performance figures, no other Ford engine could match the Lotus Twin-Cam, but several were more reliable, so during 1969 Ford's biggest problem was to choose a 'best alternative' and the cars in which it should be installed.

Choosing the cars and selecting a driving team were the biggest strategic decisions which had to be made, and all concerned agree that by the autumn of 1969 this had become the largest single programme in Boreham's motorsport planning.

**Ford-Australia: Although its massive Falcon GTs had performed well in Australia (it took third and fifth places), that had been an expensive 'horses for courses' exercise, and there seemed to be no way that the company would enter a new transcontinental event that would not visit its own territory.

**Ford-Germany: Although this team had come very close to winning

London-Sydney (a Taunus 20M RS had suffered an accident very close to the end of the rally, when it had been ahead of every rival), future policy would see it concentrating its motorsport efforts in motor racing. In the next few years, there would be the Capri RS2600, which would win a multitude of saloon car races, but rallying would be left to the British team instead.

**Moskvich: No-one knew much about this Soviet team, but every pundit agreed that while the cars were strong, they were both slow and technologically obsolete. In London-Sydney, the Type 408s had shown just how reliable they were, but they also showed just how slow they were, compared with the European machinery.

Although everyone hoped that a team would be entered for the World Cup, it was going to need a brand-new engine (and the overhead camshaft Type 412 model had just been previewed) to make it look more competitive.

**Porsche: BMC Competition Manager Stuart Turner (he moved to Ford in 1969) always used to say that his job was made a great deal easier because Porsche, the German sports car maker, was never serious about its involvement in rallying. If it had ever put as much effort in rallying, as it did into sports car racing, he said, then the 911 could be unbeatable for many years to come.

He was both right, and relieved. By 1969 Vic Elford had already won the European Rally Championship – which included the Monte Carlo Rally – in a 'works' 911, while Björn Waldegård was already showing how well German and Swedish-prepared examples could perform. Despite this, there had been little factory involvement in London-Sydney in 1968, although Sobieslaw Zasada of Poland had managed to take fourth place in a 911S.

In 1969, when the World Cup Rally was officially launched, Porsche was far too involved in building, racing and winning (it hoped) sports car races with the 908 and fearsome new 917 types, to take an interest. Any World Cup entries would have to be privately financed, though factory technical support would be available.

**Rootes/Chrysler: In London-Sydney, victory by a 'works' Hillman Hunter had been so unexpected, that very little publicity was ever reaped from that win. Not only that, but in the months that followed, and to everyone's astonishment, the US-based parent company decided to close down the 'works' Motorsport Department, slash its budget to a 'care and maintenance' level, and not get involved in major events for the foreseeable future.

The new Team Manager, Des O'Dell, was left with a well-proven type of car on his hands, but with no money and with no drivers left to deploy. In the wake of this, the winners – Andrew Cowan and Brian Coyle – defected to British Leyland, while third-crew member Colin Malkin joined Ford.

The following explains how during 1969, therefore, and into the winter of 1969, the major manufacturers concluded their preparations.

British Leyland

British Leyland had come so close to victory in the London-Sydney Marathon that its top management was convinced that it now could – and should – win the 1970 World Cup. An enormous budget was committed to the task – this included the hire of an ex-BOAC (British Overseas Airways Corporation) four-engined turbo-prop Bristol Britannia aircraft to ferry spares and key management personnel to, from, and all around South America. After the RAC Rally of 1969, the department was so swamped by the amount of work involved, the testing and the construction of all the new machines, that there was little time (or money!) available for anything else.

As it transpired, the Abingdon-based operation not only prepared eight World Cup cars, but a number of test, practice and endurance machines too. In fact from January 1970 to April 1970, four Triumph 2.5PI Mk IIs, two Austin Maxis, a works-supported Austin Maxi and a Mini 1275GT all took shape in one workshop at Abingdon, with technical advice and some parts also being supplied to several private owners.

Not only that, but the Special Tuning Department (situated literally next door to 'Comps', and closely linked in terms of expertise and facilities) also prepared no fewer than six BMC 1800s for private entrants, who provided their own finance. All those 1800s were prepared to the successful 'London-Sydney' specification of 1968.

Dunlop provided tyres in a colossal effort for this British team, and for other private owners. All in all, more than 1500 covers were involved, for Dunlop also had agreements with forty-four entries in this hundred-strong entry list. Dunlop, in fact, went to a great deal of trouble here, by providing a special batch of 'heavy duty' thick-wall SP Weathermaster tyres, which

BILL PRICE – GLOBE TROTTER

British Leyland's Bill Price was Peter Browning's deputy at Abingdon in the late 1960s and early 1970s, and was responsible for much detail planning of the World Cup effort.

After an exhausting six weeks, in which he made more contact with the rally, and the team cars, than anyone else, Bill made out this list of his movements:

Though he spent much time in the massive Bristol Britannia ('Browning's Bomber') which pre-positioned many of British Leylands wheels, tyres and spares in South America, in fact he made 44 separate flights in eleven different aircraft:

Cessna Skymaster
Beechcraft Bonanza
Piper Apache
Bristol Britannia
Lockheed Electra
Douglas DC8
Douglas DC9
BAC 111
Boeing 707
Boeing 727
Sud Aviation Caravelle

I believe that, in a 'Top Trumps' competition on this event, Bill would win hands down ...

Motorsport is expensive! British Leyland had to service seven cars, over 16,000 miles (25,750km), so to transport a mountain of spares, wheels and tyres, it chartered this four-engined turboprop Bristol Britannia aircraft to haul the material around the world. Naturally – for rally drivers have that sort of sense of humour – it was immediately christened Browning's Bomber.

might not have been puncture proof, but had much more puncture resistance than before. If ever there was detail which might just give BL (British Leyland) an advantage over Ford (whose Escorts were Goodyear-clad), this could be it.

Every team member was provided with copies of the route survey notes that Brian Culcheth, Paddy Hopkirk and Andrew Cowan had compiled in the weeks leading up to the event – and all, without exception, insisted how valuable these documents were. There was never

This splendidly posed group shot shows all seven of the 'works' cars prepared by the British Leyland Motorsport Department at Abingdon, south of Oxford. Just one of the team – Ms Ginette Derolland – is missing from the line-up. Team boss Peter Browning is in the centre, holding gamely on to the feisty young bulldog who was the event's mascot.

British Leyland needed to transport many spares and personnel from point to point in South America, using aircraft as diverse as a four-engined Douglas airliner, and a tiny Cessna for that purpose.

This was how Castrol, a major trade supporter of many cars in the World Cup Rally, advertised its presence. This explains the presence of a live, and very healthy bulldog, in some of the various teams' pre-event line-ups.

Left to right: Johnstone Syer, Brian Culcheth, Competitions Manager Peter Browning, and BL Chairman Lord Stokes, at the start at Wembley Stadium.

any doubt as to the roads and tracks they should be taking.

Because this was British Leyland, and because the *Daily Mirror* could no doubt see that 'our' team (Ford, somehow, didn't seem to count, because it was American-owned) should get the most exposure, it appears that the parent company to this newspaper, which owned both leading British motoring magazines (*Autocar* and *Motor*) was most anxious to place a couple of staff man in the rally cars.

This, therefore, is what went into the 'works' entries:

Triumph 2.5PI Mk II

Originally, it was Triumph in Coventry (with me as competitions secretary) which had started work on highly-modified Triumph 2000s in 1964. Ray Henderson then took over the task in 1965, evolved the first 2.5PI prototypes in 1967 (for the RAC Rally which was cancelled less than 24 hours before the start), and helped to settle the specification of the 2.5PIs which were eventually developed at British Leyland's 'works' team HQ (headquarters) at Abingdon. Until the end of 1969, Abingdon's first PI cars carried the original snub-nose/short-tail body style, but for the World Cup Rally itself, the restyled/long-nose/long-tail Mk II was adopted instead, for this car had been launched in October of 1969. For brevity, therefore, I have omitted references to 'Mk I' or 'Mk II' from the remainder of this book.

Documents drawn up at Abingdon in 1970 survive, which show that the preparation job sheet for these cars ran into hundreds – literally hundreds – of items, yet there is only a limited space available here to summarise. They do, however, confirm that every possible detail was

Preparation for the World Cup, at British Leyland's Abingdon workshops, with two Triumph 2.5PIs and an Austin Maxi in view.

Three fuel tanks, two spare tyres and wheels, and many tools left no space for anything else in the back of the Triumph 2.5PI.

addressed, and they reflect an enormous amount of testing, and practising, was carried out.

The monocoque body structures for the four cars, along with at least two spare shells, were specially strengthened, and supplied by Pressed Steel Fisher (a subsidiary company within British Leyland), for that company built all the production shells for this car. The decision to order spare shells paid off after the event, for this explains how it was eventually possible to repair the car which was so badly damaged in the Andrew Cowan accident in the Andes (the wreckage of which was brought back to Abingdon after the event).

Those shells included flared rear wheel arches, cooling vents (from the engine bay) in the front wings, special jacking points, aluminium doors, bonnet and boot lid, and specially altered boot lid profiles to allow

British Leyland's answer to keeping water out of the fuel injection air intake of the Triumph 2.5PI was to channel fresh air through tubes attached to the grille at the base of the windscreen.

British Leyland took ages to decide the equipment layout of the Triumph 2.5PIs – note the sheepskin seat cover, and the overdrive switch on the gear-lever knob.

two spare wheels to be carried in the boot. There was an aluminium roll cage, later found not to be rigid enough in the Cowan accident: motorsport operations did not seem to take roll-over safety very seriously in those days.

When the shell was kitted out, it was also equipped with Perspex side and rear windows, a special roof-top air intake for the cabin, and a front seat which could be converted into a full-length bed. Special vents were also let into the roof, so that the crews could keep cool (the cars did not, of course, have air conditioning), and there were drinking-water containers installed behind the front seats.

Fuel injection was retained on the engines (the power output was about 150bhp, for a TR6 camshaft and a Janspeed exhaust manifold were specified). Not only that (and this was an important modification incorporated after problems had been found on a practice car), but the fresh air intake for the inlet manifolds were re-routed, from the front of the car where water might (and did on the practice car) get into the engine, to flexible pipe-work attached to the grille at the base of the windscreen. It was that sort of detail which made pre-event practice and testing so very valuable.

Behind this was a Triumph Stag-type gearbox, overdrive which

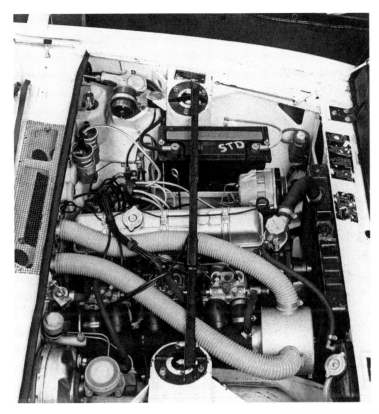

Early stages in preparation of the Triumph 2.5PI, at Abingdon. The engine/transmission assembly is ready for insertion, and those are light alloy doors.

Before settling on the specification of its World Cup cars, Abingdon spent ages on the endurance testing of a car, at the Bagshot rough-road track in Surrey. 'Fast Eddie' Burnell was usually the driver. This particular car, suitably refurbished, went on to win the Scottish Rally later in the year.

The bar across the top of the engine bay of the 2.5PIs linked the top of the front suspension struts, and added structural rigidity to the body shell to withstand the rough road going.

worked only on third and fourth gears, a 3.7:1 final drive ratio and a Salisbury limited-slip differential. A feature of the engine was the use of a special manually-adjustable device fitted to allow the crews to compensate for changes of altitude along the route. This was developed in a joint exercise between Abingdon mechanics Bob Whittington and Peter Bartram, and a Lucas engineer, which took five weeks of testing to get right.

The suspension was thoroughly reworked, for 15 inch (38.1cm) diameter Minilite wheels were chosen (the standard car had 13 inch (33cm) wheels – though the original 1964 'works' cars had used 15 inch/38.1cm wheels),

Last-minute preparation of Paddy Hopkirk's Triumph 2.5PI, at Abingdon in April 1970. It would take fourth place behind Brian Culcheth's sister car, which finished second.

these being mated to reinforced suspension, Stag brakes, and Koni shock absorbers, and inserts were fitted front and rear. They did not have power-assisted steering (PAS) – it was several more years before this would be available on the production version of this Triumph model. To boost the range of the cars, fuel tank capacity was increased to 32 gallons (145.5L), by adding extra 10 gallon (45.5L) and 8 gallon (36.4L) Marston fuel tanks on each side of the boot compartment.

One detail that puzzled restorers and observers in subsequent years was that extra roof-top driving lamps were fitted, but only at a later stage in South America. Also, the position of the lights on Brian Culcheth's car differed considerably from Paddy Hopkirk's. Pity the poor historian ...

Although the drivers were initially not enthused about using this big machine, they all warmed to it as development – and then the event itself – progressed. Not only was the PI fast and very solid, it also had good ground clearance, and rather soft and comfortable suspension. It was, in fact, very comfortable for an event which was otherwise all set to be extremely gruelling. Indeed, all the crews found it possible to sleep in the back seat when they were off duty – and were amazed that they were by no means totally exhausted when the event was over.

The saga of Brian Culcheth's very thorough recces in South America has already been covered in the previous chapter – but it was this time-consuming and sometimes boring work which helped settle the configuration of the cars – and of the crews.

After a great deal of discussion, Brian Culcheth and Johnstone

Brian Culcheth's Triumph 2.5PI pushing hard through a village on the European section.

Syer were the only British Leyland crew who chose to start with a two-up configuration. Although every other team member was advised of Culcheth's findings, all ignored his advice, and took a third crew member with them.

Paddy Hopkirk had tackled the London-Sydney Marathon three-up in a BMC 1800, and thought that it was the right decision once again for the World Cup. Paddy joined up with his then-regular co-driver Tony Nash, and with Neville Johnston, who had been his long-time business associate

in Northern Ireland, was still an established Belfast-based motor trader, and was a very capable mechanic. Although the two got on famously, Neville had never before tackled a major rally with Paddy, and would not do so in the future.

The Green/Murray team of Australians was accompanied by *Motor* journalist Hamish Cardno: although this was very much a personal gamble for British Leyland. Cardno had not even met his Australian team-mates when the entry was put in – however, Cardno was *Motor*'s

Left to right: Neville Johnston, Andrew Cowan and Paddy Hopkirk getting acquainted with their new Triumph 2.5PIs before the start of the event.

Three smart gentlemen before the start at Wembley Stadium – left to right: Brian Coyle, Andrew Cowan and 'Lacco' Ossio.

Four Triumph 2.5PIs ready to go to the start – left to right: Brian Culcheth, Neville Johnston, Johnstone Syer, Paddy Hopkirk, Tony Nash, Andrew Cowan, Lacco Ossio, Brian Coyle, Evan Green, Hamish Cardno, and 'Gelignite' Jack Murray.

Lord Stokes of British Leyland at Wembley Stadium with (left to right) Evan Green, Hamish Cardno and Jack Murray).

accredited rallies correspondent at this time, and knew his way round the sport.

Similarly, neither Andrew Cowan nor Brian Coyle had met their third crew member, Uldarico Ossio, before this project got under way. Uldarico – 'Lacco' to those who got to know him better – was however a Peruvian already notable in his own motor-sporting fraternity – and was really drafted in, not only as a co-driver and fluent Spanish speaker, but as an invaluable link between European and South American cultures. The entry numbers, crews, and registrations for the Triumphs were:

no 43	Andrew Cowan/Brian Coyle/Uldarico Ossio	XJB 304H
no 88	Brian Culcheth/Johnstone Syer	XJB 305H
no 92	Evan Green/Jack Murray/Hamish Cardno	XJB 303H
no 98	Paddy Hopkirk/Tony Nash/Neville Johnston	XJB 302H

Brian Culcheth's car – XJB 305H – was later used extensively by Culcheth in events throughout Europe, and although XJB 304H was rebuilt before the end of 1970, it was rarely used again. The other 2.5PIs were seen again, briefly on major rallies, and eventually at 'classic' level, but were not seriously rallied again at International level.

It is worth noting that one of the long-suffering pre-World Cup test cars (WRX 902H) was so strong, and so well-liked by all at Abington, that it was re-prepared in high-powered 'sprint' form (Weber carburettors instead of fuel injection, for instance) for Brian Culcheth to use in the Scottish Rally of June 1970. Not only did it perform with honour, but it won the event outright! There is no wonder that this was, and remains, Brian Culcheth's favourite 2.5PI ...

There were no team orders, incidentally. Whoever was leading the chase at the end of the event would be left, undisturbed, to take the credit. As one team member told me, with a wry smile: "Team orders? No – it was 'dog eat dog', as usual ..."

Austin Maxi

British Leyland had launched the its fourth-generation/Issigonis family car, the Maxi, complete with new-type overhead-camshaft E-Series transverse engine and five-speed/front-wheel-drive, in May 1969, this being at almost exactly the time that Peter Browning and British Leyland had begun to think about the World Cup Rally.

Although it was going to an enormous gamble to commit a quite unproven new model to such an arduous event, British Leyland top management was quite insistent. After the proposal to use Range Rovers was abandoned, for all the right publicity reasons (if not backed up by technical and motor-sporting know how) it was chosen for use by two 'works' back-up crews, one to be led by the accomplished lady driver Rosemary Smith, the other by a team of ex-RAF (Royal Air Force) Red Arrows pilots, who were accompanied by *Autocar* journalist Mike Scarlett.

Although he was an accomplished driver (as one of *Autocar's* respected road test team), Scarlett had never before tackled a long-distance rally and was, by his own admission, worried by the prospects:

"The approach came early in 1970. Up to that point I had done no

Rosemary Smith (right) and Alice Watson (with Ginette Derolland, they won the Ladies' Prize in their luridly-painted Austin Maxi) pose with the British bulldog, which was Britain's football World Cup mascot in 1970.

Nigel Clarkson (left) and HRH Prince Michael of Kent, shared a Janspeed-prepared Austin Maxi, but unfortunately crashed out in the Brazilian section.

rallying – no professional rallying, that is. It was my Editor, Peter Garnier, who first told me of the approach, and asked me to go. I had not met Terry (who was really the team leader) and Peter before the entries were made, but they took it very well.

"Incidentally, it was agreed that I would send back weekly reports on our progress, but when I called London from, I think, Santiago, I was told that there was a printing strike – the result being that my reports were not published for weeks afterwards!

"As it happened, I became a good back-seat passenger, and I was never queasy. And, like many other people on that event, the World Cup Rally taught me to sleep anywhere, on any occasion! I also did quite a lot of the driving, but it was non-competitive driving, not on the Primes. We did a bit of testing beforehand at Bagshot, and learned how to drive the car, but we didn't do any recces at all."

This crew, though led by RAF pilots who were thoroughly used to using oxygen at high altitude, took supplies along with them, but did not use it at any time, even at the height of the event in Bolivia and Peru.

In addition, a Maxi entry of military personnel, which included HRH Prince Michael of Kent, was prepared at Janspeed in Salisbury, and given a great deal of back-up from Abingdon.

[Like Andrew Cowan, and like Colin Malkin (who took up an offer from Ford), Rosemary Smith had recently come to the end of a glittering career with Rootes/Chrysler, was currently freelancing in cars as various as Ford Escorts and Porsche 911s, and was an inspired signing for this high-profile event.]

How to prepare the car? Abingdon tackled it with a combination of experience (especially with the 1800s which had tackled London-Sydney in 1968, the cars' chassis and suspensions being related) and with every ounce of engineering knowledge made available to them from Longbridge.

Early testing showed that the standard five-door hatchback bodyshell was not rigid enough for rally purposes on rough roads – Peter Browning and Bill Price described it as having a tendency to distort after prolonged testing on the Bagshot rough road facilities:

"We found that the body was beginning to 'lozenge' to one side," Bill Price recalls, "and for the tailgate to keep flying open. So we talked to the body people at Longbridge. They said 'Can't you weld the tailgate shut?', to which we said 'Yes, but how do we then get at the petrol tank?' So they said: 'Well, why don't you cut the tailgate in half ...?' So we did that, welded the top half to the bodyshell, and that made it much more rigid."

The lower half of the tailgate was then converted into a lift-up conventional boot lid, and a 29 gallon (131.8L) aircraft type fuel bag tank was installed in the boot. The rest of the shell was seam-welded in the conventional way, reinforcements were added around the front sub-frame, and a roll cage was added. The Hydrolastic suspension was beefed up, and Koni dampers were also added at each corner. Thus modified, a test car completed more than 1000 miles (1609km) of rough-road testing at Bagshot, and although there were suspension breakages, and driveshaft failures, these were systematically replaced, modified, or otherwise made 'World Cup' proof. Rosemary Smith took one on the Circuit of Ireland to get a feel for it, and won the Ladies' Prize too.

Service and repacking on the quayside at Lisbon, for the Red Arrows Maxi, which struggled pluckily home in 22nd place. Co-driver Peter Evans is with the car.

Well loaded with spare wheels, and looking quite grubby at this stage, Rosemary Smith's Austin Maxi tackles the San Remo Prime in northern Italy. After an event-long battle with Claudine Trautmann's Citroën, Rosemary won the Ladies' Prize, and finished 10th overall.

Preparation detail of the Austin Maxis prepared for Rosemary Smith, and the Red Arrows team to drive in the World Cup, included fitment of an enormous rubber bag fuel tank, and modification to the rear bodywork to convert the hatchback to a conventional boot lid. This, in fact, was a hard-working test car.

Left to right: Gavin Thompson, HRH Prince Michael of Kent, and Nigel Clarkson, (who would tackle the World Cup in a Janspeed-prepared Austin Maxi) are briefed about their cars before the start.

43

Although the Maxi production car had the new E4-Series overhead-camshaft 74bhp/1485cc engine, allied to an all-new five-speed gearbox, the World Cup cars were given a boost by adopting a prototype twin SU carburettor installation, the power of which was measured at 91bhp at 6200rpm on the Abingdon chassis dynamometer. This car, maybe, was not as fast as the 2.5PIs with which it was to run in concert, but the crews thought it was at least as powerful as they were able to cope with! The car entry numbers, crews, and registrations were:

no 70	Gavin Thompson/HRH Prince Michael of Kent/ Nigel Clarkson (As prepared by Janspeed, but with some support from Abingdon)	XMO 412H
no 74	Rosemary Smith/Alice Watson/Ginette Derolland	XJB 306H
no 96	Terry Kingsley/Peter Evans/Mike Scarlett	XJB 307H

None of these cars seems to have been used in serious motorsport after they returned from the World Cup Rally.

'My Dad's going to Mexico' – John Handley's son, along with his wife, Sonia, wishes him well at Wembley: co-driver Paul Easter waits to get on board for the first time.

Perhaps it was never going to last the distance, but this brightly painted Mini 1275GT brought real glamour to the first few days of the event. It was driven by John Handley and Paul Easter.

However, although this car was undoubtedly faster than any other entered by British Leyland on the World Cup, it was always set up as the 'hare' to all the other 'hounds' and was not expected to get to the finish in Central America. Although there were doubts that it would even reach Lisbon, and be hoisted aboard the SS Derwent, British Leyland managed to obtain support from BBC (British Broadcasting Corporation) Grandstand, which made a lot of the project, and team boss Peter Browning's instructions were, simply, to "Lead the event on arrival at Lisbon!"

Such were the team's priorities, that very little provision for spares and service in South America was ever made for this car. It was a measure of its supposed fragility, and highly-tuned state, that the chosen car was delivered to scrutineering at Wembley Stadium on a trailer, having virtually no road miles on the clock!

Although the car itself (XJB 308H) was brand-new, its engineering was a lineal; development of everything learned on the

Mini 1275GT

This was the final technical development of the Mini-Cooper and Mini-Cooper S pedigree which had been rallied by the factory since 1962.

'works' Mini-Cooper race and rally cars since they had come into use in 1962. At the height of their fame these cars had been outright winners in events as various as the Monte Carlo, the Acropolis, the French Alpine,

British Leyland's highly tuned Mini 1275GT soon retired with engine problems – though was motoring healthily enough when captured on a European Prime.

John Handley (left) and Paul Easter, ready to start the World Cup Rally in this highly-tuned Mini 1275GT. Few expected the car to reach the finish – and the team orders were "to lead into Lisbon"! Unhappily, the engine expired in Italy after only four days.

the Finnish 1000 Lakes and the British RAC Rallies – but had never been considered credible 'endurance' material – which makes the aim for some immediate publicity more understandable.

The bodyshell chosen was of the longer-nose square-style type of the Clubman/1275GT (this was done for publicity purposes, as the Clubman had only just gone on sale), and was much lightened, and was kitted out with competition-rated Hydrolastic suspension.

However, even before the event could begin, the troubles started, for although John Handley carried out much testing, he and co-driver Paul Easter found their plans for a detailed reconnaissance of the European section frustrated by awful weather, which culminated in them being stranded in the Yugoslavian resort of Dubrovnik for three days on one occasion.

Based on the definitive specification of the existing 1275S rally cars, the 1293cc engine ran on twin SU carburettors, in full Downton-type tune, and was claimed to produce 115bhp at the flywheel, which was just about as much as that engine could ever be expected to develop. Not only was an engine oil cooler tucked in behind the front grille, but there was a secondary water radiator, too. The final drive ratio was 3.9:1, the usual 'comps' straight-cut gearbox cluster was chosen, and 12 inch (30.5cm) diameter wheels with 6 inch (15.2cm) rims were fitted. The bodyshell included a roll cage, and closing panels (doors, bonnet or boot lid) were in aluminium and glass-fibre, with a huge extra bag fuel tank, by Autovita, to bring total capacity up to 22 gallons (100L).

However, everything, unhappily, seemed to go wrong with this car. There was a lot of trouble in pre-event testing and shakedown, it had to take third place in Abingdon's workshop priorities (behind the finalisation of the A-team of Triumphs, and of the Austin Maxis, too) and on the event itself there were difficult-to-trace fuel starvation problems in the Balkans. In the end, the pistons suffered, the engine began to consume vast quantities of oil, and the engine blew in a big way on a Prime in Italy (only four days after the event had started) – and, as gloomily forecast in advance – it never even had the chance to get as far as the start of the South American sections.

The car itself, though it retired before reaching Lisbon, was otherwise amazingly intact at that juncture. Suitably re-prepared, it then proved its worth by finishing second overall in the Scottish Rally of June 1970, with Paddy Hopkirk behind the wheel. Its details at the World Cup Rally were:

no 59	John Handley/Paul Easter	XJB 308H

Range Rover – well yes, but ...

Although this is a diversion, a might-have-been, even – it is worth noting that in the early stages, British Leyland was actively considering using the brand-new four-wheel-drive Range Rover for what I might whimsically call the 'B-Team' – Rosemary Smith, the Red Arrows and (at the time) the Evan Green/'Gelignite' Jack Murray combination from Australia.

When Peter Browning issued a 'this is where we are' document on 19 August 1969, he suggested that, apart from the Triumphs: "... we will be preparing a team of Range Rovers." Noting that this brand-new four-wheel-drive machine was still on the secret list, he pointed out that a pre-production car would soon be available for testing, and that public launch was currently forecast for March 1970 – just weeks before the World Cup Rally was due to start.

Because the Range Rover was to use a lightly-tuned 3.5-litre Rover V8 engine, would have amazing traction, and theoretically should have taken any or all of the World Cup conditions in its stride, this was an intriguing prospect. Unhappily, however, although Prototype no 3 was duly shipped to BL Motorsport in the autumn, things then went horrendously, and hilariously, wrong:

"Everyone now knows the story," Peter Browning recalls, "where we took this Range Rover out on test, and Geoff Mabbs rolled it, in front of the entire Range Rover board of directors ..."

If I may quote historian Bill Price on this incident:

"The entourage, including [Engineering Director] Peter Wilks, was standing on a corner near the end of the straight at the Girling test track [at Honiley – it is now a Prodrive-owned facility], when Geoff arrived at high speed. He locked his brakes in an attempt to get round, but only succeeded in going off the road, launching the vehicle into the air over a low bank. The headlamps flew out, the headlining dropped down and at least one door was damaged. The directors cringed at the spectacle, which was not helped by Geoff coming over to the assembled throng and commenting that he had 'experienced a bit of bump steer' ..."

Enthusiasm for the project seems to have died from that moment, and when it became clear that the car's launch was to be put back to June 1970 (i.e. after the World Cup Rally had taken place), the scheme was speedily abandoned.

BMC 1800

Although these were not official 'works' cars, and all were privately financed, no fewer than five

All the way from Australia, Ken Tubman's factory-backed BMC 1800 takes the start from Wembley Stadium on 19 April 1970.

This was the pre-World Cup 'christening' of the Austin 1800 which was sponsored by Motorwoman, a section of Woman magazine, and christened the Beauty Box. The drivers were (left to right) Pat Wright, Liz Crellin and Jean Denton, while the Editor of Woman (Barbara Buss) sprays the champagne. The 'Beauty Box' kept going, and finished in a very creditable 18th place.

front-wheel-drive 1800s were prepared by Basil Wales' Special Tuning Department at Abingdon, and a sixth (Car no 32, from Australia) benefited from preparation advice and parts supply. For that reason alone, these cars deserve to be analysed in detail.

The 'works' 1800 – soon christened the 'Super Land Crab' – had first been used as a serious machine in 1967, when Tony Fall had won the Danube Rally, and another car had taken a series of endurance records on the banked track at Monza in the same year. In 1968 a full team had contested the East African Safari, but there was no success, especially as two cars suffered front suspension breakages.

Then came the London-Sydney Marathon, where five much-modified 100bhp/twin-SU carburetted cars started. All five finished, Paddy Hopkirk second overall, and Rauno Aaltonen fifth. This was a great performance, but the general impression was that for the World Cup, competing cars needed to be even faster, so the 1800s were not chosen again as works cars. Several other 1800s, though, were used by private entrants:

no 3	Peter Jopp/Willy Cave/Mark Kahn	JOP 1E
no 32	Ken Tubman/Andrew Welinsky/Bob McAuley	AZN 256
no 34	Hugh Penfold/Eric McInally/Peter Jones	OOH 745G
no 54	Reg Redgrave/Phil Cooper/Bob Freeborough	OOH 744G
no 55	Lt-Comm J Mitchell/Lt A Evans/PO R Taylor	HPV 491F
no 91	Ms Jean Denton/Ms Pat Wright/Ms Liz Crellin	NOB 284F

Citroën

A positive fleet of so-called 'private entry' Citroën DS21s took part in the World Cup, but this definition seemed partly to be a ploy, so that the drivers could make a serious attempt to win the financially lucrative Private Entrant's Awards. Although this strategy was fairly obvious – and, up to a point, excusable – it meant that some of the genuine private owners further down the field could never win the prize money which would otherwise have made all the difference to them.

Although the new Citroëns were all sold to private individuals/teams, the fact that they were newly-prepared by the factory's competitions department, that all the cars carried Paris registrations, were all supported

Basil Wales' Special Tuning Department prepared five BMC 1800s, at Abingdon, to compete in the World Cup Rally – all being ready for delivery at this point.

Although Claudine Trautmann thoroughly deserved to win the Ladies' category of the World Cup Rally, her Citroën DS21's engine expired only a day before reaching the last Time Control at Fortin. It was not a good month for the Trautmanns, for husband René had crashed his DS21 while leading the event.

by Citroën factory personnel, and in almost all cases the drivers were recognised as Citroën 'works' pilots, blew that pretence out of the water from day one. One visual difference from a normal 'works' Citroën effort, by the way, was that they did not all appear in the usual 'works' blue livery. René Trautmann's car, which led the event on arrival in Lisbon, for instance, was red, and his wife Claudine Trautmann's car (a major contender for the Ladies' Prize) was white!

Although their 'private entrant' status was not challenged, I have no hesitation in listing them as a surrogate 'works' team, especially as team boss René Cotton and his wife/assistant Marlene had personally carried out a systematic recce in South America – an activity which featured in the promotional film Citroën produced afterwards, makes clear.

In one form or another, in fact, one or other of the ID/DS 'big' Citroën family had been in rallying since 1956, and the team had recorded some famous victories, including wins in the Monte Carlo Rally (1959 and

1966), Liège-Rome-Liège, Morocco and near-success in the London-Sydney Marathon, where Lucien Bianchi's leading car was eliminated by an open-road crash on the very last day when it all looked set for victory.

Three of the cars (those of René Trautmann, Claudine Trautmann and Guy Verrier) were equipped with the newly-launched fuel-injected engine, the other three having the conventional carburettor engine, all of them being of 2.1-litres. None, however, used what driver Patrick Vanson described as 'works thin bodies' (which refers to the thin-gauge steel pressings used for body skin panels in an effort to save weight), but their factory provenance was obvious.

Tyres were, of course, provided by Michelin. The cars' details were:

no 12	Robert Neyret/Jacques Terramorsi	3356 TT75
no 25	Ms Claudine Trautmann/Ms Colette Perrier	3492 TT75
no 47	Paul Coltelloni/Ido Marang	Not identified

Three of the works-prepared, but privately-entered, Citroën DS21s lined up at a Control in Europe. No 12 was Robert Neyret's car, which retired in Peru, no 25 was that of Claudine Trautmann, who was desperately unlucky not to win the Ladies' category, and no 93 was that of René Trautmann, who led the event until he crashed early in the South American section.

no 93	René Trautmann/Jean-Pierre Hanrioud	3493 TT75
no 100	Patrick Vanson/Olivier Turcat/Alain Leprince	3867 TT75
no 101	Guy Verrier/Francis Murac	3861 TT75

Ford

By any standards – and this is not to overstate what had happened – Ford had been humiliated on the London-Sydney Marathon of 1968, for although their Lotus-Cortinas had certainly been fast, they were neither strong enough, nor reliable enough to survive such a long event. For the World Cup, which was going to be much tougher – and longer – it was clear that they would have to build better cars.

So, which cars to choose? Much hinged on the reconnaissance, and the route surveys. When the Scandinavians came back from their first look-see, they were convinced that they would need big cars, and would need to go three-up. Stuart Turner, on the other hand, was not convinced, and resisted strongly. After much discussion – not bitter argument, but animated discussion – the two-up route was chosen.

Roger Clark, on the other hand, was one of the last drivers to go to

Colleagues in the 1960s, but rivals in 1970 – Ford Competitions Manager Stuart Turner (left) talking to Paddy Hopkirk (British Leyland) before the start of the event.

South America, and came back convinced that although it was going to be very tough, very long, and very tiring, it was still just a rally, and that two-up in durable Escorts was the way to go.

After much pre-event testing and assessment – Ford-Germany Taunus 20Ms, Capris, Cortinas and Zodiac Mk IVs were all considered, and it became clear that the otherwise most suitable machine, was the Taunus (of Ford-Germany) which so nearly won the London-Sydney Marathon, and which had just won the East African Safari – it was decided to build the strongest, yet mechanically simplest, Escort which could be competitive. The result was a car which was conceived, then gradually evolved, by Bill Meade, Mick Jones and Peter Ashcroft. Certain aspects of the car were also evolved after race-car designer Len Bailey had also been consulted.

Because neither of the team's high performance engines – the 8-valve Lotus-Ford Twin Cam, or the new 16-valve Cosworth BDA-type – could yet be trusted if fuel quality was in any way suspect, it was decided to run cars with a version of the well-proven overhead-valve 'Kent' instead.

51

Why drive when you can get an organiser to push the car for you? John Sprinzel doing the labourer's job with Roger Clark's Escort at Lisbon.

This was the fascia/instrument panel of a 'works' Ford Escort, on the 1970 World Cup Rally. Note – the seats have been removed to allow other detail to be photographed.

These were enlarged to 1.85-litres (with enlarged cylinder bores, and much-modified thick wall cylinder block castings), were power and endurance tuned to produce about 140bhp, and could be rebuilt very rapidly if needed. Most importantly, if a change of cylinder head was needed in – say – Bolivia or Peru, and there was an emergency, a standard production 'cross-flow' Escort or Mk 2 Cortina head would fit, and the repaired car would then run satisfactorily, if not to optimum specification.

Under the skin, too, the cars had wide-ratio, five-speed ZF gearboxes, Ford-Germany, Atlas-type rear axles, and disc brakes all round, plus the visibly unique, and obvious, roll cage arrangement which included what Rally Engineer Bill Meade dubbed 'buzzard' bars: these tubes linked the top of the front suspension struts with the top of the windscreen pillars. As is now well-known, the axle tubes wilted under the weight of all the fuel above them, and several broke or cracked in the first week. A 'fix' was designed, tested and manufactured while the cars were actually on the high seas between Lisbon and Rio de Janeiro: a Dural stiffening plate was bolted to the back of the differential casings, and clamped to the tubes themselves, effectively acting as an enormously strong bridge piece.

The boot seemed to be full of tanks, pumps and pipework. Nine gallon tanks (40.9L) were tucked into each side of the boot, and there was a 10 gallon (45.5L) central tank (making 28 gallons/127.3L in all), along with a 2.5 gallon (11.4L) dry sump tank into the bargain. Somehow, too, space was found to mount a solid post on the floor of the boot, with two spare Minilite wheels mounted on it.

Ford, along with British Leyland, put in thousands of miles (and hours), not only in testing the specification of the cars at the Bagshot rough-road facility (which was a military installation), but in several serious route survey and recce expeditions – one of which included entering Tony Fall and Gunnar Palm in the Rally of the Incas, in Peru, an event which they won

Jimmy Greaves (left) was paired up with Tony Fall (centre) for the World Cup Rally. Here, they both listen intently to Roger Clark, as he talks through some detail they have just learned at Boreham.

quite comfortably. Nevertheless, it took ages to settle on the specification of the cars, which might explain why they were not finished well ahead of the start, and why a specification failing in rear axle materials was not spotted until the event itself had actually started.

The signing of football star Jimmy Greaves to partner Tony Fall in one of the cars was a publicity master stroke, originally engineered jointly by Walter Hayes of Ford, and the *Daily Mirror*. At a stroke, it meant that so long as the car was still running, it was guaranteed full coverage in the football-orientated newspapers.

Stuart Turner, originally sceptical about the wisdom of this signing, was finally convinced when Greaves went to Boreham to drive an Escort in a press call. Drawing Turner privately to one side on this occasion, Jimmy apparently said: "If I make a prat of myself before the event, and you don't think I can do it, let's call the whole thing off! ..." – which was as honest a remark as a superstar could possibly make.

(But the event was tough for both of them. During the event, an exhausted Tony Fall was once heard to say that: "After the end, we're going to have a football match in Mexico, and we're going to use Sprinzel's head as the f****** ball ...")

For simplicity's sake, I have titled these cars 'Escort 1850' throughout, for although they were Twin-Cam or RS1600 based, they used conventional overhead-valve engines. Incidentally, they could certainly not be called Escort Mexicos, as that model was not even developed until after the event (this process came in a tearing hurry, by the way), as a tribute to the World Cup success that had just taken place. The competing cars were:

Here's a puzzle for future historians – although Roger Clark started the World Cup as no 65, it was not in this car, which was a hard-working Escort that had already competed in the 1969 Alpine Rally with a V6 engine fitted! By the way, this is the British Bagshot testing facility.

no 14	Sobieslaw Zasada/Mark Wachowski	FTW 48H
no 18	Hannu Mikkola/Gunnar Palm	FEV 1H
no 26	Tony Fall/Jimmy Greaves	FEV 2H
no 46	Rauno Aaltonen/Henry Liddon	FTW 46H
no 65	Roger Clark/Alec Poole	FEV 3H
no 85	Colin Malkin/Richard Hudson-Evans	FTW 47H
no 103	Timo Makinen/Gilbert Staepelaere	FEV 4H

FEV 1H to FEV 4H were prepared at the Motorsport Centre at Boreham in Essex, along with several recce, practice and test cars.

Because time and man-hours were both beginning to run out in the months before the start, Ford had to have three cars prepared elsewhere, from kits of parts supplied from Boreham. This explains why FTW 46H, FTW 47H and FTW 48H were all prepared outside the Boreham Competitions Department – by Clarke & Simpson (under David Sutton's control), British Vita and Clarks of Narborough (Roger Clark's business) – and were all nut-and-bolt copies of the machines being built up at Boreham.

Tyres were provided by Goodyear, which was still involved in a multi-year contract to support the 'works' Ford team, and it mounted a major operation for this, its only UK-contracted, rally team. As far as surviving records tell us, Goodyear provided its normal rubber for this event, of a type which might have been taken on the Safari rally. There would be times when the drivers wished for something more robust ...

There were no team orders and, in retrospect, several people are still surprised that Hannu Mikkola should have proved victorious. Before the start, Rauno Aaltonen and Sobieslaw Zasada were privately fancied – and in fact Rauno might have been very much in the driving seat if his gearbox tail shaft had not broken up at a very early stage during the European section.

Towards the end, too, when Timo Makinen realised that he could not now win the event, he approached Turner, and offered to 'shadow' Hannu Mikkola to the finish – offering to carry a small welding kit, and other spares, in his own Escort, just in case they might be needed when Hannu had problems a long way away from Ford service. It worked, and it worked well – sequences from Ford's film *Five for the Fiesta*, show Hannu's Escort (FEV 1H) disappearing from a shot at almost exactly the time Makinen's car (FEV 4H) appeared.

Stuart Turner, incidentally, makes the point that although the service 'umbrella' was perfectly organised (and, incidentally, Bill Barnett, who did much of this work, did not go to South America at all!), that it was one Benito Lores, a Ford dealer/administrator from Ford-Peru, who contributed

Four privately-prepared (but 'works' specified) Hillman Hunter/Hillman GT saloons, ready for the start of the World Cup. Peter Brown's JCB-sponsored car is closest to the camera, with Mike Tyrrell's car next, then Rod Badham's Berry Magicoal-sponsored car, and Alun Rees' car on its left side. Rees would finish in 15th place.

a lot to the running of the team. Within Ford, Benito became known as the 'Sergeant Bilko' of the outfit, the charming wheeler-dealer-fixer to whom border controls, Customs officials, and similar bureaucratic obstacles were an enjoyable challenge to be met, and surmounted, rather than suffered.

It was Lores who supervised the pre-positioning of the mountains of spare parts placed around the route in South America, many of which were not needed when the cars eventually arrived. Some of those spares were shipped back to the UK afterwards, but some were not. Turner is still convinced that, to this day, there may be rusty old Escorts in use in some of those countries which are running on Minilite wheels, with bullet-proof windscreens ...

(One scurrilous rumour which circulated for a long time after the event was that Ford had prepared at least one spare 'clone' Escort, which was secretly flown to South America, and which could be used while another car was being rebuilt behind closed doors. This is 100 per cent wrong, and totally misguided. As Stuart Turner retorted when he heard the rumours:

"Anyone clever enough to organise such a scam, and to take a car from place to place, without being found out at the time, would deserve my job ... And nobody applied!")

Hillman

Were these really 'works' cars? To coin a show-business phrase – 'yes-but-no-but-yes-but no ...' – for although the specification of the cars was extremely close to that which had won the London-Sydney Marathon in 1968, and the team received much 'works' advice and components, there was no actual preparation in Coventry, and very little back-up on the event itself.

Since the Hunter had won the London-Sydney Marathon in 1968, almost everything back at the factory (in Humber Road, Coventry) had changed, not least in the attitude of the owner (Chrysler), to Motorsport. Competitions Manager Marcus Chambers had been moved to an engineering job, the competitions department itself had been effectively closed down

Every competitor got the same ceremonial send-off. This was Rod Badham and Rob Lyall, the fourth car to start, ready to leave the tramp at Wembley Stadium.

– or merely put on a 'life support' system – while Marcus' successor, Des O'Dell, was only authorised to work on customer projects which would make money for the company.

This mean that although there would be four newly-prepared Hunter-based cars for the 1970 World Cup, which were virtual replicas of the victorious 1968 London-Sydney Marathon-winning Hillman Hunter, none of them were prepared in the department in Coventry. Des O'Dell somehow managed to raise the funds to fly out to South America to follow these cars (he spent many hours in British Leyland's chartered Bristol Britannia aircraft), as a 'lone-wolf' he was really powerless to affect the outcome.

The London-Sydney Hunter specification had included slightly de-tuned versions of the Sunbeam Rapier H120 engine (complete with twin dual-choke Weber carburettors, and approximately 100bhp as set up to run on poor-quality fuel), a four-speed gearbox with overdrive, and a non-standard Salisbury-type rear axle.

The bodyshells were reinforced in the normal way, including seam welding at appropriate points, and strengthening around suspension pick-ups, and a roll-over bar was specified. The firmed-up suspension rode higher than on normal road cars, both of which were necessary and desirable because this car had been designed for three-up occupation (though the Badham/Lyall crew was of only two individuals), and because the total fuel tank capacity was 37 gallons (168.2L). Minilite cast alloy road wheels were fitted. The cars' details were:

no 4	Rod Badham/Rob Lyall	MWK 938G
no 17	Peter Brown/John Bloxham/Robert McBurney	JCB 582
no 81	Michael Tyrrell/James Fuller/Bernard Unett	CMC 946H
no 83	Alun Rees/Hywel Thomas/Washington James	GEJ 166F

According to the official entry forms/car passports, no 4 and no 83

A team of youthful supporters for Sergei Tenishev's Moskvich, before the start.

Although the 'works' Moskviches were not very fast, they were very well prepared, and their drivers took the event very seriously. Ivan Astafiev was forced to retire during the South American section.

were originally Hillman Hunters, while no 17 and no 81 were Hillman GTs. The differences were purely in badging, and in original equipment, for all cars were four-door saloons, with live axle rear suspension: all cars ran in the same much-modified 'London-Sydney' form on the World Cup Rally.

Moskvich

Almost nothing was known about the five Moskvich 412s which were prepared in the Soviet Union, shipped over to compete in the World Cup, competed with honour, and were speedily taken back there, never to be seen again. They may or may not have been close to the production cars that were being produced in big numbers, but as they were not competitive and were unlikely to beat the other 'works' cars, few objections or eligibility quibbles were even raised.

Moskvich, it has to be said, had no success record in European rallying, and by any standards their cars were crudely engineered, very basically prepared, and totally uncompetitive by European standards. But

Ready to leave from Wembley Stadium, a strange car in a strange (to them) land – this was Emanouil Lifchits and Victor Chtchavelev in one of the five 'works' Moskvich saloons.

they were strong, simple to repair, and the crew were all trained mechanics – that was vitally important. Not only that, but in spite of the language barrier, all the drivers seemed to be thoroughly nice people, and were well-liked by their peers.

A team of four earlier types – 408s with the earlier-type Soviet engine – had started, completed, and finished the 1968 London-Sydney Marathon Rally with honour.

Introduced in 1969, the 412 saloon was an update of the earlier 408. It used a single-overhead-camshaft 80bhp/1478cc engine, which by all accounts had been copied from the then-modern BMW unit. However, the chassis was old fashioned, drum brakes were still fitted all round, and the top speed of this somewhat top-heavy car was little more than 90mph (144.8kph).

In rallying, even in rough and tough long-distance rallying, this Moskvich was always going to be outclassed. Although communication was almost impossible between the crews, their rivals, and the organisers on the World Cup, they were all cheerful, and were all respected by their rivals. Three of the five cars finished – in 12th, 17th and 20th positions, which was as high as could ever have been expected. The Moskvichs were:

no 21	Ivan Astafiev/Alexandre Safonov/Stasys Brundza	05-01 ABT
no 28	Leonti Potapchik/Edouard Bajenov/Youri Lessovski	05-02 ABT
no 40	Sergei Tenichev/Valentin Kislykh/Valeri Chirotchenkov	05-03 ABT
no 71	Gunnar Kholm/Vladimir Boubnov/Kastytis Girdauskas	05-04 ABT
no 84	Emanouil Lifchits/Victor Chtchavelev	05-05 ABT

Ford Escort driver Rauno Aaltonen recalls that whenever or wherever he found that he had to pass a Moskvich, that invariably there would be at least three of them driving closely in line astern. The story goes that the main reason was that the Soviet authorities deliberately kept them under-supplied with maps to stop them defecting to the West ...

Peugeot-Argentina

Although Peugeot-France was officially not interested in this event, the Argentinian subsidiary (Safrar – Peugeot-Argentina) most certainly was. Because the long-established 404 was already a very successful long-distance rally car (it had several East African victories to its credit), this was the obvious Peugeot model to use.

Information later released by team boss Claude Le Guezec showed that the cars had 504-type 1.8-litre engines, reinforced bodyshells, low axle ratios (5.21:1), and ran with three fuel tanks, their capacity totalling 150 litres (33 gallons). Preparation, incidentally, didn't begin until 23 February 1970, before the cars had to be flown to London to start the event.

Of the drivers, Larreta and Perkins were Argentine locals, while Jean-Claude Ogier was an established French driver, well-respected on the European scene, where many of his earlier rally successes had been in Citroën DS19s and DS21s. Along with Lucien Bianchi, Ogier came close to winning the London-Sydney Marathon of 1968 in a Citroën DS21, until a last day accident wiped out their chances. The World Cup cars were:

no 63	ER Larreta/J Migliore	B.131.861
no 66	Gaston Perkins/Jack Forrest Greene	B.131.862
no 76	Jean-Claude Ogier/Claude Laurent	B.131.859

Other notables

Never before, and perhaps never again, had a major rally attracted such a wide variety of cars, entrants and personalities to its lists. Even the famous Monte Carlo rallies of the 1930s, 1940s and 1950s, whose lists included titled owners whose chauffeur drove the cars, diesel-powered buses, special-bodied monstrosities, Rolls-Royce Silver Wraith limousines, Daimler mayoral carriages, and London taxi-cabs, could not match them. In rallying terms, though, there was still a fascinating eclectic list of machinery and teams. These were the most interesting:

No 2: The Porsche 911, crewed by Terry Hunter and Geoff Mabbs, looked likely to be fast and strong. Much factory advice had gone into the building of this car (the Hunter/Porsche combination had also competed in the London-Sydney Marathon), Hunter was an abrasive character who had previously driven in the BMC and Triumph 'works' teams, while Mabbs was known, and respected, at BMC team and testing level. In the event, it would be fast while it lasted. It eventually broke down in Bolivia.

No 13: The Martins – father William, and his two sons David and Julian – hailed from Kent, their 1957 Rolls-Royce Silver Cloud already being 13 years old. As far as anyone knew, the team had no previous serious rally experience, and had entered, not because they thought they might win, but merely for the adventure. Although they always drove very sedately, and were always well down near the bottom of the classification, at least they got the massive machine as far as Brazil, where their car then suffered a broken front suspension component. Although they somehow had the car repaired in the wilderness, they arrived two days late in Montevideo (Uruguay), and were forced out.

No 19: The VW (Volkswagen) Beetle, crewed by three impecunious young Mexicans (JH Perez Vega, G Hinojosa Rivero, and JA Barcena) seemed to be a classic no-hopers, where – according to them – money was almost non-existent, and there seemed to be every chance that they would become destitute even before the cars reached South America. The sob-story – 'we just want to get home' – was very effective, though.

At one stage, other kind and gullible competitors actually clubbed together to provide them with more funds. Not that this mattered in the end, for once in South America they soon disappeared from the event, and were not seen again.

No 49: The Mercedes-Benz 280E, entered by Annabels Nightclub, and crewed by Mark Birley (of Annabels), and ex-F1 (Formula 1) drivers Innes Ireland and Mike Taylor, brought a touch of glamour to the proceedings. Nor was this just a showbiz entry, for Birley had already competed with honour in the East African Safari, and Ireland had tackled the London-Sydney Marathon. None of them, however, had done any practice for the event, and the arts and crafts of navigation seemed to be distinctly lacking.

Two other privately-entered 280Es, German-prepared and driven by Edgar Hermann (ex-Safari victor) and by Alfred Katz seemed to take the event more seriously, and towards the end of the event were often well and competently placed in the Primes. Katz's car would finally finish 16th overall.

No 50: John Caulcutt's Beach Buggy was probably the least suitable of all cars entered in this event, because it was based only on a VW Beetle chassis platform, with a 1.9-litre Beetle-based engine, had a crew of three (all in their intrepid twenties), but had a glass-fibre bodyshell, with a fold-away canvas roof and no weather protection at the sides. Seasoned competitors inspected this car at scrutineering, and shuddered about its prospects for dealing with altitude and unmade roads. Naturally, they thought, it had no sensible chance of finishing, and none at all of winning any awards – and it duly retired.

No 52: Ray Richards, 40 years old, was a globe-trotting businessman, clearly out for an adventure, if not success. Entrusting the preparation to one-time British Rally Champion Bill Bengry (whose base was in Leominster), and route-finding to Bill's regular co-driver David Skeffington, he entered a new Rolls-Royce Silver Shadow. Among the extraordinary features Bengry applied to this car was an exhaust system which saw the tail pipes channelled out of the bonnet, up the front of the screen pillars, and along the roof: Bill had actually incorporated such a feature on a Ford Cortina that he had earlier prepared for the London-Sydney Marathon of 1968.

Rolls-Royce, naturally, wanted nothing to do with what it considered to be a monstrosity, which did not line-up at all with its own self-styled reputation and image of patrician excellence, so parts supply and support from Crewe were minimal. When the car duly broke its rear suspension just before the Lisbon Control, Bengry somehow had to find a local Silver Shadow in Portugal, to persuade the owner to let him take some parts from it, and got the car ready for shipment to South America: it was only then that Rolls-Royce was persuaded to supply parts to that private owner, whose car was duly restored to pristine condition.

Although it duly restarted from Rio de Janeiro, retirement followed after a crash in Brazil. Richards then flew off home to carry on his business life, but Bill Bengry eventually patched up the car, cut-off a massive corner of the route to rejoin the event on the Pacific coast, and followed the rally to the finish. Bill, in fact, used the Silver Shadow as a 'chase car' on one occasion for British Leyland, to ferry mechanics and parts to the stricken Paddy Hopkirk Triumph 2.5PI. Not only that, but he acted as a 'flying mechanic' for a number of private owners, too.

The car was later returned to standard, and apparently sold off at an auction in Bengry's native Herefordshire.

No 80: Brothers Joseph and James Sherger, British-born, but living in Kuwait, entered an eight-year-old Fiat 2300 estate car. Clearly they had little idea of the demands this event would make on a crew, seem to have done very little pre-event preparation and, in any case, chose to use a car with no previous rallying history.

Within 24 hours of starting the event from Wembley Stadium, they had apparently lost their way more than once in Germany, had already missed more than one Passage Control, and soon ran out of time, suffering from exhaustion. Although they eventually called Rally HQ in London for advice, and finally turned up at the Sofia Control, they were hours outside time limits, and they seem to have been the very first to be excluded from the rally.

Picking the entries – 'seeding' non-existent

If the starting order had been governed by an established method, by taking into account a car or driver's existing rally record, all the 'works' cars would have started at the front, and all the private owners, hangers-on and 'holiday-makers' would have followed on behind them – but this is not how the *Daily Mirror* wanted it to happen. Instead, in a glittering evening organised at London's Cafe Royal in Regent Street, the world-famous captain of the English World Cup football team, Bobby Moore, was hired to draw each name out of a box to establish the starting order by chance. This explains, of course, why Bobby Buchanan-Michaelson (multi-millionaire, eccentric, financial chancer, and sometime jailbird) came to start in the no 1 position, why the peoples' pre-rally favourite Paddy Hopkirk drew no 98, and why the ultimate winner, Hannu Mikkola, eventually started from no 18.

Of the major teams, Ford was rather lucky in this draw, for its seven cars were spread between nos 14 and 103, but British Leyland was extremely unlucky, with three of the big Triumphs seeded at 88, 92 and 98, while three of the six Citroëns were to run at 93, 100 and 101. For some, therefore, the problems of support and servicing in the first few days appeared to be difficult.

This rather idiosyncratic choice of starting order, however, would only apply to the first week of rallying (London-Sofia-Lisbon), for once the event restarted from Rio de Janeiro it would be 're-seeded', which meant that the cars would always start from overnight halts in classification order. This, therefore, meant that René Trautmann's Citroën DS21 led the cavalcade out of Rio, that Hannu Mikkola led from Buenos Aires, and that therefore Hannu's Escort would always be the first car to start from any major Time Control.

Entry list — *Daily Mirror* World Cup Rally 1970

1	Bobby Buchanan-Michaelson/Roy Fidler/Jimmy Bullough	Triumph 2.5PI
2	Terry Hunter/Geoff Mabbs	Porsche 911S
3	Peter Jopp/Mark Kahn/Willy Cave	BMC 1800
4	Rod Badham/Rob Lyall	Hillman Hunter
5	Ivica Vukova/Sreten Djordjevic/Nestor Milanov	Peugeot 404D
6	John Hemsley/Wally Easton	Peugeot 504
7	Chris Coburn/Peter Garratt/Bob Grainger	Vauxhall Viva GT
8	John Rhodes/Joseph Minto	Peugeot 504
9	Ian Harwood/Frank Pierson/Barry Hughes	Ford Lotus-Cortina
10	Cliff Woodley/Robert Locke/Philip Waller	Vauxhall Ventora
11	Paul M Donner/Martin M Donner	Ford Capri 1600
12	Robert Neyret/Jacques Terramorsi	Citroën DS21
13	David Martin/William Martin/Julian Martin	Rolls-Royce Silver Cloud
14	Sobieslaw Zasada/Marek Wachowski	Ford Escort 1850
15	Ron Channon/Rod Cooper	Ford Cortina GT
16	Jim Gardner/Laurie Ritchie	Ford Escort Elba Motor Caravan
17	Peter Brown/John Bloxham/Robert McBurney	Hillman GT
18	Hannu Mikkola/Gunnar Palm	Ford Escort 1850
19	JM Perez/G Hinojosa/JA Bercena	VW Beetle
20	Patricia Ozanne/Bronwen Burrell/Katrina Grace	Austin Maxi
21	Ivan Astafiev/Alexandre Safonov/Stasys Brundza	Moskvich 412
22	Bob de Jong/Christiaan Emile Tuerlinx	Alfa Romeo Giulia 1600 Super
23	Non-runner	
24	Edgar Hermann/Dieter Benz/Horst Walter	Mercedes-Benz 280SE
25	Claudine Trautmann/Colette Perrier	Citroën DS21
26	Jimmy Greaves/Tony Fall	Ford Escort 1850
27	Alfonso Moldini/Giuseppe Bottaro	Porsche 911S
28	Leonti Potapchik/Edouard Bajenov/Youri Lessovski	Moskvich 412
29	William Bendek/Dieter Hubner/Jorge Burgoa	BMW 2002ti
30	Christopher Marriott/John Dill	Trident Venturer
31	Non-runner	
32	Kenneth Tubman/Andre Welinsky/Robert McAuley	BMC 1800

33	Carlos Zicavo/Alcides Specos/Alfredo Verna	Peugeot 504
34	Hugh Penfold/Eric McInally/Peter Jones	BMC 1800
35	Non runner	
36	Peter Kube/Lother Ranft	BMW 2002ti
37	Tony Walker/Dennis Leonard/James Burton	Vauxhall Victor Estate
38	Fred Katz/Alfred Kling/Albert Pfuhl	Mercedes-Benz 280SE
39	Adrian Lloyd-Hirst/Brian Englefield/Keith Baker	Triumph 2.5PI
40	Sergei Tenichev/Valentin Kislykh/Valeri Chirotchenkov	Moskvich 412
41	J Rugge-Price/C Morley-Fletcher/P Beaver	BMC 1800
42	José Araújo/John Batley	Volvo 144
43	Andrew Cowan/Brian Coyle/Uldarico Ossio	Triumph 2.5PI
44	Brian Chuchua/Richard Goold/William Kirkland	Jeep Wagoneer
45	Doug Harris/Mike Butler	Ford Escort GT
46	Rauno Aaltonen/Henry Liddon	Ford Escort 1850
47	Paul Coltelloni/Ido Marang	Citroën DS21
48	Richard Skeels/John Alsop	Ford Cortina GT
49	Michael Taylor/Mark Birley/Innes Ireland	Mercedes-Benz 280SE
50	John Caulcutt/David Stewart/Noel Hutchinson	VW Beach Buggy
51	Bert Jennings/Colin Taylor	Saab V4
52	Ray Richards/Bill Bengry/David Skeffington	Rolls-Royce Silver Shadow
53	Non-runner	
54	Reg Redgrave/Bob Freeborough/Phil Cooper	BMC 1800
55	J Mitchell/A Evans/R Taylor	BMC 1800
56	Eric Celerier/Michael Gauvain	Porsche 911S
57	Non-runner	
58	R Anderson/E Willcocks/Tim Bosence	Volvo 132
59	John Handley/Paul Easter	Mini 1275GT
60	Non-starter	
61	Non-runner	
62	Carlos del Val/J Lazcano/V Ochoa	Seat 1430
63	ER Lareta/Jose Migliore	Peugeot 404
64	Gianpiero Mondini/Mario Contini	Porsche 911S
65	Roger Clark/Alec Poole	Ford Escort 1850
66	Gaston Perkins/J Forrest Greene	Peugeot 404
67	Ted Moorat/John Shaw	Peugeot 504
68	Non-starter	
69	Brian Peacock/Dave Skittrall	Ford Capri 2300
70	Gavin Thompson/HRH Prince Michael of Kent/Nigel Clarkson	Austin Maxi
71	Gunnar Kholm/Vladimir Boubnov/Kastytis Girdauskas	Moskvich 412
72	Freddie Preston/Michael Bailey	Peugeot 504
73	Anthony Pett/David Franks/Robert Robertson	BMC 1800
74	Rosemary Smith/Alice Watson/Ginette Derolland	Austin Maxi
75	Malcolm Wilson/James Walker	Mercedes-Benz 220D
76	Jean-Claude Ogier/Claude Laurent	Peugeot 404
77	Jan Leenders/Preeda Chullamonthol	Toyota Corolla
78	Emil Ipar/Enrique Esteguy/Juan Esteguy	Peugeot 504
79	Rob Janssen/Jaap Dik	Datsun 1600SSS
80	Joseph Sherger/James Sherger	Fiat 2300 Estate
81	Mike Tyrrell/James Fuller/Bernard Unett	Hillman GT
82	Non-runner	

83	Alun Rees/Hywel Thomas/Washington James	Hillman Hunter
84	Emanouil Lifchits/Victor Chtchavelev	Moskvich 412
85	Colin Malkin/Richard Hudson-Evans	Ford Escort 1850
86	Lavinia Roberts/Arthur Hazlerigg/David Jones	Ford Mustang
87	Derek Currell/Robert Currell/Frank Bryan	Peugeot 504
88	Brian Culcheth/Johnstone Syer	Triumph 2.5PI
89	Allan Keefe/James Conroy	BMC Mini-Cooper S
90	Ken Bass/Graham Waring	BMW 2002ti
91	Jean Denton/Pat Wright/Liz Crellin	BMC 1800
92	Evan Green/ Jack Murray/Hamish Cardno	Triumph 2.5PI
93	René Trautmann/Jean-Pierre Hanrioud	Citroën DS21
94	Don Soames-Waring/George Crichton/Andy Thwaite	Ford Cortina GT
95	William Cresdee/Bob Eaves/Franklin Bainbridge	BMC 1800
96	Terry Kingsley/Peter Evans/Michael Scarlett	Austin Maxi
97	Ken Haskell/David Paull/Douglas Larson	Peugeot 404
98	Paddy Hopkitrk/Tony Nash/Neville Johnston	Triumph 2.5PI
99	Kim Brassington/James Carslaw	Ford Cortina Savaga
100	Patrick Vanson/Olivier Turcat/Alain Leprince	Citroën DS21
101	Guy Verrier/Francis Murac	Citroën DS21
102	Non-runner	
103	Timo Makinen/Gilbert Staepelaere	Ford Escort 1850
104	Peter Graham/Leslie Morrish	Ford Cortina Savage
105	Bob East/Bill Chesson	Ford Escort GT
106	E Lamas-Fortes/J Rodoreda-Artasanchez/A Perez-Janeiro	Fiat 124

www.velocebooks.com / www.veloce.co.uk
All current books • New book news • Special offers • Gift vouchers • Forum

Overture and beginners: London to Lisbon

While Wylton Dickson and the *Daily Mirror* did their best to turn the start into a major 'show-business' occasion, the World Cup Rally got under way on time, in great style, and with a great amount of occasion. Although the star drivers and their cars were spread evenly across the entry (the way in which numbers had been drawn made that certain), there was personal and technical interest throughout.

This, it soon transpired, was not going to be a down-beat and altogether mundane start. Instead, arch publicist Dickson delivered a flamboyant occasion to the *Daily Mirror* by hiring Britain's world-famous national football stadium, Wembley Stadium, erecting a suitably decorated ramp on the track that ringed the famous football field, in front of one of the venerable grandstands, and making sure that each car got its minute of glory as it left the start. Everything was made more daunting by the RAC, who erected a 'Bon Voyage' sign saying: "Mexico City – 16,179 miles," (26,038km) at one point and "16,212 miles," (26,091km) at another – which caused everyone to think twice about the enormous challenge which lay ahead.

Many notable motoring personalities turned up at the start – not least Lord Stokes, the Chairman of British Leyland, who was no doubt checking on the huge bills which team boss Peter Browning was already building up. Lord Stokes, however, grinned and bore it, made the most of it, by having himself photographed with his star drivers, not least the ever-glamorous Rosemary Smith in her Austin Maxi. Every national newspaper picked up the picture of the day, which was of Rosemary Smith shaking hands with England football captain Bobby Moore, with Donald Stokes smiling benignly at the moment.

It was the sort of occasion where the world and his famous show-business

This was the route outline of the European section of the 1970 World Cup Rally. There was only one official overnight rest halt – at Monza, in Italy – during that first week.

Start
London 1
Apr 19: 10.30 01.30
Dover 2
Apr 19: 12.30 16.00
Boulogne 3
Apr 19: 18.00 21.00

Saabrucken 4
Apr 20: 02.15 06.15
Munich 5
Apr 20: 08.45 12.45
Vienna 6
Apr 20: 14.45 18.45
Budapest 7
Apr 20: 19.30 23.30

Belgrade 8
Apr 21: 01.30 05.30
Sofia 9
Apr 21: 08.00 12.00

Rodez 15
Apr 24: 04.28 13.28
L'Isle De Noe 16
Apr 25: 09.19 18.19
Arganil 17
Apr 25: 03.05 12.05
Lisbon 18
Apr 25: 08.54 17.54

Rijeka 12
Monza 13
Apr 22. 23: 18.00 04.00
Apr 23: 07.00 10.00
Menton 14
Apr 23:

Glamoc 10
Apr 22: 01.00 11.00
Sanski Most 11
Apr 22: ——— 15.00

World Cup Rally
London to Mexico April 19 : May 27

Ford

63

WHO WOULD WIN? WHAT THE BOOKIES THOUGHT

The final call on bets laid with Ladbrokes was issued as the cars left the start. These were the leading personalities:

Paddy Hopkirk (Triumph 2.5PI)	10-1
Rauno Aaltonen (Ford Escort)	11-1
Roger Clark (Ford Escort)	11-1
Timo Makinen (Ford Escort)	12-1
Hannu Mikkola (Ford Escort)	12-1
Jimmy Greaves with Tony Falls (Ford Escort)	12-1
Robert Neyret (Citroën DS21)	14-1
Andrew Cowan (Triumph 2.5PI)	14-1
Evan Green (Triumph 2.5PI)	14-1
Ray Richards (Rolls-Royce Silver Shadow)	16-1
Brian Culcheth (Triumph 2.5PI)	16-1

Ray Richards must have been flattered to figure so highly, and Brian Culcheth might just have been a bit offended ...

Just before the start at Wembley Stadium, England's football captain Bobby Moore greets Judith Clark (Roger's wife).

wife put in an appearance, where image was thought far more important than substance, and noise seemed to be an all-important factor. No doubt the *Daily Mirror* approved, but event commentator Raymond Baxter did not. It fell to the ever-eloquent Michael Scarlett, of *Autocar* (third crew in the Red Arrows Austin Maxi) to later write that:

"The proceedings were broken half way by a shatteringly noisy pop concert. The best thing said about that is that we hope nothing like that ever happens again ..."

Even so, more than 25,000 noisy and excitable spectators turned up to see the cars get away, and countless thousands also lined Wembley Way, and city streets in London, before

The pre-rally drivers' briefing for the World Cup was so boisterous that organiser John Sprinzel was obliged to use a loud-hailer to make himself heard.

Before the start at Wembley Stadium, British Leyland's chairman, Lord Stokes poses with (right to left) Evan Green, Hamish Cardno, 'Gelignite' Jack Murray, and the Australian ambassador. Their Triumph 2.5PI crashed in France, then developed serious engine trouble, before having to retire in Argentina.

Three cars lined up for the start at Wembley, in front of a big and enthusiastic crowd. Left to right: no 58 (RJG Anderson's Volvo 132), no 56 (E Celerier's Porsche 911S), and just leaving shot, no 55 (the 'Royal Navy' BMC 1800, led by Lt-Comm JJ Mitchell). None of these cars would finish the event.

the cars made their way out to the A20 on the way to the ferry in Dover. The time schedule at this stage was easy enough – easy, that is, if the car was healthy and the traffic being helpful.

Promptly at 10.00hr on Sunday, 19 April, the first car was flagged away by England football manager Sir Alf Ramsey – and just moments later the same car stuttered to a halt on Wembley Way!

Although entrant Bobby Buchanan-Michaelson (well known on the motor racing and social scene, and described to me as an eccentric multi-millionaire who had made much money on Stock Exchange deals) had commissioned the best possible privately-prepared Triumph 2.5PI, which Janspeed had helped to prepare, he had already suffered one major disappointment when his originally-chosen third crew-man, David Benson

John Sprinzel not only inspired the running of the event, but ran more Time Controls than any other official. Here he was, with a few minutes to spare, before the official 'off' at Wembley Stadium.

This Peugeot 404, driven by Ivica Vukoya of Yugoslavia, looked overloaded even before the start – and did not, in fact, survive the European section.

(motoring editor of the *Daily Express*), had withdrawn just before the start: A conflict of interests between the *Express* and the *Mirror* was suspected, and apparently could not be overcome. At the last minute, British Rally stalwart Jimmy Bullough stood in, which was encouraging for that crew, but the fact that the car halted almost at once, surrounded by a strong smell of fuel, was a bitter blow.

It took time for them to discover that the lever for Abingdon's

Two RAC hostesses looking bored with the whole business, John Sprinzel wondering how many more cars were still to start from Wembley – and the Moskvich (no 40) of Serquei Tenishev (he would finish a plucky 20th) just easing into the picture.

Andrew Cowan's Triumph 2.5PI, starting from Wembley Stadium, with Lord Stokes offering encouragement.

new-fangled manual altitude-adjustment for the fuel injection system had somehow been placed in the 'high-altitude' position, and by that time much time had been lost. To make up time, speed through the London suburbs was now of the essence, but perhaps the Triumph overdid it, as the crew were shortly pulled over for speeding in Harrow!

The rest of the 96-strong field got away with much less drama than this, though it was immediately clear that some were better prepared than others. The venerable Rolls-Royce Silver Cloud of the Martin family did not look as if would enjoy the rough stages in Yugoslavia and South America, the GP Beach Buggy looked – let's be honest – like an ill-prepared and very bad joke, while 'Gelignite' Jack Murray (second-man in Evan Green's 'works' Triumph 2.5PI) made sure that he was not ignored by setting off a gigantic thunder-flash as the car crawled up on to the ramp.

Last minute pre-event dramas included the fact that the GP Beach Buggy needed an engine change, and attention to a leaking fuel tank, before it was healthy enough to turn up at scrutineering, while Captain Gavin Thompson (in the 'Prince Michael of Kent' Maxi, no less) had suffered a road accident in his own car the day before, and needed attention to cuts and bruises before turning up at Wembley, which was no way to prepare for a 16,000 miles (25,750km) rally.

The punters already thought they knew who might win (see sidebar page 64), which should have buoyed up Paddy Hopkirk a little, though the fact that Ray Richards' Rolls-Royce Silver Shadow was placed in the Top Ten 'most-likely-to' crews said more about the status of the car than about its rallying potential. Some crews were clearly better-prepared, and more capable of winning, than others, more than one team

Only one Spanish car, this 1430, driven by Carlos Del Val, started the World Cup Rally, but retired well before the halfway point.

67

Clockwise from above: Roger Clark (right) and Paddy Hopkirk shake hands at Wembley Stadium before the start of the event. (McKlein);

Tall story time – left to right: Paddy Hopkirk, an unidentified co-driver, Alice Watson and Rosemary Smith, with their rally cars before driving them away from the factory;

Is this the most famous backdrop in the world? Millions of people will think so. Everyone will recognise that Jimmy Greaves and Tony Fall were just passing London's Big Ben, at precisely 11.00hr on Sunday, 19 April. Their Escort, much more battered before the end, would finally take sixth place;

Hannu Mikkola (left) and Gunnar Palm, who would win the World Cup Rally, ready for the start at Wembley Stadium, in London.

Carrying no 73, Anthony Pett's BMC 1800 was sponsored by Grants of Croydon, a prominent British Leyland dealership.

were clearly out for a holiday until their car broke down, or they ran out of time (and money). Even at this stage, there seemed to be no doubt that the honours would finally be disputed between seven 'works' Ford Escorts, four Triumph 2.5PIs and no fewer than six Citroën DS21s.

London to Sofia – the long drag

According to the published schedules, crews had almost exactly two days to get to Sofia, and the first major Time Control, but this promised to be a sheer accumulation of hours, as there was to be absolutely no real rallying at all in that time. Since there were times at which each Passage Control opened, it was not possible for crews to get a huge amount of time in hand, though the more determined crews were three or four hours early, and actually could go to bed for a time in Sofia!

This sector, which included the passage of England, France, West Germany, Austria, Hungary, Yugoslavia, and Bulgaria, also included a Channel crossing, a great deal of autobahn mileage and (for the seasoned professionals) a deal of boredom too.

Even so, it was not long before the incidents began to mount. Four cars were late at the first Time Control – at the Henley's garage in Dover (the Harris/Butler Escort by 20 minutes in what was their native county – they had delayed too long at a family-and-friends reunion along the way – and Chris Marriott's Trident V6 by 28 minutes) – but by daybreak on the second morning the route had joined in to Germany and Austrian autobahns, and speeds began to pick up.

Amazingly the Sherger brothers' Fiat 2300 estate car was the first to drop out due to them going astray, for even before the rally had been running for 24 hours they had missed several Passage Controls in Germany, were running very late, and seemed to be exhausted. They were not seen again until they suddenly turned up, many hours over the time limit, in Sofia – and as far as is known they never again tackled a major rally of any sort. Other cars missed Passage Controls (some of them had experienced crew members on board, which made this difficult to understand) and others struck trouble, but most kept going. The Silver Cloud needed a new starter motor, the Woodley Vauxhall Ventora suffered major braking problems, and Rob Janssen's Datsun 1600SSS suffered the first of several major engine problems (from all of which it recovered, and would reach the finish in Mexico City).

Along the way, a Control was positioned at the BMW factory in

Andrew Cowan waits to clock in at a Control in Vienna, co-driver Brian Coyle looks somewhat worried, while the Roger Clark/Alec Poole Ford Escort waits behind him.

downtown Munich, where the talk was not so much about the event itself, but about the revealing Bavarian costumes being worn by the waitresses ... OK, it was early in the event, but this was a 'man thing'.

Amazingly, though, it was the much-fancied Ford team which suffered the most dramatic set-backs at first. Not only did Rauno Aaltonen's car

sustain a major gearbox failure, but Colin Malkin's car was struck by an errant truck and was virtually written off in the collision.

The miracle of the Malkin incident was that although the new Escort (FTW 47H) was virtually wrecked, neither Colin Malkin nor his co-driver Richard Hudson-Evans were injured. As Richard later so graphically

All five Moskvich team cars, accompanied by a service estate car, lined up before clocking in at a Control in Europe. Three of the cars would make it to the finish. (McKlein)

wrote about this, during the night they were speeding south towards Sofia when a truck, coming north up the single-carriageway autoput (motorway) veered across the road, and hit the Escort: although it was not proved, it is suspected that the truck driver had fallen asleep. At a stroke, the first of Ford's seven 'works' Escorts (and the winning co-driver from London-Sydney of 1968) had been put out of the rally.

Unwittingly, Malkin's colleague Rauno Aaltonen then got involved. The erudite and thoughtful Finn had already had an eventful two days:

"My car was built by David Sutton, and I did not see it, or drive it, until I was on the way to scrutineering. I drove it there, and it had a horrible vibration. I told the Ford mechanics that this was not right, and I was told: 'That's OK, that is normal with the Escort!'"

FIRSTS AND LASTS

Ninety six cars started from Wembley Stadium on Sunday, 19 April.

FIRSTS:

The very first car to strike mechanical trouble was Bobby Buchanan-Michaelson's Triumph 2.5PI, which began to suffer from serious fuel injection problems even as it left the starting ramp in the stadium. There was a delay while repairs were made – so he was also the first to be fingered by the British traffic police, for going too fast through London to make up time!

The first car to go wrong (and effectively to be retired, though the novice crew thought they were still motoring when they reached Sofia) was the Fiat 2300 estate car of Joseph Sherger/James Sherger. The crew got only as far as Germany before missing Passage Controls, suffering from exhaustion, and originally deciding to withdraw. However, they apparently called Rally HQ in London, asking for guidance, and then carried on as far as Sofia, but were many hours out of time, and disappeared from the scene soon after that.

The first 'works' car to retire was the Ford Escort 1850 of Colin Malkin and Richard Hudson-Evans, which was struck by an errant truck on the single-carriageway autoput between Belgrade and Nis, in Yugoslavia. Although the crew were unhurt, the car was wrecked.

LASTS:

The last rally car (of 71) to be loaded on to the SS Derwent in Lisbon, was the Rolls-Royce Silver Shadow of Ray Richards/Bill Bengry/David Skeffington. After a rear hub had collapsed on the run through Portugal, much work had been needed to make it road worthy once again. This was only achieved because a privately owned Silver Shadow had been found in Portugal, and the owner had been 'persuaded' to donate a hub assembly ...

The very last car to retire from the rally was the Citroën DS21 of Claudine Trautmann/Colette Perrier, which suffered from terminal engine bothers in Guatemala, just short of the border with Mexico: Up to that point, Mme Trautmann had been the leading contender to win the Ladies' Prize – which ultimately went to Rosemary Smith's Maxi.

The last competitive section ended at Fortin, a resort town in south-eastern Mexico, on 26/27 May.

Trouble within minutes! Bobby Buchanan-Michaelson's Triumph 2.5PI was the first car to leave the start in London, but very soon it had broken down at the roadside with fuel injector settings problems.

Although the powers-that-be at Crewe no doubt shuddered, Ray Richards' Rolls-Royce Silver Shadow was well-prepared for this rally. Unfortunately, a rear suspension failure, sustained in Portugal, put the car out of the running, though it struggled on, and rejoined the event in the High Andes. (McKlein)

Claudine Trautmann's Citroën DS21, securely in the lead in the Ladies' category of the World Cup Rally at the time, takes on fuel, and gets a quick service from mechanics, at a Control in the Andes.

"But everything was in place, as we had wanted, because it was very professionally prepared – and I don't recall that I had any requests at all for changes.

"This vibration was so bad that I was convinced that something was really wrong, but the mechanics put it right, by changing the propshaft, in Germany I think.

"Then we had a little incident. We had a dry sump engine. I was sleeping, Henry was driving, we came to a petrol station, and by mistake the filling attendant started filling the oil tank in the boot, and got five litres (8.8 pints) into the wrong tank! So Henry left me sleeping, told the attendant to get a pump, and take the petrol out – 'because if you wake the man in the car, he will come and kill you!'

"Then we came to daylight, we were already through Vienna, when there came a big noise from the engine. I immediately lifted the throttle off, but the car wouldn't close the throttle! So I immediately switched off the ignition. I got the air cleaners off the Weber carburettors, and found

73

that a piece of the air-cleaner (an aluminium piece) had come loose, had gone through the carburettor, and gone into the engine! This piece was so long that it hit the valve but got no further into the engine ...

"Very soon after this the long aluminium extension which came out of the back of the gearbox broke clean off – you could see air right through it. Incidentally, I don't think this problem hit any of the other cars – it all happened, I think, because of the propshaft vibration I have already mentioned. I thought, we can't give up, we must continue as long as possible, so I bought a plastic device which is supposed to help refill oil into your rear axle, and bought four gallons (18.2L) of gearbox oil. My plan was to stop every 50 kilometres (31.1 miles), dive under the car, squirt in some oil, and get going again ...

"I also thought about how I could drive. Fifth was an overdrive, which means that you were creating more heat in the box, and you were putting more stress on the bearings as well. The lowest stress would be when we were in fourth gear, which was one-to-one gearing in this ZF gearbox, so I decided only to use fourth gear, which meant that we were quite slow as well.

"Then on the motorway before Belgrade, or somewhere near there, I suddenly saw Colin Malkin's car. So I said to Henry – 'OK, let's change the gearbox.' I started to change it, but there was one special nut fixing the clutch bell housing – anyway we couldn't get that out without dropping the engine, I think. We could get all the bolts loose except one.

"OK, we had to tighten up all the bolts again except for that one (which had never been loose), and then continued ... we were running just about last on the road at that point ..."

Brian Culcheth's 2.5PI ready to clock in at the Passage Control at Castle Schoenburg, in Vienna.

What's this? A tarmac-surfaced road on the World Cup Rally! This looks like a liaison section on the European section, somewhere in Yugoslavia.

– this, of course, is just one story, from one competitor, but with a difference. Days and weeks later Rauno would still be in the event, holding down second place, all ready to take over the lead in case team-mate and rival Hannu Mikkola faltered.

A third car then retired before the cavalcade reached Sofia – this being the ill-starred Beach Buggy of John Caulcutt. Not only had it needed a VW Beetle engine change on the night before the start of the event, but it then suffered a split fuel tank, a dramatic loss of fuel, and was well out of time when it finally limped into Sofia.

Many entrants who had planned their World Cup properly were hours early, and had reserved a hotel room in Sofia ("Sofia," wrote Mike Scarlett, "sounds like a nice soft girl, but is a hard-faced Balkan capital"), but there were mechanical troubles to be sorted out by many more. In and around all this, though, professionals like Hannu Mikkola, Brian Culcheth and Paddy Hopkirk went about their business, got their heads down for as long as possible, and mentally got ready for the first competitive section, which would follow (in what we must now call Kosovo and Montenegro, but in those days was still Yugoslavia) at the end of the afternoon.

High-speed action – at last

Originally, John Sprinzel had planned to give obeisance to the Liège-Sofia-Liège (also called the Marathon de la Route), which everyone in rallying seemed to fear, love and respect in almost equal measure, by mounting two high-speed Primes in what was then called Yugoslavia – one of them in the Titograd (now Podgorica) area, and one close to Glamoc. And why? Simply because in the halcyon days of 1961-1964, the 'Liège' (which was organised by the Royal Motor Union of Belgium) was recognised as Europe's toughest rally.

In the days when purer demands on physical endurance were tolerated, the Liège was a rally that started from Belgium, drove down through Yugoslavia to Bulgaria, and drove all the way back, without a rest of any sensible duration, and with target average speeds between Time Controls which were universally agreed to be impossible to achieve. The road sections were so tough that special stages were never found to be necessary.

The toughest part of that marathon, which had only dropped out of the calendar after the 1964 event, always started on the return trip from Sofia in Bulgaria, when the route skirted carefully around the northern border of hard-line communist Albania. The first of the impossible sections, on rough roads which were nevertheless infested with trucks and buses, invariably followed the route from Pec to Titograd (a city which is now known as Podgorica) via Pelev Brijeg, amid the mountains above the Adriatic coast regions. Pec now finds itself in Kosovo, and Podgorica/Titograd is now in Montenegro.

For Sprinzel, and for the competitors who diligently set out to survey the route in the first months of 1970, the problem was that the winter weather was very severe, and the nominated stage was impossible to survey, for weeks at a time. Bill Price recalls that he sent John Handley and Paul Easter out, in a Mini 1275GT, on two occasions, and that on both occasions they found the road completely blocked by snow, the drifts being reputedly 10 feet (3m) high. Even as late as the end of March, not a single recce crew had managed to get through that section, and to add to the confusion, a land-slide had also severed the planned route.

There was nothing new here, by the way, for even in the Monte Carlo Rally of the 1930s, when the approach route to Monte Carlo from Athens had transected the Balkans further inland, the snow drifts had invariably been feet, rather than inches, deep, so the organisers were reluctant to make any changes to their proposed route. It was only at the last possible minute that they bowed to the inevitable, cancelled their original intentions, and proposed a different, shorter and less winter-affected Prime. It was typical of both Ford and British Leyland that they hastily dispatched experts (Jim Porter and Mike Wood respectively) to the new scene, to make pace notes for their runners – which were handed out to them as they passed through the Control at Belgrade, to the north of this district.

The organisers, fortunately, were already well-prepared for an enforced change. Controllers Jim Gavin and Logan Morrison were sent out to Belgrade, picked up two Mercedes-Benz hire cars, and drove through the night to Titograd, saw the landslide for themselves (back in London, at first the team suggested they arranged to have it cleared!) – and recommended the re-route. They then stayed on, Gavin ran the start of the revised stage in Titograd, and Morrison drove the revised stage, then ran the Arrival Control in Kotor. The following day, and after using five different airlines to achieve this, the intrepid pair flew to Lisbon to await the World Cup's arrival there!

Although the respecified Prime, now linking Titograd/Podgorica to Kotor on the Adriatic coast, was further along the itinerary and only 50 miles (80.5km) instead of the original 100 miles (160.9km), it was still a perfect way to get the event under way, for it still stuck to the original 'Liège' route, and the roads were still gravel-covered, dusty, narrow, twisty and open to other traffic (in both directions!). The final approach to Kotor, which was taken in broad daylight, was down a series of tight hairpins which faced the glorious Adriatic coastline. Even so, with 65 minutes allowed for the new stage, it was just about 'on' for the determined factory-backed cars.

No fewer than six drivers (Roger Clark, Andrew Cowan, Tony Fall, Terry Hunter [Porsche 911], Hannu Mikkola and Guy Verrier) all completed it without penalty, with several others just one, two or three minutes adrift, and a total of 19 crews losing between one and ten minutes. The Martin family's Rolls-Royce Silver Cloud, on the other hand, lost no less than 71 minutes – so their assurances that the car would reach Mexico City were already beginning to look over-optimistic.

Even so, as Brian Culcheth – who had managed a more complete recce of the South American sections than any other competitor – pointed out, except for the 'headline makers', losing the odd minute would be of

Prime 1: Titograd to Kotor (Yugoslavia) – the Montenegro Prime (Target: 50 miles/80.5km in 65 minutes)

Fastest times:

Crew	Car	Penalty (mins)
R Clark/A Poole	Ford Escort 1850	0
A Cowan/B Coyle/U Ossio	Triumph 2.5PI	0
A Fall/J Greaves	Ford Escort 1850	0
T Hunter/G Mabbs	Porsche 911	0
H Mikkola/G Palm	Ford Escort 1850	0
G Verrier/F Murac	Citroën DS21	0
J Neyret/J Terramorsi	Citroën DS21	1
R Trautmann/J-P Hanrioud	Citroën DS21	1
B Culcheth/J Syer	Triumph 2.5PI	1
P Hopkirk/A Nash/N Johnston	Triumph 2.5PI	1
J Handley/P Easter	Mini 1275GT	2
R Aaltonen/H Liddon	Ford Escort 1850	3
S Zasada/M Wachowski	Ford Escort 1850	3

no importance, when penalties in the Andes would probably be measured in hours!

There was no need, surely, for heroics at this juncture, but with the adrenalin pumping a few competitors (and cars!) didn't see it like that. Timo Makinen's Escort suffered from a sheared distributor driveshaft, but coasted the last section of the Prime, through the hairpins, to the end of the Prime, and Ford service. John Handley's extrovert Mini 1275GT was already misfiring, while Evan Green's big Triumph charged off the road on the very first corner when he found his brake pedal going all the way to the floor, but the problem was soon sorted: more worrying was the fact that this Triumph had already started to misfire, and fuel injection problems were suspected.

A start, at least, had now been made. The walking wounded walked (or drove) even slower than before, the few deluded private owners who had not prepared their cars properly were about to retire, but during the night more than 80 crews now struck out in a north-westerly direction, up the Adriatic Coast, and prepared to tackle the next Prime. This long trek involved a drive through Dubrovnik, almost to Split, before turning inland to Glamoc, which now finds itself in Bosnia.

Compared with the first, Prime 2 (the 'Serbian Prime') linked Glamoc to Bosanska Krupa (also in Bosnia), along a rather ill defined gravel-surface (sometimes very rough) 119 mile (191.5km) route by way of Sanski Most, for which a mere 2hr 50 minutes had been allowed – which translated into a 42.3mph (68.1kph) target average. By modern, 21st century, standards, that doesn't sound much – to which I can only remind everyone that this was in the deepest, most fearsome, 'Liège' country, where road surfaces

Rugge-Price's BMC 1800 hurrying along on one of the European Primes.

were atrocious, signposting was almost non-existent, and there seemed to a vast, creaking, smelly truck around every blind corner.

Why this route and why this Prime? Once again, it was laid out as a tribute to the last great Liège, where it had figured as one of the great car breakers of the event, and where Rauno Aaltonen's Austin-Healey 3000 had done so much to secure its leading margins.

This was where the first major snag turned up for almost every crew. The Road Book, to quote more than one crew member, was quite "distressingly vague" in some ways, and rarely defined the route to be taken in detail. There was no question of a 'Tulip' road book being provided, nor of any direction arrows being placed on the ground to make route-finding any easier.

In the case of Prime 2, competitors were left to find their own way between Sanski Most (a Passage Control) and Bosanska Krupa (the end), using one or other of the unmade, badly signposted and rugged roads connecting the two. As a study of the maps confirms, there were at least two obvious routes – and both had been extensively recced by the professional teams.

This, though, was going to be no picnic, not only because there was much mist in the early miles, and the tracks were gravel covered, but there was still old snow and ice (which remained from the harsh Balkan winter). Realising that they had a great deal of time in hand, several professional crews elected to wait for full daylight before they started the Prime. The serious problem, however, soon followed, as Brian Culcheth later told me:

"There was a problem on an early Prime in Yugoslavia. Ford and Citroën had recced one way through, and we had recced another – and on the event there was a bridge down on our way. We had to go back and rejoin the other route. We met someone coming back, and that was a big diversion. That cost us 15-20 minutes. Every one of the Triumphs lost a similar amount of time there."

Indeed they did – and so did many other teams. But there were other problems, too. Not only was there also a short diversion around a bridge, which had only been temporarily repaired, but there was one point at which

three stranded trucks blocked the way. The plank bridge looked distinctly dodgy, so much so that Tony Fall/Jimmy Greaves refused to tackle it, returned to the nearby Passage Control at Sanski Most, and went the long way round; whereas Hannu Mikkola (who was still at the young, gung-ho, stage of his career) took a run at it, jumped high enough to clear a gap in the middle of the bridge, and went on his way.

Roger Clark, of all people, rolled his Escort at quite an early point, only 12km (7.5 miles) after the start of the stage, ended up on the roof, and saw most of his petrol drain away before he could be righted. This took so long (the rally cars were already quite spread out) that, by the time Terry Hunter arrived in his Porsche 911 and provided some muscle to help set the stranded machine back on its wheels, and had bustled back to the start to pick up more fuel, well over an hour had been lost. As privateer Rob Lyall described (see sidebar, page 78), Roger actually muscled in the queue for petrol, filled up the Escort's tanks, then dashed off by the alternative route, asking Lyall to pay for the fuel ...

At this benighted spot on the Yugoslavian map, there were as many stories as there were rally cars. *Motor* journalist Hamish Cardno saw some of the drama from the back seat of the Green/Murray Triumph 2.5PI:

"We came down a hill through some very rough road works, to find the road completely blocked by three large trucks. The middle one was broken down, another couldn't be moved for some reason we couldn't establish, and the third had stuck in the mud trying to get past. We had been there for quite some time, arguing with the Yugoslavian lorry drivers then trying to find a way round, when a Citroën arrived. Shortly after it came one of the Peugeots, then Paddy Hopkirk's Triumph, then the Red Arrows Maxi. Eventually, about 20 of us managed to push the stuck lorry free, and carry on ..."

Rival journalist Michael Scarlett (from *Autocar*, in the Red Arrows car) confirmed this from a different viewpoint, his post-rally pictures showing the privately-entered Citroën raised to 'jacking height' and making for the undergrowth trying to find a way round – which it failed to do.

This hold-up caused wholesale time-loss to many cars, which, on a

Finding the road blocked by a broken-down truck in the second Prime, Paul Coltelloni's 'private' Citroën DS21 hoisted its skirts, set the suspension on high, and tried to drive round, through the trees. He failed!

smaller rally, might have resulted in cancellations and delay allowances being applied. On the World Cup, however, John Sprinzel and John Brown had already emphasised just how much the crews were expected to fend for themselves. If they found a blocked road, and there was an alternative itinerary which was found to be open then – tough. In the event, there were grumbles, but no more than that.

The accidents, some trivial, but some terminal as far as rally cars were concerned, came thick and fast – which maybe explains why the Spa-Sofia-Liège 'classic' had been forced out of Yugoslavia a few years earlier. The Antiguan Chrysler Hunter hit a truck (and could not continue), Dennis Cresdee's 1800 finished up off the road, and was damaged, Jean Denton in the 'Beauty Box' BMC 1800 hit a bicycle (which actually had two boys on it!), while José Araújo's Volvo 142S also hit a cyclist.

The Cooper/Channon Cortina suffered broken engine mountings (this

---

PAYING FOR IT ALL ...

No, this is not the point at which I reveal how much the Daily Mirror pumped into the World Cup Rally (but think of £250,000 in 1970 currency, and keep on counting ...), but it's worth remembering just how a rally car's co-driver had to manage the funds he carried.

Because the passage of Europe-London-Sofia-Lisbon was positively brief by what would follow, it was enough to carry a few Deutschmarks, Bulgarian dinars, Italian lira, French francs, Spanish pesetas and Portuguese escudos. For sure there was no time to stop and visit one's friendly roadside bank ...

(As an example, when Roger Clark needed fuel in Yugoslavia, and was in a great hurry, he got fellow competitor Rob Lyall to pay the garage for him – and Rob did not get his money back, in an unsuitable currency, until the event reached South America.)

South America was a totally different problem. Not only did each country have its own currency, but in most cases inflation was rampant, and neighbouring countries (who were sometimes not friendly towards those neighbours) would usually not accept that currency, no matter how friendly they were at the time! Add in the fact that several border crossings were so remote from civilisation that there were no banking facilities for miles (and there was no time to indulge in queueing and formalities, anyway ...) and a World Cup competitor's problems become more and more clear.

Team managers and their assistants were invaluable (if one could find them, in a hurry), but many crews resorted to carrying wads of that much-derided, but universally accepted currency – the US dollar.

Prime 2: Glamoc to Bos Krupa (Yugoslavia) – the Serbian Prime
(Target: 119 miles/191.5km in 2hr 50 minutes)

Fastest times:

Crew	Car	Penalty (mins)
R Trautmann/J-P Hanrioud	Citroën DS21	4
G Verrier/F Murac	Citroën DS21	6
H Mikkola/G Palm	Ford Escort 1850	7
R Aaltonen/H Liddon	Ford Escort 1850	8
T Makinen/G Staepeleare	Ford Escort 1850	14
P Vanson/A Turcat/A Leprince	Citroën DS21	15
B Culcheth/J Syer	Triumph 2.5PI	26
P Hopkirk/A Nash/N Johnston	Triumph 2.5PI	26
J Handley/P Easter	Mini 1275GT	27
R Neyret/J Terramorsi	Citroën DS21	28
J Bloxham/P Brown/R McBurney	Hillman Hunter	32
I Marang/P Coltelloni	Citroën DS21	36

With virtually no outside assistance, Ron Channon and Rod Cooper kept their privately-supported Ford Lotus-Cortina in one piece, and finally finished in 14th place.

would also happen to Rauno Aaltonen's Escort, but weeks later), while Dutchman Bob de Jong's Alfa Romeo Giulia Super broke its transmission. This was already turning into a real endurance rally, even though just two Primes (and, in World Cup terms, very short Primes) had taken place.

From a study of the Prime times, it was clear that none of the 'works' Escorts had suffered from the truck blockage, as their three fastest runners lost just seven, eight and fourteen minutes respectively, while Trautmann and Verrier's Citroëns swished imperiously through (on the same route) to lose a mere four and six minutes respectively. On the other hand, Paddy Hopkirk and Brian Culcheth (Triumph 2.5PIs) lost 26 minutes, and were not best pleased.

Unhappily, two cars (both from the high-profile British Leyland team) were already suffering from engine misfiring problems. The Aussies' 2.5PI had not only suffered failing rear shock absorbers, and a failed bearing in the rear axle, but the engine had been running on five (of six) cylinders for some time. Much work would be carried out at Monza, before the cars clocked in at Parc Fermé – but there was worse to follow.

The BBC-sponsored Mini 1275GT was in even more dire straits. A misfire, thought to have been caused by fuel feed maladies, had affected the car in the very first Prime, and now it had much work to do. Although the Mini actually took ninth fastest time on Glamoc – Bosanska Krupa – it was clearly in trouble, and staggered into Monza sounding awful. Because

Time for a rebuild at Monza – this was Brian Culcheth's big Triumph, which eventually finished second overall, and was hours early at this point. The competition numbers had been blanked out to comply with the wishes of local Italian authorities.

this problem resulted in a weak mixture from time to time, it was almost inevitable that there would be more, and more major, dramas to come – they duly followed in the next Prime, when a big bang signalled the end of a cheeky little effort.

Following the dramas of this early Prime, most crews were relieved to make for the first overnight rest halt at Monza, just north of Milan. The route from Bosanska Krupa led to Senj (on the Adriatic coast) to Rijeka, then into Italy, then finally swiftly and smoothly along an autostrada towards the legendary Italian F1 circuit – Monza. Although no speed test was scheduled on the circuit, the fact that many teams were planning to carry out major rebuilds made it certain that there would be large and enthusiastic crowds on hand, to see the fun.

Even the crews that had temporarily lost their way on the Serbian Prime had lots of time to spare here, with up to three or even four hours for factory mechanics to work their customary miracles, and (once in Parc Fermé) another six hours where only the drivers could work on the cars.

Although it was very early days, at this point Citroën was happy to claim 'bragging rights' in the current general classification. René Trautmann (DS21) had lost five minutes, Guy Verrier (DS21) had lost six, while Hannu Mikkola (Escort 1850) had lost seven minutes.

This was a day when seasoned crews discovered that they might occasionally build up a lot of time in which repairs could be completed – though in many cases they would have to complete the job themselves, inside the Parc Fermé compounds.

Ford, as one might expect, were ready to carry out restorations in the same way that they might on a European event. Not only did Timo Makinen get his damaged distributor drive completely renewed, but Ford had time (and appropriate equipment) to hoist the engine out of the car to get the job done.

After spending a full two days stopping regularly, and squirting oil into his Escort's gearbox, Rauno Aaltonen finally found time to get a more permanent fix.

They shall not pass! After their lengthy pre-arrival service at Monza, cars had to go into a Parc Fermé, which was firmly policed by Dean Delamont of the RAC.

Tony Ambrose, John Sprinzel, Colin Taylor, an assistant from the local motor club, and John Brown, celebrate the safe arrival of the World Cup contestants at Monza, for the first official overnight halt.

"We were running just about last on the road at that point," Rauno recalls, "because every 50km (31.1 miles) we had been stopping to pour more oil into the gearbox.

"But there was still time for service. So we continued, after Sofia, to the Adriatic Coast, and our luck was in, for there was such a heavy fog, and because it was dry and the roads were dusty, there was fog and dust mixed – visibility was nil. This is how we climbed up very rapidly from something like 91st place on the road in Sofia to about 14th. And every 50km (31.1 miles) I was still stopping to squirt oil into the gearbox ...!

"Finally we got to Monza, and by that time Ford had already made telephone calls, and a man had flown in, from the ZF factory in Germany on the Bodenzee. The man came, dissembled the box, told us it really was 'no problem' – we had enough time before clocking in. He had a little box of bits – not enough bits as far as I could see. He said we wouldn't need any more – this fix will hold 'for ever'.

"So we said what is 'for ever'? He said at least 5000km (3107 miles), and I said we have only 25,000km (15,534 miles) still to go ...

"After this, though, we could start using fifth gear again, and to start to drive normally. From that point, we did no more work on the gearbox. Anyway, after Monza we never had much time to stop at service ..."

The ZF man's fix was mainly involved in working on the innards of the gearbox, while Boreham mechanics worked their own wizardry, with sealant, Araldite and other magic potions, on the gearbox extension itself, for the regulations did not allow them to make wholesale changes.

For the truly professional drivers, so far this was 'just another rally', with rivals to be beaten, problems to be solved, service crews to be consulted at regular intervals, and rest to be taken wherever possible. For the amateurs and pure adventure seekers, it was another matter entirely.

I was running the Arrival Control at Monza, and clearly recall seeing the sheer exhaustion, the staring eyes, the dishevelled appearance and – in some cases – the realisation that the dream was about to end, there and then. Several crews had clearly not planned very far ahead, a number of

Because of the relaxed time schedule in the European sections, the World Cup cars usually had a lot of time for service and repairs. This was the pre-arrival area at Monza, near Milan, with the Culcheth and Hopkirk cars receiving attention.

US-based Jeep trader Brian Chuchua thought that this enormous 4x4 would be ideal for the World Cup Rally, but he was outpaced by the more nimble European machinery – and had to carry out his own service and repairs. His machine did not make it to the finish.

them had no hotel reservations for that night, and were obliged to sleep in service vans (if they had any), on any bench or table that they could find – but not in the cars themselves, which were out of bounds overnight.

The American Brian Chuchua's massive Jeep Wagoneer (a huge estate car, which looked as big as some of the buses already encountered) seemed to be hale and hearty, Chuchua seemed to be disappointed by his lack of pace (he would be 61st at Lisbon) – or, rather, surprised by the pace of the European cars – but the professionals had not been expecting any better. He would certainly get to South America, but would shortly disappear from the column.

The numbers were already coming down – Chris Coburn's Vauxhall Viva GT was out, with a leaking radiator, Woodley's Vauxhall Ventora had gone off the road, Gardner's Ford Escort Elba motor caravan had burnt out all its electrics, Mondini's Porsche 911 had crashed, Marriott's Trident had virtually collapsed, its suspension severely damaged, Lavinia Roberts' Ford Mustang had crashed, and Keefe's four-door Mini-Cooper S failed to complete Prime 2. Before the rally cars arrived in Lisbon three days later, there would be more carnage – much more of this.

Monza to Lisbon – civilisation, at last?

After a night's rest close to Monza, crews then set out on what would be a very scenic passage of Northern Italy and Southern France, before pointing westwards towards Lisbon, and the boat which was scheduled to take them on to South America.

Jeremy Rugge-Price drove one of the several well-prepared BMC 1800s to start the World Cup. Seen here on the early UK section, it did not make the finish, however.

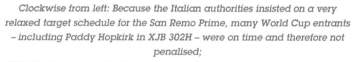

Clockwise from left: Because the Italian authorities insisted on a very relaxed target schedule for the San Remo Prime, many World Cup entrants – including Paddy Hopkirk in XJB 302H – were on time and therefore not penalised;

FEV 1H, at a very early stage in the World Cup Rally, with Hannu Mikkola (not wearing a crash helmet, at the wheel on the San Remo Prime. Co-driver Gunnar Palm is more cautious ...;

Alun Rees' Hillman storms over the San Remo Prime in northern Italy. He kept the car (which was running in 'Cowan/London-Sydney' trim) going until the end, and finished 15th. (McKlein);

Paddy Hopkirk's Triumph 2.5PI, pushing on hard over the San Remo Prime in Italy, only days after the start of the World Cup Rally. (McKlein)

Prime 3: the San Remo Prime
(Target: 72 miles/115.9km in 2hr 0 minutes)

Fastest times:

Crew	Car	Penalty (mins)

This schedule was easy, the result being that the following 23 crews all completed it without penalty:

Crew	Car	Penalty
T Hunter/G Mabbs	Porsche 911	-
R Badham/R Lyall	Hillman Hunter	-
R Neyret/J Terramorsi	Citroën DS21	-
S Zasada/M Wachowski	Ford Escort 1850	-
R Cooper/R Channon	Ford Lotus-Cortina	-
H Mikkola/G Palm	Ford Escort 1850	-
E Hermann/D Benz/H Walter	Mercedes-Benz 280SE	-
Ms C Trautmann/Ms C Perrier	Citroën DS21	-
A Fall/J Greaves	Ford Escort 1850	-
A Katz/A Kling/A Pfuhl	Mercedes-Benz 280SE	-
A Cowan/B Coyle/U Ossio	Triumph 2.5PI	-
R Aaltonen/H Liddon	Ford Escort 1850	-
ER Laretta/J Migliore	Peugeot 404	-
R Clark/A Poole	Ford Escort 1850	-
G Perkins/J F Green	Peugeot 404	-
B Culcheth/J Syer	Triumph 2.5PI	-
E Green /J Murray/H Cardno	Triumph 2.5PI	-
R Trautmann/J-P Hanrioud	Citroën DS21	-
P Hopkirk/A Nash/N Johnston	Triumph 2.5PI	-
P Vanson/A Turcat/O Leprince	Citroën DS21	-
G Verrier/F Murac	Citroën DS21	-
T Makinen/G Staepelaere	Ford Escort 1850	-
E Lamas-Fortes/A P Janiero	Fiat 124	-

Even though it was situated in a very picturesque part of Italy, and the Italians were as super enthusiastic about the event as anyone could have hoped, Prime 3 – the San Remo Prime – was a disappointment. Although the route was mountainous, and loose-surfaced (scenes from publicity films made for showing after the event are spectacular, to say the least) the schedule was far too relaxed. No matter how much pressure had been applied before the event, the authorities had insisted on two hours being allowed for the 72 mile (115.9km) Prime – the result being a very easy-to-attain target.

No fewer than 23 cars (listed in the Prime times shown above) completed the stage inside the target, some of them by at least 10 minutes. These, incidentally, were the 'usual suspects' – all six 'works' Escorts, all four Triumph 2.5PIs, and five of the six factory-prepared Citroën DS21s were among them – which truly set the scene for the rest of the event.

Still looking very smart, and on its way to a fine performance in the French Prime, Andrew Cowan's Triumph 2.5PI eventually crashed badly in Argentina, and was written off.

The one major retirement on this Prime was the gallant little Mini 1275GT of John Handley/Paul Easter, which finally blew its fuel-starved engine in a big way. Initial reports that the car had crashed were soon discounted – the structure, in fact, being in such good shape that it was speedily refurbished back at Abingdon, for Paddy Hopkirk to drive in the forthcoming Scottish Rally. All in all, this was not a good day for British Leyland, for the Green Triumph 2.5PI was now misfiring badly, running only on five cylinders, and emergency service near San Remo established that a valve guide had broken. Since a new cylinder head was not immediately available, and would undoubtedly break the regulations if fitted, this team was in trouble.

The first big challenge of the day, in fact, came over what was known as the Alpine Prime – a magnificently demanding 67 mile (107.8km) passage of roads in the Alpes Maritime north of Cannes, where many a French Alpine Rally had been won and lost in recent years. Along the way, and for all the obvious romantic rallying reasons, Sprinzel and Brown had placed a Passage Control at the summit of the Col du Turini – a location which was usually encountered in the depths of a Monte Carlo Rally winter, but was now basking in a Mediterranean spring.

To fire the imagination of all classic rally enthusiasts, I need only point out that this Alpine Prime linked a rural cross roads called Les Quatre Chemins (literally – four roads) with the village of Rouaine, by way of Sigale and Entrevaux. Used for the very first time on the French Alpine Rally in the early 1960s, sections of this Prime had set fear into the heart of drivers when originally set at a target average of 60kph (37.3mph), but

Still going well at this stage, in Europe, Evan Green's Triumph 2.5PI suffered an accident in France, which crippled it severely.

for the marathon it was set at no less than 72kph (44.7mph)! All this, mind you, with the roads theoretically not closed to the public, though the access junctions were firmly controlled by the French police. To eliminate short-cuts, there were Passage Controls in Sigale (Tony Mason in charge) and Entrevaux (Mike Preston).

Although this Prime was as nothing compared with what would follow in South America (and, at least, all the roads were tarmac-surfaced), it was so serpentine, narrow, and tiring that, to get the flavour, I commend it to any enthusiast visiting the area in future years. Start at Les Quatre

There was plenty of glamour behind the entry of this Mercedes-Benz car – the fashionable London nightclub, Annabel's, entered the car, and it was crewed by Annabel's owner, Mark Birley, along with retired race drivers Innes Ireland and Mike Taylor.

Prime 4: Quatre Chemins-Sigale-Entrevaux-Rouaine (France) – the Alpine Prime
(Target: 67 miles/107.8km in 90 minutes)

Fastest times:

Crew	Car	Penalty (mins)
R Neyret/J Terramorsi	Citroën DS21	0
H Mikkola/G Palm	Ford Escort 1850	0
A Fall/J Greaves	Ford Escort 1850	0
R Trautmann/J-P Hanrioud	Citroën DS21	0
T Makinen/G Staepeleare	Ford Escort 1850	0
R Aaltonen/H Liddon	Ford Escort 1850	1
R Clark/A Poole	Ford Escort 1850	1
T Hunter/G Mabbs	Porsche 911	2
B Culcheth/J Syer	Triumph 2.5PI	2
G Verrier/F Murac	Citroën DS21	2
Ms C Trautmann/Ms C Perrier	Citroën DS21	4
A Cowan/B Coyle/U Ossio	Triumph 2.5PI	4
P Hopkirk/A Nash/N Johnston	Triumph 2.5PI	4

Chemins, just 30 kilometres (18.6 miles) north of Grasse, then follow D10, D17, D10 again, D911 to Entrevaux, D610 and D10 once again ...

Because of the high speeds demanded, the daylight conditions, and the pressure that crews were now under, this was bound to be the scene of many dramas – and so it was. Although five cars (three Escorts and two big Citroëns) beat the target, the most significant news was that the Green/Murray/Cardno Triumph 2.5PI crashed in a big way. Other team members had already warned Green that this was a long rally, where early heroics were not needed, but the impression given is that he was already driving a little bit 'over the top'.

As Cardno later wrote:

"About 10km (6.2 miles) from the start of the Prime [with Evan Green driving] ... he accelerated out of the corner, there was a bang like a pistol shot, we veered to the left slightly then shot off the road, to the right and into the trees. We hit one fairly small tree with the right-hand rear door, then smacked head-on into a much larger tree and dropped down to come to rest at a crazy angle about 15ft (4.6m) down from the road ..."

To cut a long story very short, the left front wheel had broken off, causing the accident, it took more than two hours to summon help, to get a breakdown truck to pluck them out, for a local mechanic to bodge up the car enough to tackle the Prime (at very limited speed), and to get it to Abingdon service at Rouaine. At the same time, the fuel injection supply to the damaged cylinder was disconnected (a pipe was led to the outside

FORD, ESCORTS AND BROKEN AXLES

Ford's Stuart Turner freely admits that the team was incredibly lucky on this event. If the event had not been split into European and South American sections, with two weeks in between while the cars were on the high seas, the Escorts would not have lasted very long, and all would either have retired, or limped along after many hours of delays for repairs. As he later wrote in his best-selling autobiography Twice Lucky:

"After just seven days ... our so-called Escort wonder cars were beginning to break up. They were quite a bit heavier than standard with 28-gallon (127.3L) fuel tanks in the boot, and in that first week we found that all the axles had started to break up, with the tubes actually splitting away from the casing in the centre.

"Bill Meade had flagged his concern over axles well before the event, and Len Bailey (Ford's resident racing/rally car design contractor) had agreed to have some made with tubing to aircraft specification. Something went awry, however, because we ended up with standard cold-drawn tubing, which was 50 per cent softer than the standard Ford material we'd used in testing ..."

Driver Roger Clark, whose Escort had suffered first, takes up the story in his own book Sideways to Victory:

"Bill Meade, Mick Jones and I had sat down in Lisbon before we flew home, and pondered the problem. There wasn't time to consider any elegant changes to the axles, and there was no question of changing them because they had been marked with radioactive paint by the organisers, at the start.

"Whatever we devised would have to be something we could fix, by strapping or welding, to axles already in place. To save time, any lash-up job we developed should be capable of being fitted without taking the axles out of the car.

"Between us we developed a Dural bridge-piece which fitted inside the rear cover of the diff, with the cover bolted on top of it, and a couple of U-bolts to hold the piece to the axle."

To prove the fix, Roger, in fact, spent a hectic few days on the rough-road test track at Bagshot, trying to jump an old Escort test car (with the new 'fix') higher, faster and more heavily than it ever been done before, and found that he could not damage the axle. Then it was a matter of producing six kits, making sure that they could all somehow be stowed into mechanics' or a team manager's airline baggage, and then getting them to Rio de Janeiro.

In the interval between the cars being unloaded from the ship in Rio de Janeiro, and before they tackled the first Prime in Brazil, all were pulled over to hastily requisitioned workshops, the brace kits were fitted, after which lots of fingers were firmly crossly, and they were sent on their way.

And, as we now know, they worked ...

I hesitate to guess what is going on here in Portugal, except that kingpin organiser John Sprinzel has his arm round Ginette Derolland, who was a crew member for Rosemary Smith's Maxi.

world, where one of Mr Joseph Lucas' injectors regularly sprayed fuel ...). This soon made 'Gelignite' Jack Murray feel very ill, a hospital visit was required in Pamplona, Spain, three Passage Controls then had to be missed to keep the car in the running at all costs, and even though the cylinder head was changed before the car was loaded on to the ship in Lisbon (something specifically against the regulations ...), this was an unhappy episode, for the 2.5PI was now running 69th out of 71 runners.

Other cars, too, dropped out, these including Buchanan-Michaelson's hapless Triumph 2.5PI (which had given trouble within minutes of the start from London) suffered terminal fuel injection problems, while Mark Birley's Mercedes-Benz 280SE in which ex-F1 drivers Innes Ireland and Mike Taylor were star crew members, went off the road. Competitors who began to mutter that all this proved that the event was going to be too tough had obviously not assessed what was still to come, for with only

The Australian-built BMC 1800, driven by Ken Tubman's team, still looked clean and smart at this stage – before the rigours of the South American section began.

four Primes already run off – three of which had been cleaned by several competitors – this was only the beginning. Even so, the next two days (Thursday night, Friday and Friday night) were purely routine – 'mileage, just mileage' – as the route wound through southern France, and Spain, to get to Portugal.

In the meantime, the real technical drama – the saga of the axle problems on the 'works' Escorts – had begun to evolve: this is described in some detail in the sidebar on page 87. It was Roger Clark's car which

showed off the first symptoms, when it arrived at a Ford road-side service point with an obvious oil leak from the axle. One axle tube was found to have cracked, very close to the diff casing, so much so that it was in danger of coming away from the diff casing completely: Rauno Aaltonen, who followed the hapless Clark's car at one time, swears that he could see the inner half shaft rotating inside the crack, so obvious was the failing.

After a lengthy delay at a nearby garage, some temporary welding was carried out, but was not entirely successful, and a gloomy Roger was not at

It's a long way down from there, if the crane driver sneezes! This was Lisbon, with one of the Triumph 2.5PIs being lifted aboard the Derwent.

Seasoned ex-rally driver Tiny Lewis (crouched by the rear wheel of Rauno Aaltonen's Escort), with Henry Liddon and Gilbert Staepelaere alongside him, during a servicing session in Lisbon.

Seventy-one cars lined up, and ready for loading onto the Derwent, at the close of the European section in Lisbon. The three cars nearest the camera were no 18 (Hannu Mikkola's Escort), no 12 (Robert Neyret's Citroën DS21, and no 101 (Guy Verrier's Citroen DS21). Only the Escort would make it to the finish).

Prime 5: Arganil to Pampilhosa – the Portuguese Prime
(Target: 45 miles/72.4km in 65 minutes)

Fastest times:

Crew	Car	Penalty (mins)
H Mikkola/G Palm	Ford Escort 1850	0
A Fall/J Greaves	Ford Escort 1850	0
R Aaltonen/H Liddon	Ford Escort 1850	0
R Clark/A Poole	Ford Escort 1850	0
R Trautmann/J-P Hanrioud	Citroën DS21	0
T Makinen/G Staepeleare	Ford Escort 1850	0
G Verrier /F Murac	Citroën DS21	1
S Zasada/M Wachowski	Ford Escort 1850	3
B Culcheth/J Syer	Triumph 2.5PI	3
P Vanson/A Turcat/ O Leprince	Citroën DS21	3
R Neyret/J Terramorsi	Citroën DS21	6
I Marang/P Coltelloni	Citroën DS21	8
J-C Ogier/C Laurent	Peugeot 404	8
P Hopkirk/A Nash/N Johnston	Triumph 2.5PI	8

all sure that he would even reach Lisbon. Hours later, and before arriving at yet another Ford service point, the temporary weld failed again. At the next point, the resident expert was Nobby Clark of British Vita (a company which had built one of the seven 'works' Escorts). There seemed to be enough time – just time – for what was going to be a lengthy rebuilding job. Nobby took the axle off the car, disappeared down the road with it to a local garage, had it welded up, strengthened, with extra beam stiffeners included, and sent Roger and Alec Poole on their way after a mammoth delay of six hours!

Too much lateness to make up? Not at all – for Roger then raced across France, across Spain, and into Portugal, found that he had time in hand before the Arganil Pime – and was relaxed enough to 'clean' that stage, which he duly did. Other Escorts, but not all, were in similar trouble – for the Fall/Greaves car also suffered a similar breakage, and the other machines showed signs of an impending breakage. It was typical of Hannu Mikkola's luck (and driving methods, maybe) on this event, that his car (FEV 1H) did not show any signs of failure ...

Just before arrival in Lisbon, Prime 5, later described as being almost 'forestry stage' in character, was situated near Arganil. So easy had the open-road schedule been during the previous two days that some crews had time for several hours sleep, before they chose to attack this Prime in full daylight. Not that it was going to be too demanding of them, for the factory

Two of the well-placed Triumph 2.5PIs – no 98 was Paddy Hopkirk's car, no 88 was that of Brian Culcheth – pause before clocking in at a Control during the European section.

teams had all had time to practise it in previous weeks, so with just 45 miles (72.4km) to be tackled in 65 minutes, it was clearly cleanable.

And so it was. Even though they were now desperately worried about the state of the rear axles under their cars, five of the six surviving Escorts beat the target (the sixth car, driven by Sobieslaw Zasada, lost just three minutes), while René Trautmann's Citroën DS21 joined them. It was enough, at least, to cheer them all up, for a rest, and a two-week hiatus in this monumental event, were just over the horizon.

Then came the main road journey to the Lisbon Arrival Control (where I was officiating), which was in a filling station close to the centre of the city, after which just 40 minutes of 'neutral section' was allowed to reach the Alcantara Docks. After this the cars had to go through Customs formalities, and to drain their fuel tanks, before they were individually lifted into slings and hoisted aboard the SS Derwent, which was due to weigh anchor on that very evening. No matter what excuses a rally crew came up with, and no matter how much special pleading took place, that departure time would certainly be confirmed.

By Saturday afternoon, the approaches to the Arrival Control in Lisbon (and even the quay itself) began to resemble an expensive, and high-tech, breaker's yard. All of the works teams had extensive re-building facilities available, and the more resourceful private owners were making frantic changes and repairs before losing sight of their cars for the next two weeks. British Leyland's strategy was thrown into disarray because its spares truck had been held up at the French/Spanish border for many hours, while Ford was not only carrying out a full-scale refurbishment of all its machines, but was already scratching its head over finding a solution to the rear axle breakage problems: this was not an isolated case, for sure, but seemed to be an endemic problem on all six of its 'works' cars.

This Lotus-Cortina Mk II was well-prepared, and looked very purposeful – note the exhaust system exiting over the line of the roof of the car – but retired well before the event reached the high Andes sections.

The Citroën 'private owners' for their part, looked relatively serene, but needed no more than routine maintenance and a change of wheels and tyres. For the French, though, this was the calm before the storm: although a good recce had been carried out of the South American sections, very little spares provisioning had been made, and (if only their rivals had known it) the rest of the event would fall into the 'high hopes' category.

At this point, the two cars which seemed to create most of what we might call the 'Fleet Street' (where London's national newspapers were still concentrated) stories were Evan Green's sadly-ailing Triumph 2.5PI, and Ray Richards Rolls-Royce Silver Shadow, while the other Rolls-Royce (the stately Silver Cloud) was eventually able to reach Lisbon, but only by missing Controls (it was classified 71st and last ...).

Although it had been patched up after its big crash in France, the big Triumph really was in a pitiable state, with suspension and body damage needing attention, and a terminally damaged cylinder head. Heroic work by the mechanics from Abingdon not only provided a brand-new cylinder head and accessories, but also a new rear door from one of the practice cars, and rearranged front suspension. As good as new? Certainly not – but it was serviceable, even if the sump guard and most of the auxiliary lights would have to be screwed into place in Rio de Janeiro ...

And how long did it take? Hours, for sure, but according to journalist Hamish Cardno:

"The latest we could book into the Lisbon Arrival Control was nine minutes past five. At five minutes to five – the engine still without air cleaners and other detail points – we fired up and drove off to the Control, where we booked in at two minutes past ...

"We had 40 minutes' neutralisation to reach the Control at the Parc Fermé on the docks – but the Control did not close until 19.55. We rushed back to Goncalves and set to work on the car again. Eventually it was finished and we screamed off to the docks where we booked in at 19.36 ..."

The Silver Shadow needed equally drastic mechanical surgery, but in this case it was driver Bill Bengry who had to act as his own mechanic.

GLUTTONS FOR PUNISHMENT

Saturday, 25 April to Friday, 8 May – no fewer than 14 days – covered the time between the end of the European leg, and the start of the South American section of the event. Some crews lazed around – the Copacabana beaches in Rio de Janeiro were very seductive – and a few flew ahead to carry out last-minute recces in the Brazilian and Uruguayan sections which were soon to follow.

Roger Clark and ace-mechanic Bill Meade flew back to the UK to design, engineer, test and manufacture the axle braces which would ensure that Ford's Escorts would complete the event. A few, myself included, had to return to the UK to take up the 'day job', if only for a short time.

One team, however – Citroën – saw little point in doing nothing. For no sooner had the DS21s reached Lisbon than Guy Verrier (third) and Robert Neyret (seventh), along with Citroën 'works' Team Manager René Cotton, and a team of experienced mechanics, flew off to North Africa, to pick up a new set of cars, and to compete in the rough-and-tough Rally of Morocco, which ended in Casablanca!

These were three ugly short-wheelbase/two-door prototype DS21s which carried different rear-end styles (the third car was driven by local hero Jean Deschazeaux), which fought among themselves for the lead on what was a very demanding event. In the end, only 12 of the 63 cars completed the event. Two of the Citroëns retired after mechanical breakdowns, but Robert Neyret/Jacques Terramorsi started from no 1, and finished first. Not only that, but the Consten/Todt Group 1 DS21 (they were not involved in the World Cup) took second place.

Interviewed after the finish of the Morocco Rally, Neyret said: "It was harder than the first part of London-Mexico, and I tremble a little to think how many Moroccan Rallies are waiting for me in South America ..."

After which Neyret, Verrier and their co-drivers hopped on another plane and flew over to Rio de Janeiro ...

Service, repairs, but certainly not a bodged job – this is one of the 'works' Escorts on the dockside in Lisbon.

Before it reached Portugal, this ultra-expensive vehicle had suffered a rear wheel hub bearing failure (subsequent investigation showed that it had never been grease-packed, even when new). The crew had no such spares on board, no service crew to greet them, and no conceivable way of getting replacements from the UK in a hurry. Somehow or other (and the can-do business acumen of owner Ray Richards must have had something to do with this), a Silver Shadow private owner was located within 100km (62.1 miles). He was subsequently 'persuaded' to donate the appropriate corner from his own car, and Rolls-Royce was then shamed into air-freighting suitable parts to that Portuguese owner, whose car was sitting on blocks in his garage! Only ace-fixer Bengry, co-driver David Skeffington, and tycoon Richards could have achieved this sort of thing – yet somehow it was exactly what the world of rallying seemed to expect.

When the dust had settled, the state of play could then be surveyed. Twenty five cars had already dropped out – some due to accidents, some due to mechanical bothers, and a few due to exhaustion among their crews – and battle

Gunnar Palm (left) and Hannu Mikkola were not yet in the lead when this picture was taken at Lisbon, but would take over within two days of the restart from Rio de Janeiro.

lines had already been drawn between the three major 'works' teams – Ford, British Leyland and Citroën. (However, I still insist that the Citroëns were really 'works' cars, even though they were nominally entered as 'private owner' cars.)

Amazingly, four of the five Primes so far held had proved to be cleanable – which was not at all what the organisers had hoped, but they had not been able to set ultra-demanding target times in some cases – and the redoubtable René Trautmann found himself leading, with a penalty of just five minutes, which was two minutes ahead of Hannu Mikkola's Escort, and four minutes ahead of his team-mate Guy Verrier. Four Citroën DS21s, four Escort 1850s and two Triumph 2.5PIs occupied the 'top ten' positions, so there was satisfaction, to a degree, for all concerned.

95

Just before the restart in Rio de Janeiro, rally leader René Trautmann sorts out a detail with John Sprinzel and Controller Jim Gavin (centre).

British Leyland, though, was nursing a private grievance, for its decision to go in a particular direction on Prime 2 (the Serbian Prime) had cost them at least 15-20 minutes each). Although sixth and eighth at this stage was good, it was not good enough for the ambitious Brian Culcheth, who was not about to waste the months he had already invested in the event: he personally thought he should have been in the top four at this juncture, and would have to claw his way back up the leader board in Brazil and beyond.

Some observers were amazed that so many crews (including, frankly, some of the 'no-hopers') had actually reached Lisbon, and would eventually find themselves in South America, but the truth is that the route, so far, had not been as tough, or as tiring to the crews, as had originally been forecast. Although there had been only one scheduled overnight halt in seven days – at Monza – most crews were not exhausted, as there had been other chances to make up time, to sleep at service points, and generally just to husband all reserves for what lay ahead.

And what did lie ahead? Only those professionals who had already practised some of the South American sections could related the unknown to what had already been experienced. To the crew members who were heard to say (and I did, indeed, hear this said): "Gawd, that was really, really tough ...", a sage like Henry Liddon would merely smile, twinkle his eyes behind his spectacles and say:

"Gentlemen, the first two Primes in Brazil are each longer than anything you tackled in Europe. The rally is just about to start ..."

The real rallying, it seemed, still lay ahead – in Brazil ...

Results after European Section – Lisbon – 25 April 1970

Total mileage covered so far: 4500

Top Ten in general classification:

Place	Crew	Car	Penalty (hours-minutes)
1	René Trautmann/Jean-Pierre Hanrioud	Citroën DS21	0-05
2	Hannu Mikkola/Gunnar Palm	Ford Escort 1850	0-07
3	Guy Verrier/Francis Murac	Citroën DS21	0-09
4	Timo Makinen/Gilbert Staepelaere	Ford Escort 1850	0-21
5	Patrick Vanson/Olivier Turcat/Alain Leprince	Citroën DS21	0-31
6	Brian Culcheth/Johnstone Syer	Triumph 2.5PI	0-32
7	Robert Neyret/Jacques Terramorsi	Citroën DS21	0-35
8	Paddy Hopkirk/Tony Nash/Neville Johnston	Triumph 2.5PI	0-39
9	Rauno Aaltonen/Henry Liddon	Ford Escort 1850	0-44
10	Tony Fall/Jimmy Greaves	Ford Escort 1850	0-45

71 cars were still running.

Interlude
South Atlantic crossing

Once the cars were loaded on to the SS Derwent in Lisbon, there was really only one choice for the crews to make. Were they going to spend the next two weeks lazing around, and waiting for the restart, or did they have the resources to fly over to Brazil and carry out some last-minute route surveys and practice – or do some Brazilian sun-bathing instead?

Well before the start, those who thought that it might be relaxing to cruise slowly across the South Atlantic with their cars were speedily told that this would not be possible. For a start, the Royal Mail Lines SS Derwent was a pure freight ship, which did not cater for passengers in any numbers, and for another thing, there was always the (remote) chance that such passengers would somehow gain access to their cars, and carry out repairs and refurbishments along the way.

The organising team had arranged alternatives. One was for hotels to be available for crews to laze around in Lisbon (in Portugal, it was a very balmy season in April, of course), or they could fly to Rio de Janiero, where they might also laze around in the Hotel Gloria, which was not only Rally HQ, but was also within easy strolling reach of the fabulous beaches of that vibrant resort and city.

Lining up the 'works' Escort to be slung on board the Derwent at Lisbon are (left to right) Patrick Mennem of the Daily Mirror, Henry Liddon, a photographer, and Rauno Aaltonen. At that moment, Rauno was not at all sure whether his car's gearbox would withstand much more punishment – five weeks later he finished in third place!

Immediately after arrival in Lisbon, of course, there was the usual round of official receptions and a prize giving where trophies and prize money connected with the European section were awarded. For some, however, there was no rest. Ford's engineers and driver Roger Clark flew back to Boreham post-haste to develop and manufacture the axle braces, which could then be fitted before the cars restarted in the South American section, while Citroën team boss René Cotton, and two of his star drivers took relatively short-haul flights across to Morocco, where they were scheduled to compete in the Rally of Morocco (which they duly won!).

All crews eventually used one or other of the specially-hired Boeing

Service alfresco in the shade. Work going into one of the 'works' Escorts in Lisbon

707s from TAP (the Portuguese national airline) or Varig (Brazil's leading international airline) to reach Rio, and several of them immediately set out to carry out last-minute route surveys and practice sessions of routes in Brazil which had only recently been changed.

One particular 707 was almost entirely filled by drivers, co-drivers, mechanics and team personnel. As Controller Jim Gavin recalls:

"You know how every airline captain calculates his take-off run from the estimated weight of the craft, and the outside temperature? They assume that every passenger had a particular amount of hand baggage ... Well, on this occasion, most of the passengers were carrying spare parts, cylinder heads, crankshafts and heaven knows what in their hand baggage, and they staggered up the aeroplane steps lugging all this kit – how on earth they got in the overhead lockers I will never know.

"Alec Poole and Roger Clark were on board, both of them were avid 'take-off timers,' and Alec reckoned that a run of 45 seconds was about right for a fully-loaded 707. So they started their stop watches when the brakes came off ... round came 40 seconds, not a damned thing, then 50 seconds, then more than a minute, and finally it staggered off the ground – not soaring, but just enough to keep flying, get the undercarriage up, and climbing.

"They heard more 'clicks' on that take-off run than if there was a plane-full of crickets on board ..."

In the meantime, the SS Derwent weighed anchor in Lisbon at midnight on the Saturday, and began its steady progress across the South Atlantic. It would be nearly two weeks before crews and rally cars were reunited.

Peace, for a few days at least, with a group of the cars lined up and ready to board ship in Lisbon. Claudine Trautmann's Citroën DS21 is closest to the camera, with the Jimmy Greaves/Tony Fall Escort ahead of her, and Zasada's Escort ahead of that.

5

Rio de Janeiro to Santiago

When the rally finally restarted from Rio de Janeiro, almost everyone involved – competitors, organisers, mechanics and pressmen – were bored to death, champing at the bit, and ready to start motoring again. The *Daily Mirror*, in particular, had closed down its coverage for two weeks – not even a vibrant daily newspaper could find words to describe drivers reclining alongside swimming pools – and in any case, in their opinion, there was some real sport, football no less, to be covered at this time.

Behind the scenes, however, the organising team was having to deal with reports of serious flooding, which might mean the truncation, or even the cancellation, of an early Prime. This was just the first of several geographical near-disasters which would afflict this monumental event.

As already noted, the entry fee for competitors in the event included a transatlantic airline ticket – which effectively meant using a Boeing 707 owned by airlines TAP of Portugal or Varig of Brazil to do the job in one long hop from Lisbon to Rio de Janeiro, and it also included hotel accommodation at either end of that journey. Rally HQ in Rio was the Hotel Gloria.

A few of the professional drivers spent their 'down-time' looking ahead, to parts of the route (particularly the Brazilian Primes, which most had not yet even seen) – and in some cases reporting back to the organisers about the impossibility even of getting through certain sections.

Confident that he would get that far, Paddy Hopkirk decided to fly up to Central America and have a look at the two Primes – one in Costa Rica, and one in Mexico itself – and he has always insisted that this was a good investment, as he was to set the fastest time on the Costa Rican Prime, and win substantial cash prizes for his pace in the Central American section.

Ford, British Leyland, too – and Citroën, to a lesser degree – had a look at the Brazilian stages, for the two-week gap between the World Cup arriving in Lisbon, and it restarting from Rio de Janeiro, gave drivers time to fill in their knowledge for what was to come. It mattered not that they were professionals, for conditions (road and especially bridge) in this part of the world could best be described as unique.

Brian Culcheth confirms this:

"Johnstone and I left Lisbon the day after our arrival there, so we had time to have a quick look at the first two Primes in Brazil and get an up-to-date picture. The highlight of this little trip was that we got bogged down in mud after taking three hours to cover as many kilometres. With a lot of pushing from various locals, we managed to get back down the way we had come onto a more driveable surface. The locals informed us that it would take 12 hours sunshine before the road was passable – and it was

Every travelling controller was issued with this large-scale map of South America, to remind him of the sheer scope and scale of the 1970 event.

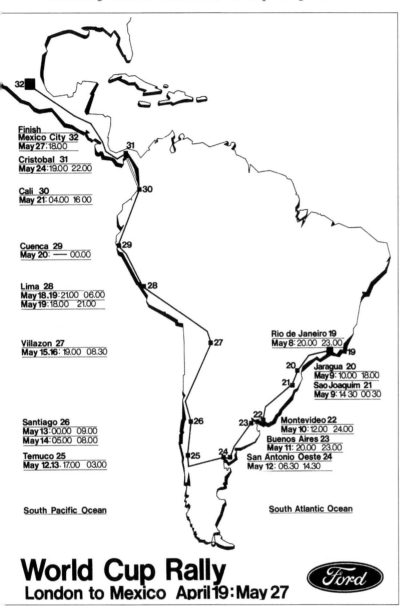

Finish
Mexico City 32
May 27: 18.00

Cristobal 31
May 24: 19.00 22.00

Cali 30
May 21: 04.00 16.00

Cuenca 29
May 20: —— 00.00

Lima 28
May 18.19: 21.00 06.00
May 19: 18.00 21.00

Villazon 27
May 15.16: 19.00 08.30

Santiago 26
May 13: 00.00 09.00
May 14: 05.00 08.00

Temuco 25
May 12.13: 17.00 03.00

South Pacific Ocean

Rio de Janeiro 19
May 8: 20.00 23.00

Jaragua 20
May 9: 10.00 18.00

Sao Joaquim 21
May 9: 14 30 00 30

Montevideo 22
May 10: 12.00 24.00

Buenos Aires 23
May 11: 20.00 23.00

San Antonio Oeste 24
May 12: 06.30 14.30

South Atlantic Ocean

World Cup Rally
London to Mexico April 19 : May 27

The South and Central American sections of the World Cup Rally described almost a complete clockwise circuit of this vast continent. Two ferry crossings were involved – at Point no 24, across the River Plate, and between Points 30 (Buenaventura) and 31 (Panama) in the Pacific Ocean.

still pouring down. Eventually the rally organisers had to cut this bit of the route out, for some four days later it was still impassable ..."

And, as Hamish Cardno later wrote about his escapades in the 'Australian' Triumph 2.5PI:

"First of all we tried to find a quick route through São Paulo – but there isn't one. Then we came to a point on our route notes – made earlier this year by other members of the British Leyland team – where road works were shown and the signposting was a bit complicated. Now it is all different again ...

"For the trip we had hired two standard cars ... after only 700 miles (1126.5km) on these roads we had punctures, exhaust systems falling off, windscreen wipers packing up, and the suspension systems of both cars got a bit tired ...

"The roads we had been looking at were not rough in the sense of having great ruts or potholes – most of them seem to be made of very hard-baked clay. When it is dry this is like driving over a cobbled road with half the cobbles missing, giving a corrugated effect which provides probably the hardest known suspension test.

"When the rains come it is equally rough, but as slippery as sheet ice. After several hours of tropical rain it becomes a quagmire ..."

While the organisers sat back in the Hotel Gloria in Rio, this and other news began to filter back about conditions in the remoter part of Brazil. It soon became clear that it was the second Brazilian Prime – the so-called Rio Grande Prime (Ituporanga to Canela), which was originally to be a monster of 240 miles (386.2km), and for which four hours was to be set as the target time – which might just bring the event to a halt. As luck would have it, the super-experienced controllers due to take charge of that section were David Seigle-Morris, Donald Morley and Erle Morley – so it was typical of John Sprinzel that he sent them up-country, two or three days ahead of the event, to report back.

If they could get through, he reasoned, then the World Cup would still go that way, but if they could not, he would have to consider cancellation. The news from the Morleys, when it came back over Brazil's creaky telephone system, was about as bad as it could be, for there were flooded roads, flooded bridges, bridges washed away, bottomless mud patches (all this was as Brian Culcheth had already reported), and no guarantee that conditions would improve in the next few days.

Prime 7, therefore, would have to be shortened, and it was – to 120 miles (193.1km) for which a mere 1hr 40 minutes would be allowed, which meant a target average speed of 72.2mph (116.2kph)! It was this sort of decision which would have to be made, time and time again, in the days and weeks which followed.

And if this news was not enough (and word travelled fast, not only among the 'works' drivers, but among the privateers who tended to stay close to the factory representatives whenever they could ...), there was the bigger problem. They still had nothing to drive!

Rally drivers forcibly separated from their precious cars tend to get nervous, so there was great relief when the news of the SS Derwent's safe arrival in port on the Wednesday was received. That, of course, was just the start – for how quickly could the cars be unloaded, and would promises made many moons ago be kept?

Patient diplomacy before the event, however, to ensure that Brazilian import regulations were sufficiently eased (or, shall we say, 'bent') to allow 71 rally cars to be allowed into the country, had clearly paid off, and the cars were speedily released. Even so, dealing with Customs formalities seemed to take up most of Thursday, 7 May.

By mid-day on the Friday, local rallying and motor club enthusiasts had caused a positive fleet of breakdown trucks, petrol supplies, and emergency service facilities to be assembled close by (it was at this point that one otherwise cynical competitor was heard to say: "Blimey, Sprinzel has thought of everything ..."). Indeed, it seemed, he really had – and this was all born of his previous bitter experiences all round the world, from the number of times he had suffered less-than-perfect support on other long-distance events.

Getting the cars from the quayside, to actually getting the rally under way into the Brazilian night, was going to be quite complex. First of all, they would have to be funnelled down to a Holding Control in the middle of the city, then they would have to be subjected to what was the 'ballyhoo' start, with lots of flag-waving and high officials in attendance, followed by the real beginning of the South American section, from a filling station on the city outskirts.

It was my job to oversee the despatch – minute by minute – of all 71 cars, from the quayside. By mid-afternoon, the location at Pier Maua was well organised, with the cars lined up in classification order, all of them being lined up on the baking hot wharf. Baking hot? I can vouch for this, because no sooner had the cars gone I visited a nearby Cable and Wireless survey ship, was offered a cold beer or two, and noted that the first one or two did not even seem to touch the sides!

Not all the cars fired up at once, before leaving for the three-mile (4.8km) trip down to the Holding Control in front of the Hotel Gloria, but as long as a co-driver turned up with his Road Book at the Control table, the rescue crews could do the rest. A few machines had suffered from their two weeks of idleness below decks – a puncture here, a flat battery there, empty fuel systems in several machines – but the biggest drama seemed to surround the Citroën team, of which all six DS21 cars were still hale and hearty. First of all, there was a mix-up over ignition keys, for an entire unsorted batch of Citroën keys was handed over by the shipping company, and had to be filleted, while Claudine Trautmann found a flat battery in her car, and her husband René Trautmann complained that the height control adjustment on his DS21 had been damaged, blaming it most volubly on the shipping line which had handled the car.

Then, as Rauno Aaltonen recalls:

"The Fall/Greaves Escort, was lucky to stay in the event. On the dockside Jimmy Greaves put his brief-case on the roof of the Escort, complete with money, papers, pace notes, everything – then forgot about it. They drove off from the quayside, and the brief-case flew off the roof. The next car, I don't know who it was, immediately found it in the road, picked it up, and gave it back to Tony and Jimmy!"

Next, and it was typical of the dramas which always seemed to surround the Rolls-Royce Silver Shadow on this event, its owner, Ray Richards, arrived at the Pier Maua to collect his car, but did not have the Road Book with him, which the controller needed to stamp before releasing it ...

But it could have been worse. The cars were all there, all without exception were eventually persuaded to fire up and turn into working rally cars again, and since most crews had already taken the precaution of doing a dummy run from one location to another (using taxis, of which Rio had many ...), with just one hour allowed to complete three miles (4.8km) to get from the quayside to a holding Parc Fermé at the Hotel Gloria, there were few dramas.

Amazingly, some dedicated factory service crews managed to carry out more work on their cars before they had to go into Parc Fermé – with work beginning on fitting axle braces to the six 'works' Escorts, and with transmission renewals starting on the Triumph 2.5PIs. On the whole, though, all were itching to get under way.

To keep the media happy (not only the *Daily Mirror*, you understand, but Brazil's local radio and TV networks) John Sprinzel and Wylton Dickson had managed to turn the official 'ballyhoo' start into a genuine flag-waving/big crowds/music blaring 'event' outside the architecturally spectacular Brazilian Museum of Art, where the Brazilian flag was enthusiastically waved by no less than the Brazilian Minister of Transport.

I was doing no more than watching this extravaganza (the following morning I was due to fly off to Montevideo to await the rally's arrival in Uruguay), but was amazed to see how similar was the behaviour of this massive crowd of young people to a plague of locusts. The ever-amiable Richard Harper, who was in charge at this point, saw his Control equipment (including the Control banner, and 'this way' arrows) appropriated even before the first cars arrived from the Hotel Gloria. Any rally car which stopped was subject to minute scrutiny from the crowd, and if a sponsor's sticker could be peeled away, it would be ...

As Michael Scarlett later told me about his experiences inside the Red Arrows' Maxi:

"Everyone had to knock, tap, slap, feel, touch, push, prise, pull, tear or twist everything on the outside of the car. I could never keep a goldfish now; I know just how they must feel ...

"We lost one complete rally number sticker, several other advertising stickers and, after someone's careful attention to the boot with a penknife, found ourselves driving, as Terry put it, an 'Austin two-rivet-holes' after the Maxi name plate was pinched ..."

Action – at last

All that, of course, was just for publicity purposes – and, good grief, was there a lot of that! Even so, this was all just a prelude to another Control on the edge of the city. This is where the real World Cup Rally began. Competitors who had just spent days either sun-bathing, sight-seeing, getting some work done or – occasionally – receeing some of the route which was to come, were suddenly faced with the enormity of what lay ahead. Once they had left down-town Rio de Janeiro, they were faced with non-stop rallying through Brazil and Uruguay, a 41 hour sector which included two long and demanding Primes – and all of it on roads and tracks which none of them, surely, had ever rallied before.

Minute-by-minute, 71 cars left for the Brazilian hinterland, now

Prime 6: Ventania to Bateias (Brazil) – the Parana Prime
(Target: 125 miles/201.2km in 1hr 30 minutes)

Fastest times:

Crew	Car	Penalty (mins)
R Aaltonen/H Liddon	Ford Escort 1850	15
S Zasada/M Wachowski	Ford Escort 1850	15
T Makinen/G Staepelaere	Ford Escort 1850	15
H Mikkola/G Palm	Ford Escort 1850	16
A Fall/J Greaves	Ford Escort 1850	17
P Hopkirk/A Nash/N Johnston	Triumph 2.5PI	18
T Hunter/G Mabbs	Porsche 911	19
R Clark/A Poole	Ford Escort 1850	19
B Culcheth/J Syer	Triumph 2.5PI	19
A Cowan/B Coyle/U Ossio	Triumph 2.5PI	20
R Neyret/J Terramorsi	Citroën DS21	23
R Trautmann/J-P Hanrioud	Citroën DS21	24
G Verrier /F Murac	Citroën DS21	25

running in classification order – which at this point put René Trautmann's Citroën DS21 on the road, closely followed by Hannu Mikkola (Ford Escort 1850), Guy Verrier (Citroën DS21), Timo Makinen (Ford Escort 1850), Patrick Vanson (Citroën DS21) and Brian Culcheth (Triumph 2.5PI).

A very determined Rauno Aaltonen lay ninth – with the two utterly different cars of the Evan Green 'Australian' Triumph 2.5PI, and the Martin family's stately but hopelessly uncompetitive Rolls-Royce Silver Cloud bringing up the tail.

Aaltonen, no question, had embarked on a do-or-die mission at this point:

"Even before we left Lisbon, it was time to discuss with Henry [Liddon, his co-driver]. We decided that it was highly unlikely that we would ever see Mexico. We were certain that this car could not finish. So we went absolutely to the limit, and it went perfectly well. We won every Prime [before Montevideo] except one, in Uruguay, where we had a very rough road with big rocks, so we had a puncture, and we did not win that one. But everything else we won quite a lot of cash – for the prize money was something like £500 for fastest time in each Prime. That was good money for those days ... It meant that we were climbing up the leader-board, very quickly ..."

In fact Rauno would climb to fifth in the next two days, and there was more to come ...

First of all, competitors had to face a 10 hour slog north, then west, out of Rio de Janeiro, and eventually south-west through São Paulo (after Rio, this was Brazil's 'second city', but even bigger and more traffic-clogged than that), to Ventania, where Travelling Controller Peter Harper

was scheduled to send them on their way over Prime 6, the Parana Coffee Prime – to Bateias, which was once again close to the South Atlantic Ocean. That Prime, at least, would be tackled in full daylight, as would Prime 7 (the much-shortened Rio Grande Prime), which linked Ituporanga with Canela.

Was that enough for the time being? Indeed no – for the rally cars then had to fight their way south-west once again, to cross the Brazilian-Uruguayan border before making their way to Prime 8 (the Uruguay Prime). If they had enough time to spare, they could delay tackling this stage until after dawn on 10 May, but this meant assuming that the balance of the sector – from Salto (which was on the very edge of Uruguay, close to the Argentinian border, before making almost due south to Montevideo (the capital of Uruguay) – would allow then to make up time.

Sounds straightforward enough? Yes, perhaps, but only if one's car was still strong, one's maps were adequate, and one's navigation was well-drilled. The start of the South American section, too, looked positively European at first – green, with flowing hills, but no fearsome climbs, descents, or altitudes, and no bleak 'outback' to be conquered – but this merely lulled the senses of those who still had not grasped the sheer enormity of that rest of the event.

In the meantime, some of those cars which were either 'walking wounded' when they disembarked on the dockside at Rio, and might still have a 'to-do' list of work to be completed, spend the first hours at the side of the road, in garages, often on stands, and usually with vital pieces hanging off.

The Silver Shadow had its other rear corner/hub changed as a precaution (that arch-realist Bill Bengry had seen what he was changing before Lisbon, did not like what he found, and somehow got hold of another sub-assembly to take across the South Atlantic with him), while the other Rolls-Royce (the Silver Cloud) soon dropped out with broken front suspension components. The so-called impecunious Mexican students started from Rio, but were not officially seen after that – one presumes that they eventually found their way back to their home country by private enterprise – but maybe the VW Beetle is still rusting away somewhere in Brazil.

Andrew Cowan's 'works' Triumph 2.5PI received the replacement overdrive – the original had been giving him trouble for days in Europe, but time could never be found to replace it on the European side of the ocean. It took two hours in the suburbs of Rio, while engine and suspension patch-up work on the 'Australian' 2.5PI continued (though the engine on that machine did not sound at all well ...). Adrian Lloyd-Hirst's privately-prepared Triumph PI also needed a front suspension rebuild, which could not be completed before he ran out of time.

Finally, on the Saturday morning, came the first competitive motoring of the South American section, as crews tackled Prime no 6 (the Parana Coffee Prime from Ventania to Bateias). This one, though, was different. Back in Europe (way back – was it really more than two weeks since any of the crews had been driving at rally speeds?), for of the first five Primes had been cleaned by several drivers, and René Trautmann had only missed the target in deepest Yugoslavia by four minutes.

Here, though, was a 125 mile (201.2km) challenge where no-one got nearer than 125 minutes off the target. Mostly held on smooth dirt, on twisty but public roads where other traffic was occasionally encountered, this was much like European rallying, but on a large scale. Those running near the back of the field had a rather more tough time, perhaps, as Mike Scarlett in the Red Arrows Maxi confirmed:

"A wide red-earth road between banks; the dull impression faded when we rounded a corner to meet a little van cringing to one side coming the other way, then things like a horse and cart, a herd of cattle, the odd lorry, and so on. Another not very closed road ..."

Later in his story, Mike also pointed out another hazard:

"On both these [early] Primes, we met the much-publicised two-plank bridges, mainly only a worry when one came upon them suddenly round a blind corner ..."

First impressions showed this sort of Prime to be ideal Ford Escort territory, for six of the fastest eight times were set by a 'works' Ford, with only Paddy Hopkirk's Triumph and Terry Hunter's Porsche breaking up their monopoly. At a stroke, therefore, Trautmann's Citroën lost the rally lead – he was eight minutes slower than Hannu Mikkola here, and therefore trailed him by six minutes.

However, competition was still close – the fastest cars lost 15 minutes, while even though tenth fastest must have been a disappointment, Andrew Cowan was only 10 minutes further adrift. Worse, though, was the fact that 10 cars did not complete that Prime before Gerry Ryan closed his Control, at Bateias, at 14.55hr. For the organisers, this was perhaps worrying. If an average of 10 cars disappeared after every Prime, would there be any survivors by the time the event reached La Paz, in Bolivia, or Lima, in Peru? The Andes Primes, after all, could be even more demanding than the relatively 'normal' Primes in Brazil and Uruguay.

Prime 7: Ituporanga to Canela

Next came the Rio Grande Prime, the section which had already caused so much heartache back at Rally HQ in Rio in the days leading up to the restart. Much shortened, but given an even more insane target average speed than the original, this now faced crews with a 120 mile (193.1km) thrash over verdant, rolling countryside, still over roads not closed to the public, but still encountered (for those near the head of the column) in daylight.

According to the time sheets this was almost, if not exactly, a rerun of Prime 6, for five 'works' Escorts occupied the top five positions, with Terry Hunter's Porsche 911S sixth, and Brian Culcheth's Triumph 2.5PI down in seventh place.

An insane target average? For sure (though you might like to use the word 'unattainable' instead) – just take one look at the times recorded, where Rauno Aaltonen was fastest of all, but still 35 minutes (not seconds, minutes) late, while Andrew Cowan and Paddy Hopkirk (twelfth equal in the big Triumphs) each lost a massive 50 minutes.

The valiant private owners were hoping that the 'works' machines might be too razor-edge in their tuning, and might wilt under the pressure of long Primes – but unhappily for them, they were wrong. With the single

Prime 7: Ituporanga to Canela (Brazil) – the Rio Grande Prime (Target: 120 miles/193.1km in 1hr 40 minutes – much shorter than originally-intended 240 miles/386.2km in four hours Prime, the change being due to impossible road conditions)

Fastest times:

Crew	Car	Penalty (mins)
R Aaltonen/H Liddon	Ford Escort 1850	35
R Clark/A Poole	Ford Escort 1850	37
H Mikkola/G Palm	Ford Escort 1850	38
A Fall/J Greaves	Ford Escort 1850	38
T Makinen/G Staepelaere	Ford Escort 1850	38
T Hunter/G Mabbs	Porsche 911	40
B Culcheth/J Syer	Triumph 2.5PI	42
R Trautmann/J-P Hanrioud	Citroën DS21	43
G Verrier /F Murac	Citroën DS21	44
S ZasadaMachowski	Ford Escort 1850	49
R Neyret/J Terramorsi	Citroën DS21	50
A Cowan/B Coyle/U Ossio	Triumph 2.5PI	50
P Hopkirk/A Nash/N Johnston	Triumph 2.5PI	50

exception of Terry Hunter's Porsche 911S (sixth fastest here), the leader board was completely dominated by Ford, Triumph and factory-supported Citroën machines.

Hunter, indeed, was going faster, and more consistently, than all but he had expected. The 911S, which was supported by Bio-Strath (who marketed health-food products), was probably faster in a straight line than any of the factory machines, but was of course limited by a lack of factory service. Hunter himself was an ex-Triumph, ex-BMC Mini 'works' driver, while his co-driver Geoff Mabbs was still well connected with the British Leyland team – and had been personally responsible for demolishing the only Range Rover test car which had been assessed before a choice of cars for the World Cup had been made.

To give an idea of the huge gulf which was now beginning to separate the 'gentlemen' from the 'players' – or the amateurs from the professionals – it is worth noting that at least nine cars lost more than two hours here (this on a Prime with a target time of only 100 minutes ...).

In the end, five cars dropped out on the Rio Grande Prime – which brought the running total down to 56 (out of the 96 that had originally started from Wembley Stadium) – and unhappily for the publicity seekers one of these was the Royal Hussars' Austin Maxi, whose driving team included Prince Michael of Kent. This car went off the track on the Prime, badly damaging the entire front suspension, steering and driveshaft details on the right side of the car. With no access to service or repairs, the Maxi had to abandon – which at least gave the enthusiastic Prince Michael time

The 'Royal' Austin Maxi still looking smart, on the European section – but it crashed, and had to retire, in Brazil.

to carry on around South America, by joining the organising team as a travelling controller.

This was also the juncture at which the headline-making Rolls-Royce Silver Shadow had one incident too many. It left the track, and could not be retrieved in time. Later – much later – it would be put to rights. Owner

Ray Richards flew back to Europe to get on with his business life, while driver Bill Bengry cut across country to Chile, where he joined the rally 'caravan' and played the part of an informal 'sweeper' and 'emergency service'/taxi machine for the rest of the event. Without Bengry and the Silver Shadow, for instance, Paddy Hopkirk's Triumph 2.5PI would have

The Royal Hussars and the 17th/21st Lancers, two noted British Army regiments, sponsored this Austin Maxi, which was driven by three of their serving officers – Gavin Thompson, HRH Prince Michael of Kent, and Nigel Clarkson. Prince Michael later joined the organising team in the latter stages of the event.

had to retire when it broke a transmission shaft well short of any help from the mechanics ...

Other casualties were Brian Chuchua's enormously heavy Jeep Wagoneer, Bill Chesson's privately-prepared Ford Escort, Tony Walker's Vauxhall Victor estate car, and Rugge-Price's BMC 1800.

Now, though, it was time to make for the Brazilian/Uruguayan border at Santana do Livramento, to drive on through the night, and to tackle the third Prime, the only one in Uruguay, where the target average speed was set at no less than 83.3mph (134.1kph).

Unhappily for Ford, and even before the rally reached the start of the next Prime, Roger Clark's Escort was wiped out in a bizarre accident. As Roger later wrote in his autobiography:

"We had just come out of the Rio Grande Prime, and Alec Poole [his co-driver] was driving. I was kneeling on the passenger seat, with my back to the windscreen, rummaging in the back of the car for a sweetie or something, when all of a sudden there was an almighty crash, my backside hit the dashboard, my ankle twisted under me, and when I eventually managed to look round, I found the Escort well-and-truly rammed up the back of a defenceless VW Beetle ...!"

Before they could tackle Prime 8, of course, the rally cars had to run the gauntlet of border officials from one South American nation to another – to try to do it quickly, to try to do it without fuss, and to hope that there would be no diplomatic, commercial or administrative hang-ups.

Most crews managed all this without too much hassle – for most of them it was early morning, which meant that border officials were fresh and well-briefed – but Rod Cooper/Ron Channon, in their Ford Cortina GT, caused all sorts of drama when they got through Customs, found their engine running badly without noticeable oil pressure, and did a quick (and illegal) U-turn to get immediately back to the Castrol service point on the Brazilian side of the border.

One crossing in this informal style was apparently OK, but three crossings – into Uruguay, then back into Brazil, and finally back into Uruguay again – was something else. The guards, they say, got so excited that guns were drawn, much gesticulating took place, the absence of appropriate 'multiple-entry' visas was mentioned, so it took time before the Castrol experts did their stuff, the car was restored to health, and the Cortina GT went on its way ...

Once the rally cars got into Uruguay, it was almost as if they had gone through a time tunnel, into another age and previous motoring age, for the economics of this nation meant that virtually no modern cars had yet been imported, and many cars of a great age were still pottering around the streets and roads. To the locals, therefore, a VW Beetle (yes, a Beetle, for this car was already to be found almost everywhere in remote parts of the world) was modern, rare, but somehow normal. Picture, therefore, the consternation of those who were still used to seeing Ford Model Ts of the 1920s, and 'stove-bolt' Chevrolets of the 1930s, and were now confronted by what to them must have seemed like space-age Escorts, Triumphs, Citroëns and Porsches. Not only modern (futuristic, to them) cars, but sometimes luridly painted, and driven in a very extrovert manner.

Prime 8: Tucuarembo to Salto

"It was with one of these old cars," Michael Scarlett recalls, "that our Red Arrows Maxi had its famous shunt in Uruguay."

An old lady driving an early-perpendicular Ford Prefect of 1940s vintage drifted out of a side road into the path of the speeding Maxi, did not even seem to see it, and the Maxi had no chance of stopping.

Prime 8: Tacuarembo to Salto (Uruguay) – the Uruguayan Prime (Target: 125 miles/201.1km in 1hr 30 minutes)

Fastest times:

Crew	Car	Penalty (mins)
A Cowan/B Coyle/U Ossio	Triumph 2.5PI	14
B Culcheth/J Syer	Triumph 2.5PI	18
H Mikkola/G Palm	Ford Escort 1850	19
T Hunter/G Mabbs	Porsche 911	20
A Fall/J Greaves	Ford Escort 1850	20
R Aaltonen/H Liddon	Ford Escort 1850	20
P Hopkirk/A Nash/N Johnston	Triumph 2.5PI	23
G Verrier/F Murac	Citroën DS21	23
P Vanson/O Turcat/O Leprince	Citroën DS21	25
T Makinen/G Staepelaere	Ford Escort 1850	26
J Bloxham/R McBurney/ P Brown	Hillman Hunter	27
R Neyret/J Terramorsi	Citroën DS21	27
S Zasada/M Wachowski	Ford Escort 1850	30

"Terry was driving at the time, we had only just left the end of the Prime, and a British Leyland service point – that was about five kilometres (3.1 miles) back up the road – he did his best to avoid her, but caught one corner of the old Ford. This did a lot of no good to the Maxi – the front suspension and steering rack of the Maxi was seriously damaged – and we knocked over the old Ford, which ended up on its roof in the middle of the road."

The startled lady's Ford Prefect was restored to its wheels as soon as possible, which was just as well, for there was a little dog and a couple of chickens in there as well. She departed quite happily, knowing that she had been a bad girl.

Somehow, the mechanics back up the route got to know of the accident, rushed down the road, found the crippled Maxi, and set about restoring it to something like health. It took hours, of course, and the Maxi was never again likely to be in with a chance of major awards, but it made it all the way to the finish, weeks later, in Mexico City.

The location of a Prime, in that friendly but financially backward country, therefore, was a real culture shock. This Uruguayan Prime, linking Tacuarembo to Salto, was set at an almost insanely high average speed – 125 miles (201.2km) in just 1hr 30 minutes – so it was no surprise to find that everyone lost time. This was the first of several Primes were the big Triumphs were expected to take time out of the under-geared Ford Escorts, and so it transpired. Andrew Cowan's Triumph set fastest time, with Culcheth's sister car just four minutes adrift. Culcheth later confirmed that it was on this section that his clutch master cylinder failed, but as he was

The Anderson/Willcocks/Bosence Volvo 132 completed the European section, but expired in South America.

spending many minutes in top gear, or overdrive top (where a clutch was not needed to affect the change) continuously at between 80 and 100mph (128.7 and 160.9kph), he had managed perfectly well without it!

For him, however, there was one actual hold up, due to a puncture, towards the end of that Prime:

"On the whole event, we had eight punctures. The Uruguay puncture was the most costly, because in the end we were second fast to Andrew, who got the Prize Money instead of us!

"Hannu, I reckon, had far fewer punctures than us on the event [in spite of Dunlop's thick wall SP44s], and the reason for that, I reckon, was that he was running first on the road in South America. The puncture I had in Uruguay, for instance, was caused because previous cars had sent rocks flying into our path ..."

That astonishing pace, incidentally, was set-up even though the Triumph spent many miles towards the end of the Prime trying to get past a BMC 1800 in a dust cloud (he did now know they were there ...).

Although the Triumphs beat the Escorts for the first time on a long Prime, the real sensation occurred just a few kilometres into the Prime when Citroën hero René Trautmann went off the track in a big way, virtually writing off his DS21. Having lost the lead to Hannu Mikkola on a previous Prime, he was no doubt well hyped-up on what was supposedly a stage which would favour a fast car with long-travel and supple suspension.

Although Trautmann had practised this Prime himself (he was not merely relying on

Although this Citroën DS21 was prepared by the factory in Paris, and René Trautmann was the team leader, he was entered as a private entry. He led the World Cup Rally throughout Europe. Unhappily, he crashed the car in the early stages of the Brazilian section. (McKlein)

Looking weary, Johnstone Syer climbs out of the second-place Triumph of Brian Culcheth, at a South American Time Control.

OOH 744G, the gallantly-driven BMC 1800 of Reg Redgrave, Bob Freeborough and Phil Cooper, press on in South America. They would finish ninth overall, and second in the Private Entry category.

other people's survey notes), only a few kilometres into the section he encountered a section which had recently been diverted to get around a damaged bridge (this, apparently, had been notified to the organisers, and in general to the drivers). Approaching this at extremely high speed in the dark – this was a fuel-injected DS21, which was apparently running the still-experimental five-speed gearbox, by the way – not even Trautmann could slow the DS21 enough for it to scrabble into the diversion.

The result was that it left the track, somersaulted several times, and ended up severely damaged, well off the road. Second-hand reports from the end of the stage included one driver (unidentified) who commented: "Even for a Citroën it was a very odd shape indeed ..."

Although Trautmann could not make permanent repairs (and, of course, there was very little organised Citroën service on this event) he somehow manhandled a very battered DS21 to the end of the Prime. Some

reports put their Prime penalty at 3hr 43 minutes (Andrew Cowan's Triumph lost just 14 minutes ...), but the fact is that he retired at that point, did not turn up at the Time Control in Montevideo, and was therefore out of the rally.

For those crews and their cars, who were still hale and hearty, this exciting World Cup marathon was now beginning to settle into a pattern. Except for Terry Hunter's Porsche 911S (it was fourth fastest on the Uruguayan Prime, only six minutes behind Andrew Cowan's Triumph), the Prime leader board would always be stuffed with up to five Escort 1850s, three Triumph 2.5PIs, and three Citroën DS21s. The Escorts would usually be fastest where the going was twisty and, somehow, more 'European', the Triumphs would always be competitive where they could stretch their legs and use their high, overdrive-assisted, top speeds, and the Citroëns could be relied upon to show well wherever the going was rough.

And as to the rest of the entry? Cars like Rosemary Smith's Austin Maxi were still going remarkably well – the driver's experience and finesse made up for the fact that the car was still under-developed as a rally car. The Moskviches were – well, just Moskviches – which meant that while they were remarkably slow, they were also very sturdy. Their crews made up for a lack of European languages with a relentless cheerfulness which endeared them to everyone else.

Incidentally, other crews found that it was always unwise to have to follow them on narrow tracks, because they were either not willing to be passed, or could not see behind them in dust clouds. As Citroën private owner Patrick Vanson told me many years afterwards:

"We once had trouble getting past the Moskviches, which always seemed to be running together – if one had a problem, they all stopped, to sort out the problem. Once we managed to get past them, then a long time afterwards we came to a point that we could not hold on any more and we had 'to pick the flowers' (translated, this is a French euphemism for 'spend a penny', or 'have a toilet break' ...). So we decided that we weren't about to be overtaken by the Moskviches again, so we decided to put the Citroën sideways across the narrow road. I seem to remember that Tubman in a BMC 1800 also started to catch up with us, and we saw him coming, but we managed to finish what we had to do, and we got going again before we were caught ..."

The no-hopers had already been filtered out in Europe, the spongers had already dropped out, the gallant-but-underprepared were gradually breaking down in South America, and those cars which were based on already-proven engineering, but were not very fast (the various BMC 1800s and the Hillman Hunters were perfect examples) were plodding steadfastly on.

Surprisingly, the engine in Peter Jopp's Special Tuning-built BMC 1800 went on to three cylinders, and a complete cylinder head change had to be tackled in a competitors-only Parc Fermé in Montevideo. Rod Badham's Hillman Hunter (a newly-built 'clone' of the model which had won the London-Sydney Marathon in 1968) broke its radiator, and Bert Jennings' Saab V4 found that its rear axle was completely adrift. Even Doug Harris discovered that a Ford Escort 1300GT, though prepared with as much borrowed expertise as Boreham could provide, was gradually shaking itself to pieces, and needed extensive bodging work to keep the suspension and steering in approximately the right places.

Every competitor, it seemed, had a colourful story to tell – stories which often involved local cars, local wildlife, or local customers. It was immediately clear, for instance, that life was considered very cheap and, especially in the remote villages, there seemed to be no control over young children, dogs or other animals.

Nothing, however, could match the story – perfectly genuine, and authentic, as other crews later confirmed – that involved Rauno Aaltonen's Escort in Uruguay:

"It was before Montevideo," Rauno recalls, "there was a village, a lot of spectators, a dirty bit of road going through it, and in the middle of the village a 90 degree corner. We were driving carefully, there was no point in having an accident there, nor of hitting a spectator ...

"There then came a big American car, a really big one, with no shock absorbers, which was floating up and down. It overtook us, the passengers all having Mexican-type hats, very dark-complexioned people. They came to this 90 degree corner, going far too fast, understeered off, went into the crowd. Then they got back – I don't know how many were injured.

"So we then got round the bend, and there, 50 metres (164.1ft) later, a policeman tried to stop that car, but the driver just went past the policeman. He, who had his gun out already, stopped us, jumped in on to Henry's lap, speaking Spanish which I think meant 'follow that car' ...

"I caught up the man immediately, went to the side of his car – the windows were open – the policeman waved his gun, pulled the trigger, but

the gun didn't fire. I was completely amazed by all this, because if he had killed the driver with another shot, then the American car might swerve the wrong way and hit me ...

"So when he did this, I braked hard, pulled back and forced him to stop the car. The policeman then jumped out – and we disappeared immediately! We weren't used to this sort of thing in Europe ..."

By the time the cars arrived outside Montevideo – I was running the Arrival Control, at the toll bridge on the river Santa Lucia, and had been prepared for a very long wait between cars, particularly towards the tail – a number of them needed a lot of work, just to keep going at all.

Amazingly, Evan Green's 'Australian' Triumph 2.5PI was still running, even though its engine could only fire on five cylinders; the well-known French driver Jean-Claude Ogier had to retire after hitting a cow that proved to be even more solid than Ogier's Peugeot; Claudine Trautmann's DS21 (now leading the Ladies' category by a considerable margin) ran over some of the debris, but her car suffered no more than body damage.

As to the Brits, Phil Cooper had been off the road in one of the Special-Tuning-built BMC 1800s, but was carrying on; Jean Denton's 'Beauty Box' car (consistently but not rapidly driven) would need a new starter motor before the restart); and Major Ted Moorat's Army-sponsored Peugeot fell foul of the rough roads when its ignition coil became detached, and fell down in the engine bay, to damage the fan and the radiator.

Happily for East-West détente, the Soviet 'works' Moskvich 412s were still plodding along, if not fast, certainly reliably – though one of them was tipped unceremoniously on its side so that the mechanics could work on repairs. On its side? Clearly Moskvich had been studying BMC methods, for it was Abingdon that had invented this method for its Minis, a process that had appeared in several newsreels and rally films in recent years.

By the time the surviving cars, and the officials, went to bed in Montevideo on the night of Sunday, 10 May, only 52 cars remained in the event – which meant that 19 had already been lost. Was this too tough? Would there be any healthy finishers by the time the event reached Central America? Experienced observers thought that there would be plenty left – not least because at Montevideo the leader board was dominated by five 'works' Ford Escorts, three Triumph 2.5PIs, and three big Citroëns.

One story, which chronologically should be in the next section, refers to the Rolls-Royce Silver Cloud, which arrived in Montevideo many hours after the Time Control had closed – indeed, just as the crews, en masse, set off towards the ferry to Argentina. Although we all knew that the car had been forced to retire in Brazil, the Martin family had not given up all hope. Finding a craftsman in a remote little township, they had persuaded him to mend the broken front suspension. It took him all day to accomplish this, and he charged them a mere £10 (or its Brazilian equivalent) for the work.

According to the Martins, the craftsman then proudly told them: "Now I will be able to tell my children, and my grandchildren, that I have repaired a Rolls-Royce. In fact I will even paint 'Repairer of Rolls-Royces' outside my garage door ..."

The *Daily Mirror* 1970 World Cup Rally 40

Results after Brazilian and Uruguayan sections – Montevideo – 10 May 1970

Total mileage covered so far: 6500

Top Ten in General Classification:

Place	Crew	Car	Penalty (hours-minutes)
1	Hannu Mikkola/Gunnar Palm	Ford Escort 1850	1-20
2	Timo Makinen/Gilbert Staepelaere	Ford Escort 1850	1-40
3	Guy Verrier/Francis Murac	Citroën DS21	1-41
4	Brian Culcheth/Johnstone Syer	Triumph 2.5PI	1-51
5	Rauno Aaltonen/Henry Liddon	Ford Escort 1850	1-54
6	Tony Fall/Jimmy Greaves	Ford Escort 1850	2-00
7	Paddy Hopkirk/Tony Nash/Neville Johnston	Triumph 2.5PI	2-10
8	Patrick Vanson/Olivier Turcat/Alain Leprince	Citroën DS21	2-15
9	Robert Neyret/Jacques Terramorsi	Citroën DS21	2-15
10	Andrew Cowan/Brian Coyle/U Ossio	Triumph 2.5PI	2-19

52 cars were still running.

Across the River Plate

Never before had a rest halt on a major rally seemed so welcome, and never before had the next day proved to be so relaxing – until the next Prime started from Saladillo, in Argentina, at 21.00hr on a star-lit night. A few amateur historians had already scanned the River Plate (the estuary which had to be crossed later in the day) for signs of the wreckage of the German battleship Graf Spee, but were disappointed, whereas most competitors had a long lie-in before starting the next leg to Santiago, the capital of Chile.

It was, of course, much easier to say this than to achieve it. Although the World Cup organisers had effectively neutralised the entire route from Montevideo, via the trans-Plate ferry, and through the frenetic hotbed of motor traffic called Buenos Aires, to a small town called Saladillo in Argentina (where the next Prime was due to start), from that point on they had set a very fast and demanding 1800 mile (2897km) route, which would include two horrendously long and fast Primes in the Argentine Pampas. With very little spare time for them to enjoy Argentinian scenery, or even to halt for a time in the 'Alpine' resort of Bariloche, they were being asked to do all this in 28 hours – an average speed of 64mph (103kph).

On Monday, 11 May 1970, much of the day's motoring was to be scenic, if somewhat frenetic – the important point was that it was to be the first of 10 days of really hard motoring over some of the worst, the roughest, the twistiest, and the highest roads and tracks in the whole of South America. If ever there was a moment at which seasoned crews formed a lasting hatred of the organisers and their devious rallying minds, this was it.

It all started very gently from the overnight Parc Fermé outside the Colombia Palace hotel in Montevideo, when the entire field of rally cars, and some service support cars, were released at once, to make a pleasant dash up one of Uruguay's most modern highways, to the port of Colonia. Then, as now, Colonia is a sleepy little town (no more than 20,000 inhabitants) in south-western Uruguay, its principal importance being that it houses the ferry terminal for a regular trans-Plate crossing to Buenos Aires itself.

Travel expert Mike Broad of the organising team had block-booked one of the pair of boats which carried out a regular shuttle, whose journey time was three hours. During this crossing, although there was no chance for crews to carry out any work on their cars, this certainly allowed the South American media – reporters, interviewers and TV crews – to get all their material in advance of arrival in Argentina.

Although Peter Graham's Cortina Savage finally broke its previously sick transmission on the way out of Montevideo, and several other cars seemed to have had repairable accidents (with each other!) on the way up the coast road, the rest of the cavalcade made it to Colonia on time. After the ferry trip, they saw their machines unloaded into the hot afternoon traffic of Buenos Aires, dealt with the Customs and Immigration people of yet another country, and set out south-west to the little town of Saladillo, which was about 125 miles (201.1km) away.

For the World Cup cars, by all accounts, getting out of Buenos Aires was one of the most exciting interludes in the entire event, as the local auto club had laid on individual police escorts from the ferry terminal, through the city, and out towards Saladillo. These could best be described as enthusiastic but not totally in control, though all of them seemed to exhibit a great deal of machismo (look this up in an English-Spanish dictionary!). All in all, the crews seemed happier when they were finally set free once again, to find their own way.

Not that this was always easy, especially as the available maps were sometimes old and less than detailed. Confirmation that maps and routeing instructions were not always entirely clear came from Paddy Hopkirk, who

Bravely driven by Tish Ozanne, Bronwen Burrell and Tina Kerridge, this privately-entered Austin Maxi was finally eliminated after it had struck trouble on the Pampas Prime – but has survived, intact, to be seen at latter-day classic events.

my colleague Jim Gavin set to start the cars on the Prime which followed at once. The story of how one hire car was definitely on its last legs, that it eventually expired in the Pampas, and how Gavin eventually gave back the keys to the office in Buenos Aires, is for another day. A short flight across the River Plate, and the collection of hire cars, was much more restful than expected.

Expecting nothing but a small audience, some sheep and cattle (Argentina had millions of them) – for this was to be an evening occasion – the controllers found that the place had already been transformed into what looked like an 'out-station' for a European rally, with service points set up by the major factory teams and their suppliers, so that any work needed before battle recommenced could easily be achieved. It was at this point that more dedicated high-tech butchery from the Abingdon mechanics saw the Red Arrows Maxi restored to something approaching road-worthiness, and that crew was now doubly determined to make it to the finish.

By the time the cars arrived, thousands – and I mean thousands – of enthusiasts had arrived from Buenos Aires to see the fun. The local club had built a stockade for the controllers and rally cars to use, but that didn't really help. Argentinians can climb over fences, right? Well – they did – and when Hannu Mikkola was finally flagged off at 21.00hr, the atmosphere was like Trafalgar Square on New Year's Eve ...

The Citroën 'private owners', incidentally, were definitely feeling twitchy at this juncture, for they had no support rendezvous – but on the other hand their DS21s were still behaving suspiciously well.

One high-profile car – the Green/Murray/Cardno Triumph 2.5PI was now terminally ill, for the engine had finally and irrevocably gone back on to five cylinder in Uruguay, the diagnosis was that a piston had definitely failed, but that time could not be found to make the change until the cars reached Chile in 24 hours' time. On the second of the Argentinian Primes, however, the death rattle was finally heard, the piston had broken, there was a hole in the side of the cylinder wall – and that was that.

Prime 9: Saladillo to Espartillar

What followed, in retrospect, was a big disappointment, for although both of the Primes located in Argentina covered dust track surfaces, they turned out to be 'cleanable' – and by a considerable margin too. Earlier in the year, when Brian Culcheth had practised these Primes in a Triumph 2.5PI recce car, he had concluded that time could be taken away from the Fords – but he proved to be wrong. Inexplicably, he thought, the Saladillo-Espartillar Prime had been set at a mere 57.1mph/91.9kph (200 miles/321.9km in 3hr 30 minutes, which sounds difficult, let's be honest ...), but this was no more demanding than a long British Rally Special Stage, for instance.

"For us," Brian Culcheth remembered in later years, and still with a trace of bitterness audible in his voice, "the biggest disappointment was in the Primes in Argentina, which we cleaned with many other cars. Why were the average speeds set at only 57mph (91.7kph) and 63mph (101.4kph)? After all, they had set the Uruguayan Prime at 83mph (133.6kph). On the fastest Argentine Prime, my Triumph averaged 108mph (173.8kph), and I still beat Hannu Mikkola by 12 minutes – but of course that didn't count.

found himself resting in the back seat of the big Triumph at one moment in mid-Argentina, peered out of the window to look at the stars (Paddy was an avid and knowledgeable star-gazer), and decided that their car was going in entirely the wrong direction. A further study of maps proved him right – hobbies can be useful at times ...

Once again I somehow got ahead of the game, for in my next assignment as a travelling controller I was to run the Time Control in Saladillo, with

Terry Hunter's Porsche 911S was the only true private entry to give the 'works' cars a fright – but it suffered serious engine problems in Argentina, and finally expired in Bolivia. (McKlein)

There was a 200 miler (321.9km) in Argentina, then a 380 miler (611.6km), where we had expected to take up to 30 minutes off Mikkola, but we both cleaned both of them, so it was all a waste ..."

When the route was finalised, the tracks across the Pampas were both rough and unkempt in many ways, so John Sprinzel thought his original schedule would be enough to penalise everyone, especially as the Prime was to be run in darkness. Clearly, though, he had not reckoned with the local authorities in Argentina. Apparently when they saw what tracks had been chosen, and what the forecasts about 'their' surfaces actually were, they immediately sent out some heavy-duty graders, which made them much easier. The locals, apparently, were delighted, but never really knew that it was the World Cup Rally that had inspired this action!

On the day itself, the weather was good at first, the tracks being smooth, dry and very dusty, so the only problem was if one car tried to pass another without the leading car realising this. As it happened, no fewer than 19 of the 50 runners were un-penalised, with the Ford and Triumph cars ahead of time by a considerable margin. The usual suspects, of course, all made it early to Espartillar, where the first cars arrived before midnight, and Controller Gerry Ryan had a very easy time, but when the media saw that not only had Rosemary Smith's luridly-liveried Austin Maxi made it on time, but so had one of the gallant Moskviches too, there were big smiles all round.

The dust, however, was a big problem, and one that finally caught up with Terry Hunter's Porsche 911S. Still well-placed at Montevideo (no service support, please note), the engine began to suffer from dirt ingestion on Prime 9, and a great deal of time was lost stopping (in the dark, naturally ...), stripping out the air cleaners, building it all up again, then carrying on. This explains, for sure, why the 911S was not among the 19 cars to clean the Prime – but it was back on form for Prime 10, which it would clean

Later in the evening, the private owners – who were inevitably

Prime 9: Saladillo to Espartillar (Argentina) – the Pampas Prime
(Target: 200 miles/321.9km in 3hr 30 minutes)

This Prime was much less demanding than the organisers had hoped, for it had been graded extensively between the route survey and the event itself.

No fewer than 19 cars cleaned the Prime, these being:

Crew	Car
P Jopp/W Cave/M Kahn	BMC 1800
R Badham/R Lyall	Hillman Hunter
R Neyret/J Terramorsi	Citroën DS21
S Zasada/M Wachowski	Ford Escort 1850
J Bloxham/R McBurney/P Brown	Hillman Hunter
H Mikkola/G Palm	Ford Escort 1850
A Fall/J Greaves	Ford Escort 1850
L Potapchik/E Bazhenov/Y Lesovski	Moskvich 412
P Kube/L Ranft	BMW 2002ti
A Cowan/B Coyle/U Ossio	Triumph 2.5PI
R Aaltonen/H Liddon	Ford Escort 1850
P Coltelloni/I Marang	Citroën DS21
G Perkins/J F Green	Peugeot 404
R Smith/A Watson/G Derolland	Austin Maxi
B Culcheth/J Syer	Triumph 2.5PI
P Hopkirk/A Nash/N Johnston	Triumph 2.5PI
P Vanson/O Turcat/O Leprince	Citroën DS21
G Verrier/F Murac	Citroën DS21
T Makinen/G Staepelaere	Ford Escort 1850

Prime 10: S Antonio Oeste to Bariloche (Argentina) – the trans-Argentine Prime
(Target: 380 miles/611.6km in 6hr 0 minutes)

This Prime was much less demanding, and much faster, than the organisers had hoped, for it had been graded extensively between the route survey and the event itself.

No fewer than 13 cars cleaned the Prime, these being:

Crew	Car
T Hunter/G Mabbs	Porsche 911
R Neyret/J Terramorsi	Citroën DS21
S Zasada/M Wachowski	Ford Escort 1850
H Mikkola/G Palm	Ford Escort 1850
A Fall/J Greaves	Ford Escort 1850
A Cowan/B Coyle/U Ossio	Triumph 2.5PI
R Aaltonen/H Liddon	Ford Escort 1850
R Janssen/J Dik	Datsun 1600SSS
B Culcheth/J Syer	Triumph 2.5PI
P Hopkirk/A Nash/N Johnston	Triumph 2.5PI
P Vanson/O Turcat/O Leprince	Citroën DS21
G Verrier/F Murac	Citroën DS21
T Makinen/G Staepelaere	Ford Escort 1850

running towards the rear – began to experience rain. British Leyland fortunes slumped severely in this part of the world, for not only did some of the 1800s begin to suffer from various maladies, but Tish Ozanne's privately-entered Maxi slid off the track and could not be retrieved, while the Red Arrows Maxi also went hedging and ditching, but was finally levered back on the track

Prime 10: San Antonio Oeste to Bariloche (the Trans-Argentina Prime)

Many hours later, and having driven further south during the night through Bahia Blanca, the World Cup arrived at San Antonio Oeste, a large regional town on the Atlantic coast, on the Golf San Matias. There it was that first of the true monster Primes – a 380 miler (611.6km) all the way west across Argentina to the ski resort of Bariloche – was due to start. Veteran rally driver Tiny Lewis would run the start, while Peter Harper would be in charge of the finish.

This Prime was huge. At 380 miles (611.6km), it was longer than the combined length of all the Primes which had been run in the European section, and was twice as long as any single Prime so far previously set on this event – it was three times longer than any except for Prime 9, which had just been tackled – and was expected to be very difficult. Which, indeed, it would have been if the authorities had not repeated their pre-rally re-grading trick and render it harmless.

380 miles (611.6km) in a set time of just six-hours sounds horrifying enough, but it simply did not turn out like that. To give a clearer idea of just how long it actually was, all the 'works' teams had arranged to have emergency service/refuelling dumps in the middle of this monster. For British Leyland and Ford, for instance, Castrol had set up a temporary depot in Maquinchao, and made sure an English-speaking Castrol employee was on hand. Neither the Escorts nor the Triumph 2.5PIs could carry enough fuel for such a long Prime. And what did the private entries do? They had to find a local petrol station in one of the towns along the route – fortunately it was daylight, and these, such as they were, were open.

As it happened, no fewer than 13 crews cleaned this Prime, and no-one should be surprised to learn that this list included five 'works' Ford Escorts, three Triumph 2.5PIs, and three Citroën DS21s. Not that this was always achieved without drama and, admittedly, some subterfuge.

Rauno Aaltonen, who had climbed up to fourth and was still hopeful of catching his team-mates (Hannu Mikkola and Timo Makinen) now

Andrew Cowan's Triumph 2.5PI approaching a Time Control in the South American section – this car would end up severely damaged after leaving a dust and fog-wrapped track in Argentina.

Crossing short wooden bridges like this one was safe enough, even at speed, but it was essential to hit the planks absolutely straight on. This, by the way, is a so-called main road in Argentina.

related the sort of story which regular keeps chat-show audiences in fits of laughter, though he assures me that it is absolutely genuine:

"We were on this Prime across the pampas, which was on dirt and very very fast, but one track only. Well, we got a puncture on the right rear wheel. We started our usual procedure, but as I was tightening up the wheel nuts, we heard a phizz, as the left rear wheel/tyre went flat. So we changed that quickly, but now we had no more spare wheels.

"We carried on – and then we had a third puncture, and no spare wheel

to use to change. Well, we couldn't carry on driving – so we stopped, jacked up the car, took the wheel off, and then wondered – so I thought – we would wait. We would have to wait for another Escort – and I knew that Zasada was in the next Escort.

"He came, his engine was running, he stopped next to me, asked if we were all right, I said we were alright but ... what about his car? He said it was OK, so I put my head into his car, and said 'What about your water temperature? And your oil temperature?'

"In the meantime, Henry [Liddon – co-driver] had taken a tyre lever and was breaking into Zasada's boot with it! Zasada's engine was revving quite high, so I guess he couldn't hear what Henry was doing ... this is a true story, I promise. Henry, being a gentleman, only took out one spare wheel, took it out, and closed the boot lid very gently, I saw this, and said to Zasada: 'OK, now you go ...'"

There is more:

"So now we changed the wheel, and at this point Tony Fall's Escort arrived, but with very yellow lights. His alternator had failed. So I said: 'Let's make a deal? I will take you to the end of the Prime. If we have a puncture, you will help, and I will be your lights? If you do not make this deal, you will have to stop here, and be out of the rally.'

"It was a beautifully clear night, bright stars, and totally quiet. Tony agreed to this, so we set off driving, very fast, but side by side, so I didn't break his windscreen. You could see meeting traffic, but if Tony had to drop back, he did it quickly, and a long way, so that I did not smash the windscreen. Well, we managed, and we got to Bariloche, and we were not penalised ..."

For some people, however, the mechanical dramas had begun even before the Prime started. As the Red Arrows Maxi scribe, Mike Scarlett, later wrote:

"The way to the trans-Argentine Prime ... in Tuesday's dawn was across mainly pretty dull flat land. The last was the longest straight road I've ever met – 45 miles (72.4km) without a kink through a huge sea of wide open greenland, boring, earth road, mostly smooth enough, 'rather like the Nullaboor' according to Terry.

"Good thing it was too, for Peter, who was driving, suddenly announced: 'We've got no brakes.' The pedal went to the floor, with only slight retardation ... As the road was mainly flat and utterly clear of other traffic, Peter achieved what he said was a lifetime's ambition on a slight downhill section – 100mph (160.9kph) without brakes ..."

A pipe bleed nipple, it seems, had unscrewed itself, and BMC mechanics soon put things to rights at the next service point.

Running very close to the front of the field, though, Brian Culcheth summed up the whole day like this:

"Nearing the refuelling point we were catching the Vanson Citroën, but the dust was too thick for us to try to pass him. At the refuelling point

Brian Culcheth, third at the time, and looking for second place, on one of the Primes in South America.

Castrol did an excellent job in getting us topped up in record time, and we pulled out just as the Citroën was leaving its own refuelling bay ...

"Nearing the end of the Prime we were running well ahead of schedule and began to ease the pace a little, so that we finished 30 minutes inside the time allowance. These two Argentinian Primes had been a great disappointment, for the Triumph could have taken at least 30 minutes back from the Ford Escorts had the time allowances not been so generous ..."

For all the leading drivers, in fact, the southern route in the Argentine had been a frustrating period, where no amount of pre-event practice, and little of the cautious approach to car preparation, had paid off. And now, if such a thing was possible on this event, a stretch of boredom set in. After completing Prime 10, close to Bariloche, and crossing the border into Chile at Paso Puyehue, 47 cars picked up the much-vaunted Pan-American Highway (which traversed the entire length of Chile) and set out on what passed for an international highway, to the capital of the country, Santiago.

Except that this was still being run to a demanding time schedule, for the 'works' cars which had easily cleaned the two previous Primes there appeared to be no problems. Others, such as the Badham/Lyall Hillman Hunter (who unfortunately suffered a road accident – see the sidebar on page 129), Ken Bass' BMW 2002 (which didn't have all its forward facing lamps after tail-ending another rally car in Uruguay), and the Donner brothers' Capri (which had suffered from a lengthy navigational error), made much heavier weather of it all.

Rally leader Hannu Mikkola, however, was still running first on the road, and eventually reached the Holding Control 25km (15.5 miles) south of city with a good deal of time in hand. Once the first group of rally cars had been assembled, they were then shepherded in to the city-centre Parc Fermé (Hannu arrived at 00.30hr on Wednesday, 13 May).

Although the crews then realised that they would have not one, but two, nights in comfortable beds, they all had to be reasonably bright and chipper to take part in something of a show-business occasion on the Wednesday afternoon, which was witnessed not only by Ford's film crew, but by any other media members who had travelled that far.

This polyglot line-up of World Cup cars was taken inside the chain-link fencing of a Parc Fermé in South America. In view are Triumph 2.5PIs, Citroën DS21s, Ford Escorts and a Porsche 911S. The winning car – Hannu Mikkola's Escort – carried competition no 18.

More corralled cars, same Parc Fermé, this group including Moskvich, BMW 2002ti, Peugeot 504 and Ford Capri types.

Private entrants tended to carry their spare wheels on the roof, for they usually had no outside service assistance to help them.

Behind cage-like wire fencing, but having to do all the work themselves, crews had three hours to carry out maintenance and repairs on their rally cars. The only 'help' they could get from mechanics was in the form of shouted instructions through the wire. I was one of the controllers trying to make sense of this hilarious occasion, at one point having to resist bribery from the formidable Mick Jones, mechanic of Ford (though, one must admit, the choc ice was very tasty ...), to allow him to get closer to Messrs Fall and Greaves ...

In general, it seems, all the crews took matters very seriously, entering the wire 'cage' with mountains of spares and special tools, and it was clear that a number of the 'works' drivers had already been put through a series of rebuilding seminars before the event started. Some were more ambitious than others, but all appear to have completed their tasks in the time allowed.

By this time the well-placed Porsche 911S of Terry Hunter/Geoff Mabbs was in dire trouble with its fuel supply and air cleaner problems, where dust ingress had worsened, but most crews were concentrating on preventative maintenance. Working on Doug Harris' 1.3-litre, privately-entered, Ford Escort GT, co-driver Mike Butler took off the cylinder head, decarbonised it, reset all the valve gear, and reassembled

it for further action; several cars received new shock absorbers and even complete suspension struts; and almost all of them were given time to get rid of the rubbish that had piled up inside their cramped cabins in previous days.

Amazingly, none of the Citroën crews bothered to turn up at all – which might speak volumes of confidence in the preparation of the DS21s, but probably meant that none of the drivers were truly confident at the prospect of working on such complex machines.

In the meantime, the published results showed that 43 cars were still running, that far too many crews (in the organising team's opinion) had been un-penalised on the Montevideo-Santiago leg, and that the factory-built, or factory-backed teams were now many minutes (if not hours) ahead of any private entrants.

Behind the scenes, though, big dramas were brewing. Ahead lay a concerted assault on the high altitude roads and tracks of the Andes, in Chile, Argentina, Bolivia and Peru – yet one vital section of that route was known to be blocked with snow, the weather was closing in, and all manner of changes might have to be made.

Time, though, for another night's sleep, which would be in tranquil contrast with what was about to follow ...

6

Santiago to La Paz – high altitude & high drama

Even before this part of the event – the truly critical leg in the entire World Cup – began, a major crisis had hit the organising team. At the time, fortunately, it was well hidden from the competitors and the media, but for a while it looked as if the cars might not be able to get out of Santiago, the capital of Chile, and along the minor and high-altitude routes into Argentina and Bolivia for the huge Primes, which were going to be so important to the rally leaders.

"Before the rally cars arrived, when we were already in Santiago," John Sprinzel told me, "all of us – Dean Delamont, Tony Ambrose, John Brown and myself – were all in the main HQ hotel in Santiago. We got a message from Argentina, telling us that there had been an avalanche, there was still snow which was blocking the route, and they didn't think we would be able to use the original route.

"At the same time we had a message from Peter Harper, one of our travelling controllers, telling us that he was snowed in somewhere and couldn't get his scheduled aircraft flight to his next Control. David Seigle-Morris had burnt two old hire cars in the north of Chile, and he was stuck too. The fact was, too, that we couldn't get over the Agua Negra pass at that moment – we had, in fact, hired a little plane to see if the promised bulldozer had been up there to clear it (and they hadn't) – so at that moment we were just ready to scream at each other. We had no idea as to how we were going to get out of the hole. The rally was due to arrive the following day. It looked desperate. Without a solution, we would have had to cut out Bolivia, lose the difficult Primes before La Paz, and go up the Pan-American Highway through the Atacama desert."

All manner of panic measures were needed to sort this one out, and subsequently several critical timings had to be changed. In the end, another Controller, Dr John Teall, was sent smartly up to see the railway company, to persuade those in charge that they should make sure the shared railway tunnel (shared, that is, with road traffic, from time to time) through a particularly crucial part of the route in the Andes would be given over entirely to the rally for several hours – and a sheaf of cash helped to ensure

that. Because John Brown had planned alternative routes some weeks, if not months, in advance, such a problem – and solution – had already been foreseen.

"Secondly, we got a message through from Peter Harper (don't forget that inter-continental phones were difficult in those days ...), and maybe Tiny Lewis, to say that they had managed to get an aeroplane out of wherever they had been stuck. Seigle-Morris finally found another hire car, managed to shorten and re-route the cars' passage, while John Brown had to drive up to the repositioned Control, because Seigle-Morris was still too far away, and time was running out!"

That all happened in one day, and one evening – and was the biggest single crisis this event encountered. Not that it was all cleared up without making other changes. The author, for instance, who had spent the day in Santiago, cooped up inside the wire-fenced school playground where there was a crews-only Service Park, running that operation, was suddenly sent off to Salta in Argentina, to get to the end of the 510 mile (820.1km) Gran Premio Prime at La Vina. This was not in his original schedule ...

The other major problem facing the organisers was that far too many cars had cleaned the entire Buenos Aires-Santiago section, and that, in addition, many more cars than expected were still running when the event reached Santiago and the two-night halt. Quite suddenly, what had been promised as the 'world's toughest rally' began to look distinctly survivable.

Neither John Sprinzel nor John Brown were happy to let this continue, so hasty steps were taken up to tighten up the next two stages. Even so, those plans would be blown out of the water when Prime 11 had to be shortened drastically, but the massive Prime 12 (510 miles/820.8km, no less) would have one hour chopped from its target schedule, turning that challenge from 'difficult' to 'ludicrously impossible'. In fact it was wise to chop that hour, but as it happens, Mikkola lost only 45 minutes on the new schedule, which means that he would have 'cleaned' it at the original nine hour pace. That is how hard the top drivers were going on this event!

In the first weeks of 1970, survey crews found that much of the route in South America was in bleak, totally uninhabited, and featureless territory. This was part of the High Andes route in Bolivia and Peru ...

Flat out for 57 hours

Almost everyone connected with the event still rates the Santiago-La Paz-Lima sector of the event, over the highest roads and tracks in the Andes, as the crucial days which finally sorted out the outcome of the event. In particular, gritty professionals like Brian Culcheth kept on referring to the 57 hours which settled everything – 57 hours being the overall time schedule for the route linking Santiago to La Paz, by way of two borders (Chile to Argentina, Argentina to Bolivia), high altitudes, and three enormously long, and viciously demanding Primes. It was almost as if '57 hours' had been engraved on his lasting memory of the entire event.

By any measure – whether analytical, or in Hollywood-drama terms – this was make-and-break time, this when the rally might be won and lost. The cars which got to La Paz with the least trouble, and which left their over-stressed crews in good physical shape, would surely become

favourites for victory a few days (and several more countries!) hence. If there was time, it would be instructive to see which cars and drivers benefited from the three monstrous Primes (totalling 900 miles/1448km!) included in the 57 hours, and which suffered.

Any pre-rally thoughts of pacing oneself, of being frightened of the altitude/lack of oxygen/exhaustion factor, would have to be speedily forgotten, and it seems that all but what a few scathingly called 'the tourists' (who were no longer driving hard, but just hoping to pick up a finisher's award) now began to drive absolutely flat out. There was no longer any question of the 'works' crews pacing themselves, for from this point all of them trusted their cars to keep going in awful conditions, and on the visual evidence it seems that all of them drove flat out from this point to the very end.

"For me," Paddy Hopkirk says, "it was a case of going as fast as

... where the altitude sometimes exceeded 15,000 feet (4572m).

possible, for as long as possible, because we had to face the chance of the unexpected cropping up – maybe a landslide, maybe a road being blocked, maybe broken-down vehicles getting in the way. We were so unfamiliar with this part of the world – I had never been out here before the recce, don't forget – that we thought that might just have been a hi-jacking, the roads could have been blocked against us, we might not have been able to get across the border."

By this time the cars were often so strung out over the vast distances of this event that one competitor rarely saw his closest rivals, and sometimes wondered if, in fact, he was on the correct route:

"Hannu was usually way ahead," Brian Culcheth told me, "and I was third on the road most of the time, because Rauno was running second. I would say that up to Santiago we had only been driving at 'eight tenths'. After that – me, certainly – we were always driving at 'ten-tenths' ..."

For many of the private owners, it was a question of survival –

rallying survival, that is – for they were likely to be taking several hours (not minutes ... hours) longer on the massive Primes, had no welcoming service crews to keep their cars in good shape, and had to pace themselves, mentally and physically.

As one cynic reminded me when this book was being compiled: "If the Health and Safety lobby had existed in those days, and if their people had been out in South America, they would have closed down the World Cup at a stroke ..."

It was in this part of the world, in particular, that the rally became so strung out, and so many cars retired, that surviving rally cars would often rush along the route, never seeing any of their rivals. Hannu Mikkola makes the point that as he was in the lead by this time, and was starting from all Time Controls first on the road, he never saw any of his rivals for days at a time. Rauno Aaltonen and Brian Culcheth, both chasing Mikkola as much as they could, and sometimes closely matched in penalties, rarely saw each other, except at major Time Controls where there might be some time in hand.

As a travelling controller on the event, I can confirm this. Officiating at the end of the massively long (510 miles/820.8km!) Rodeo-La Vina Prime, I could see the last 10 miles (16.1km) or so across a parched, tree-stunted landscape: any rally car would forecast its arrival with a big plume of dust, and would not then arrive for up to 10 minutes. The first rally car which I greeted was Sobieslaw Zasada's Escort, which was, in fact, penalised by 73 minutes at this point, after which Brian Culcheth's Triumph 2.5PI arrived, having lost 85 minutes – and no more than six other cars (including the two leading Citroëns) arrived in the first two hours. Later in the day, when the stragglers limped in, the wait between arrivals seemed to be interminable. For officials, at such times, it helped to have a good book to use as 'fall-back' or 'time-filling' occupation ...

For those who had neither recced the route or studied the challenge which lay ahead, the schedule from Santiago (Chile) to La Paz (Bolivia), looked quite relaxed – 57 hours being allowed to complete 1950 miles (3138km), at a target average of only 34.2mph (55kph). Easy peasy? Well, maybe at sea level, maybe with a fresh car and fresh crews, and maybe without three Primes (two of them enormously long) to be tackled, but ... although the truly seasoned crews found ways and means of building up timeliness (so that some sleep could be snatched before Primes were tackled, and so that a Prime start time could be chosen to ensure a maximum of daylight), it was always going to be exhausting.

The restart from Santiago came at the gruesomely early time of 05.00hr on Thursday, 14 May, with all the competitors realising that they would not see another bed until the Saturday evening in La Paz! Just two hours up the road came the first of the Primes, a much-shortened sector whose original route had been savaged by the weather.

Prime 11: Putaendo to Illapel

In the original scheme of things (and as practised by Ford and British Leyland survey teams several weeks earlier, this Prime should have led north from Putaendo before striking inland, eastwards, over the Agua Negra (Black Water) pass, which at 15,650 feet (4770m) was set to be the second highest in the entire route. As already explained, because of a combination of landslides and heavy snow falls, the Agua Negra was closed.

Here was a major problem. In the original scheme of things, the Putaendo to Sotaqui Prime was to have been set in five hours, and would certainly have been more than 300 miles (482.8km) long. But now it had to be drastically shortened. The chosen re-route involved a loop back southwards in mid-Prime towards Santiago, and a Prime finish at Illapel, which left only 121 miles (194.7km), none of it at very high altitude.

With a target time slashed to a mere 1hr 30 minutes – this equated to a target average speed of 80.7mph (129.9kph) – no-one even came close to making it on time. As rough and demanding as any other Prime on the event, this one seemed to be run in undulating country, mostly rolling hillside, with many scrubby bushes and extrovert cactus plants. It also seemed to be infested with donkeys and other animals which, for the first few cars at least, seemed to be wandering around the track when they arrived.

Perhaps the swiftest 'non-works' car in the event was Terry Hunter's Porsche 911S, which was sponsored by Bio-Strath. It finally expired in the high altitude stages of Bolivia.

It accounted for only one retirement (Major Ted Moorat's Peugeot 504 finally broke its rear axle, cracking the casing, and spilling all the available lubricant), though Terry Hunter's hard-pressed Porsche 911S was still in big trouble, and lost more than three hours, stranded at the side of the road, with engine and ignition bothers. Paul Coltelloni's Citroën DS21 had a major accident – his car hit a solid wall at high speed – which damaged the front suspension and the steering rack.

It was by this time that the sensible mid-field runners – cars like

Prime 11: Putaendo to Illapel (Chile) – the Chilean Prime
(Target: 121 miles/194.7km in 1hr 30 minutes – this being much shorter than originally intended, due to blockage of the Agua Negra pass by heavy snow falls)

Fastest times:

Crew	Car	Penalty (mins)
T Makinen/G Staepelaere	Ford Escort 1850	45
A Fall/J Greaves	Ford Escort 1850	50
H Mikkola/G Palm	Ford Escort 1850	51
R Aaltonen/H Liddon	Ford Escort 1850	53
P Hopkirk/A Nash/N Johnston	Triumph 2.5PI	53
B Culcheth/J Syer	Triumph 2.5PI	54
R Neyret/J Terramorsi	Citroën DS21	57
S Zasada/M Wachowski	Ford Escort 1850	58
G Verrier/F Murac	Citroën DS21	64
R Janssen/J Dik	Datsun 1600SSS	64
P Vanson/O Turcat/O Leprince	Citroën DS21	68

the steadily driven German Mercedes-Benz types, Rob Janssen's Datsun 1600SSS, the surviving Mosviches, and hard-working but increasingly battered BMC 1800s such as those driven by Peter Jopp, Reg Redgrave and Ken Tubman, all began to make their point. None of them were going to win – none had ever been capable of winning – but all seemed to be determined to make it to Mexico City. More work was done on the Austin Maxis: although these were hitherto unproven rally cars, they were standing up quite valiantly to the shocks, and endurance, of this event.

The leader board on this Chilean Prime tells its own story – and confirms that every Ford, Triumph and Citroën driver was now going just as fast as he or she possibly could. Four 'works' Escorts led the list (this time it was Timo Makinen who was fastest of all – just five minutes ahead of Tony Fall/Jimmy Greaves' sister car and except for the valiantly driven Datsun of Rob Janssen, all the other top runners were Triumph 2.5PIs or Citroën DS21s.

Once again, it was clear that neither Paddy Hopkirk nor Brian Culcheth (in the Triumph 2.5PIs) could make any impact on the flying Fords – and both could only hope that the much lighter Escorts would eventually prove

The winning Ford escort – FEV 1H – tackles yet another stony, loose-surfaced mountain track on the way to La Paz.

High in the Andes, connecting Chile with Argentina, the World Cup route used this tunnel – which was shared with an express train service.

Prime 12: Rodeo to La Vina (Argentina) – the Gran Premio Prime (Target: 510 miles/820.8km in 8hr 0 minutes)

Fastest times:

Crew	Car	Penalty (mins)
H Mikkola/G Palm	Ford Escort 1850	45
R Aaltonen/H Liddon	Ford Escort 1850	61
S Zasada/M Wachowski	Ford Escort 1850	73
B Culcheth/J Syer	Triumph 2.5PI	85
P Hopkirk/A Nash/N Johnston	Triumph 2.5PI	92
G Verrier/F Murac	Citroën DS21	94
R Neyret/J Terramorsi	Citroën DS21	95
T Hunter/G Mabbs	Porsche 911	136
A Fall/J Greaves	Ford Escort 1850	147
P Vanson/O Turcat/O Leprince	Citroën DS21	154

to be very fragile. Little did they know that it was precisely such fragility – and, in particular, a spate of wheel stud failures – which would hit the Fords on Prime 12. Not that this was any consolation as the cars left Illapel, where they had lost precious minutes to the Escorts.

For the rest of the day, the 42 survivors drove east, out of Chile, into Argentina, by a revised route which avoided the Agua Negra pass, which was still well-and-truly impassable. The alternative, over a route which sounds romantic, but actually made both organisers and competitors nervous, was to cross into Argentina by way of a dual-purpose single-track tunnel at Limite, which was mainly used by trains, but could also be passed (when the authorities permitted it) in cars.

The nervousness was not caused by having to dodge frequent trains – from Santiago to Mendoza there was a scheduled express passenger train, but apparently this ran only once every week, and the rest of the service was similarly sparse – but by the condition of the surfaces. Clearly the authorities were quite used to this occasional use by motor cars, but a series of logs had to be installed at the Argentine end by local workman to make it all viable, while local police, customs and railway officers all had to be consulted, to ensure that the tunnel would only be used by World Cup cars for some hours.

Prime 12: Rodeo to La Vina – the Gran Premio Prime

Now it was deep breath time, for the Prime the crews were about to tackle in the Andes of Argentina was a real monster. Starting at Rodeo, and ending at La Vina (a village some distance due south of Salta, which is to the north of the country), this was originally scheduled as a 510 mile-long monster,

for which a target time of nine hours was set. This was to be a truly horrid Prime, mainly run off at high altitude, on dry, dusty, unsurfaced tracks. This, competitors suddenly realised, was where the World Cup might be won or lost. Whether to carry oxygen or not, whether to plan for daylight or night-time motoring, or not, where to refuel, and what time to choose to start the Prime, were all factors. For the 'works' teams, finding fuel was not going to be a problem, for they had made provision before hand, but for the private owners it was a serious consideration.

Neither Ford (with tank capacities of 28 gallons/127.3L) nor British Leyland's Triumphs (heavier cars, but carrying 32 gallons/145.5L) could hope to complete this monster stage without at least one stop. Happily Castrol had already made arrangements – not only to provide top-up facilities close to the start line, but also to provide fuel at Tinogasta, which was more than half-way along the stage. Maybe these were not Formula 1-style pit stops, but at least they were specially-placed facilities which could usually dispense high octane fuel from massive barrels.

But ... nine hours? In view of recent events, was this still a reasonable target? In fact, as a direct consequence of the way that so many World Cup cars had recently beaten the scheduled targets of the two Primes in Southern Argentina, John Sprinzel now decided to tighten up the Rodeo-La Vina Prime. On each and every copy of the Road Book, the number '9' was firmly scored out, and '8' was inserted in its place. A few heroes – and, believe me, on this event there were plenty of those – were now being challenged to beat a target of 63.75mph (102.6kph) throughout a long, lung-wrenching, and difficult Argentinian day: until Sprinzel's cruel, sweep of the pen was imposed, the target average had been a mere 56.7mph (91.3kph).

Even so, there was just one minor bonus resulting from this geographical upheaval. Because Prime 11 would be considerably shorter than originally planned, and the transport section which followed it had been shortened too, many rally cars arrived at the slightly relocated start of the Rodeo-La Vina Prime many hours ahead of schedule. Not only that, but because of the way that the overall timing of the event was worked out, the Start Control at Rodeo would be open from 20.00hr to 07.00hr on the following day – a total of 11 hours.

So, here was a fascinating conundrum to be worked out. The deep-thinking teams and individuals realised that they could gamble by starting the Prime quite late – well into the night, in fact – thus ensuring that they would be tackling much of the latter end of this Prime (when they were tired) in daylight.

Brian Culcheth, who had surveyed this section on more than one occasion in the preceding months, had this to say:

"That stage in Argentina started in the dark, but because of the five hour gap in the fifty-seven (hour) schedule which I now thought was available, Andrew Cowan decided to wait for daylight before starting [and the result of this decision is described below ...]. I thought, well, suppose I waited until daylight, but suppose I got a problem on the Prime, and I had taken several hours rest and waited for daylight, I might put myself under tremendous pressure."

Brian and his co-driver Johnstone Syer, therefore, had a rest before the Prime began (several hours sleep, in the car, with a mechanic briefed to awaken them at a specific time), but still elected to tackle the early part of the Prime in darkness. In fact they started fourth, behind Sobieslaw Zasada's Escort, and two of the Citroëns.

"My whole strategy throughout the event was to travel as light as possible, and not to carry loads of bits, because I thought that if I had trouble I wasn't going to win anyway. My whole feeling, all the time, was to do everything to the minimum ..."

As it happened, one of the biggest hazards of the Rodeo-La Vina Prime was the dust that formed when any car passed along the tracks. As luck would have it, on that day there was little wind, so the dust hung in the air for quite some time. This was the occasion when Paddy Hopkirk reached a BMC refuelling point, complaining bitterly that Culcheth had been holding him up in the dust. Culcheth, in turn, told him that it had been Guy Verrier's Citroën that was laying the dust in the first place.

Brian has often been quoted about this Prime:

"It was just like driving from Edinburgh to Dover, mainly in fog, on unmade roads strewn with rocks and animals, just as fast as you could. The first 400 kilometres (248.5 miles) were hell, for we were in the continuous dust cloud of the leading cars. Again the speedy Castrol refuelling came to our aid. With one Citroën delayed with some fault, and the other slow in refuelling, we were away before them.

"At the next service point at the end of the two Primes, we were 88 minutes late, but third fastest, and just had to collapse into a bed for two hours – completely exhausted."

The scenery, if anyone had any time to look around them, was stunningly beautiful, though the truly high passes were yet to come in the next sector of the event.

Andrew Cowan's accident

It was almost entirely due to the hanging dust on this Prime that Andrew Cowan then crashed his Triumph, and was lucky not to be left with any permanent injuries. The crew was also lucky that other rally crews stopped (some of them for hours) to render assistance, for this was a part of the world which was a long way from what we effete Europeans called 'civilisation.'

This was the scenario. Andrew had elected to wait for some hours before tackling the Prime, so that he could do his fast driving in daylight. Andrew's co-driver Brian Coyle was alongside him in the front of the car, while their third-crew man, Lacco Ossio, was strapped in to the rear seat.

Andrew, who had been in 10th place as the cars left Santiago, was hoping to claw back time, especially from the Citroëns, and was going as fast as possible. At one point, in mid-stage, he caught up with a cloud of hanging dust, and quickly realised that this was being stirred up by Jean Denton's 'Beauty Box' sponsored BMC 1800. Some time later, Jean told me that because of the dust she had created herself, she did not know that the Triumph was catching up, or she would most certainly have pulled over.

"Andrew Cowan went off the road," Bill Price later wrote, "near Salta just before the end of the Prime, when following in the dust of the BMC 1800 ... They had been preparing to overtake and in the dust and the rising sun, mistook the direction that the road was bending. The car landed on its roof about 20 feet (6.1m) below the road, completely wrecking it. The crew miraculously survived, though incurring head injuries, and a cracked vertebra in the neck sustained by Andrew Cowan.

"The first car along was the Australian Ken Tubman, who left his crew tending the bloodstained victims which he rushed ahead to La Vina for a doctor and ambulance: before many hours had elapsed they were safely in hospital ..."

In fact, both William Bendek (a Bolivian-entered BMW) and Alun Rees (Hillman Hunter) were also on the scene, and every effort was made to help the hapless Triumph crew. All incurred Prime and road penalties, of course, but there seemed to be no ill-feeling or protests about any of that.

My view of these traumatic events came by being the travelling controller running the end-of-stage point at La Vina, and for that reason I was quite unable to leave my post to go to their aid. At this 'ghost town' location there was no more than a house or two, and several World Cup service crews – the miracle being that some sort of telephone service also existed! The arrival of a much-distressed Jean Denton was the first news of the disaster – and the amazing thing was that the emergency services could react so quickly. At the end of the day, I visited the hospital in Salta where the crew had been taken, and was relieved to see what loving care was already being given to them.

The car, of course, was completely trashed, but for all the usual bureaucratic, financial and Customs reasons, the wreckage had to be

José Araújo, of Argentina, was not popular with other competitors, because he was slower than most, yet used baulking tactics to stop other cars getting past him. His Volvo 144 eventually dropped out in the high Andes section.

brought back to Abingdon. Amazingly, within months, it was sold on, in a package deal which included one of the special 'Pressed Steel' bodyshells, was reborn, and still appears at classic events all around Britain!

All this tended to obscure what was happening to the rest of the field, where there was movement, real movement, which affected the standings. At the very peak of the event, Hannu Mikkola determined to make his lead unassailable, while Rauno Aaltonen did his best to cut the gap (there were no team orders at Ford ...), but other Fords were suffering a spate of problems.

Hannu himself was lucky to avoid crashing into one of the emergency vehicles which he found rushing up the Prime (against rally traffic) to get to the scene of Andrew Cowan's accident, miraculously did not suffer from

Could there really be any roads down there? This was the view from the British Leyland Britannia aircraft as it approached the major airfield at La Paz, in Bolivia.

knock at the door, a guy asked if I was Mr Mikkola, I was stupid and said 'Yes' – and he hit me immediately. There were two other guys controlling Gunnar, but Gunnar was calling for Timo, and we knew we would then be on the right side. I was wrestling with this guy, Gunnar got to the door, Timo appeared, then they left ..."

Rauno Aaltonen, running behind Hannu, did not have such an eventful time, but was ultimately was not as lucky as his team-mate, and suffered from several punctures, though he was never reduced to the subterfuge of 'borrowing' spares from another Escort (as previously related in Chapter 5). At first glance, it looks as if Rauno, 16 minutes further adrift of Hannu, was lagging behind, but if we allow at least five minutes to change each punctured wheel, then the gap suddenly seems to be minuscule. Zasada was also fast – but, as we shall see, his moment of non-glory was still to come.

And what about the others? Both Brian Culcheth and Paddy Hopkirk put in sterling performances in what were much heavier cars than the Escorts (all the 'works' Fords, and all the 'works' Triumphs, by the way, stopped for fuel at Tinogasta), but both lost more than 40 minutes to the 'Flying Finn', and by now must have realised that they were not about to win this event unless something awful happened to one or other of the Escorts.

a spate of punctures (Goodyear's performance on this rally was not as good as everyone had hoped), and stormed into the Arrival Control at La Vina as if the devil himself was behind him. Calculations showed that he took only 8hr 45 minutes for this monstrous challenge – which means that if John Sprinzel had not quite arbitrarily cut an hour out of the schedule, he would have cleaned it by a comfortable margin.

Not that it was all easy for Hannu:

"There was this Argentine guy called Araújo, who didn't let us pass for 100km (62.1 miles). It was very dusty and I got so mad. Then we passed him, but drove through some potholes, so that broke a rear shock absorber. We had a service in the middle of the stage, so we stopped. Gunnar said we should stop and change, and I said we couldn't do it. Gunnar, he had been doing the recent Safari in the Taunus, and that car had coil spring suspension, so that when you break a shock absorber it is completely uncontrollable, and it breaks the axle. However, on the Escort where we had leaf springs, the leaf spring is its own shock absorber – it was working, but not so well – so I said 'We go.' Gunnar said 'No, we have to fix it', then I said again 'We go.'

"The following morning in La Paz, we had breakfast – Timo, Staepelaere, Gunnar and myself – and then I went to bed. There was a

In fact, if they had only known it at the time, two of the Fords – those of Timo Makinen and Jimmy Greaves – suddenly struck trouble on the Gran Premio Prime, and for a time it looked as if they might not even finish it. Both of them suffered from an epidemic of broken wheel studs at the rear, and although this could not be directly blamed on the previous axle problems, there is little doubt that the heavy weight of the massive fuel tanks, which sat above and behind the axle, might have had something to do with it.

On both cars the studs broke, taking wheel nuts with them, and allowing the Minilite wheels to come loose, to start wobbling around, and to give instant warning to the crew that something was badly wrong. Changing studs would have been possible, but not every Ford crew was carrying such spares (in one of the sister cars, Rauno Aaltonen was carrying nuts and studs, but was running ahead of these breakdowns, and could therefore not help), and the only solution seemed to be to use the black art of bodging ...

Timo Makinen, it seems, used brute force. Sure in the knowledge that if he could get to the next Ford service point (which he knew to be at the end of the Prime, in La Vina), that new Minilites would be available, he eventually got around the problem by ramming the wheels back into place,

Timo Makinen was unlucky with breakdowns, broken wheel studs, shattered disc brakes and more, but kept going, and finished fifth overall.

and (admittedly) expertise than some of his colleagues.

Tony Fall and his football-superstar co-driver, Jimmy Greaves, had even worse lucky. Afflicted by the same stud-breaking epidemic, they could not devise permanent ways of getting rear wheels to stay in place. After gathering some 'unofficial' assistance from Ford mechanics, these were detached before the car came into sight of the Prime finish, which meant that the car had to be pushed – on three wheels and a brake disc, for the last short distance. Thereafter the car was soon repaired – but much more was to occur to them in the next two or three days.

Much more was to happen on this enormously long Prime which, together with the two which followed – one in Bolivia and one in Peru – settled the order for good and all. The Freeborough/Cooper/Redgrave BMC 1800 (which had been enjoying a spirited battle with the Citroëns for the lead in the 'private owner' category) hit a horse, which despatched the poor animal, and left the 1800 with badly dented bodywork. Terry Hunter's Porsche once again seemed to be on full song – it was eighth fastest on Rodeo-La Vina – but could not now make up for the huge delays suffered in the Chilean Prime.

Citroën, for its part, found the DS21s very suitable for this long and rocky test, though their lack of outright performance was always going to be a problem. Having set fifth (Guy Verrier), sixth (Bob Neyret) and tenth fastest (Patrick Vanson) on this Prime alone, they remained a threat – reliable, as it looked at the time but all that was soon to change – to the British factory machines. Amazingly, Vanson's excellent time on the Prime was partly affected by a delay caused by a deranged fuel supply system, something which on board mechanic Alain Leprince was able to rectify.

The privately entered Hillman Hunters, on the other hand, were suffering badly from a lack of factory support. Team boss Des O'Dell (who was hitching rides around the route in British Leyland-hired planes) was always on hand to give technical support, but it was the mechanics that were missing. Two of the Hillmans suffered identical brake failures, where

and jamming the heads of ratchet spanners into the mangled remains of the broken studs.

Hours late, and (for Timo) driving with real circumspection, he finally limped into La Vina, where his car was quickly restored to health. From that moment, it seems, Timo realised that he could never win the event, so in a real long-term act of generosity he continued, effectively to act as a 'sheep dog' for the other Escorts, carrying more spares, equipment

KBO* – UNTIL OTL**

Let's never forget that 96 cars started this Intercontinental Marathon, and that many of them had to rely on their own resources just get to the finish. A few were lucky, but many ran out of time, money, and parts to keep going. The fortunes of Hillman Hunter no 4, driven by Rod Badham and Rob Lyall, is so typical of what happened to many who retired along the way.

A 'replica' London-Sydney Marathon winning car was a good choice, sponsorship from Berry Magicoal of Rugby was welcome, the crew were experienced at British and European level, and both were experienced drivers, mechanics and fixers. On the other hand, they had to carry their own spares, and could neither afford nor find the time to carry out any reconnaissance, not even in Yugoslavia.

By comparison with what was to follow, the London-Sofia-Lisbon sector was a breeze. Although they got lost for a time in the Serbian Prime (as did many crews), they cleaned the San Remo Prime, and suffered no mechanical dramas before the Hunter was loaded on to the Derwent in Lisbon.

The trouble started in Brazil, as Rob Lyall told me:

"It was on a Prime in Brazil, maybe it was in Uruguay, where we damaged the radiator, and had to change it.

"Then we got into Chile. I was driving down the main street of a little village – and you should remember that the World Cup average target average speed through Chile was above the legal maximum speed in that country ...

"There were hundreds of people on the road side, and a policeman was waving us on. I was driving at about 50mph (80.5kph), and a kid on a bike came out from the right, and I couldn't do anything, I hit him, and he came through the windscreen, and landed on my lap. I was blinded anyway – and I think it was dusk.

"Unfortunately the youngster, who was about 14 years old, he died, and we got chucked into jail! For a time, they couldn't get a judge to come and get us out. But there had been a schoolmaster who saw the thing, and a policeman who saw the thing, so there was no real problem in the end, but we lost so much time, and we were running behind the whole event. I reckon we were at least 12 hours, if not more, behind anyone else – and, of course, we now had a car with a lot of problems.

"We had a 'shatter screen' to start with, which more or less blocked the hole, and then somewhere else we borrowed a screen which we taped into position over the shatter screen. Then with all the dust, and the roads were quite amazingly rough that everything was shaking loose, you'd get an inch of dust on the floor, so that every time you hit a bump, the dust would come up over the maps and into your nostrils ...

"I think we were probably several hours behind the last car in the event. We had more trouble because the door locks in the rear doors, which had been wedge-locked and Loctited in place, rattled free, and fell into the bottom of the doors, which meant that we had to hold the rear doors closed by bungee straps!

"We then ran off the road because the dust had got between the taped on screen and the shatter screen – early in the morning, Rod came up to a corner in the foothills of the Andes, I suppose, and there was a right-hander, which he missed, and we went off, and crunched it. So we got out, and we got that going again ..."

All this was without service of any sort.

"Then, after the night halt in Santiago, in Bolivia, we were still running very late, Rod came round a corner, there was nothing in sight, except for an old woman leading a donkey, Rod couldn't dodge, and his reaction was: 'Which shall I hit?' We hit the donkey, which got up and ran away, went flying off into the boonies, with this old lady hanging on to the other end of the rope.

"Now, we'd gone with 'roo bars on the front of the Hunter, just in case we hit anything – and they had been pushed back into the front wing. Oh, and by the way, we couldn't open the doors. It had pushed the radiator back on to the fan ... this was not a good day!

"At this point I said: 'You know I think I saw a soldier not too far back.' Then a lorry came along. We stopped the lorry, and asked him to give us a lift back to the Army camp. So I left Rod there, and got back to this Army camp in the lorry, where I was immediately arrested.

"However, they forgave me, they got a message through to John Sprinzel, telling them that we had an accident and we had retired, but we were not hurt. That was premature. In the meantime I remember playing football in the army camp, and there were condors sitting on a fence nearby – waiting for lunch, I guess.

"This lorry driver, who was going back to his village, said there was someone there who could maybe mend the car. So we did the deal, for him to tow us to the village. So he agreed to do that, couldn't start his truck, reached under his seat and took out a 2lb hammer, hit something on the engine, after which it started. It was years before I realised what he did – because the truck had a magneto and it was sticking ...

"We got the car in tow, and got to the next village, which was maybe 40km (24.9 miles) away. It was like a Western film set – a wide street, dirt surface, mud huts, nobody about ... He stopped outside this house, there was sacking over the door way, and inside was a phenomenal mechanic's shop, with all the tools, shiny and neat.

"The mechanic said he'd like to help, but he couldn't because he couldn't get the bonnet up to look and see what the damage was. Then out of the blue came an American – he was teaching the locals to rear sheep, and he'd come along in a Jeep. He said 'What if we got the lorry at one end, the

[continued overleaf]

129

[continued]

Jeep at the other, and towed it apart!' Which we did, and we got the bonnet open. The fan blades had come up through the top of the header tank – and we thought that was that.

"All of a sudden, out of the blue, this army officer, who was the commander of the 'secret army camp', arrived. So I challenged him and said: 'Well, the British army could sort this out …' – at which he said 'Well, get the radiator out …' which we did. He took it away, two hours later he was back, with the whole thing beautifully repaired/remade.

"We had been there for hours. Well, off we eventually went on … then the car started overheating. We thought the radiator must have gone, and we stopped and looked, but the radiator was OK. It was the fan blades which had chopped through the bottom hose – so how could that have happened?

"We suddenly realised that the engine was able to move. What had happened was that the bosses for the engine mount into the cast iron block had pulled out. There was now really no engine mounting on one side!

"Eventually we got a tow to the next village, which took another couple of hours, and found a guy there who thought he could probably weld it. So we took the whole thing apart. Well, he found a bucket of water, he threw in some pellets to make some acetylene gas … and eventually he did it.

"So off we went, kept going, and sometime after that it broke again – and I remember Rod saying: 'Get out, get a block of wood, and we will jam it up under the sump guard.' I distinctly remember then saying: 'But we haven't seen a tree for 500 miles (804.7km)!'

"Anyway we managed to block the engine with a trolley jack sitting on the sump guard, and off we trotted again, running very very late by now. We must have been in Peru by this time, because the route led along the ridges of the Andes, and then turned left, and down to Lima.

"The main source of income in Peru at that time was tin from the tin mines. The tin was brought down from 12,000 to 15,000 feet (3658 to 4572m) by lorries. These had been stopped to let the rally cars go through – but when we got there, very late, the lorries had been let go, and they were packed up in long lines. I remember that we were going in rivers and banks to try to get through. Well, eventually we got down to Lima, and I believe it was John Brown on the Control at the edge of the city, and he had kept it open about 20 minutes more than he should have done, on maximum lateness, and we arrived about 5 minutes after he had packed up.

"So we were out …"

That, though, wasn't the end of the story:

"I wanted to get home, because I needed to start work again. So set out to try to buy airline tickets. However, to buy a ticket, I had to be able to show my passport, which I did, and they said: 'But there's no entry stamp.' I said 'Yes, because I'm on the World Cup Rally, and we have retired,' and we had our own rally passports which were stamped at the borders.

"They said that didn't count, they couldn't do anything for me, because my passport wasn't stamped, which meant that I wasn't there … And I remember Erle Morley, who was a travelling controller on the event, coming up behind me, and asking me: 'Do you have trouble then?' …

"They said I could buy my way out of this problem, but it would have to be in local currency, but at that time I only had American dollars! He said I could go to the black market, and I actually asked him where I would find it! Eventually I did get everything sorted out. And every time I met Erle Morley for the next 30 or 40 years, he would say: 'Did you ever get out of Peru?' …"

– and that was only the shortened, sanitised, version. In May, in South America, there were dozens of such stories.

* KBO – a famous Churchillism, meaning Keep Buggering On

** OTL – Outside Time Limits

the pipes leading to the rear drums split, and let out hydraulic fluid. The Badham/Lyall car continued to have its awful trek through South America, this time suffering broken engine mountings (see the sidebar on page 129).

The biggest disappointment at this juncture was to the Freeborough/ Cooper/Redgrave BMC 1800, which, as mentioned, ran into a horse on the road between Rodeo and La Vina and incurred severe body damage. It had been enjoying a truly spirited fight with the so-called privately-entered Citroëns. Rosemary Smith's Austin Maxi was still making good progress, but she was slowly losing ground to Claudine Trautmann's big Citroën, even though the French woman's car almost ran out of fuel on its approach to the La Vina Control.

Prime 13: Villazon to Potosi (the Bolivian Coffee Prime)

Crews who completed the Gran Premio Prime – and only seven had managed this in less than 10 nerve-wracking, lung-searing, hours – could not look forward to a few hours of relatively relaxed motoring. The word 'relaxed', however, deserves explanation, for it is worth noting that (by Western European standards) the route now led on distinctly down-at-heel roads and tracks through Salta, to San Salvador de Jujuy, and on to the Argentinian border town of La Quiaca.

This, according to the maps (which were poor, in all truth) made it clear that this was the major (the only direct …) route between two South American capitals – Buenos Aires in the south, and La Paz, the capital of Bolivia, in the north. It soon became very clear that few drivers would tackle this road as a tourist destination, if only because it was routed through deserted (but increasingly tropical) countryside, was virtually uninhabited, and was often running at 10,000 to 12,000 feet (3048 to 3658m).

To get a feel for the terrain, in times like today it is instructive to visit Google Earth or other internet mapping services, to see just how welcome any isolated habitation actually was, for in their own way border towns and intermediate trading posts were like oases in the desert.

The 41 crews which were still running eventually found their way to the Argentinian border town of La Quiaca, picked their way through its crowded streets, then made for the border crossing to Bolivia over what was called the 'International Bridge'. No sooner had they done this when they entered Bolivia, in Villazon, where Controller Gerry Ryan had set up shop for the start of the next Prime.

After what had immediately gone before, what was to follow sounded much more civilised, and more bearable, but think again. Maybe it was considerably shorter than before – but it was still a 270-miler (434.5km), another monster by European rally standards. Not only that, but the target time was a mere five hours, which equated to 54.0mph (86.9kph).

Does that sound reasonable? Well, yes, but ... first of all, remember that this one Prime was the same distance as, say, London to Carlisle, or

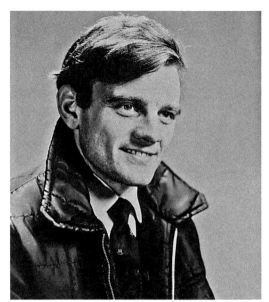

Rod Badham (left) and Rob Lyall tackled the World Cup in a 'London-Sydney replica' Hillman Hunter, with major sponsorship from Berry Magicoal of Rugby, in Warwickshire.

Prime 13: Villazon to Potosi (Bolivia) – the Bolivian Coffee Prime
[Target: 270 miles/434.5km in 5hr 0 minutes]

Fastest times:

Crew	Car	Penalty (mins)
S Zasada/M Wachowski	Ford Escort 1850	47
B Culcheth/J Syer	Triumph 2.5PI	47
G Verrier/F Murac	Citroën DS21	54
H Mikkola/G Palm	Ford Escort 1850	56
T Makinen/G Staepelaere	Ford Escort 1850	59
R Neyret/J Terramorsi	Citroën DS21	66
R Aaltonen/H Liddon	Ford Escort 1850	66
P Hopkirk/A Nash/N Johnston	Triumph 2.5PI	69
A Fall/J Greaves	Ford Escort 1850	91
J Bloxham/R McBurney/P Brown	Hillman Hunter	104
G Perkins/J F Green	Peugeot 404	104
R Freeborough/P Cooper/ R Redgrave	BMC 1800	104

Well into the South American section of the event, Rosemary Smith's Austin Maxi received service from the BMC mechanics. Ace technician Doug Watts is looking less than pleased at this moment.

London to Edinburgh, all on truly basic tracks (for the cars would leave the main 'highway' in Tupiza, before heading north to Potosi). Not only that, but there was not a single point at which it would be running at less than 10,000 feet (3048m), and there were some sections which approached 14,000 feet (4267m) and more.

Remember, also, that at these altitudes, due to the thinning air, the power developed by the engines would be considerably reduced. A Ford Escort 1850, for instance, might have been rated at 140bhp at sea level, but at these heights the peak power developed would be much less than 100bhp, and performance was therefore reduced.

Because of the way that the time schedules were laid out on the World Cup, cars running early as they crossed into Bolivia would have been able to start the Prime from 19.00hr on the evening of Friday, 15 May, but many were running so far down the lists that they did not start fast motoring again until the early hours of the 16th.

Because the reputation of this Prime had gone before it – drivers in practice cars had returned, wide-eyed, with stories of the altitude, the condition of the tracks, the desolation and, in some cases, the seeming incomprehension and disinterest of the locals – almost everyone seemed to be going more slowly than before. Such was the isolation of Potosi, as an end-of-Prime location, that the organisers had needed to find a private plane so that Controller Jim Gavin could get there at all!

"There was no easy way to get to this one-horse silver-mining town," Gavin later confirmed, "but Sprinzel had done a deal with the authorities. I got to La Paz, and the arrangement was that I would be flown there in one of the president's (Signor Martinez) aeroplanes. I was to go with a *Daily Mirror* photographer/reporter called Kent Gavin (no relation).

"We got up to the airport at La Paz very early, looked for the presidential plane, could find nothing which looked Presidential, but found a little single-engined Cessna instead. At that point, the *Mirror* reporter flatly refused to go to Potosi – he'd had awful experiences in light planes during the Biafran war in Nigeria, and swore that he would never again fly in anything with less than four engines!

"So I travelled alone, with two pilots. Eventually we took off for Potosi, it was a very bumpy flight, and at one point we were in formation with a Condor. I think he was waiting for lunch ..."

Amazingly, of the 41 cars which started this Prime in Villazon, all but two reached the finish at Potosi, and struggled on to La Paz. The one high-profile casualty was Terry Hunter's Porsche 911, which simply 'dropped off the organiser's radar' – a reason for retirement was apparently never posted. The other was Astafiev's 'works' Moskvich, which rolled in the Prime – and although this car had never been in the running for performance prizes, it was one which had always been greeted warmly at earlier Controls.

The brave, and the determined, were still going very quickly. Brian Culcheth set equal fastest time overall (he had certainly not wasted those long and boring practice days in this part of the world), his penalty of 47 minutes being exactly matched by Zasada's Escort. For Zasada, though, it wasn't all good news, for his Escort also began to suffer from broken wheel studs, which caused Ford mechanics to call ahead, to La Paz, and

have their local distributor (Ford seemed to be well-represented in this part of the world) get a batch of studs newly machined up overnight.

Guy Verrier's Citroën was going as well as ever, and was only seven minutes adrift, while the usual stars – four more Escorts and Paddy Hopkirk's Triumph 2.5PI, all showed well. For the first time, however, a Hillman Hunter made an appearance – John Bloxham's JCB car (JC Bamford Excavators Limited was their sponsor) being tenth fastest overall, while the battered Freeborough/Cooper/Redgrave BMC 1800 was still obviously in mechanically good shape, as it matched the time set by the Hillman.

Who was relatively slow at this point? Hannu Mikkola was clearly not rushing too much (he already had his eye on producing a virtuoso performance in Peru, which lay ahead), Patrick Vanson was just behind the leader board, and Tony Fall/Jimmy Greaves lost no less than 44 minutes to Zasada's sister car. For this, however, there was an excuse, as one result of the stud-breaking episode on Rodeo-La Vina meant that he was running with only three sound studs on each wheel. A full and comprehensive repair would be made in La Paz but that, as the Road Book so succinctly spelt out, was twelve to fifteen lung-searing hours away.

To use the modern vernacular, Bolivia was, quite simply, something else. Road conditions were primitive at best, the local populace seemed to be quite unaware of what this rally was all about, and almost everyone connected with the World Cup Rally had to build their own infrastructure, and make their own arrangements. Back in La Paz, however, the authorities had so much power that they had closed the appropriate roads to all but rally traffic – though this did not seem to apply to animal-drawn vehicles (of which there were thousands), or, of course, to the loose animals themselves.

As ever, the erudite *Autocar* writer, Mike Scarlett, gave the best description of what he observed from the back of the Red Arrows Austin Maxi:

"During the day, the countryside never changed – a distant backcloth of low hills rising abruptly out of the endless plateau, the car seeming almost to be standing still on a moving ribbon of straight stony road rather than the other way round. The way was only enlivened by the most primary colourful costumes of the universally brown-bowler-hatted Indian women, and the wonderful smiles, white teeth in brown Tibetan faces, of everyone at the roadside. Indian men and boys looked all the more Himalayan with their ear-flapped headgear. Houses were mud-bricked low huts, mostly sited nowhere. Cows, donkeys, sheep, all rather scrawny, were scattered about the lean-scrubbed plain: the odd herd of llamas, most aristocratic and cameelious, looked more at home. The road was pure Bagshot ..."

(The 'Bagshot' reference, of course, was to the testing ground, and not the affluent High Street! Except that I don't understand how Scarlett could link the Andes with the Himalayas and Tibet, this was a wonderfully compact description of an amazing landscape.)

Rally leader Hannu Mikkola described the challenge like this:

"It was very difficult, coming to Potosi. That last 280km (174 miles) was one of the hardest I have done. I am sure it was the lack of oxygen and that – I started to notice that I was braking very early – and sometimes I

Co-driver of Moskvich no 21, Alexandre Safonov, rushes to the controller's table, at the end of a Prime in South America.

didn't brake at all. Sometimes I was very sleepy – and sometimes Gunnar was hitting me with the Road Book to keep me awake!

"I was very tired. When we came out of the Prime at Potosi, Zasada collapsed. Then we had a road section where we knew we would have more than an hour in hand. Gunnar said he would drive – he drove for 10 minutes, then he set an old-fashioned timer, and suggested we sleep for 10 minutes at the side of the road! Then he drove a bit more, then I took over, and drove to the end of the day."

By this point, of course, everyone was dog-tired after the exertions of recent hours, which made it a relief that the route from Potosi (a silver mining town) to La Paz was relatively unadventurous. The Control at Bolivia's capital city was located alongside the International Airport at El Alto de la Paz, where every service crew for every car that was to receive support would be concentrated. According to the optimistic schedule prepared by many optimistic competitors, they should be able to place their cars into Parc Fermé at La Paz airport before bedtime on Saturday, 16 May, secure in the knowledge that they would have 24 hours rest before having to move out again – towards Titicaca, Cuzco, and the terrifying prospect of the longest Prime of all, in Peru.

Incidentally, was it really only seven days since they had all tackled the first South American Prime, in Brazil, on the other side of this vast continent!

Top of the world

Everyone approaching La Paz, by whatever route – road, train or aircraft – soon realised that they were reaching the capital city of Bolivia, but that this was not only a land-locked nation (approach to the Pacific Ocean had to be by way of the

Rosemary Smith's stripey-liveried Austin Maxi, high on the Col de Portillo, in the South American section.

The Donner brothers – Paul and Martin – worked miracles to get their privately-prepared Ford Capri all the way to the High Andes, before it finally broke down.

northern tip of Chile – and those two countries were often at loggerheads about access, or ancient territorial claims) but one which seemed to live at the top of the world.

The centre of the old city lies at an altitude of 12,000 feet/3658m (this makes it the highest capital city in the world), but is actually in a valley.

The international airport, where the World Cup cars would be housed, was on top of the nearest plateau, literally at El Alto (The Height), at more than 13,000 feet (3962m). A measure of the height, and of the thinness of the air, is that La Paz airport has one of the longest main runways in the world!

Everywhere in South America, the World Cup Rally drew large crowds. These cheerful little boys were found in Bolivia.

(A measure of this is, that when the British Leyland Cessna arrived overhead from Salta (from where I had thumbed a lift), the Control could not be roused, for it was siesta time. To "waken them up", as the Cessna pilot joked, he therefore landed the Cessna, took off again, and landed again – all along the length of that single runway ...!)

Ford driver Rauno Aaltonen, analytical as always, later recorded just how badly he and his co-driver Henry Liddon must have been affected by the lack of oxygen:

"We were in a silver mining town, where there was a Control, not yet in La Paz. That is where I was close to Zasada, who was met by a Ford film crew, who asked him how he felt about the altitude. He said he felt fine, then fell down unconscious in front of the camera because of a lack of oxygen!

"There was a point when we were driving, somewhere in Bolivia, and Henry suddenly stopped reading the notes. I looked across, and he looked unconscious! We were very high. We did have oxygen in the car, but we didn't have enough to use it all the time. We had an emergency bottle.

"There was froth coming out of Henry's mouth. I was very afraid that this was something serious. So I stopped immediately, it was in a Prime. I got the emergency oxygen bottle, and squirted in to Henry's mouth. In no time he woke up, made no comments, picked up the pace notes, said '300, Fast ...' – and carried on as if nothing had happened.

"Incredible. Then, in the same mountainous area, I can remember coming down hill, very fast, and there was a hairpin bend at the bottom. I wanted to slow down, of course, and found that I could not move my right leg! I was on full power, but couldn't move my leg. The brain was working, but I just couldn't move my leg.

"So, I had time, I put my right hand out, grasped the knee, pulled it back, and placed the leg on the brake – and it worked. Once again this was due to a lack of oxygen. That time, already, I had a glider pilot's licence, so I was used to going to great heights and feeling the effects – and I knew the danger of a lack of oxygen, and how you could have hallucinations and things.

"Now we come to a part, incidentally, where Henry was driving. It was later, still on poor roads, but the maps we had were only one-to-one million, so you couldn't see any details. It would show you a mountain in a different colour, but few details of the road, and hardly any place names. It didn't help that we had a speedometer which was 27 per cent wrong, because of the shorter final-drive (with an overdrive fifth). The distance measurement on the speedometer, also, was 27 per cent wrong!

"Of course, at that moment, the cable to the Halda had broken, so we had to do the navigation by adding 27 per cent of the indicated mileages. OK, but it was an easy section, so Henry was driving, I was sleeping, and I think there were four or five cars following us – in every car the co-driver was driving.

"Henry started driving faster and faster, and I woke up, then he really shook me by saying: 'Rauno, we have to change. I don't know where I am. Something is wrong.'

"I got behind the wheel, accelerated, made a handbrake turn, and started going back the way we had come. All the cars following me did the same, all swapped drivers, and we all started going really fast. Suddenly the road turned from dirt to tarmac, and in front of us there were houses, built on to the mountainside. People had heard four cars coming up the hill, the lights came on, windows opened ...

"We had to continue until it matched with the maps, but it took hours and fuel was a problem. Anyway, we continued and we eventually got it right, and we made the next Control on time ..."

From Potosi to La Paz, there were hundreds of miles of nothing much, but all at a high altitude, and the amazing thing is that 39 cars actually made it all the way. Although crew exhaustion must have been a real factor

Although Guy Verrier was a regular member of the Citroën 'works' team, he competed in the World Cup Rally as a private entry. Driving this DS21, he was always very well placed until his co-driver crashed the car on the approach to La Paz, and it later expired before it could reach Lima.

Most professional crews had time to spare when they arrived in La Paz. Timo Makinen's Escort was virtually rebuilt before it went into Parc Fermé.

by this stage, there seems to have been only one significant accident, when Francis Murac (the co-driver to Guy Verrier's Citroën DS21, which was still very handily placed in fourth position) nodded off, and crashed the car. The miracle is that the chassis survived, though the bodywork was considerably mangled.

For those crews who had time, there were many opportunities to get the rally cars rebuilt before they were driven into Parc Fermé at El Alto de la Paz. Something approaching garage facilities were set up by the most serious teams, major rebuilds were attempted, and completed, and even though the altitude (and lack of oxygen) ensured that most people suffered from headaches, nausea and sheer, worrying shortness of breath, the jobs were done.

Not everyone made it to La Paz without drama. There was real excitement for British Leyland on the run in, for it was here that Paddy Hopkirk's Triumph broke a quill shaft in its rear axle. Although this was a known weak spot in the Triumph's chassis-mounted differential (it had happened on Triumph-built 'works' 2000s as early as 1965, for instance), the crew did not carry spare parts to repair such a breakage, though did, at least, set about dismantling the broken component.

With approximately 50 miles (80.5km) still to go before Hopkirk could reach La Paz, and the comforting embrace of British Leyland mechanics, the car came to a halt. Fortunately, Peter Jopp, Mark Kahn and Willy Cave's BMC 1800 arrived on the scene. Now it can be told that Peter Jopp – who was well down in the running, and had a very sick car himself at this time – promptly offered a tow, and started tugging the stricken car towards La Paz. Such an operation was strictly illegal in rallying terms, and could have resulted in disqualification, but the team was desperate.

As Peter Jopp later commented, as quoted in Paddy's autobiography: "We towed the Triumph for about 60km (37.3 miles), stopping several

Several British Leyland cars, including Triumph 2.5PIs, Austin Maxis and BMC 1800s, group together for service.

times to conceal the tow rope whenever a helicopter buzzed around. We were constantly watching in the mirror, worried that we would be seen by another competitor giving an illegal tow ..."

As Team Co-ordinator Bill Price later told me:

"We were sitting at La Paz, and the local radio was broadcasting a commentary all the way along the Andes, from way back – at least 100 miles (160.9km) back.

"The Stead brothers [British Leyland importers in Bolivia], whose Spanish was good, of course, were listening, and suddenly said: 'The local radio has just told us that Paddy Hopkirk has just broken down, with a broken diff ...'"

Even then, everything might have been lost, for much time had passed, and Paddy might have been late on arrival at La Paz. Other BMC runners also brought news of the breakdown to British Leyland in La Paz, where Manager Peter Browning commandeered a local driver in a Jeep, to take a mechanic back up the route, carrying a new axle.

But there was more confusion to come. When the 'Beauty Box' 1800 arrived, the girls handed over a handwritten note from Paddy pointing out that it was the quill shaft which had broken.

Undaunted, British Leyland then sent off mechanic Den Green, in another 'chase car', complete with quill shaft, also against the flow of rally cars. This, though, was always going to be slow, and time consuming. Amazingly, Den Green then encountered Bill Bengry, in the infamous Rolls-Royce Silver Shadow, which had rejoined the route, though not as an active competitor. Bill immediately offered to use the Rolls-Royce as a high-service chase car, drove a luxury car back up the route against rally traffic, eventually found the convoy, and saw the car repaired at the side of the track. So much spare road time seemed to be built in to the schedule at this juncture that Hopkirk's car was still un-penalised when it reached the Bolivian capital, with just 10 minutes to spare.

Although Brian Culcheth's Triumph was still mechanically sound, and the driver much refreshed after his sleep outside the car after the Rodeo-La Vina Prime, his car was nevertheless also in the wars. As Brian later told the author, it was also repaired by what could be described as unconventional methods:

"Our windscreen was now so badly cracked from the previous peppering received in Uruguay, that we decided to have it changed in La Paz. This was a decision for which we nearly paid dearly, for when the mechanics got the old screen out in many pieces, they then found the replacement screens sent from England were the wrong size, and fell hopelessly through the large 2.5PI screen area.

"Stuart Turner, Ford's Competitions Manager, very generously came to our rescue and loaned us an Escort screen, which fitted height-wise, but was about two-and-a-half inches (6.4cm) short on each side, so the gap was made up with cardboard and various strips of sticky tape, making us a bit short of vision."

(Later it was discovered that the screens supplied, via British Leyland's parts network, were actually for the Triumph 1300, and had been wrongly labelled in the warehouses back in the UK.)

No matter how bodged up the repair looked, it was clearly an enterprising operation, for it was in this condition that the car survived for another 10 days, and would reward its determined crew with second place overall.

The story so far

In almost every way, the situation at La Paz was critical to the way that the World Cup Rally would develop. In effect this night stop was half way through the most demanding section of the event – the High Andes sectors – for there had been three extremely taxing Primes before La Paz, and another two Primes would follow before the cars reached the end of the South American section at Buenaventura in Colombia. Not only that, for although the previous Primes had been long, high, and very exhausting, that which was soon to follow in Peru looked like being the most difficult of all.

All the teams and individuals now had time to sit back, rest up for one precious day, and reflect. Ford had now imposed itself on the leader board, with Hannu Mikkola's Escort more than an hour ahead of Rauno Aaltonen's sister car. Brian Culcheth's Triumph was handily placed in third, a mere three minutes behind Rauno, and confident that he could eventually overtake him, while Guy Verrier (though in a badly damaged Citroën DS21), was fourth, only 15 minutes back.

More drama, though, was yet to unfold.

They might not have been fast, and their Soviet crews could not speak any Western languages, but the entire rally warmed to the five 'works' Moskvichs that started the World Cup Rally. No 71 was driven by Gounnar Kholm, and finished a gallant 17th on the event.

Results to La Paz, Bolivia – 17 May 1970

Mileage so far completed: 10,250 miles (16,496km)

Top Ten in general classification:

Place	Crew	Car	Penalty (hours-minutes)
1	Hannu Mikkola/Gunnar Palm	Ford Escort 1850	3-52
2	Rauno Aaltonen/Henry Liddon	Ford Escort 1850	4-54
3	Brian Culcheth/Johnstone Syer	Triumph 2.5PI Mk II	4-57
4	Guy Verrier/Francis Murac	Citroën DS21	5-12
5	Sobieslaw Zasada/Marek Wachowski	Ford Escort 1850	5-40
6	Paddy Hopkirk/Tony Nash/Neville Johnston	Triumph 2.5 Mk II	5-44
7	Robert Neyret/Jacques Terramorsi	Citroën DS21	5-53
8	Timo Makinen/Gilbert Staepelaere	Ford Escort 1850	6-08
9	Patrick Vanson/Olivier Turcat/Alain Leprince	Citroën DS21	7-38
10	Jimmy Greaves/Tony Fall	Ford Escort 1850	7-55

39 cars were still running.

7

La Paz to Buenaventura — by way of Cali, Colombia

Now for The Big One. Competitors might have been sleeping blissfully in their high-altitude hotel rooms, fretting over the mechanical state of their increasingly battered cars, or merely whinging about the high altitude, the lack of oxygen, the nausea and the breathlessness but, subconsciously, they were probably thinking about what lay ahead.

On paper it all sounded straightforward enough – La Paz in Bolivia to Lima in Peru would cover 1150 miles (1851km), in a target time of 25 hours, which was 'only' a required average of 46mph (74kph). That sounded easy enough – except that the altitude factor was not mentioned. It wasn't easy – as the stats show – for only 30 of the 39 starters would survive the 25 hours, and only four of them – two Fords and two Triumphs – would make it to Lima on time.

After a full night's rest, and a full day in which to worry about what was to come, the competitors regained their car from Parc Fermé at the airport at El Alto de la Paz, where the first car was due to leave at 22.30hr on Sunday, 17 May. The first cars left in a rainstorm, which was welcome, but the weather cleared up during the night, and the usual hazards of dust had reappeared by the time the sun rose.

In theory, the next few hours motoring should have been a tourist's paradise, except for two factors – one was that this sector was taken at night, the other being that it was all at very high altitude where the air was thin, and the affect on the human body was depressing.

Controller Mike Broad, at least, made life easier for competitors by stationing himself at the Bolivian/Peruvian border at Desaguadero to see that all got through smoothly and efficiently. Desaguerdo was a town split into Bolivian and Peruvian sections, and was placed on the only main through road, from La Paz to Lima, on the shores of the southern-most tip of Lake Titicaca (which sits at an altitude of 12,500 feet/3810m, and is one of the highest commercially navigable lakes in the world). This, though, was no time for sight-seeing, or box-ticking.

This transport section, and what was to follow, was much more demanding than the forecasts suggested. In fact, for years to come, whenever World Cup veterans got together to chat about the 1970 event, their stories almost inevitably homed in on the monumental Prime in Peru, which linked Cuzco to Huancayo.

Because it came immediately after the overnight halt at La Paz, every crew was more or less rested, every crew knew just how close (or otherwise) he was to his nearest rival, and every one realised that this was to be one of the most extreme high-altitude challenges of all time. And high it certainly was. With Cuzco sitting at 11,000 feet (3353m), and Huancayo sitting at almost the same level, there was simply no respite for crew or cars, especially as some of the passes linking the two centres reached 15,000 feet (4572m) and more.

Prime 14: Cuzco to Huancayo – the Incas Prime

This, the most difficult Prime of all, started at the very exit of Cuzco, a city more usually visited for its cultural heritage, and of course as the jumping off point for a visit to the amazing historical relics at Maccu Picchu. This time, though, on the very exit of town, it was the launching pad for this monster Prime. In bald terms, this Prime measured no less than 560 miles (901.2km) and was almost all on loose surfaces at high (sometimes very high) altitude. In many cases, the drops off the side of these tracks could be horrendous – as Tony Fall (who had competed there in a Peruvian event in 1969) was telling anyone who would listen. Organiser John Sprinzel, determined to ensure a real result on this one stage alone, allowed no more than 11 hours for it – and expected to see every crew considerably penalised. He was not disappointed.

In a Prime so long that at least one, if not two, refuelling stops would be needed, Castrol set up a service halt in mid-stage at Chinchero for its contracted runners ("Service point will probably be supervised by Ken Berry, who is Racing Consultant for our Peruvian Agents ..."), while major teams set up at least two other emergency service points, one in Chinchero, the other in Ayacucho (where petrol was also being stored for the favoured few). The first cars started this enormous Prime at first light in the morning

Travelling Controller Logan Morrison setting up shop at the end of one of the Primes. One of the Triumph 2.5PI practice cars, complete with roof rack, is in the background.

British Leyland used this small twin-engined Cessna as often as it used service cars during the European section of the World Cup Rally.

of 18 May, and spent all day driving north-west, but none of them (not even Hannu Mikkola) managed to complete it until night was once again falling.

It was an incredible challenge, which no-one who tackled it is ever likely to forget. A few – only a very few – competitors were going flat out (if only to ensure that they did not arrive late in Lima itself), but that included the leading Ford and British Leyland crews, and many others were pacing themselves at no more than eight-tenths effort. Hannu Mikkola, already securely in the lead, took no less than 12 hours 21 minutes to complete the stage, yet he beat team-mate Rauno Aaltonen by a mere 11 minutes, and Brian Culcheth's Triumph by just 18 minutes in all. Minutes – yes, minutes, not seconds – but by 1970 World Cup standards these gaps were tiny. And, as Roger Clark had quipped when he reported his practice in this Prime before the event started:

Prime 14: Cuzco to Huancayo (Peru) – the Incas Prime
(Target: 560 miles/901.2km in 11hr 0 minutes)

Fastest times:

Crew	Car	Penalty (hours-mins)
H Mikkola/G Palm	Ford Escort 1850	1-21
R Aaltonen/H Liddon	Ford Escort 1850	1-32
B Culcheth/J Syer	Triumph 2.5PI	1-39
P Hopkirk/A Nash/N Johnston	Triumph 2.5PI	2-11
Ms C Trautmann/Ms C Perrier	Citroën DS21	2-58
T Makinen/G Staepelaere	Ford Escort 1850	3-04
P Vanson/O Turcat/A Leprince	Citroën DS21	3-25
R Freeborough/P Cooper/R Redgrave	BMC 1800	3-28
R Smith/A Watson/G Derolland	Austin Maxi	3-50
K Tubman/A Welinsky/B McAuley	BMC 1800	4-01
A Fall/J Greaves	Ford Escort 1850	4-05
W Bendek/D Hubner/ J Burgoa	BMW 2002ti	4-07
A Rees/H Thomas/W James	Hillman Hunter	4-09
G Perkins/J F Green	Peugeot 404	4-35
L Potapchik/E Bazhenov/Y Lesovski	Moskvich 412	4-41

"The drops off the side of the tracks could be really frightening. Some of them were so far that your clothes would have been out of fashion before you hit the bottom ..."

It was the sort of Prime where superlatives were needed to describe everything that went on. Although it was possible – just – to treat this as an ultra-long transport section (the Arrival Control at Huancayo was open for 10 hours – from 17.00hr to 03.00hr the following day!), this was still an exhausting section: the tenth fastest competitor – Ken Tubman in his BMC 1800 – took 15 hours to complete the job, and was then faced with driving for several hundred more miles to get to the end of the leg in Lima.

Hannu Mikkola and Gunnar Palm, who now seemed to be in that trance-like state of super-beings who just knew that they were going to win the event, were fourth to start the Prime, first to reach the Ford service point at Chinchero, first to reach the end of the Prime at Huancayo, and first to scorch into Lima at dead of night, ready for another rest halt.

Hannu, who was never one to make too much of his achievements (as far as the media was concerned, he left the eloquent, likeable and very persuasive Gunnar Palm to do most of the talking), but he obviously thought about, and planned, his driving:

"In the beginning I thought my rivals might be Rauno and Timo. Citroën were very fast in the first week – they were faster than us, which surprised me, but our car was a very good handling car, but it was not powerful at all.

"Maybe I was lucky. There were two major problems with the cars during the event. There was the axle problem in Europe, and then it was the wheel-nut problem in South America – and I didn't suffer from any of it.

"Maybe sometime at the very end of the rally I could have minor problems, but at that time Timo (who could no longer win the event) was carrying lots of spares, and was driving after me, so that if something happened he could help me. He is very mechanically minded.

"You had to get used to the very long stages – like over 900km (559.2 miles) – you couldn't push all the time, you had to find a nice pace, and to believe that it was the right speed. You had to believe that you could do 12 hours at that sort of driving pace. To me it was a matter of keeping going.

"I never again did anything so tiring, so demanding. It was not just one long stage, but you had already had other super-long stages – you were doing something like 2000km (1243 miles) in one series.

"I always remember driving this 900km (559.2 miles) Prime, and we were all waiting until 06.00hr to start. I think Timo was the first to start, and I was fourth to start (all of us in Escorts) – I think we started at two minute intervals. After about 40km (24.9 miles) I was already first on the road, and we just kept going, and we didn't see anybody. We had service in the middle – and I remember I had a Coke and two hard-boiled eggs. That was lunch, we had been driving for about six hours, and this was the point at which we got new tyres. We drove until about 18.00hr and we had a puncture just 20km (12.4 miles) from the end. We went to change it, and I could hear the other rear tyre going down too – they were completely finished. So we changed them both, and still didn't see anybody catch us."

Paddy Hopkirk, similarly, told me just how seriously they all had to treat this monstrous Prime:

"The 560 mile (901.2km) Prime from Cuzco to Huancayo, including the Ticlio Pass after the Prime – that was at 15,870 feet (4837m) – was gruelling, with the altitude averaging 13,000 feet (3962m), and an average speed set at 50mph (80.5kph). I was glad to have the oxygen bottles on board at this altitude, and with the adjustable metering unit the [2.5PI] engine ran without the over-fuelling problems which some cars experienced."

The story of this Prime is not really who was fast and who was not – after counting Mikkola, Aaltonen, Culcheth and Hopkirk the rest were 'also-rans' – but who had the most trouble, and who dropped out. Tony Fall and Sobieslaw Zasada had major problems, which took hours to fix, as did Timo Makinen, while the two most prominent Citroëns both disappeared.

Even before the start of the Prime, Guy Verrier's DS21, fourth when it left La Paz, stopped with a completely collapsed hydro-pneumatic rear suspension, and also suffered from a holed fuel tank: both these failures, Verrier, suggested, were inspired by the crash which the car had suffered on its way to La Paz. Close by, Bob Neyret's car suddenly stopped, with a broken engine timing chain – which left Citroën down to only three runners (from six starters), of which Paul Coltelloni's machine looked ready for the scrap yard, and Claudine Trautmann's car was suffering from engine bothers.

It was Ford, however, that provided the media with stories of knock-about comedy, though it did not feel like it, perhaps, at the time. Tony Fall

The fact that Paddy Hopkirk's car has the extra roof-top lights fitted, means that this action shot was taken in South America. Paddy finished fourth overall ...

and Jimmy Greaves, who had shrugged off their wheel stud breakage problems in Argentina and Bolivia, were ready to make a big effort in Peru (Fall, after all, had recced this section in autumn 1969), but the fates thought otherwise.

Not only did the newly-manufactured wheel studs on their car stretch, and allow a wheel to come off, but at one time a hub and half-shaft also detached themselves. By the time the pantomime was complete, the crew had suffered 10 punctures, and had been reduced to changing inner tubes and changing covers at the side of the road.

As Tony told me immediately afterwards:

"By the time the eighth one happened, we were absolutely shattered. We changed the tyre and decided to have a five minute rest at the side of the road, even though Stuart would be mad with us afterwards. As I passed the other rear wheel I kicked the tyre in disgust, and the damned thing went down! There was only one thing to do, we lay down and nearly went hysterical with laughing ..."

At one point, the tyre supply situation was so desperate that co-driver Jimmy Greaves was obliged to flag down a bus, in order to go ahead and try to bring back some tyres from a Ford service point that was further along the Prime. Later, when Fall started gingerly driving along the road, he encountered a dejected Greaves at the roadside, who informed him that the bus had turned off the route before the service crew could be found!

It was early in the Cuzco to Huancayo Prime that Sobieslaw Zasada's Escort became the reluctant centre of attention from several other crews. Not only was there an accident which delayed him by several hours, but this had a ripple effect on several other competitors. One

... while Brian Culcheth (whose car never carried roof-top lights) was trying just as hard, and finished second.

Whatever happened to Timo Makinen's Escort, FEV 4H, after the event was over, and the publicity died away? Where is it now?

has to remember, of course, that four factory Escorts left the start of the Prime in line astern (Hannu thinks this was at two minute intervals), with Brian Culcheth's Triumph and Paddy Hopkirk's Triumph close behind.

Brian Culcheth recalls: "We never came close to being hit by another car, truck or bus on the rally. The nearest problem was that at one point we nearly hit Zasada's Escort (I was livid with him). He had crashed, in the dark, we came round a corner, and he was right across the road. We had no choice, we went up the bank, somehow got round him – it was just an instant decision. I think his crash had just taken place before us."

Rauno Aaltonen was in the middle of a pace notes crisis (it was caused by a typing error back at Boreham) at the same point, and is sure that the same crisis had already caused Zasada to crash:

"We were in top gear, it was reasonably straight, Henry had made the notes, and of course I trusted him whatever he said. Over this brow we rushed, and I could immediately see the very sharp right ...

"Well, I put the car totally sideways, trying to slow down, and there was a curve carved into the mountain, with a vertical bank on one side. Halfway round the corner I found Zasada's car on its side, on its door, because he had been using the same notes ...

"I had no way to stop, and I was coming rather fast – I will never forget the scene, that Zasada and Wachowski were trying to get up the bank like baboons to get out of the way ... I couldn't stop and I think I hit his car gently, but I didn't stop, because I knew that the next car to come would be Timo – with the same notes and going just as quickly Zasada was still

The 'Beauty Box' BMC 1800, sponsored by Woman magazine, kept going sturdily throughout the six weeks of the World Cup Rally, and eventually took 18th place.

trying to get his Escort back on its wheels when Timo arrived – same scenario again ..."

As a result of this crash, Zasada's Escort had suffered a badly smashed-up front suspension strut, and had body damage all along the near side of the shell. Nothing daunted, however, Zasada somehow got the car back on to its wheels, and drove it haltingly back up the Prime, to find the Ford emergency service crew (which included Boreham stalwart Norman Masters) still in Cuzco, though almost ready to leave.

Unhappily there were no specialised spares on hand, so the only thing to do was the cannibalise a standard 1100 Escort which was parked nearby, leaving Zasada's rally car with a drum-braked standard-setting strut on one side, and with disc brakes and competition settings on the other three wheels. Thus bodged up, the Poles set off, at no great pace, but stopped at one of the mid-Prime service points, where a full and final repair was completed! Zasada's total penalty for that Prime was a whopping eight hours ...

Brian Culcheth, in the 2.5PI which was destined to take second place, observed:

"Soon after the start of the Prime, we came across Zasada's Escort which had hit the bank and looked badly damaged. Drama again – we came into a corner, saw part of a disc brake, then a warning triangle, and then Timo Makinen's Escort at the side being repaired – two Fords down, two to go!

"The nature of this fantastic road is such that you can see the road most of the time, winding ahead up one mountainside, then down the other, and so on. So for most of the Prime we could see the Escorts of Mikkola and Aaltonen, all the time, and they could see us closing in.

"What a battle – three cars fighting for the

Alfred Katz's Fixo Flex-sponsored Mercedes-Benz 280SE made few headlines throughout the event, but by driving sensibly, and by having a sturdy Mercedes-Benz to drive, managed 16th place.

lead, all driving as hard as they knew how. Aaltonen then had a puncture, and we moved into second place, blowing the horn as we passed the Escort on its jack. 200 kilometres (124.3 miles) later we had a puncture and Aaltonen repassed us for second place – and this is how we battled the whole way ..."

This, indeed, proved to be the 'killer' Prime, for nine of the 39 cars which left La Paz that morning were eliminated before the Arrival Control in Lima closed. In almost every case, this was because the hard-pressed cars had finally let the teams down. Then, for some crews, the drama really started, for it was often possible to have repairs made, but then almost impossible to arrange to get the cars out of Peru once again, unless they crossed the border at La Tina. Since, in some cases, this had all happened days earlier, and the cars had entered Peru by distinctly abnormal methods, there was the possibility that the mobile wrecks would be impounded permanently.

Among those who suffered badly from the rigours of the Bolivian and Peruvian tracks, of the altitude, and of the general exhaustion that was setting in was the JCB Hillman Hunter, which suffered a major front suspension failure, needing repairs to the steering knuckles/front hubs on both sides of the car.

The Jopp/Kahn/Cave BMC 1800, which had been one of the first to help Paddy Hopkirk when his Triumph broke down before arriving at La Paz, had suffered all manner of dramas during the event, finally limped into Lima having had a serious rear suspension failure. This happened on other 1800s in the same part of the continent, thus proving that testing to destruction could sometimes produce consistent results.

There was much disappointment, too, for the gallant also-rans, some of whom became 'also-retired', thus putting an end to their stout efforts. Everyone was sorry to see Major Freddy Preston's Peugeot 504 stopped with terminal fuel injection problems, and there was much sympathy for the under-financed Donner brothers (and their privately-prepared Ford Capri), for they had no oxygen supplies, suffered badly from altitude-sickness and complete exhaustion (for they were their own service crew) and had to retire.

Two of the BMWs were in trouble, but still limping along (Ken Bass' car ruined its front suspension struts, and had no spares, while Peruvian resident Peter Kube found that his rear suspension was cracking up. Both were struggling along – which ensured that they got a great reception on arriving in Lima – but on the other hand Jose Araújo's Volvo disappeared with damaged front suspension, and no-one seemed to be sorry at all. Araújo (the Argentinian) had got himself quite a reputation on this event for being almost impossible to pass (a matter of Latin pride was involved, it was thought), and there was also the little matter of his altercation with Hannu Mikkola ...

Three all-female crews were still in the running, with Claudine Trautmann's Citroën DS21 leading that particular contest (but there were mechanical problems on the horizon), Rosemary Smith serenely carrying on in spite of crew sickness, and an overheating engine, and the Jean Denton's 'Beauty Box' 1800 running some hours behind, now with a cracked sump/transmission case which was going to a good test case

for Araldite as the cars cooled overnight in Lima. At the time, few had expected any of the female crews to reach the closing stages of what was an extremely gruelling marathon.

For some, the delays caused by mechanical failings and punctures stretched into hours. These days, on World Championship rallies, cars do not lose tyres after punctures (and the 'mousse' inserts mean that they are sometimes partly reinflated), but on the World Cup a puncture could be crucial. As already noted, Tony Fall and Jimmy Greaves' Escort eventually ran out of rubber and inner tubes, Greaves' subsequent bus journey, in the search for Ford service, is now a rally legend. Making a prat of himself, he might have thought? No way – on this event, Jimmy was one of the real heroes ...

Even so, by the time the event arrived in Peru, the rallying survivors were beginning to live like zombies. Ten days after the World Cup Rally had restarted from Rio de Janeiro, they had driven thousands of miles, crossed several Latin American countries, yet they had enjoyed only three official night halts.

For the author, it was a spine chilling experience to run the Arrival Control in the outskirts of Peru, which was actually located outside the gates of the General Motors car and truck assembly factory in the city. News, by radio, began to filter through from Huancayo soon after 19.00hr – almost everyone, it seemed, was much penalised at that point – and it did not look as if any car would arrive in Lima on time.

In spite of the location of the Peruvian capital – Lima is at sea level, and only 12 degrees of latitude south of the Equator – it looked like being a long, cold, night, and all the forecasts were that arrivals would be widely spaced. How wrong we all were.

Amazingly, those who might be described as the 'usual suspects' – Mikkola and Aaltonen (Escorts), Culcheth and Hopkirk (Triumphs) – all appeared, comfortably ahead of schedule. Hannu Mikkola, in fact, had not only set the fastest time on Cuzco–Huancayo (81 minutes down on the target time), but had been driving flat out ever since, as the route led over the monumental Ticlia pass, then gradually down to sea level via La Oroya.

At least 80 minutes before Mikkola was due to clock in, he screamed straight past the Control, on his way to the Ford service point which had been set up further down the road – he must have been pulling up to 100mph (160.9kph) at that point (in suburban Lima!) – and it was not long before Aaltonen's Escort repeated the trick.

Once those four leading crews had clocked in, however, the carnage exacted by this overpowering Prime, and the cumulative effect of racing at high altitude for several days, all became apparent. Arrivals were widely-spaced, the cars were often in pitiable condition, and the boredom factor soon settled in. By the time the Arrival Control closed at 06.00hr on 19 May (the Control had been open for nine hours), only 30 cars had arrived.

So was it now time for the organisers to ease up on their demands? All except the very few competitors who were hoping to improve on their positions thought so. But, as for the organisers? No, not at all. Just take a moment to look at the official Road Book times covering the city of Lima,

Ken Bass kept his BMW 2002ti going well through many of the roughest and highest tracks which the World Cup demanded, but could not quite reach the end of the South American section.

where the cars were to be locked away in a compound at the Automobile Club of Peru:

Arrival: Lima (Parc Fermé)   21.30 (18 May) – 06.40 (19 May)

Departure: Lima (Departure Control) 18.00 (19 May) – 21.00 (19 May)

For the true heroes like Hannu Mikkola and Brian Culcheth, this meant that they could enjoy an overnight rest of perhaps 18-20 hours. For mere mortals, who might have been hours late on the shattering Cuzco-Huancayo Prime, only 12 hours or even less was available for sleep – real, horizontal sleep, in air-conditioned comfort. How much longer could human beings cope? Was it any wonder that Brian Culcheth later emphasised, and re-emphasised, that this was the toughest, fastest and most tiring rally that the world had ever known?

Into Ecuador

The restart was made, with due pomp and ceremony, from the Automobile Club of Peru, on Sunday evening, Tuesday, 19 May, in front of enormously enthusiastic crowds. The rally leaders and their cars, who must have looked like alien gods to the locals, for they rarely travelled outside their own country in those days, got an ecstatic send-off, but the biggest cheers were reserved for Peter Kube's BMW 2002ti, which was a Peruvian entry, and for William Bendek's BMW, for he was from neighbouring Bolivia.

For almost all the 30 runners, the next, overnight, run to the Ecuadorian border at La Tina was almost as welcome as a rest cure, for it was on the Pan-American Highway, this lengthy section being of smooth tarmac, and led through Trujillo, and Piura, before striking inland for the border town itself.

Although most of the top crews were rested, with cars restored to something close to 100 per cent state, for some of them, the problems started again, at once. Although Rauno Aaltonen's Escort had now stormed up into second place, he had all manner of mechanical dramas to overcome, for which time had not been available before he checked in to the Lima Control. Even though he had recorded second fastest time on the Incas Prime, before he got through to Lima he had hit a large rock in the middle of the road (had Hannu Mikkola's earlier progress dislodged it, by chance?), which bent the special crossmember rather badly:

Although the signboard confirms that the scene is only 14 kilometres (8.7 miles) from Lima, this shows just how basic the road surfaces were for much of the World Cup Rally. One of the big Citroën DS21s is using every available inch of its suspension wheel movement to keep up the pace.

"Quickly I had to adjust the steering rods to get it roughly right again. We continued, and at emergency services I got Henry to write on a piece of paper: 'Please telephone so-and-so at Lima, we need a crossmember ...'

"We got to Lima, but there was no crossmember, though one was promised. So we checked into Parc Fermé, and soon, while we were sleeping in Lima, a mechanic arrived with a special crossmember – by air, with a crossmember in his baggage, all the way from Boreham!

"Ford had telephoned Boreham from Lima, Boreham had sent Stuart McCrudden on an aeroplane, with a crossmember as hand-baggage ... he got to me, through Miami, Mexico City, then on to Lima. As soon as we checked out of Lima, we drove for 100 metres (321.8ft), then stopped, Ford service was there, jacked the car up, the crossmember came off, and I think it took maybe two hours to change, for it was quite complicated.

"Everyone had now gone, long ago, so then there was a race – and then our alternator failed ..."

It was that sort of event, which true professionals like Aaltonen treated as a constant, six-week challenge. Something, somewhere, somehow, was always likely to happen.

Although Peter Jopp's co-driver Willy Cave had received news, in Lima, that he was wanted back at his 'day job' with BBC TV (a general election had just been called ...), the team decided to keep going if possible. That was not, in fact, for long. The 1800 needed much expert work from Abingdon's mechanics, on the bodged up rear suspension repair, and eventually limped off towards the Ecuadorian Prime, but the car's transmission eventually failed before it reached the border, and JOP 1E became one of the ultimate retirements from this incredibly demanding event.

To the great relief of the organisers, two South American residents made it to the finish. One of them was William Bendek of Bolivia, whose BMW 2002ti survived, to finish in 13th place.

Peter Jopp (left) and Willy Cave struggled valiantly to keep their BMC 1800 (registered JOP 1E) going, but it finally broke down on leaving Lima, in Peru.

Prime 15: Macara to Cuenca, the Ecuadorian Prime

In the next few hours which followed his road-side rebuild in Lima, Rauno Aaltonen thought all his troubles were over – but hitting that huge rock had done more damage to the Escort than he had thought, for damage to the crossmember (which include the engine mounting bracketry, eventually caused the engine mounting to collapse too:

"The engine mounting on one side of the car broke, and it also tore the mounting – the steering column was going through it. This meant that the engine dropped down on one side, the steering column was jammed, and was very difficult to turn at all. So there was really no steering unless I accelerated, at which point the engine would twist and lift up on that side, then I could turn the shaft ...

Peter Jopp, Mark Kahn (of the Daily Mirror) and Will Cave kept going, valiantly, in their BMC 1800, until the World Cup reached Peru, but it had to retire with irreparable mechanical problems soon after leaving the Lima halt.

Prime 15: Macara to Cuenca (Ecuador) – the Ecuador Prime
[Target: 250 miles/402.3 in 3hr 00 minutes]

Fastest times:

Crew	Car	Penalty (hours-mins)
R Aaltonen/H Liddon	Ford Escort 1850	1-51
P Hopkirk/A Nash/N Johnston	Triumph 2.5PI	1-57
H Mikkola/G Palm	Ford Escort 1850	1-57
T Makinen/G Staepelaere	Ford Escort 1850	1-58
B Culcheth/J Syer	Triumph 2.5PI	1-59
A Fall/J Greaves	Ford Escort 1850	2-00
S Zasada/M Wachowski	Ford Escort 1850	2-07
W Bendek/D Hubner/J Burgoa	BMW 2002ti	2-30
R Freeborough/P Cooper/R Redgrave	BMC 1800	2-33
G Perkins/JF Green	Peugeot 404	2-40
A Rees/H Thomas/W James	Hillman Hunter	2-45
R Smith/A Watson/G Derolland	Austin Maxi	2-47
C Trautmann/C Perrier	Citroën DS21	2-54
K Tubman/A Welinsky/B McAuley	BMC 1800	2-56
R Channon/R Cooper	Ford Lotus-Cortina	2-50

"So we learned how to drive the car in a different way – for about 1000km (621.4 miles) – before we could get it repaired."

The same problem, too, afflicted Timo Makinen's car, this also needing a bodge repair, then a lengthy rebuild at the next Ford service point, before it could be restored to health. In spite of the time, effort and budget which had been applied to these cars, the Escorts were demonstrably not bomb-proof. On the other hand, they had extremely resourceful drivers, magnificent mechanics out in the field, and the big advantage in Latin America, of a dealer service network which was so valuable at times.

It was on this stretch that the lead in the Private Owners' category changed yet again. Because both Guy Verrier's and Bob Neyret's Citroën DS21s had both dropped out before arrival at Lima, the battle for that category was suddenly developing into a close contest between a third Citroën – that of Patrick Vanson – and the BMC 1800 of Freeborough/Cooper/Redgrave.

Up to the start of the Ecuadorian Prime, Vanson led that contest, then fell back when the complex hydro-pneumatic suspension of the DS21 gave trouble, and a lot of time was lost. The BMC 1800 then took over the lead, but was itself delayed when a rear swinging arm in the rear suspension broke, and had to be replaced after a big delay. Back to square one, with Vanson now seventh – behind four 'works' Escorts and the two surviving Triumph 2.5PIs.

While the tired crews were resting in Lima, the organising team had once again trimmed the time to be allowed for a Prime. Taking the view that it was better to penalise everyone by a ludicrous amount, than have

Rauno Aaltonen and Henry Liddon, crash helmets in place and concentrating hard in their Ford Escort on one of the Primes in South America. Aaltonen had a troubled start to the event, but fought his way all the way to second place in South America, and eventually settled for third overall.

the top four or five crews all cleaning the Prime, the 250 mile (402.3km) dash was now to be set in three hours instead of four – an 83.3mph (134.1kph) target average – over foggy and mostly jungle-lined tracks, from the Ecuadorian border at Macara, to Cuenca by way of Zaraguro. For the drivers, who might indeed be rested after the awful exertions of Bolivia and Peru, this might almost have felt like a frolic, for the much-reduced cavalcade realised that this was to be their final flat-out test before the end of the South American section.

With Hannu Mikkola now well ahead, and with Paddy Hopkirk now probably too far behind the leading trio to upset the order (even though there were three long Primes still to go ...), there seemed to be little incentive for anyone to go absolutely flat-out over this Ecuadorian stage. The battle for second place, between Aaltonen's Escort and Culcheth's Triumph 2.5PI, though, was still in the balance – and there was also the fact that the Lima-Cali road section itself was by no means a 'touring section', as it was set at 51.4mph (82.7kph), with one potentially troublesome border crossing (Ecuador to Colombia, where Controller Richard Harper was in attendance) still to be accomplished.

As Culcheth later commented:

"This Prime was over a very smooth dirt road, and provided one of the greatest displays of sideways rally driving ever seen. Aaltonen (Escort) and I kept up the battle for second place – he was the fastest, and we were fourth fastest, being slowed by a puncture. Ecuador provided the greatest crowds seen during the rally – in every town we went through, thousands of people lined the streets. At the refuelling place, the police had to use tear gas to control them. It was a tremendous sight, with people hanging out of buildings, climbing up trees, climbing on to the car, and all going wild with excitement ..."

By this late stage, in fact, the World Cup Rally had split itself into two major groups – on the one hand, the professionals in factory-backed

All Ford historians affectionately call this the 'cactus shot' – for it shows Hannu Mikkola and Gunnar Palm, at high speed, in typical South American scenery.

The pace notes on this Prime must have been easy to compile, as the last few miles were almost straight, with no hazards except for the wildlife.

machines, still trying for every minute, and every possible advantage, and on the other, the balance of the field, who were striving, as delicately as possible, to reach the finish.

Penalties recorded on the Ecuadorian Prime tell their own story for fastest (Aaltonen) and seventh fastest (Zasada's Escort) were separated by 16 minutes, the eighth car (Bendek in his BMW 2002ti) was a further 23 minutes behind that, and even the battling lady crews (Rosemary Smith and Claudine Trautmann) were a full hour behind the fastest time.

As expected by the professionals, the overall timing, in fact, was so tight that only four cars reached the Cali Control on time (35 hours, without rest, after leaving Lima) – the three leading Escorts, and Culcheth's Triumph. There might also have been a fifth – Paddy Hopkirk's Triumph – except that he shunted the car on the approach to Cali. Paddy later admitted that there was no excuse for his little incident, for no other vehicle was involved. He had, in fairness, been trying very hard to get back on terms with Culcheth's car, which had left Lima more than an hour ahead of him

Oh Paddy, what happened? Actually, Paddy was trying so hard on the last section into Cali in Colombia, that he went off the road and crumpled his Triumph. The mechanics later discovered a severed brake line which must surely have affected the car's behaviour.

(on penalties), but although there was no likelihood of him closing the gap in just one or two Primes, he was really having a go.

"I was just stupid," Paddy now admits, "There was nothing coming the other way. I just lost it, locked up the front end, and went straight off into a ditch, and pushed the front in. I can tell you, I felt a complete ******, especially when I had to ask the British Leyland mechanics at Cali to make repairs. In fact the radiator and the oil cooler were both damaged, but my co-driver, Neville Johnston, did a wonderful job, and managed to get us going. Then at Cali, after the restart for the run down to Buenaventura, the mechanics did some more panel bashing, to keep us going ..."

There was no good reason for it, Paddy reckons (though the fact that the mechanics discovered a broken rear brake pipe that had caused partial brake failure must have been a very viable excuse by any standards), but because these Triumphs really did seem to have been prepared like tanks, the machine somehow survived the major shunt.

After much hard work, which involved crowbars and big hammers to the bodywork, not to mention some replacement of lamps and other front-end auxiliaries, front suspension changes, and a new cooling radiator, the car did not look much better, and would certainly never win a concours competition, but apparently felt almost like new.

"I felt completely incompetent, and I shouldn't really have been going

Paddy Hopkirk would rather that no-one ever published pictures of his battered Triumph 2.5PI. The car still looked a mess at the finish – but not nearly as bad as it had done immediately after the crash in Colombia.

and fired up the engine, to his utter dismay he found that there was no oil pressure, with a big warning light telling him to switch off at once.

Ford mechanics were not allowed in Parc Fermé at this point (as at previous locations, shouted instructions across a fence, or through wire mesh, was the best and only alternative), so Hannu and Gunnar Palm had to carry out their own investigation. It wasn't long before the two discovered that the dry sump oil tank, in the boot, was almost empty – and of course there was no rhyme nor reason for this to be so. As I reasoned, afterwards, when trying to decide what had happened, although 'sabotage' might have been suspected, this was altogether impractical, as an Escort dry sump tank could only be emptied by a syringe, and this would have taken time, and would have been obvious to bystanders.

Ford mechanics were adamant that they had not drained the system before the car went into Parc Fermé, yet there was no evidence of oil pools or leaks on to the ground under the car. A mystery? Indeed, a real mystery, which has never been solved. The good news for Hannu was that he refilled the system, crossed his fingers, fired up the engine again – and it lasted, without lasting problems, to the end of the event.

According to the Road Book, the road section from Cali in Colombia, to Buenaventura (the major sea port on the Colombian coast where the World Cup cars would start their fourth, and last sea voyage of the event) was meant to be easy – after a night's sleep in Cali, a four hour 'Neutralised Section' which would merely channel the surviving cars down from Cali to Buenaventura itself – but for several competitors it was anything but that. The road itself was mainly through jungle, was narrow, twisting and – as ever, it seemed, in South America on this event – was infested with trucks and over-crowded buses. The only good news, though, was that it was almost all downhill, for Cali – at 1000 metres (3280ft) of altitude – was still up in the mountains, whereas Buenaventura, of course, was down at sea level.

For the rally cars, therefore, the problem was not of getting to Buenaventura on time (the schedule was relaxed, and no penalties were to be exacted in any case), but of getting there without suffering the heart-attack of meeting oncoming traffic round the blind corners which abounded on that section.

None of the rally leaders suffered from what I will call 'Mercedes-Benz-truck roulette'– but others were not so lucky. The leading Fords and

that quickly ... My excuse, and I will give this as an excuse, is that I think it was the one Prime that I had not recced. The moral of the story is that I should have practised every inch of the route, and I hadn't done that ..."

Other late-event dramas, before Cali, befell Claudine Trautmann's Citroën, whose engine was becoming sicker, and consuming more oil, by the day, while Peter Brown's JCB-sponsored Hillman Hunter bent its propshaft, and the vibration eventually fractured the transmission casing, so the car could go no further.

Cali to Buenaventura – the final hours in South America

For the next few days, it seemed, everything that happened after arrival at Cali came as an anti-climax. The roads were gradually returning towards sea level, the pressure of rally timing was off, and there was the enchanting prospect of a weekend to be spent aboard a luxury liner, on the warm Pacific Ocean.

Before the run down began, on what proved to be an almost suicidally narrow road to the port of Buenaventura, the rally cars, all 26 of them, were placed in a Parc Fermé.

Except that one or two cars suffered pilferage (those were the cars which were so damaged that their doors could not be locked), all seemed healthy enough to fire up again at departure time.

Except one – and this is where, for 40 years, there has been an abiding mystery. When rally leader Hannu Mikkola climbed into his Escort 1850,

Patrick Vanson's Citroën DS21, sponsored by Klippan safety belts, the company for whom Patrick worked, looked quite good from this angle, though the left rear corner had been destroyed in an accident between Cali and Buenaventura.

Triumphs – Aaltonen and Mikkola, Culcheth and Hopkirk – made it to the quayside, but others were not so lucky. Looking back after 40 years, the leading private owner, Patrick Vanson, still thinks that it was a miracle that he and his Citroën DS21 survived:

"It was at the very end of the South American route, between Cali and Buenaventura – just like Paddy, who also had an accident in this country – it was because the road was only the width of one car, and there were many buses running. They couldn't stop, they wouldn't stop – so we went round a right-hand corner, I will always remember it, we hit this bus, there was a terrible noise and we thought it must have taken the left-side back wheel clean off.

"We got out, and we were nearly crying because it was near the end.

Then Alain Leprince said: 'He hasn't touched the rear wheel,' and although we could literally tear off the rear wing and throw it away, we actually fixed it back on. It was very mangled. From somewhere, too, Alain found a wood panel, which was used as 'glass' for the rear door!"

(Patrick also recalled that a repair might have been easier if a Citroën support car could have reached them – but this car had just suffered a similar accident even closer to Cali, with similar results!)

Major John Hemsley's Peugeot 504 also suffered even more on this short transit section than it had done in the previous week or so. Like Vanson, Major Hemsley also hit an oncoming truck and almost, but not quite, turned the 504 into a complete write-off. As everyone who knew him can confirm, Hemsley was quite determined to finish the event, so

Although British cars dominated the final leader board in the World Cup Rally, Patrick Vanson of France took seventh place in his own Citroën DS21, and won the Private Entrant's Trophy. Patrick is closest to the camera, with co-driver Olivier Turcat on the left of the shot, and mechanic Alain Leprince in the centre.

even though the left front wing had been torn off, the left-side door was smashed, the windscreen was totally shattered, and most of the extra driving lamps had gone, the car somehow kept on going.

Functionally, the biggest single problem was that the steering wheel, too, was badly damaged, and would need replacing just as soon as possible, but somehow Hemsley got this mobile wreck to Buenaventura, and would carry out more repairs in Panama City.

By this time, too, the engine in Claudine Trautmann's big Citroën was in a pitiable state, drinking colossal quantities of oil and although she still held 10th place overall, and had the Ladies' Prize competition almost within her grasp, it wasn't certain that she would make it to the finish.

In spite of this, just three cars were late on arrival at Buenaventura – Doug Harris' gallant Escort 1300GT, Hemsley's Peugeot 504, and Paul Coltelloni's Citroën DS21, which had really been in the wars, and seemed to have been repaired by many different hands, in many different ways, along the route. Smart or not? Let's just say that Citroën would never have used it in a display advertisement!

Two of the three BMWs which left Lima didn't make it to Cali, and yet again Rob Janssen achieved a miracle in once again patching up his Datsun 1600SSS to get it to the finish. I can do no better than quote his own words from a report submitted at the time.

Every picture tells a story – although the Redgrave/Freeborough/Cooper BMC 1800 finished in a sturdy ninth place, at the close of the event it had lost one of its rally door plates to a souvenir hunter.

Brian Culcheth's Triumph 2.5PI being hoisted aboard the MS Verdi, at the end of the ultra-gruelling South American section. Third overall at that point, he would overtake Rauno Aaltonen's Escort on the final run through Central America, towards Mexico. (McKlein)

"The next problem was water, easily seen at the bottom of a nearby ravine, but almost unreachable. Nothing daunted, Janssen lowered his co-driver Jacob Dik down into the ravine on the car's tow rope, found it impossible to haul him back up complete with a brimming waster carrier, so attached the tow rope to the car, gently drove out into the road again, and plucked him up in the minimum of time ..."

For everyone who made it that far, of course, it was worth it, because John Sprinzel's organising team had already decided – and said as much – that any rally car that clocked in to Cali before that Control closed, would automatically qualify as a finisher. Twenty-six crews did that,

"At one stage the car's radiator had sprung a leak and, lacking a suitable repair kit, Janssen had to look around for ideas. In the end the intrepid crew tore out some of the car's plastic trim, melted it with their portable welding gear, used the still pliable plastic to seal the radiator, and all was well.

all of them made it to the MS Verdi for the transit to Panama – and the celebrations could now begin.

But only for a short time. The Verdi, for sure, was a fine vessel, but beyond it lay Central America, and the final push towards Mexico City.

Results to Cali, Colombia, then Port of Buenaventura – 21 May 1970

Mileage so far completed: 13,450 miles (21,646km)

Top Ten in general classification:

Place	Crew	Car	Penalty (hours-minutes)
1	Hannu Mikkola/Gunnar Palm	Ford Escort 1850	7-10
2	Rauno Aaltonen/Henry Liddon	Ford Escort 1850	8-17
3	Brian Culcheth/Johnstone Syer	Triumph 2.5PI Mk II	8-35
4	Paddy Hopkirk/Tony Nash/Neville Johnston	Triumph 2.5 Mk II	10-44
5	Timo Makinen/Gilbert Staepelaere	Ford Escort 1850	11-42
6	Tony Fall/Jimmy Greaves	Ford Escort 1850	17-06
7	Patrick Vanson/Olivier Turcat/Alain Leprince	Citroën DS21	19-00
8	R Redgrave/R Freeborough/P Cooper	BMC 1800	21-38
9	S Zasada/M Wachowski	Ford Escort 1850	21-43
10	Ms C Trautmann/Ms C Perrier	Citroën DS21	23-46

26 cars were still running.

Second interlude
A liner from Ecuador to Panama

Buenaventura (Colombia) to Cristobal (Panama)

To get the battered survivors of the World Cup Rally from South America (where the roads had been awful, and the altitudes often extreme) into Central America was always going to be a real logistical challenge, and took many weeks of pre-event planning to sort out. In 1970 there was still no way that cars could be driven overland between Colombia (the north-western extremity of South America) and Panama itself – simply, there was no road, and the mass of untamed jungle filling the space was known as the Darien Gap.

Even at the time, construction of a new road was planned for the future, but to this day (40 years on ...) this final link in the fabled Pan-American Highway – measuring 87km (54.1 miles) – has not yet been built.

As with the task of getting rally cars from Europe to Brazil earlier in the event, such a challenge involved routeing every vehicle from Colombia to Panama, and this could only be achieved by sea.

Having swallowed this decision, there were several alternatives. Perhaps it could have been possible to route the rally cars all the way up to the north coast of Colombia (which might have included the bonus of visiting Bogota), or even into Venezuela, but this would have added 'dead' mileage to the overall route. Instead, and as already noted, the final competitive section in the South American section of the World Cup Rally had to end at the city of Cali, after which the timing was neutralised so that the cars could find their way westwards, down the mountainside, to the port of Buenaventura.

The organisers considered chartering an entire ship, but this made no commercial sense, and instead they agreed to take space in the Italian Lines MS Verdi, a modern ship (launched as recently as 1963) which already plied an ideal route across the corner of the Pacific Ocean, which linked Buenaventura (leaving the dock at 16.00hr) with the Panama Canal, passage through the canal, to a scheduled docking point at the port of Cristobal (which was an offshoot of Colon), on the very edge of the Caribbean Sea, and at the northern tip of the Canal.

Near the end now. Timo Makinen's car waits to be hoisted aboard the MS Verdi, at Buenaventura in Colombia. Left to right are David Skeffington (co-driver of the Rolls-Royce Silver Shadow which followed the event even after it had officially been retired), Bill Bengry (the driver of the Rolls-Royce), and Timo's co-driver Gilbert Staepelaere.

Time for a beer (or three ...) at the end – left to right: Ron Crellin, Gilbert Staepelaere, Johnstone Syer, Mick Jones (Ford mechanic), Jimmy Greaves, Liz Crellin, Tony Nash, Stuart McCrudden (Ford-Boreham), and Pat Wright.

By comparison with what had gone before, a short weekend in the stylish modern Verdi was like heaven on earth, and proved to be an ideal way of preparing for the last harum-scarum dash up through Central America which was to follow.

Paddy Hopkirk, who had just suffered the horrors of a real flea-pit in Buenaventura, summed up perfectly:

"The hotel in Buenaventura was disgusting, with one rusty fridge, covered in ants and maggots ... In contrast, when we got on board the Verdi, it was like Claridges – it was super luxurious, and we had a great party that night en route to Panama ..."

The ship was crowded with other passengers, most of whom lionised Jimmy Greaves who (according to another competitor) "scored more often than he would have done in the soccer team ..."

Except for the fact that berths could not be booked in advance – Controller Jim Gavin knew this, made sure that he boarded before any of the cars were craned aboard, and secured Cabin no 1 (the best – naturally) for himself – there were really only two irritants in the two-and-a-half-day passage that ensued, for those rally teams still in the event. One was that, although the scenery was beautiful, and passage through the Canal was tranquil, the Verdi took up to 10 hours to complete the 77km (47.8 miles) length of the Canal (this was normal, because of the various enormous locks involved), and then tied up for the night at Cristobal with the cars still stowed on board. That it had begun its cruise past Bilboa (the port for Panama City) at the start of this transit did not go down well with crews who were, by this time, anxious to make it to the finish. It would be more than 24 hours before they and their cars, returned to the capital city.

On its way through a huge lock in the Panama Canal, the MS Verdi carries a precious load of World Cup Rally cars. The VW Karmann Ghia is an interloper, but other cars in shot, and on deck, are the leading Escort, Paddy Hopkirk's Triumph 2.5PI, and Rosemary Smith's Austin Maxi.

Party time in the swimming pool of the MS Verdi – en route from Buenaventura to Panama – where Hannu Mikkola and Gunnar Palm relax after two weeks of flat-out motoring in South America.

8

Panama to Fortin – all over bar the shouting?

Was this marathon ever going to end? Would we ever reach a Time Control, knowing that there would be no more flat-out driving in dreadful hire cars to come, no more scary encounters with trucks and buses on awful roads, and no more breakdowns scores of miles from anywhere. To those of us who had already been involved for more than a month – whether competitors, mechanics and team personnel, officials, or plain enthusiasts, by late May it began to feel like that. Exhausted people would mutter the names of John Sprinzel and John Brown in dark corners, hiss at the indignities which had already been inflicted by them, and vow to take up a less stressful occupation in the future. Yet we all came back for more, convinced that this might just be the first and the last of the real high-speed marathons.

A few individuals, for sure, went slightly 'stir-crazy'; no doubt you have heard that sturdy American expression? It refers to the way that for prisoners, confinement eventually drives them mad. Maybe what took place in Panama City on 24 May wasn't quite like that – but it certainly felt like it.

As far as the 26 competitors were concerned, the problem was that the beautifully equipped MS Verdi had already been acting like a luxury prison for three days, yet there still seemed to be no immediate plans for the event to be relaunched, in a helter-skelter dash up through Central America, to Mexico City itself.

As already noted, the regular timetable for this ship saw it spending much of Saturday, 23 May 1970, easing its way gently through the magnificent Panama Canal, negotiating its huge locks (amazingly, the Pacific, the Atlantic Oceans and the water in the centre of Panama itself do not have quite the same sea level datum in that part of the world!), and eventually mooring at a dock in Cristobal-Colon in the evening.

So far, so good, but the passengers then stayed on board all night (they had, at least, been allocated comfortable cabins to sleep in, and the bars remained open ...), while the dockers of this North American-controlled port complex got on with the job of unloading all 26 cars, lining them up neatly on the quayside. Only one rally car – the Mercedes-Benz 280SE of

Fred Katz – showed any temperament, but this was merely by showing off a flat tyre, which was a positive pin-prick of a problem after the hazards which all the surviving crews had already shrugged off.

Even then, however, that was not the end of the waiting, for the cars were still officially in Parc Fermé and could even be approached by their crews, no work on them was allowed at this point, and no-one could get at them. The organisers had no intention of moving the survivors until the end of the afternoon, as the scheduled restart from the centre of Panama City was not due until 20.00hr.

The way to get round the 'stir-crazy' syndrome seemed to be to take it all as lightly as possible, and to look ahead. Rumour has it that Brian Culcheth (one of the few competitors who had surveyed the route which still lay ahead, and who was still driving flat out at all times) arrived for breakfast on the ship, rubbed his hands, beamed around the restaurant, and said:

"Great. Nearly finished. Only 51 hours to go!"

Fine, and in the context of this monumental event, those (to be precise) 51 hours and 30 minutes through increasingly civilised countryside looked like a mere addendum to what had already gone before, a mere diversion. Consider, though, that there would be no scheduled rest halts until the cars would arrive in the resort town of Fortin in Mexico, and that two lengthy Primes – one in Costa Rica and one in Mexico itself – still lay ahead. And that, in Europe, a schedule like this would have covered more than half of a major rally like the Acropolis, the Spa-Sofia-Liège, or the RAC – and would have been considered very tough.

So, it was still breakfast time, the crews could not get access to their rally cars until the late afternoon, Cristobal-Colon was just like any other massive, industrialised, dockyard in the world – and what could be done? Fortunately, local enthusiasts from the Panama Racing Club, excelled themselves, by providing an informal taxi and courier service, offering tours, trips and hospitality in general, which some crews accepted with ill grace – though most of them had already booked into a hotel in the middle

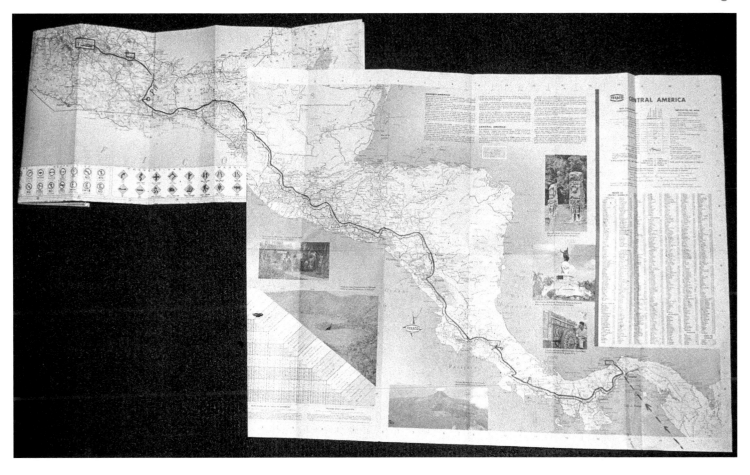

This carefully drawn map shows the route that the 26 surviving World Cup cars were asked to follow, between Panama (bottom right) and Mexico City. More cars were to drop out along the way.

of Panama City to build up a bit more sleep in advance of what was to follow.

I now re-enter the story in a minor capacity, for it was apparently the rainy season in Panama, and during the day that the heavens opened, allowing several inches of torrential warm rain to fall in a seemingly endless deluge. Having already been banished from a hotel for the day, to supervise Parc Fermé, and to see that the cars eventually left for the 50 mile (80.5km) journey to downtown Panama City, I 'travelling controller Robson' now had nowhere to shelter except in a seedy hire car – and it leaked. Later, when John Sprinzel was threatened with a bill for new shoes and rainwear, his only response was to laugh.

According to the Sprinzel master plan, an easy two hours was to be allowed for cars to make the 50 mile (80.5km) journey south, through Panama, from Cristobal to Panama City itself, and I prepared to release

them, one-by-one, minute-by-minute, at the end of the afternoon. This, though, was not what the Panamanian police had in mind (though they had not yet discussed this with the World Cup organisers), and they sent Officer Rodriguez to impose what, to them, was a tidier solution.

What they intended to do (and would I, as the official in charge at Cristobal please tell the crews ...?) was to line-up all the rally cars behind a police VW, and lead them into Panama City in a sedate convoy instead. Cue 'Robson' to make phone calls back to Rally HQ in Panama City, for the organisers to talk to the chief of the Traffic Guard (Major Roberto Diaz) – who was in any case scheduled to wave off the cars from the Conoco station – and for everything to be unscrambled yet again.

What happened in the end (and in a way that ruffled egos were eventually smoothed down) was that the convoy project was dropped, the rally cars left Cristobal at one minute intervals as originally intended

Service with a smile, with Abingdon's 'Fast Eddie' Burnell – in overalls – looking after Rosemary Smith's red-and-white striped Austin Maxi, and Reg Redgrave's BMC 1800.

– and Police Officer Rodriguez was then happy to follow the last car. Not only that, but he received an 'official' invitation to the party which later developed at the Conoco station – and probably dined out on his experience for years to come.

Once the cars left the Main Control at the Conoco petrol station, on the Pacific sea coast of Panama City itself, what remained looked simple enough. The only major towns and cities listed were David, San Jose, Managua, Choluteca, San Salvador, Guatemala City, Oaxaca and Fortin – but this disguised the fact that the route led all the way up the narrow land strip which is Central America. From Panama, the cars would travel through Costa Rica, Nicaragua, Honduras, El Salvador and Guatemala, before entering Mexico itself.

That meant enduring no fewer than six border crossings. As already explained (see the sidebar on page 22), when making this journey as a normal tourist, or on commercial business, each border could have been responsible for hours of delays. Fortunately, hundreds of hours of patient diplomacy beforehand, not least by making a circular tour of all the embassies in London to make arrangements (where personalities like Jack Sears had a big and most successful input), ensured that this did not happen.

For the rally cars, most border crossings were achieved in a matter of minutes, and it must have helped that some of John Sprinzel's most noted controllers (David Seigle-Morris, Val Morley and Donald Morley among them) were on hand to vouch for the grubby, often battered, rally cars as they approached the checkpoints.

By this time, a number of cars still running in the event were, frankly,

in the walking wounded category. Some looked battered, some had received a number of rebuilds along the way, and a few were not certain to finish the event (though, as noted, they would already qualify as 'official' finishers, that classification having been issued at Cali, three days earlier).

As was now normal on this event, where the leaders ran at the front of the queue, it was Hannu Mikkola's Ford Escort that was first to leave Panama City at 20.00hr on Sunday, 24 May, with 25 other crews, some in cars which were decidedly second-hand, leaving behind them.

Somewhere between Cristobal and Panama City, one car, the white Citroën DS21 driven so gallantly by Claudine Trautmann (it was officially placed 10th overall at Cali) was really in a terrible state, and needed major repairs. With little factory support at this juncture (she was, after all, a 'private entry' ...) she had to organise assistance to weld-up the front suspension mountings on her car.

That, however, was a minor problem compared with what was already developing on the car, whose engine was developing a colossal appetite for oil. Piston rings, for sure, had broken, and with neither time nor resources to do anything about this, the French lady could only hope that her car could stagger up through Central America to the finish.

Why was this a big deal, and was 10th overall all that important? Simply because she was leading the Ladies' Prize competition by a big margin: to win this would be financially very valuable to her, and would provide a really important tag for Citroën's advertising which might surely follow. With all this in mind, Claudine, whose husband had crashed out of the event while leading it in the first days of the South American section, kept plugging away.

The run westwards towards Costa Rica should have held no perils for the rally crews, as the 350 miles (563.3km) was over good tarmac, all at night, and was running to an easy schedule. Easy? Relatively so, for although there was an overall open road speed limit of 80kph/50mph, the Panamanian authorities had let it be known that they were not about to harass the contestants of this very important international event on this occasion ...

Everything, therefore, was set for a gentle run towards Canaos, in Costa Rica, where the next Prime would begin. Unhappily, tragedy then struck the Citroën team, and the rally itself, for it was on the run-up through Panama towards the border with Costa Rica (it was dark, of course), that

The gritty performance of Tony Fall and footballing superstar Jimmy Greaves, in FEV 2H, was one of the surprises of the World Cup Rally. After suffering many mechanical breakdowns, punctures and axle breakages, mostly in the high Andes, they struggled through to take sixth place.

near Penemone, Paul Coltelloni's big Citroën DS21 was hit, virtually head on, by a local's car. Coming in the opposite direction, and reputedly badly lit, it suddenly swerved across the road in front of him (trying to reach a poorly-lit petrol station on the other side of the road). The Citroën was completely wrecked, and Coltelloni's co-driver, Ido Marang, suffered severe head injuries from which he died shortly afterwards.

Coltelloni himself was knocked about, and badly shocked, but at least he (and the unconscious Marang) were both dragged out of the wreckage before the Citroën burst into flames, and burnt itself out. This accident, of course, could have happened anywhere on this rally, or on any public highway along the way. There was no question of the Citroën being in poor condition – it was not, and was well-equipped with headlamps and spot lights – while Coltelloni himself was well rested, having spent the previous night in bed, on board the Verdi.

This was awful, but it rapidly became clear that there was nothing the organisers, nor Citroën, nor the Citroën team, could have done to make sure it never happened. Even so, it cast a pall on the last few days of the event.

In the meantime, Tony Fall and Jimmy Greaves continued their perpetual battle against misfortune – for if any other car had suffered more punctures in this event, then it was not known to the rest of the crews, and if any other crew had suffered from breakdowns so far from service and support, it was not publicised. This time the intrepid crew suffered an accident, which sounds rather less traumatic than it actually was.

At least there were no injuries – at least not to human beings, that is – for this accident occurred when the Tony Fall/Jimmy Greaves Escort hit a stampeding horse at high speed. There was simply no way of avoiding the shunt, the poor animal was immediately killed in the impact, and in hitting the Escort its body caused damage to the roof, and of course it also shattered the windscreen. Fortunately the 'buzzard bars' did their job, and the basic shape of the bodyshell was preserved.

Not only that, but the animal's head was badly cut in the collision, which resulted in a great deal of animal blood being sprayed around inside the cabin. The Escort was sent spinning down the road – fortunately no other cars, private or competition, were involved – and when Fall (who was driving) finally regained control, he discovered that the entire laminated

Major John Hemsley kept his Peugeot 504 going, through thick and thin, but eventually suffered an accident on the way to the ship at Buenaventura, and the battered car then expired on him in the second to last Prime. Ford photographer Ken Shipton – camera slung round his neck – treats this all as a day's work. The suave-looking gentleman in the leather jacket is Controller David Seigle-Morris.

screen had been smashed into the car, and that both Greaves and himself had slivers of glass in or close to their eyes.

It was the sort of impact where the only thing to do was to stop, to take stock, and to carefully get rid of all the glass that the duo could find. Naturally they were not carrying a spare screen – not even a 'shatter screen' – but somehow they got themselves to a Ford agent who had been prepared for just such a visitation well in advance of the rally. After much 'heavy repair' (which means that brute force, rather than delicacy, was involved), a replacement screen was somehow persuaded to stay in place, and the car (FEV 2H) survived to the end.

Following the tragic accident to Coltelloni's Citroën, and the less serious accident to the Greaves/Fall Escort, the 'World Cup' was now down to 25 runners, though because of the state of some of those still present, it might be easier to specify, say, 20 runners, and a few might still not make it.

Major John Hemsley's Peugeot 504 was in a pitiable state by this time, its chassis well out of true, a non-standard steering wheel having been added in Panama City, and it was only just able to drag itself along. The accident with a truck on the route from Cali to Buenaventura had almost been the final straw. In fact, although the BAMA-backed Peugeot would start the penultimate Prime, in Costa Rica, it did not finish it. That reduced the runners to only 24, and there was more disappointment to come.

Major John Hemsley battled his way through South America in this Peugeot 504, but an accident with a truck damaged the car very severely, and it finally expired just hours from the finish at Fortin, in Mexico.

winning the stage with a time six minutes faster than Hannu Mikkola ... When we got back to England, I was entertained to lunch at the Costa Rican Embassy, and they presented me with a certificate recording my win on their Prime, and the fastest time ever across Costa Rica. Our performance on the Panama to Mexico section also won us the Mexico Coffee Institute Award, with prize money of £500!"

It was on this Prime, however, that one of the last major changes in running order took place. Rauno Aaltonen's Escort, which had been a secure 18 minutes ahead of Brian Culcheth's big Triumph as the cars left Panama City, suddenly stuttered to a halt in mid-Prime. Culcheth passed the stricken vehicle, which was at the side of the

Prime 16: Canaos to Cartago – the Costa Rica Coffee Prime

The Costa Rican Prime started immediately after the cars had crossed the border from Panama, into that country. Competitors had been told to expect conditions to be much worse that in Panama – and they were not disappointed. Not only was the Prime run off in darkness, but the surface rapidly changed from tarmac to smooth dirt, then to rough, ungraded, dirt, followed by a climb to 10,000 feet (3048m) in the Costa Rican mountains, and more of the same for hours and hours ...

According to the Road Books, all the cars would have to tackle it in darkness, which was probably just as well, as the target time for this 220 mile (354.1km) section was set in a mere 2hr 30 minutes! That was an average speed target of 88mph (141.6kph), and under the circumstances it was always going to be completely impossible. Incidentally, according to the original printed Road Book, three hours should have been allowed, but John Sprinzel and John Brown had been so impressed by the pace of cars on early Primes that they had culled a full 30 minutes off the target.

This cut, in fact, was not necessary, for even Paddy Hopkirk (who was still out to make a point against his team-mate/rival Brian Culcheth) would lose 41 minutes, Hannu Mikkola would lose 46 minutes, and Culcheth himself dropped 51 minutes.

Even 40 years later, Paddy recalls the stage – and has a special reason for doing so:

"This was the Prime we had practised between finishing the European section and restarting from Rio," Paddy said, "and it paid off, with us

Prime 16: Canaos to Cartago (Costa Rica) – the Costa Rica Coffee Prime
(Target: 220 miles/354.1km in 2hr 30 minutes)

Fastest times:

Crew	Car	Penalty (hours-mins)
P Hopkirk/A Nash/N Johnston	Triumph 2.5PI	0-40
H Mikkola/G Palm	Ford Escort 1850	0-46
B Culcheth/J Syer	Triumph 2.5PI	0-51
S Zasada/M Wachowski	Ford Escort 1850	1-07
R Janssen/J Dik	Datsun 1600SSS	1-09
A Fall/J Greaves	Ford Escort 1850	1-09
R Smith/A Watson/G Derolland	Austin Maxi	1-11
T Kingsley/P Evans/ M Scarlett	Austin Maxi	1-21
P Vanson/O Turcat/A Leprince	Citroën DS21	1-25
A Rees/H Thomas/W James	Hillman Hunter	1-26
K Tubman/A Welinsky/ B McAuley	BMC 1800	1-27
R Channon/R Cooper	Ford Lotus-Cortina	1-27
R Aaltonen/H Liddon	Ford Escort 1850	1-33
W Bendek/D Hubner/ J Burgoa	BMW 2002ti	1-36
T Makinen/G Staepelaere	Ford Escort 1850	1-37

Somewhere inside that devastation is the remains of a Datsun 16000SSS, which the indefatigable Rob Janssen drove on the World Cup. According to all the odds, it should have expired several times, but Janssen somehow kept it going. Apart from suffering sundry accidents, it also underwent several complete engine rebuilds, including the piston replacements.

track, its bonnet up, and its crew looking frantic, and realised that he had probably inherited second place.

At the end of the Costa Rica Prime, that 18 minute deficit had been converted into a lead of 24 minutes. Even if Aaltonen could get the car going again, surely not even the brilliant Finn could make up that much time on the one remaining Prime in Mexico. It wasn't a question of prestige, or of prize money – but simply of practicalities. Rauno Aaltonen himself takes up the story:

"Now we came to the very end, of the event, somewhere near Mexico, my car suffered three punctures, and suddenly my engine lost power. It got worse and worse and worse – I was sure it was a fuel supply problem.

"I had to stop. I had to check the fuel flow through all the filters, which took a lot of time. Eventually I found a supply pipe to the Weber carburettors – under the Webers where I could not see it, of course, was bent, and this I think had started to happen when the engine was going up and down on the broken engine mounting. Now it was kinked enough to cause trouble when we were going uphill and the Webers needed more fuel ...

"It took us about two hours finally to solve the problem. That dropped us from second to third place, and I had no way of making it back ..."

Not that this was the only incident those protagonists suffered. After starting just ahead of Aaltonen, and starting just two minutes apart, this meant that Culcheth had a shrewd idea of the precise location of the other. Even so, it almost ended in tears. First of all, the big Triumph suffered not one, but two punctures, the wheels having to be replaced. Then it started to rain, the wipers became snagged up in the 'temporary' gaffer tape surrounding the inherited screen, and finally the windscreen itself began to come out, so had to be refixed.

Both, in other words, had suffered badly, but Aaltonen afflicted most, he dropped one place, from second to third.

This, on reflection, was the near-the-end Prime where most upsets were caused. Apart from the Aaltonen-Culcheth upset, drama was also brewing in the Ladies' category, as Claudine Trautmann found her Citroën barely able to drag itself along, and as it seemed to be consuming as much engine oil as petrol, the assumption was that the engine could not last for long. That was the bad news for her – but the good news for Rosemary Smith (whose luridly liveried Maxi had proved to be remarkably reliable) was that she gained no less than 34 minutes on that Prime alone.

Because Major John Hemsley's Peugeot did not finish the stage (hours later, Travelling Controller David Seigle-Morris actually found him in mid-stage when clearing the route after every other car had gone through ...) the World Cup was now down to 24 runners. With Claudine Trautmann's Citroën expected to die at any moment, and with Rob Janssen's Datsun still struggling along (it side-swiped yet another truck, and destroyed much of the bodywork, before the end of the Central American section), close to the exclusion times for the Primes and Controls, that figure looked all set to be

Reg Redgrave's immaculately prepared BMC 1800 fought tooth-and-nail for the Private Entrants' Award, eventually finishing ninth overall.

reduced in the next few hours: amazingly, though, Janssen's Datsun set the fifth fastest time on the Costa Rican Prime!

Fortunately, the pace now eased. Once the cars had tackled the Costa Rica Prime, they were able to potter on, on main road routes, through Nicaragua, Honduras, El Salvador and Guatemala, before they reached the border with Mexico. Here, though, came a brief moment of farce. To ease their passage, the organisers had arranged to send a travelling controller – twice French Alpine Rally winner (and one-time BMC 'works' rally driver) – Donald Morley to that border, to make sure that officials were well-briefed.

Amazingly, when Morley arrived, well ahead of the potential schedule which he had been given, he discovered that all but one competitor – which

was the Ford Escort GT of Doug Harris/Mike Butler – had already passed through. Some, it seemed, had passed through up to 11 hours earlier. Claudine Trautmann's Citroën, however, did not quite reach Mexico, for it expired in Guatemala, when the engine finally collapsed: in the latter stages it had apparently been consuming one gallon (4.5L) of Total oil every three miles (4.8km) ... So, only 23 runners remained.

And so the World Cup Rally finally entered its destination country, Mexico, where the football World Cup was due to start in a few days. One Prime remained, and one Main Control – the resort town of Fortin – lay ahead, but the major battles all now seemed to have been resolved. The main road run from the border to Oaxaca in Mexico – by way of San Cristobal and Tuxtla Guiterez – was easy enough, and the 'works' crews

all made sure that they were able to get some real sleep in Oaxaca before the final Prime began.

The last of the organisational nightmares then erupted. For a variety of reasons, way back in 1969 the route chosen for the final Prime (Prime 17, the Aztec Prime) in Mexico had not been surveyed in detail. Accordingly, when John Brown and Dean Delamont flew in to Mexico City, hired a VW Beetle, and set off south, they were not at all sure what to expect. Official permissions were still lacking, and it was all very complicated.

Brown and Delamont then drove the stage, but at one point found a very promising gravel road, which was being widened, and from time to time was closed so that explosives could be used to clear more ground. When John Brown arrived at this point, he found that road gangs were busily dynamiting the road to make improvements for the population at large. At the very last minute, therefore, Brown had to rush around, make decisions on the hoof, bribe various officials and workers with the ubiquitous American dollars, and plead with them to hold off for three hours or so, until his 23 precious rally cars could pass. It could, of course, have been worse – for many more rally cars might, just might, have been involved. The team knew, however, that just 24 rally cars had left the end of the Costa Rican Prime, and that just 23 had crossed the last border where travelling controllers had been in place.

And it worked! Under some pressure, no doubt, from the Mexican auto clubs (who wanted the world thinking the best of their efforts, and of their sporting nation in general), the contractors guaranteed to hold off for the afternoon and evening while the World Cup Rally passed through – on the basis that they would be told

Timo Makinen started the event as a favourite, but his Escort suffered mechanical problems. Later in the World Cup, he carried many spare parts in his Escort, so that he could act as a 'travelling mechanic' to support Hannu Mikkola.

the very moment that the final car on the road (which looked certain to be the Harris/Butler Escort GT) had passed by. Later, of course, the organisers discovered that the contractors' plant had broken down on the afternoon in question, and that no further earth-moving would have been possible on the day in question.

In the end a modified Prime, that not even super-professionals like Henry Liddon and Brian Culcheth had surveyed, went ahead, with just 90 minutes being allowed as a target for a 106 mile (170.6km) route. Needless to say, this target proved to be quite impossible to achieve and, frankly, because the gaps were now so large, many crews no longer needed to go flat out.

As it transpired, this was very much a 'schools out' type of occasion, as unless any of the cars had suffered as breakdown, then no significant changes in the order would have been possible. There was, however, time for a bit of team managers' gamesmanship to be played out, so British Leyland made sure that second-place man Brian Culcheth's Triumph was actually first to get into the stage, which theoretically meant that he would never encounter the hanging dust of a rally car in front of him, which might otherwise make him lose time. (Culcheth, on the other hand, was an 'old hand', and realised that this might mean him meeting the occasional truck, van, private car, or stray animal which had not already been frightened out of the way – so he drove carefully and took account of that).

BL team boss Peter Browning then made sure that Paddy Hopkirk's Triumph then set off second, which ensured that no car (no Ford Escort, in particular) could get through to challenge Culcheth without tackling two thick dust clouds.

As it transpired, the fastest time was set by Rauno Aaltonen, who waited for some time before he actually tackled the Prime, started a mere two minutes behind Culcheth on the Prime itself, caught and passed him in the middle of it, but clearly could not get clear.

He lost no fewer than 56 minutes on what was an impossible time schedule. Still irritated beyond measure by the mechanical problems which had taken so long to solve on the previous Prime, he had been hoping that he could catch up the 24 minutes by which he trailed Culcheth's Triumph. This, however, did not happen, for Culcheth was also still going flat out (as he reminded me, he had been at ten-tenths since the event had left Santiago in Chile many days previously ...), so he could only claw back three of those minutes, with Paddy Hopkirk three minutes further adrift.

Hannu Mikkola, for his part, knew just how far ahead of everyone else he actually was, was determined neither to crash, to meet any other vehicles, or to suffer punctures, and swept serenely through the 106 miles (170.6km). By his own admission, he was just cruising at this stage, enjoying the scenery, and went on to lose 71 minutes, which, in the context of the overall timing, was of no importance at all.

Hannu Mikkola confounded all the pundits by winning the World Cup Rally in such a composed manner. He had, after all, only won his first world class rally in mid-1968, did not take part in the London-Sydney Marathon, and had not competed in any long-distance event previously.

Prime 17: Oaxaca to Tuxtepec (Mexico) – the Aztec Prime
(Target: 106 miles/170.6km in 1hr 30 minutes)

Fastest times:

Crew	Car	Penalty (hours-mins)
R Aaltonen/H Liddon	Ford Escort 1850	0-56
B Culcheth/J Syer	Triumph 2.5PI	0-59
P Hopkirk/A Nash/N Johnston	Triumph 2.5PI	1-02
S Zasada/M Wachowski	Ford Escort 1850	1-09
H Mikkola/G Palm	Ford Escort 1850	1-11
T Makinen/G Staepelaere	Ford Escort 1850	1-12
A Fall/J Greaves	Ford Escort 1850	1-16
A Katz/A Kling/A Pfuhl	Mercedes-Benz 280SE	1-21
A Rees/H Thomas/W James	Hillman Hunter	1-23
T Kingsley/P Evans/M Scarlett	Austin Maxi	1-23
R Smith/A Watson/G Derolland	Austin Maxi	1-29
W Bendek/D Hubner/J Burgoa	BMW 2002ti	1-29
R Channon/R Cooper	Ford Lotus-Cortina	1-32
K Tubman/A Welinsky/B McAuley	BMC 1800	1-36

After finishing seventh overall, and winning the Private Entrant's Award, Patrick Vanson took out his Citroën DS21 for this stunning action shot.

So now, after weeks of concentration on awful roads, after climbing to great heights, suffering so much from a lack of oxygen at times, and having to deal with primitive motoring (and sometimes living) conditions, for 23 surviving rally crews, it really was almost all over. The run to the hillside resort of Fortin took up much of the afternoon and evening, which gave every surviving crew much time to reflect.

Not only had Hannu Mikkola driven at an absolutely blistering pace whenever it was essential, but he had also ridden his luck at all other times. With only one near-miss to report (a crumpled rear wheel arch extension told its own story ...), and only one mechanical mystery (the 'self-emptying'

dry sump tank) to worry about, he had an almost serene run from start to finish.

Controlled so capably by co-driver Gunnar Palm throughout the event (who once, let us not forget, threatened to bail out and fly home at an early stage if Hannu did not slow down considerably) he had settled the event by his performance in the Andes, but thereafter drove no faster than necessary. All of which was a great surprise to his rivals and – yes, he admitted it, but much later – to his team manager, who had originally looked on Hannu as the pace-maker, for he had thought that Rauno Aaltonen in particular, and maybe Timo Makinen, would be consistently faster.

To this day, second-placed man Brian Culcheth is convinced that he could have won the event, instead of taking second place as he did – no other competitor had prepared so well, so frequently, or in such detail, and none could have wrung the big Triumph's neck more competently than he did. Let's play down the rumours of other finishers being saved by 'illegal' transmission swapping, or the fact that it was only an 'act of God' that saw Ford's Escorts marooned on board the SS Derwent for two vital weeks, which gave Ford time to design, test and manufacture the rear axle braces that were to allow it to continue in South America. Without those braces, for sure, not a single Escort might have finished, in which case Culcheth would have been a worthy winner in what was undoubtedly a very sturdy car.

And why did Fleet Street's favourite, Paddy Hopkirk, not beat Culcheth? Except for the self-inflicted wound of crashing off the road just before the end of the South American section, for Paddy it was only the gradual accumulation of minutes, behind Culcheth, which made that certain. Mathematically, the extra weight of a third crew member, which must have affected performance, particularly at altitude, might just have made all the difference. Let's not forget, however, that third crew-member Neville Johnston 'paid for' his passage by stripping out the rear axle of the stricken Triumph before La Paz. Without the time that saved before BMC mechanics arrived on the scene, Paddy would have been late, and penalised, on arrival at that Control ...

As to the other Fords – Rauno Aaltonen deserved second place, not third, if only for the number of incidents and breakdowns that he had overcome along the way. Lesser mortals might have given in, but as Rauno said later: "A rally driver must never give in. Never. Never. Never. Henry and I were determined to finish while the car was still mobile. And we did ..." Timo Makinen, for his part, had suffered more than his share of mechanical dramas, Zasada had not been as fast, nor as lucky as forecast (maybe it was significant that he did not drive again for Ford ...).

Everyone, on the other hand, was full of praise for the way that Jimmy Greaves and Tony Fall ('The Unlikely Lads') kept going, kept on bodging up their car, and managed to stay friends throughout it all. Footballing superstar Greaves must have known that there was a more elegant and more pleasing way to reach the Aztec Stadium in Mexico City than in a battered rally car, but he never gave in, nor even threatened to fly home in disgust. And how many other footballing legends have ever taken a local bus through the Andes in the search for wheel and tyre repairs?

As to the others, Patrick Vanson, that smoothly-spoken and competent Citroën pilot thoroughly deserved the Private Entrant's prize (and the money which came with it!) for taking seventh place. Vanson, like every other Citroën team member, suffered from not having made a personal route survey, but on the other hand he was lucky enough to survive an accident on the horrible road down to sea level from Cali to Buenaventura.

Citroën, though, needed some luck, especially after rally leader René Trautmann had crashed out in dramatic style, after his old colleague and mentor Paul Coltelloni had suffered an awful accident, and after Claudine Trautmann's car had laid down and died after suffering for so long.

There were as many stories to tell, as there were finishers' medals. Rosemary Smith kept going when all about her were crashing, or suffered broken down cars. To complete the World Cup in an unproven type of car (the Maxi was a brand-new rally car, let's not forget) was one thing, but to do it so competently, gracefully, and in a good pace was quite another. Co-driver Ginette Derolland's illness (thought to be gastro-related) at one point was survived with great stoicism.

Three of the five Moskviches made it to the finish, and the rest of the world knew no more about them at the end than they had done in the beginning! With penalties of at least 25 hours (not minutes, but hours) more than the winning Escort, this flagged up just how much

Gounnar Kholm was one of the three Moskvich drivers who got their rugged Russian cars through to the end – taking 17th place.

Above: Although a Hillman Hunter had won the London-Sydney Marathon of 1968, the same cars had less luck on the World Cup of 1970. Alun Rees of Wales had a well-prepared Hunter, though, and finished 15th.

Left: Leonti Potapchick was very cheerful as he lined up at Wembley Stadium, ready to start the World Cup Rally. He would finish in a storming 12th place overall.

Right: Jean Denton's hard-working, but somewhat crumpled, BMC 1800 was sponsored as the 'Beauty Box' machine, but was in acute need of a make-over by the end of the event;
Far right: Gaston Perkins of Argentina made very few headlines on the World Cup itself, but used his Peugeot 404 well – cars like this had already won the Safari more than once – to finish 19th.

Rauno Aaltonen, third overall in his Escort, receives a colourful welcome at Fortin, the end of the final competitive section in the World Cup Rally.

Two ecstatic, but exhausted heroes at the end of the World Cup Rally –
Hannu Mikkola (left) and Gunnar Palm. The same duo would win the East
African Safari in 1972 – after which Palm retired from the sport.

the Moskvich was lacking in performance, but the crew made up for much
of this with their cheerful determination.

It was the cars at the back – Janssen with his Datsun 1600SSS, which
seemed to be rebuilt (maybe re-manufactured, or certainly reassembled,
would also be appropriate ...); the Red Arrows Maxi (which was so far
behind the other Maxis that the British Leyland mechanics saw less of
it than they might); and the gallantly-driven, much-rebuilt Escort GT of
Doug Harris and Mike Butler, which was the source of much gossip at
Fortin.

Doug Harris and Mike Butler kept plodding along, in their 1.3-litre Escort,
eventually finishing 23rd and last in the World Cup Rally. They had no
outside assistance, and deserved all the plaudits that came their way.

The Red Arrows Austin Maxi was battered, but patiently and lovingly repaired by the mechanics, to allow it to finish the event, in 22nd place. In a way, the crew was disappointed that it could qualify as 23rd and last!

Fortin was in party mood when the World Cup crews arrived, with many of the locals dressed in native costume, and ready to celebrate anything for which an excuse could be found. John Sprinzel and I were rostered to run the Time Control, but on this occasion there was no idling around for hours, and time to be killed.

No fewer than 21 of the 23 cars arrived at Fortin within an hour of the Control opening, and the other two – the Red Arrows Maxi, and Harris' Escort – were known to be some distance away. But who would be last?

"Actually," Mike Scarlett told me many years later, "in the Red Arrows Maxi we thought we might be the last finisher – and there was to be a prize for that! We stayed up late at Fortin, hoping that no-one else would come. We knew that Doug Harris, in a privately-entered Escort, was still out there somewhere. By 02.00hr he still hadn't arrived, so we went to bed happy. Then we got up again, we found that Doug had arrived at about 08.00hr, and he was last after all ..."

So now it was party time ...

9

Party time

Although some of the organising team (myself included) had to man the Time Control at Fortin until the end of the event, for everyone else it was truly party time. After six weeks and 16,000 miles (25,750km) of motoring, at last it was time to relax. Fortin to Mexico City? Well, that was tomorrow's problem, and that could wait, right? A few (only a few?) tequilas were waiting to be sunk before then, and anyway, the morrow would bring a strictly controlled convoy run behind important Mexican police chiefs and dignitaries, mainly on speed-limited motorways. That was the official theory, at least ...

Oh really? Maybe the organisers hoped that they could keep everything in order, but John Sprinzel knew full well that high spirits were just waiting to be unleashed, and he must have feared what was to follow on 27 May.

Officially, the Time Control at Fortin would not close until 12.00hr on 27 May (which was precisely the time at which the run into Mexico City was due to start), but this was always going to be a theoretical 'last minute' concession. As it happened, all but two of the gallant runners who had survived the final day, and the last Prime of all, arrived soon after the Control opened up on the previous evening. In the meantime, rally officials kept in touch with events at the Aztec Prime Arrival Control, Tuxtepec, and knew that the last two competitors would be very late – but would still qualify.

Breaking almost every rule that the FIA could no doubt have applied if it had known it was happening, the organisers either went off to party, or retired to bed, leaving a note at the reception desk of the hotel which effectively said: "When you arrive, call us, and we will clock you in!" Their sleep was little disturbed: Robert Janssen's battered Datsun rolled up at about 02.00hr, having completed an eventful event by scraping along the side of a truck, and destroying most of the right hand side of his car, but nothing else disturbed their rest.

In the meantime, for others the party went on all night, for the very last official finisher (the plucky Escort 1300GT of Doug Harris and Mike Butler) did not arrive until 08.00hr, by which time the rallying world was still coming rather blearily back to life. Doug and Mike had missed a phenomenal party, where any number of competitors (and those team managers and organisers who could not see what might happen) had ended up in the swimming pool, fully dressed and neither ready nor willing to take an impromptu swim.

The morning after the night before, the 23 finishers (many of them nursing hangovers, sometimes of heroic proportion) lined up behind two police cars and a handful of officials. Although there were still 200 miles (321.9km) to go, the Road Book called this a Neutralised Section, which was probably just as well. I can do no better than quote from my own words, penned at the time:

"Fortin to Mexico's Aztec Stadium was over 200 miles (321.9km) and, against all the better judgement of the enthusiasts on the committee, a convoy was planned for the day. This meant that happy and exuberant rally crews were expected to drive sedately in line astern behind two police cars and a couple of officials [I was one of them] all the way to the city."

John Sprinzel, glad to see a successful end to this monumental event, was in a Dodge Dart hire car, the President of the Mexican motoring association ANA (Automóvil Club de Mexico) was in his own car, and in theory the police cars were there to ensure that fair play and common sense prevailed. Although British Leyland did not have the representation in this country to conjure up 'official' cars, Ford most certainly did, and had not only found an up-to-date, massive Galaxie saloon, but had even arranged for its UK boss, Bill Batty, to arrive in time to join the fun – while Ford's photographer (the intrepid Ken Shipton, who seemed to have popped up anywhere and everywhere in previous weeks) was actually sitting in the open boot of the Galaxie, taking pictures of the boisterous rally drivers and their cars behind him.

"The truth of the matter is that almost everyone was as good as gold, maintaining station where publicity demanded it, and sucking along in their wake a long tail of service cars, practice cars, press, mechanics and local enthusiasts. All in all, the convoy, most spiritedly led by police at a highly illegal 70mph/112.7kph (for a 50mph/80.5kph toll road, that is) must have totalled about 60 cars and, from the comments at the finish, must have been very exciting in the middle of the pack: it is always more difficult to trail in a convoy, than to lead it. Trucks imperiously waved into the side of the road by the mobile police may have expected two or three VIP cars to break through, but this was just ridiculous.

"On the dual carriageway stretches nearer Mexico City the experts got rather bored and spent some time formatting in four-abreast or Vic formation for the benefit of *Daily Mirror* photographers [Paddy Hopkirk's

'Now, let's get this convoy into some sort of order!' This was the scene just before the ceremonial run into Mexico City, from Fortin, actually began. Hannu Mikkola's winning Escort is only partly in shot, Bran Culcheth's second place Triumph (no 88) is behind it, with Rauno Aaltonen's Escort (no 46) behind that.

The ceremonial drive into Mexico City started from Fortin. At this point the exhilarated drivers were still behaving themselves – I was actually travelling in the 'big American' on the left of the group, but ...

big Triumph being one of the first to break ranks], one formation suddenly becoming very lively when Timo Makinen dropped a fizzing fire extinguisher through the open window of Rauno Aaltonen's Escort. Rauno promptly passed it across the car, where Henry Liddon politely handed it on to another Escort – that of Tony Fall – which was formatting alongside! Just in fun, you understand – and this must have been one of the finest officially-approved, and officially-policed open road races yet seen ..."

It was all very fast, with the convoy running at illegal (for this toll road) speeds, but as the police cars at the head were setting the pace, no-one seemed to be perturbed about this. Not only that, but for this occasion, the toll barriers had all been lifted, so that the convoy had a high-speed free run to the outskirts of the city.

Hannu Mikkola recalls going just as carefully and smoothly as possible (he was not about to join in the same party tricks as Timo Makinen had started, and anyway he was nursing a hangover – (the reinvented, teetotal, version of Hannu was still some years into the future ...) but he did get involved in one rather unsavoury moment, as Rauno Aaltonen recalls:

"Later Hannu, me and a third Ford were driving along this motorway quite normally, and suddenly a Mexican VW Beetle arrived, with five or six people in it. They kept carving about between us, making rude signs. By this time we were not under stress, and there was nothing to lose, so I nudged the rear corner of the Beetle, spun him half way round. and then slowed down to give him space. Hannu saw this in his mirror, carried out an emergency braking manoeuvre, so the spinning VW hit Hannu's car a

... one or two drivers were getting bored, and all manner of over- and undertaking was about to take place. Two of the 'works' Escorts, and Patrick Vanson's Citroën, are in shot, with several private motorists muscling in on the act. They would shortly be muscled out of line by exuberant drivers ...

'Keep in order, boys' – this was the ceremonial run in, en route to Mexico City. This picture is taken out of the back window of Brian Culcheth's second place car, closely followed by Aaltonen's Escort, Hopkirk's damaged Triumph, Makinen's Escort following, and the Greaves/Fall Escort bringing up the rear.

Gilbert Staepelaere (Timo Makinen's co-driver), and Jimmy Greaves, after it was all over, in Mexico City.

little, which made him spin even more – and at this moment I again gave him a little push. I think that between us we managed to make him spin twice more. He left everyone alone after that ..."

In sporting terms, it was a tragedy that hard-done-by competitors like Claudine Trautmann (whose Citroën DS21 had expired less than a day and 300 miles/482.8km from Fortin) could not stagger to the official finish, but it was amazing that so many crews (including the indefatigable Bill Bengry in the Rolls-Royce) managed to make it all the way up the spine of South America in spite of being officially out of the event.

City cavalcade

But still it was not quite all over. As the convoy reached city limits, it was finally persuaded to get back into something like classification and single file order, and await new official shepherding. A different group of police, this time on smart American-built Harley-Davidson motorcycles, took over the sheep dogging duties, and set off on circuitous, but picturesque, tour of the boulevards surrounding the city centre itself – this being necessary to channel the cavalcade from its entry from the east, to the Aztec Stadium, which was several miles out on the south side of down-town Mexico City.

Organised chaos, perhaps, or just chaos? This was the ceremonial procession of rally cars, on its way from Fortin to Mexico City. At this precise moment, Hannu Mikkola's car appears to be under the control of two police Harley-Davidson motorcycles.

Parc Fermé at Fortin before the run into Mexico City began, with some very battered cars in the line-up. Rob Janssen's Datsun 1600SSS was a moving wreck by this point, and the miracle is that it even made it to the end!

Corny, maybe, but good for a headline! After their arrival at the Aztec Stadium in Mexico City, Tony Fall (left) and Jimmy Greaves hand over a turf from Wembley Stadium. F1 World Champion Graham Hill is in the background.

According to the Road Book, four hours had been allowed to get from Fortin to Mexico city limits, though everyone comfortably beat that, while just one more hour was allowed for this automotive snake to reach the Stadium itself. All well and good, you might say, except that the roads were not closed off to other traffic, the pace was quite brisk – and at this moment, too, it began to rain.

As my *Motoring News* report on this harumscarum occasion noted:

"Met at city limits by fleets of police motorcyclists, the rally cars were then taken on a whirlwind and considerably frightening tour of the city, in which they were encouraged to shoot red lights, to drive at speeds of 70mph (112.6kph) or even more, and generally behave in an antisocial way unthinkable in Britain or Europe. That there were no serious shunts is a minor miracle, though one or local cowboys received 'accidental' scrapes on their front fenders when they tried to muscle in on the act ..."

The 'act' was faithfully recorded by Rob McAuley of Australia's camera, who was given special dispensation not to travel in Ken Tubman's BMC 1800 (in which he had completed the event), while Ken Shipman was finally pitched out of the open boot of the Galaxie as it crossed a particularly bumpy stretch of local street: although Ken sprained a wrist, he calmly carried on taking pictures until he could be rescued by another car!

By now, though, it really was all over, and every rally car (including Rauno Aaltonen with a flat tyre on his Escort ...) made it to the car parks outside the Aztec Stadium. True to its whole-hearted support for the event which it

Hannu Mikkola and Gunnar Palm are surrounded by well-wishers at the finish, at the Aztec Stadium in Mexico City. F1 World Champion Graham Hill is on the right of this group.

Victory is very sweet – Hannu Mikkola (right) and Gunnar Palm, on the roof of their Ford Escort, at the Aztec Stadium, in Mexico City.

had sponsored, the *Daily Mirror* arranged for double F1 World Champion Graham Hill to greet crews at the finish, along with the FA's (the Football Association) elder statesman Sir Stanley Rous, along with Edward Pickering (Chairman of the IPC Magazine Division – which owned the *Daily Mirror* at the time).

And that, almost, was that. Hannu and Gunnar posed with Graham Hill, champagne was sprayed, garlands were awarded, photographs were taken, and the sizeable crowd (who were, frankly, more interested in seeing Jimmy Greaves than they were in seeing Hannu!) cheered, waved, and generally added to the atmosphere. There was, of course, no likelihood of any car eligibility problems – the very generously-worded regulations, which allowed all manner of modifications, had seen to that many months earlier – so the event could soon turn to celebration all round.

Everyone who finished, one might say, was a winner at this level,

Hannu Mikkola, Ford-UK Managing Director Bill Batty, and Gunnar Palm, at the finish Control in Mexico City. Success has just begun to sink in ...

'It's over at last – let the celebrations begin!' – or was Ford mechanic Mick Jones, atop the Escort of Rauno Aaltonen, saying something much more basic? This was the Aztec Stadium, in Mexico City, and it really was all over.

Left to right: Patrick Vanson, Olivier Turcat and Alain Leprince looking smooth and relaxed in front of the Citroën DS21 which eventually won the Private Entrant's Award. The pristine condition of the car must mean that this shot was taken in Europe before the gruelling motoring really began.

Hannu Mikkola wasting a bottle of good champagne after the finish of the World Cup Rally. Left to right: Rauno Aaltonen, Henry Liddon, Gunnar Palm, Hannu Mikkola, Gilbert Staepelaere and Timo Makinen. FEV 4H was driven into fifth place by Timo and Gilbert.

whether it was the Ford or the big Triumphs at the front, or whether it was Janssen's Datsun, the Red Arrows' Maxi, or Doug Harris' Ford Escort GT at the rear. When the time came to hand out the prizes, there was genuine sympathy for Claudine Trautmann, who looked certain to win the Ladies' Prize in her Citroën DS21 until the very last day.

Special applause greeted Rosemary Smith, who finally lifted that Ladies' Prize, while rowing along a rather uncompetitive Austin Maxi, and

dealing with crew illness on the way, and for Patrick Vanson of France, who won the Private Entrant's Award in his factory-built Citroën DS21.

There was also genuine pleasure in seeing special awards going to Rob Janssen, for somehow keeping the battered Datsun going to the end of the event, and to that gentlemanly Australian, Ken Tubman, who sacrificed a higher position by spending three hours on the spot at the scene of the Cowan accident, to see what help he could give.

The morning after the finish (left to right) Rauno Aaltonen, Gunnar Palm, Bill Batty (Managing Director, Ford of Britain), Hannu Mikkola and Stuart Turner (Ford Competitions Manager) talk to the media about the event.

The *Daily Mirror* summed up perfectly, on its back page, when the event had finished: 'Magnificent Mikkola' was its splash, which was all that needed to be said ...

That said, the prize giving and banquet which surrounded these ceremonies was quite shambolic. The sponsors seemed to be more interested in impressing each other, along with local club officials, rather than in congratulating the hardy crews, the presenter/MC was singularly badly briefed, and didn't seem to care about that, while no-one seemed ready, able, or even willing to congratulate the core of the organising team for the magnificent job they had done.

After the win, the press calls began. This was Ford-UK's Managing Director, Bill Batty, with Hannu Mikkola, Stuart Turner and Gunnar Palm, in Mexico City.

The top three Ford Escorts in the World Cup Rally, and their crew, celebrate after the event. Left to right: Rauno Aaltonen, Henry Liddon, Gunnar Palm, Hannu Mikkola, Gilbert Staepelaere and Timo Makinen.

Perhaps the biggest insult of all, which was only rectified by Sprinzel himself at the last moment, was that no invitation to the celebrations had been originally extended to Wylton Dickson, who was finally whisked out from London to Mexico City at the last minute, on the very afternoon of the ball.

In the end it fell to the Private Owner prize winner, Patrick Vanson – who was, and is, not only a very competent rally enthusiast, but a consummate professional when it came to running such occasions in his own business – to do those honours. He got a huge response – which put the official attitudes to shame. When that happened, even Sprinzel, a seasoned rally veteran on the one hand, and still exhausted on the other, was delighted to see that it had all been worthwhile.

After the ball …

When the dust had settled, the last bottle of champagne had been drunk, and publicity had turned sharply towards the football World Cup, the *Daily*

WELL-EARNED PRAISE

When it was all over, Ford-UK's chairman, Stanley Gillen, was so relieved to see the result, that he penned this note to Stuart Turner:

"All of us here have watched your progress to Mexico with great excitement. Every morning the first thing we have looked for was yesterday's rally results.

"The whole company – right across Europe – has been behind you and we have had many messages from the Companies on the Continent.

"It is difficult to know who to single out for praise because I know that the drivers and the mechanics have been up against some very hard physical conditions. You too, of course. But I think that, above all, this has been a triumph of organisation and I know that you are entirely responsible for this.

"So, many congratulations. We are very proud of you and your men – so please give them my regards too.

Very sincerely,

STANLEY GILLEN"

FORD'S WORLD CUP – THE COST OF WINNING

With Stuart Turner's permission, I have quoted a passage from his best-selling autobiography Twice Lucky, *which shows that fortune follows the brave:*

"An ideal result? Well, yes, but although Ford's Managing Director, Bill Batty flew out to Mexico City to greet the winners, and Ford made a film called Five for the Fiesta, *I got back to find a crisis over costs waiting on my desk! In the nine months leading up to the event, it seems, we had spent £127,666 – some £87,666 (or 220 per cent) over budget – and questions being asked were: 'How did I account for this? And where is the money to come from?'*

"I could account for it easily enough, but while I thought that £4,500 insurance for Jimmy Greaves, £10,000 for special charter aircraft to get the cars back to the UK for magazine tests, and £9,900 for 900 new Minilite wheels was all justified, there were those who gulped at the sums.

"If nothing else, the post mortem showed me how carefully Ford monitored its spending, and how it always wanted to get top value. I also realised that as far as the finance people were concerned, the worst crime I could commit was to go back and ask for more money.

"But I recall this as a 'tut tut' rather than a 'this is terrible' session with the accountants (it might have been a lot more painful if we hadn't won), but we still had to make serious cuts in the programme for the rest of the year ..."

In recent years, I have been privileged to study original documents covering this crisis. Naturally it was Walter Hayes who poured oil on troubled waters, by pointing out that: "This overrun situation is a little hard on Ford of Britain because they are standing the whole cost of the World Cup Rally, although the benefits have been just as great in places as far away as South Africa and Australia ..."

The same documents add more detail to those sums just quoted above – and include the cost of building seven rally cars (£14,000), rally car and driver costs on the event (£6,840), and the cost of airfares for recces, management and mechanics (£16,600). To get a feel for these costs at modern currency levels, and the challenge of mounting a truly serious effort becomes clear. Stuart Turner makes it clear that, in his opinion, if Ford had not won the event so convincingly, then he might just have lost his job.

Over at British Leyland, as we now know, Competition Manager Peter Browning had similar fiscal challenges, and an even more difficult task in convincing his chairman, Lord Stokes, that finishing second and fourth overall, plus winning the Ladies' Prize, had all been worth it.

Mirror had a chance to reflect. Although there is no doubt that they had reaped an enormous amount of coverage and publicity (there seemed to be headlines in the sports pages on most days ...) it was also clear that the paper had spent a great deal of money.

How much money? That was never made clear, but it was certainly well north of the £250,000 (in 1970-value currency) which was originally mentioned. So had it all been worth it?

Although the *Mirror* was well used to spending highly on promotion, this had obviously been an extremely major operation (one only had to survey the day-after-day coverage to appreciate that). But was it all worth it? Let's just say that the *Mirror* never again backed such a grandiose motoring project – and one doubts very much that anyone ever dared to ask ...

Ford, of course, was absolutely delighted with the result, for if the Escort had never again won an event, the amazing success that it had on the World Cup reinforced a sporting reputation that it would never lose. This is emphasised by the alacrity with which Walter Hayes arranged for Ford-of-Britain Managing Director Bill Batty to fly out to Mexico City, and the beaming smiles of the posed 'tea party' in the grounds of the HQ hotel tell their own story. (Or was it that Hayes already knew just how much Ford had overspent its budget, and was determined to head off the criticism before it even erupted ...?)

Once it had won the World Cup Rally, Ford was very proud of FEV 1H, and has kept it around as a 'family pet' ever since. Here, in 1985, it was posed, at Boreham, with an early example of formidable Group B RS200 rally car. There was no question of a replica being built, of course – for the FEV 1H which survives to this day is the real deal. Ford's Bill Meade, who was mainly responsible for engineering the Escort, is in the dark anorak at the nearside of the RS200.

LONDON TO MEXICO IN 1995 – RE-CREATING AN EPIC

Twenty five years after the real, the unique, and the only, London-Mexico World Cup Rally had been run-off, celebrated motorsport entrepreneur Nick Brittan set out to organise a rerun. Because of the age of eligible cars, factory teams were not involved, and not even Nick could organise an event which included every feature of the original. As a result, the only car with a resemblance to a 'works' entry was a 16-valve BDA-engined Escort (registered H1 FEV – a genuine purchase by Ford, to nearly replicate the priceless 1970 winning-car), which was prepared by David Sutton's experienced historic business, and was driven by Hannu Mikkola and Gunnar Palm.

A much simpler route than the original, with no fewer than 42 short special stages, started from the Ramada Hotel at Heathrow Airport on 22 April 1995, and led directly to Spain and Portugal, before the cars were flown across the South Atlantic from Lisbon, in gargantuan Antonov aircraft, before restarting from Rio de Janeiro in Brazil. After that they visited Brazil, Paraguay, Argentina (but only just), Bolivia, Peru, Ecuador and Colombia, on the way to the Colombian port of Cartagena. After a ferry trip to Panama, the survivors then drove up the spine of Central America, to finish at the ritzy Mexican resort of Acapulco on 21 May. Compared with 1970, there were many night/rest halts, and road conditions were much smoother and less damaging than before.

According to the rather vaguely-worded regulations, eligibility for this event was restricted to 'classic' cars of a type which were in production when the original World Cup Rally was promoted in 1970, and – again according to the regulations – organised service and 'flying mechanics' were not allowed. That ruling seemed to have been circumvented in more than one case.

Because of the costs involved, only 59 cars took the start, with Hannu Mikkola and Roger Clark (both in newly-built '25 year old' Mk I Escorts) at the front. Ross Dunkerton and Bruce Hodgson of Australia, Tony Fall, and disabled F1 driver Clay Regazzoni were in the list, along with ex-Red Arrows pilot (and 1970 Maxi driver) Terry Kingsley: amazingly, though there were numerous Ford Escorts, not a single Triumph 2.5PI started the event.

After a series of heart-stopping mechanical problems (which at one time apparently involved a cylinder head gasket change on the complex BDA engine – by the crew themselves! – victory once again went to Hannu Mikkola, who had been reunited with Gunnar Palm for the first time in 23 years. Ross Dunkerton (Datsun 240Z) was second, Dean Rainsford's Ford Mustang was third and Janos Balazs' Porsche 911 was fourth.

No fewer than 45 of the 59 starters made it to the finish, which tells us much about the more relaxed nature and time schedule of the event. Joint-favourite Roger Clark (co-driven by Tony Moy) was not among them, for his engine overheated in Brazil, after just nine stages.

Brittan, they say, lost a lot of money in mounting that enterprise, and certainly no-one else has ever tried again to revive the event in South America!

Some ended up looking smarter than others – Fred Katz's big Mercedes-Benz looks tidier than the Red Arrows' Austin Maxi, but, as you might expect, Rosemary Smith's red-and-white Maxi looks neater than all of them.

Not only that, but there seems to be no doubt that Ford's feat in winning the world's toughest rally in what was effectively a very simple Escort, complete with a 'Kent' overhead valve engine was a great influence on the speedy work which went into creating a new model – the Escort Mexico. The styling people looked long and hard at the striping livery (in various different ways) which had appeared on the Escort rally cars, and it is therefore no coincidence that the *Telegraph Magazine* livery which graced Mikkola's car was virtually replicated on the Mexico road cars which followed in December 1970.

Stuart Turner, of course, was vastly relieved

In 2003, the World Cup-winning Escort was brought out of retirement, and driven up the hill at the Goodwood Festival of Speed ...

(see the sidebar on page 189 for details of a huge financial overspend), and to this day is sure that the World Cup victory led to the launch of the Mexico car, the Mexico Racing Challenge, and the Mexico Rally Championship, which gave great momentum to Ford's Advanced Vehicle Organisation (AVO) network, which was expanding hard at that time.

Although British Leyland returned from Mexico with a much-enhanced reputation for running unfamiliar cars (both the Triumph PI and the Maxi were little-known to it when it began work on the project), the phenomenal effort in taking second and fourth places in among the phalanx of Escorts was never totally appreciated by British Leyland management, yet it was an amazing achievement.

People in Berkeley Square presumably subscribed to the American saying that 'second place is for the first of the losers ...' – which was extremely unfair, and unkind. It has to be said, however, that British Leyland

... looking just as good, and as purposeful, as ever.

made the most of the success when they got back to London, mounting a magnificent post-rally party at the Royal Lancaster Hotel, congratulating all the crews, and making the most of what had been achieved.

Although one can see why finance-orientated directors blanched when they looked at the finalised accounts which Abingdon presented to them for approval, but the fact is that to win, this was always going to be an enterprise where it helped to have a budget of 'bottomless-pit' proportions.

Even so, it can be no coincidence that, within weeks, the decision came down from high, that the world-famous BMC/British Leyland Competitions Department was to be closed down, after which it was almost inevitable that team boss Peter Browning would also resign.

In later years there would be (slightly) longer events, but none ever attracted the serious battle between factory teams which had been a feature of this one, none of them was a slickly organised, and none of them seemed to

Famous car, equally famous driver? In 2003, at Goodwood, FEV 1H was driven up the hill by no less a driver than Malcolm Wilson, who had already been running Ford's World Rally Team for some years.

have considered every eventuality, and vagary of weather, road conditions, and political realities. For all those reasons, the *Daily Mirror* World Cup Rally was unique, and it was a real pleasure and privilege for everyone – competitors, sponsors, teams and officials, even to be involved.

The very last word goes to John Sprinzel himself:

"I honestly thought that we – all of us, including the *Daily Mirror* – did a good job in making the 1970 World Cup happen, and bringing in

such a high standard that there are still people today whose eyes light up and sparkle when the event is mentioned.

"If I have one regret, it is that we couldn't schedule any Prime at a target average of 100mph (160.9kph) or more – and yet people achieved more than that on Primes in Argentina and Uruguay!

"I was never tempted to try again. I figured that we could never repeat it. I just didn't think we would be that lucky twice ..."

Final results — Mexico City — 27 May 1970

Place	Crew	Car	Penalty (hours-mins)
1	Hannu Mikkola/Gunnar Palm	Ford Escort 1850	9-07
2	Brian Culcheth/Johnstone Syer	Triumph 2.5PI	10-25
3	Rauno Aaltonen/Henry Liddon	Ford Escort 1850	10-46
4	Paddy Hopkirk/Tony Nash/Neville Johnston	Triumph 2.5PI	12-26
5	Timo Makinen/Gilbert Staepelaere	Ford Escort 1850	14-31
6	Jimmy Greaves/Tony Fall	Ford Escort 1850	19-31
7	Patrick Vanson/Olivier Turcat/Alain Leprince	Citroën DS21	22-03
8	Sobieslaw Zasada/Mark Wachowski	Ford Escort 1850	23-59
9	Reg Redgrave/Phil Cooper/Bob Freeborough	BMC 1800	24-42
10	Rosemary Smith/Alice Watson/Ginette Derolland	Austin Maxi	30-35
11	Ken Tubman/Andrew Welenski/Bob McAuley	BMC 1800	32-36
12	Leonti Potapchik/Edouard Bazhenov/Youri Lesovski	Moskvich 412	34-06
13	William Bendek/Dieter Hubner/Jorge Burgoa	BMW 2002ti	35-14
14	Ron Channon/Rod Cooper	Ford Lotus-Cortina Mk II	36-43
15	Alun Rees/Hywel Thomas/Washington James	Hillman Hunter	37-50
16	Alfred Katz/Alfred Kling/Albert Pfuhl	Mercedes-Benz 280SE	38-05
17	Gounnar Kholm/Vladimir Boubnov/Kastytis Girdauskas	Moskvich 412	38-52
18	Jean Denton/Patricia Wright/Liz Crellin	BMC 1800	39-16
19	Gaston Perkins/Jack Greene	Peugeot 404	40-46
20	Serguel Tenichev/Valentin Kislykh/Valeri Chirochenkov	Moskvich 412	41-05
21	Robert Janssen/Jacob Dik	Datsun 1600SSS	46-01
22	Terry Kingsley/Peter Evans/Michael Scarlett	Austin Maxi	46-25
23	Doug Harris/Michael Butler	Ford Escort GT	66-08

– three other cars, which had reached Buenaventura, but not Fortin and Mexico City, also qualified as finishers:

Claudine Trautmann/Colette Perrier Citroën DS21
J Hemsley/WJ Easton Peugeot 504
P Coltelloni/I Marang Citroën DS21

The author — a personal marathon

From the day I got John Sprinzel's phone call in 1969, to the day I walked back into my workplace in June 1970, I lived, breathed, and thought about little else but the World Cup Rally. At the time it was the most enthralling motoring adventure I had ever tackled – and it still is.

Along with other lucky and (frankly) very hard-working travelling controllers on this event, there was much excitement, many unforgettable experiences, an amazing number of startling vistas, crowds, ceremonies, airports and border controls to be endured – but at the time, somehow, there never seemed to be time to sit back, relax, and enjoy it all.

Because I was a salaried employee in the motor industry in those days, I had to take all my annual leave in one lump, and beg off a few days unpaid leave into the bargain, even to make this schedule possible – which explains why I had to high-tail it back to work, from Lisbon, in the middle of the event, for the two weeks when the rally cars were entombed in the SS Derwent as it crossed the South Atlantic.

Accordingly, I notice from my schedule that my only real 'down time' came in Lima, Peru, towards the end of the event. Otherwise I was on the move, working, or preparing to make another move. Fifteen flights, and 15 nations in six weeks? Was it a record? Not at all, for I know that stalwarts like Bill Price of British Leyland completed 44 separate flights in 11 different aircraft, three of which were privately hired!

Maybe I didn't work as hard as the competitors themselves, but this was my personal schedule in those weeks:

Saturday, 18 April 1970: In London, at pre-event scrutineering

Sunday, 19 April: At the start in Wembley Stadium, London.

Monday, 20 April: Flew to Sofia, Bulgaria (via an aircraft change in Prague).

Tuesday, 21 April: Running the Control at Sofia, Bulgaria

Wednesday, 22 April: Flight from Sofia to Milan, Italy.
    Then: Running the Arrival Control at Monza, near Milan. Cars in Parc Fermé overnight.

Thursday, 23 April: Flew from Milan to Lisbon, Portugal.

Saturday, 25 April: Running the Arrival Control at Lisbon.

Sunday, 26 April: Flew back to the UK, and back to work for two weeks!
    In the meantime, rally cars were in transit across the South Atlantic, on the SS Derwent.

Thursday, 8 May: Flew overnight, from London to Lisbon, then Lisbon to Rio de Janeiro, Brazil.

Friday, 8 May: Cars unloaded from the SS Derwent at the docks in Rio de Janeiro. Running the Departure Control from the dockside, ready for cars to leave for down-town Rio.
(Evening): In a group at the official restart from downtown Rio de Janeiro.

Saturday, 9 May: Flew from Rio de Janeiro to Montevideo (Uruguay), via São Paulo

Sunday, 10 May: Running the Arrival Control at Montevideo.

Monday, 11 May: After the overnight halt, flew from Montevideo to Buenos Aires (Argentina). Then took a hire car to Saladillo, south-west of Buenos Aires.
(Evening): Running the Start Control of the Pampas Prime.
Then drove back to Buenos Aires.

Tuesday, 12 May: Flew from Buenos Aires to Santiago (Chile).

Wednesday, 13 May: Running a closed-to-service-crews Service Park in Santiago.

Thursday, 14 May: After overnight halt, at Departure Control from Santiago.
Then flew to Salta, in northern Argentina, picked up a hire car, and drove on to La Vina, the end of the Gran Premio Prime.

Friday, 15 May: Running the Arrival Control at the end of the Rodeo-La Vina Prime.
Then down to the hospital in Salta to check up on the injured Cowan/Coyle/Ossio crew.

Saturday, 16 May: Flew from Salta to La Paz (Bolivia) in a British Leyland-hired private aircraft.
Later: Helping run the Arrival Control (for the overnight halt) at La Paz.

Sunday, 17 May: Flew from La Paz to Lima (Peru).

Monday, 18 May: Running the Arrival Control in Lima, prior to the overnight halt.

Tuesday, 19 May: Running the Departure Control from Lima

Saturday, 23 May: Flew from Lima to Panama City (Panama).

Sunday, 24 May: Took a hire car to Cristobal Dockyard. Ran Neutralised Section Control (for Cristobal to Panama City sector).

Monday, 25 May: Flew from Panama to Mexico City (Mexico), then took a hire car back to Fortin, east of Mexico City.

Tuesday, 26 May/Wednesday, 27 May: Along with John Sprinzel, ran Arrival Control at Fortin, the end of the competitive section of the event.

Wednesday, 27 May: Rode in cavalcade of cars from Fortin to the Aztec Stadium in Mexico City. Then to the final hotel, then to the dinner/celebration in Mexico City itself.

Thursday, 28 May/Friday, 29 May: Flew back to UK by BOAC, via Nassau and Bermuda.

– and then, from the following Monday, back to work after an unforgettable experience ...

Aftermath

When the leading teams and individuals returned to Europe, those who had been successful basked in the glory of great publicity, and those who had not, licked their wounds and wondered how to put the best gloss on it all.

Ford, naturally, made the most of their famous victory. No sooner had the winning Escort, FEV 1H, returned to the UK, then it was refreshed (though by no means completely rebuilt), and loaned to the leading magazines for them to enjoy. This is an edited extract of what *Motor's* Michael Bowler had to say after trying it out in Southern England:

It could have been one of those nasty cheap imitations that spring up in the dealers' showrooms after such a success, but it wasn't. It had that air of well-used dustiness which no aerosol can imitate, the half-empty Thermos flasks hanging on the back seat, the biscuits, the mechanical noises all telling the tale of two men and 16,000 miles (25,750km). Ford were so impressed with the condition of the winning Escort that they fed it straight to *Motor* after only the briefest of checks to make sure it was legal.

We filled up the middle of three tanks at Brentford [this was the location of Ford's press fleet garage ...] and drove straight across the centre of London in heavy traffic on a stifling day – the tank had a slight leak and smelt. To a car that had scaled the heights of the Andes and roared across the plains of the Argentine, London presented no problems. It was just as happy to inch its way forward in the queues as any other car. Tick-over was a bit fluffy as the Webers needed adjusting, and the exhaust system needed attention, but it didn't boil (standard fan and standard-looking radiator) and the plugs didn't oil up.

Even in that first short spell it was obviously extremely comfortable. Superb hammock seats hold you all the way up your back and the ride was remarkably good with none of the jerky stiffness that one expects from a competition car. For obvious reasons, it was a left-hand-drive car and the major controls were ideally placed: one expects that the co-driver does complex things like deciding which light switch to operate. The clutch was quite firm but un-juddery, the brakes heavy despite twin-circuit braking with two servos, and the accelerator required a hefty push to prop the butterflies open. The gearbox was superb – a ZF five-speed box (homologated for Group 2) with a Porsche-like gate ...

Despite its five speeds it is geared to do only 16.5mph/1000rpm (26.6kph/1000rpm), which means it lost out considerably to the Triumphs on maximum speed, but gained on acceleration, particularly with its light weight, and high but reliable output of 140bhp at 6000rpm.

As tested, the car was on its Goodyear Rally Special tyres – similar to the G800 Grand Prix. For standing starts it paid to get them spinning and keeping the engine above 5000rpm for the best figures.

The first time we exceeded 80mph (128.7kph) it produced the major sounds of a hard life – propshaft vibration. Between 80 to 100mph (128.7 to 160.9kph) it rumbled and howled like a dervish, but it was suddenly all peaceful again for relaxed 100mph (160.9kph) cruising. The engine sounded fine, there was little wind noise, and nothing rattled in the suspension department. No doubt crash hats kill off all the noises on special stages, not to mention the rocks bouncing off the underside, but on any normal surface it was impossibly noisy between 80 and 100mph (128.7 and 160.9kph).

The suspension has been drastically modified, not only to give a less tiring ride, but also to keep the wheels on the ground even when bumpy. But larger suspension movements also meant more roll; and with huge tyres on very wide Minilites, the grip was high enough to produce a lot ...

The preparation was certainly very good because this car hardly suffered at all, apart from occasional damper changes and the bracing required after Europe to stop the rear axle splitting. Durability and the first class pair of Mikkola and Palm led to a victory by over an hour from the Culcheth/Syer Triumph. A remarkable achievement.

Incidentally, even in its after-16,000 mile (25,750km) condition, *Motor* found that the Escort reached 60mph (96.6kph) in 8.9 seconds, 0-100mph (0-160.9kph) in 29.5 seconds, and reckoned that it would reach 114mph (183.5kph) at 7,000rpm in fifth gear. All these times were broadly comparable, by the way, with those of a standard RS1600 road car.

Whatever happened to ... ?

The drivers and their cars

The winners

Hannu Mikkola (Finnish, professional rally driver) became one of the world's most successful rally drivers in the 1970s and 1980s. He won the Safari Rally of 1972, the RAC Rally four times, was the first to win in the Audi Quattro, and became World Rally Champion in 1983. Along with Gunnar Palm, came out of retirement to win the London-Mexico Retrospective Rally of 1995, in a newly-built Ford Escort.

Gunnar Palm (Swedish) won the 1972 Safari Rally with Mikkola, then retired to become a successful public affairs manager with Ford of Sweden.

Second place

Brian Culcheth (British, professional rally driver) carried on as a professional driver through the 1970s, in Triumph 2.5PIs, Dolomites, and TR7s, plus Morris Marinas, then had great success in Opel Kadett GT/Es. Retired from rallying at the end of the 1970s, and eventually bought and run an ironmongery business in Porlock, Devon.

Johnstone Syer (Scottish) carried on as Culcheth's co-driver for some years. After retirement, he returned to his native Scotland to run the family photography business.

Third place

Rauno Aaltonen (Finnish, professional rally driver), later driving for Datsun, for Lancia and BMW. From the mid-1970s, set up business consultancies, not only with manufacturers such as BMW, but in teaching the art of driving. Was still amazingly active, even in the 2000s.

The Escort (FEV 1H) became a star of Ford's heritage collection, preserved in original condition, and has often been shown and demonstrated at classic events all over the world. Nowadays it is rarely driven, and is irreplaceable.

This Triumph 2.5PI Mk II (XJB 305H) was used successfully in Europe by Culcheth in the early 1970s, then left to rot at Abingdon. Later scrapped by British Leyland's Motorsport Department, on orders from top management.

The Escort (FEV 46H) did not rally again, but was loaned out for rallycross use by Rod Chapman. It finally died of old age in the mid-1970s. Scrapped.

Henry Liddon (British, motor trader, later professional co-driver, later rally co-ordinator), stayed with Ford in the 1970s, co-driving with Timo Makinen until 1976, their successes including three RAC Rally victories in 1973, 1974 and 1975. Later joined Toyota Team Europe, becoming Ove Andersson's team manager. Killed in a private plane crash on the Ivory Coast Rally, in Africa, in 1987.

Fourth place

Paddy Hopkirk (British, professional rally driver), already an icon of British rallying, originally retired from rallying within months of the World Cup Rally, but occasionally appeared again, notably in the 1977 London-Sydney Marathon where he took third place in a Citroën CX2400

The Triumph 2.5PI Mk II (XJB 302H) was soon sold off by British Leyland, into private hands. Believed written off after a rallying crash, but the wreckage survives to this day.

Tony Nash (British, motor trader) retired soon after the World Cup Rally, and returned to the Bristol area, where he restarted his career in the motor trade. Was not again closely involved in motorsport, and died in the 1980s.

Neville Johnston (Irish, motor trader/businessman). Did not compete in any further major rally, but returned to his business career in Northern Ireland, and competed in motor racing as a hobby. Tragically killed in a motor racing accident in later years.

Fifth place

Timo Makinen (Finnish, professional rally driver) went on to great fame in the 1970s with Ford, driving Escorts to win the RAC Rally three times in 1973, 1974 and 1975. Left Ford after 1976, then drove for FIAT and (briefly) Triumph. Excelled in the Round South America Marathon of 1978 (in a Mercedes-Benz 450SLC), but a crash spoiled his result. Competed in some historic rallies of the 1980s, but otherwise returned to his native Finland, and gradually dropped out of the motoring scene.

After the World Cup, Ford used the Escort (FEV 4H) as an exhibition car in Europe for some time though it did not rally again. After being sold to Ford of Germany in 1973, it dropped out of sight. Believed scrapped.

Gilbert Staepelaere (Belgian, semi-professional rally driver) carried on as a successful rally driver at European level in the 1970s, winning more events in Escorts than anyone else the world. Late in the 1970s, reverted to a public relations post with Ford-Belgium, and retiring in the 1990s.

Sixth place

Jimmy Greaves (British, International footballer) never rallied again, although his achievements on the World Cup were widely praised. Early in the 1970s, with his football career on the pitch at an end, he eventually became a successful footballing pundit on British TV. Fought and apparently conquered an alcohol-related illness, but carried on successfully on TV to the end of the 1990s. Became a popular after-dinner speaker, and was soon established as one of football's 'living legends'.

The Escort (FEV 2H) was not used again in rallies and, according to Ford's records, was sold to Jimmy Greaves in 1971. It disappeared from view many years ago, and is believed to have been scrapped.

Tony Fall (British, professional rally driver), carried on for years as a successful professional driver. In the 1970s, with Lancia, BMW and Opel, before setting up his Opel rallying business in the UK. Promotion to run Opel's world-wide rallying operation from Germany, which included developing the Cosworth-engined Ascona 400 and Manta 400 models which brought a World Championship to Walter Rohrl, ended when he left the company in the late 1980s following a scandal over missing sponsorship funds. Back in the UK, he eventually took control of the Safety Devices roll cage concern, and continued to enjoy classic rallies in his Datsun 240Z. He died, too early, while officiating on the Classic Safari Rally of 2007.

Seventh place, and leading private owner

Patrick Vanson, (Anglo-French, business executive), mixed rallying with work as a publicity chief with the Klippan safety belt concern in France. Already successful in BMC cars, and Citroën DS types. Soon retired, to join Lanson Champagne concern in Australasia.

Olivier Turcat (French, corporate lawyer), mixed amateur rallying (with Vanson) and a business career. A very competent co-driver.

Alain Leprince (French, motor mechanic/engineer), was working for René Cotton at Citroën in 1970, and was loaned to Patrick Vanson for the World Cup Rally. Later joined the Renault F1 team as an engine technician.

The DS21 (3867 TT75), returned to France, and was eventually restored to health as a road car. Almost certainly scrapped.

The World Cup Rally – same name, later events

Four years after the original event had been run, Wylton Dickson promoted a second World Cup Rally in 1974, but economically this could not have come at a more difficult time. Originally planned to link London with Munich in West Germany (the location of the 1974 Football World Cup), and to take place in the spring of 1974, it was launched just as war erupted once again in the Middle East, after which the 'energy crisis' developed, oil supplies were drastically curtailed, and the outlook for pleasure motoring, and motorsport, suddenly looked bleak.

Predicted as early as mid-1973, and launched officially in October 1973 (just before war broke out in the Middle East!), the event was to be sponsored by the finance house UDT (United Dominions Trust), would have covered 12,500 miles (20,117km), and would have been spread over 20 days in May 1974.

The proposed route had not then been surveyed, though a map was issued. From London, cars would have made for Lisbon, then crossed the Straits of Gibraltar, crossed the Sahara desert to Tamanrasset, turned east at Kano in Nigeria, then passed through Khartoum, Saudi Arabia, Amman in the Middle East, struck north to Moscow, then turned west through Krakow, to reach Munich. Twenty countries were to be visited, and there was to be one early 'special stage' in the UK before cars even crossed the Channel.

This original route, as proposed, was extremely ambitious (there would be thousands of miles of desert or jungle, and extremely high temperatures), but as the cars were supposed to go through Saudi Arabia, Jordan, Syria and Iran (but not Israel) on the way to the Soviet Union, the outbreak of war soon meant that this was abandoned; the event would have to be drastically shortened, and simplified.

Not only that, but support from the 'works' rally teams (which were under pressure to look responsible after petrol shortages erupted, for motorsport was banned for a time in several countries, including the UK) was lukewarm at best, and soon it disappeared almost completely. One particular press conference which Wylton Dickson held in York before the start of the RAC Rally probably sealed its fate, as he virtually accused 'works' teams of not being brave enough to enter 'his' event – and they didn't like him very much either.

Although the route was finalised by Henry Liddon and Jim Gavin (it covered 14 countries and 10,975 miles/17,663km), it could only attract 69 entrants, and was so curtailed that the entire Middle East and Soviet sectors had to be abandoned. The route taken still started from London and ended in Munich, but made more directly for Kano, doubled back on itself (which meant that there were two complete crossings of the Sahara desert), reached Tunis, and visited Sicily, Southern Italy, Greece and Turkey before making a beeline back up through Yugoslavia for the finish at Munich.

(I, incidentally, was offered a travelling controller's job on the event, but as this would have involved the running of only two Controls in Algeria, with nothing to do in the intervening two weeks, I turned down this 'holiday' opportunity.)

Andrew Cowan and Johnstone Syer, driving a factory-built Ford Escort RS2000, started as pre-rally favourites, with Shekhar Mehta (Lancia Fulvia HF), Bob Neyret (Peugeot 504) and Sobieslaw Zasada (Porsche

911) strongly fancied, though few were expected to set such a blistering pace as Hannu Mikkola had set in 1970.

In the end, the Safari desert took a ferocious toll of the field, only five cars reached the half way turning point at Kano, though a dozen more reached Tamanrasset, waited around, and rejoined on the way back. On this basis, just 19 cars qualified as finishers, the winner being the Andre Welinski/Ken Tubman/James Reddiex Citroën DS23, with Christine Dacremont's Peugeot 504 28 hours (not minutes, not seconds, but hours) behind in second place.

Although Wylton Dickson insisted that UDT were delighted with all the exposure they got, and waved sheaves of cuttings to prove it, the fact is that with the single exception of *Autocar*, most of the enthusiast's press treated it as a minor diversion. Citroën made nothing of a victory by a beautifully-prepared private entry, which was of a car which was already obsolete ... and that was that. After such an intellectual (and, I guess, financial) battering, Dickson then lost interest in promoting another 'World Cup'.

British Rally enthusiast/classic rally organiser Philip Young, however, did not. As he told me:

"I went to see Wylton Dickson, and subsequently registered the name World Cup Rally for a London to Cape Town route [for a classic rally] that was to have taken place in 1992. A local war and a closed border caused the Foreign Office to lean on me heavily to cancel the event. This was a bitter pill to swallow as the edict came three months before the 'off' with everything in place.

"The name was then used for four events which I organised, that used similar regulations, and concept, as the 1970 epic, for a London-Marrakesh-London for 1400cc hatchbacks, in 2001. There were three others that followed on, London-Athens, London-Tunisia, and finally the toughest of the bunch, London-Dakar, in 2005."

Philip's events, though enjoyed by the well-to-do classic fraternity, did not attract any interest from factory teams, and the concept now appears to have died.

RALLY GIANTS™

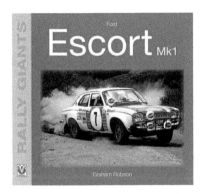

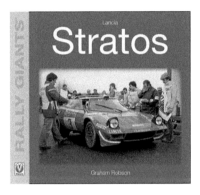

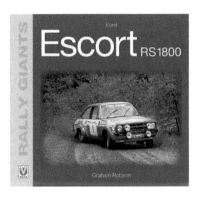

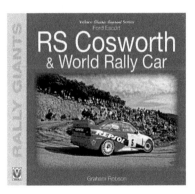

These fascinating books describe the birth, development and careers of some of the most famous and succesful cars in rallying, providing a compact and authoritative history of where, when and how they became so important to the sport.
These titles are now back in print due to popular demand. Also available in ebook format, see https://digital.veloce.co.uk

Paperback • 21x19.5cm • 128 pages • 100 photographs

For more info or to order any Veloce book, call +44 (0)1305 260068 • Email info@veloce.co.uk
• Visit us on the web at www.veloce.co.uk / ww.velocebooks.com

Also from Veloce Publishing –

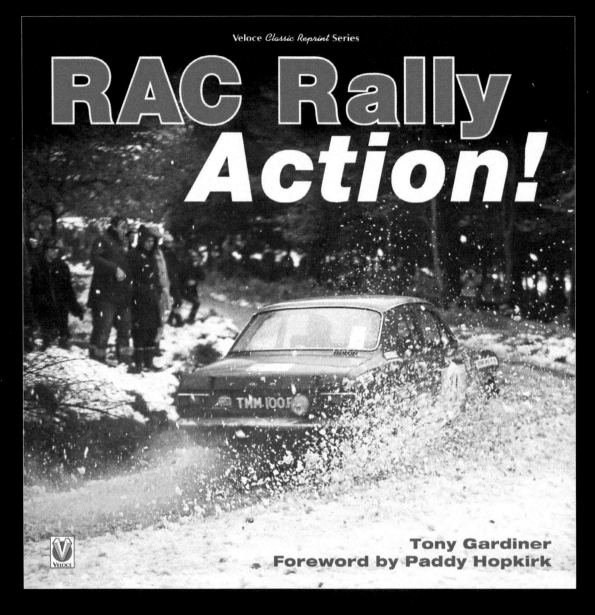

Veloce *Classic Reprint* Series

RAC Rally
Action!

Tony Gardiner
Foreword by Paddy Hopkirk

The next best thing to being there! Covering the pre-WRC 'Rally of the Forests' period. An incredibly detailed and highly illustrated review of a great era of rallying. Over 250 photographs, most of which are published for the first time. Reproductions of rally documents including regulations, programmes, road books, and crew notes.

ISBN: 978-1-787112-29-2
Paperback • 22.5x22.5cm • 208 pages • colour pictures

For more information and price details, visit our website at www.veloce.co.uk • email: info@veloce.co.uk • Tel: +44(0)1305 260068

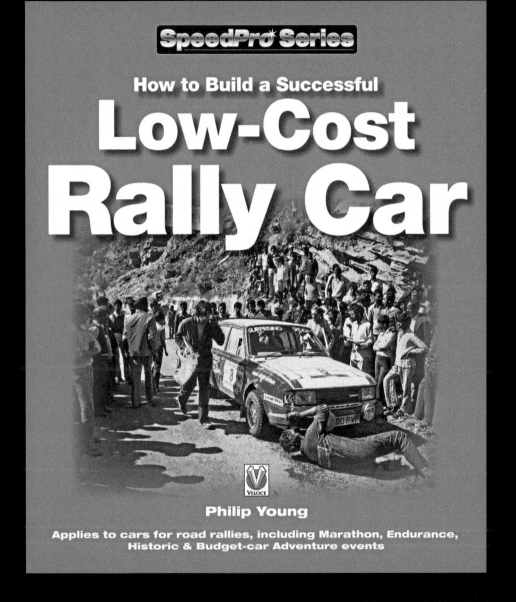

Simple, cost-effective, basic and reliable tips to ensure that any rally car stands a chance of reaching the finishing line. If you are planning a road-based rally, don't even think of leaving home before reading this book and implementing the tried and tested mods it describes so well.

ISBN: 978-1-84584-208-6
Paperback • 25x20.7cm • 96 pages • 154 colour and b&w pictures

For more information and price details, visit our website at www.veloce.co.uk • email: info@veloce.co.uk • Tel: +44(0)1305 260068

Index

LINE

"MARU"

STATEROOM

ANCHOR LINE

CABIN

NAME
SHIP'S NAME
SAILING DATE
DECK   ROOM No.   BERTH No.

TO BE FORWARDED TO
YORKHILL QUAY, GLASGOW

WANTED
NEW YORK

LABEL No. 7

CH00687564

UNITED STATES LINES

American Way to and from Europe

CUNARD LINE.

PARIS

Kindly place this Label on the **END** of the package.

CABIN
P&O

S.S.   Berth No.

Passenger's
Name.

NAME
STEAMER
FROM
DATE

ROOM   No.

C R

WHITE STAR LINE

NEW YORK   LIVERPOOL

FOR
**STATE
ROOM**

**FIRST
CLASS**

STATEROOM No.

K.

BERTH NO.

French Line
PIER 88 NORTH RIVER
NEW YORK

YORK
LINE
BAGGAGE FOR
CK *P*
ER
OY

Compagnia Italiana Transatlantica
Rome Steam Navigation Company

2

SECOND CLASS
SECONDA CLASSE

per S/S *GIUSEPPE MAZZINI*
from ZANZIBAR to LONDON (Via Port Said).

Passenger's Name

MONTHLY FAST LINE
Zanzibar-Mombasa-Genova

MATSON

NAME *Eunice H. Avery*
STEAMER *Mariposa* STATEROOM *157* DATE *June 20*
PORT OF DEPARTURE *Melbourne* PORT OF DESTINATION *San Francisco*

MATSON LINE · OCEANIC LINE

BAGGAGE WANTED IN STATEROOM

SECRETS OF THE
GREAT
OCEAN
LINERS

JOHN G. SAYERS

Bodleian Library
UNIVERSITY OF OXFORD

First published in 2020 by the Bodleian Library

Broad Street, Oxford OX1 3BG

www.bodleianshop.co.uk

ISBN 978 1 85124 530 7

Text © Bodleian Library, University of Oxford, 2020

All images, unless specified, © Bodleian Library, University of Oxford, 2020

All rights reserved.

No part of this book may be reproduced, stored in a retrieval
system, or transmitted in any form or by any means, electronic,
mechanical, photocopying, recording, or otherwise, without
the written permission of the Bodleian Library, except for the
purpose of research or private study, or criticism or review.

Jacket design by Dot Little at the Bodleian Library
Designed and typeset in 11 on 16 Monotype Baskerville
by illuminati, Grosmont
Printed and bound by Toppan Leefung, China,
on 157 gsm Oji Zunma matt art paper

British Library Catalogue in Publishing Data
A CIP record of this publication is available from the British Library

CONTENTS

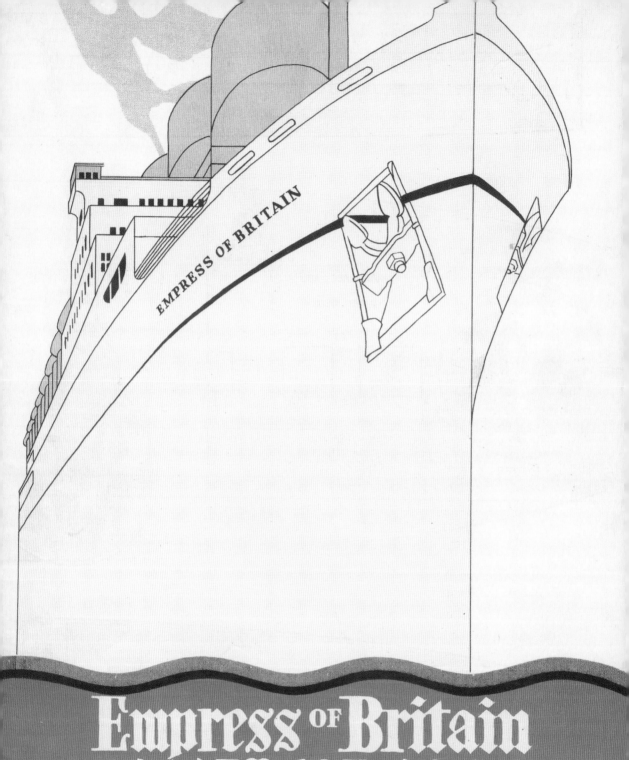

Empress of Britain
APARTMENT PLAN
CANADIAN PACIFIC
WORLD'S GREATEST TRAVEL SYSTEM

PREFACE

In the very early 1950s my parents took me to England, their country of birth, to visit relatives they hadn't seen since before the Second World War. In an era when commercial trans-atlantic flights were in their relative infancy, we went by ship – Cunard's tired old RMS *Franconia* eastbound, and the same company's superliner, RMS *Queen Elizabeth*, westward.

Some fifteen years later, when I saw a grouping of five souvenir ocean liner lapel pins at a Sunday morning antiques fair in Woodstock, near Oxford, I knew that I had to collect them. Then I found enamelled souvenir spoons, napkin rings, tea strainers and other such mementoes. As the collecting bug took hold, my focus turned to other North Atlantic ocean liner material, and eventually to other routes.

Ephemera, the bits and pieces of everyday life on board, help to reconstruct the diverse pleasures of a voyage. The berthing card that you received upon boarding, for example, gave you your first task – booking a table for dinner. At about the same time

you would peruse the passenger list for names of the rich and famous. If you were in Cabin or Tourist Class, your passenger list had a red, white and blue cover, and the prospect of seeing the names of the rich and famous was minuscule. If you were in First Class, the cover of your passenger list was lettered in gold, and your search could turn up film stars, high-ranking politicians, generals, high clergy, stockbrokers and even the Duke and Duchess of Windsor, as we will see in the course of this book.

The ephemera that I found were particularly useful in providing images of the steamships and their interiors during the golden period of ocean liner travel between the late nineteenth century and the Second World War. They also provided brochures, sailing schedules, voyage logs, cruise information, letters written on board, diaries and a host of other secrets. This book is designed to disclose the secrets of that fifty-year golden age, which were buried in shipping-line internal memos, passenger notes and records, and other shipping documents.

The book's progress is chronological, from the early stages of planning a voyage to disembarking on arrival, following the same sequence that my parents went through so many years ago. I conclude with two chapters on liners in wartime, and on the pall of some shipping disasters that brought home the reality that there is no such thing as an unsinkable ship.

Ocean liners were a home from home, and they needed to be able to accommodate passengers of all ages and all budgets. The glamour is in the mighty liners that plied their trade across the globe. World cruise voyages were particularly exotic. Passengers needed not only the money but also the time to leave their businesses or other responsibilities for a few months, and they were treated like royalty. But the story would be incomplete without the counterpoint of the poor and desperate people who fled across the Atlantic seeking a better life in North America.

This voyage owes a debt to Julie Anne Lambert, Librarian of the John Johnson Collection of Printed Ephemera at the Bodleian Libraries, who has worked hard over the years accommodating the deluge of thousands of items of material in the Sayers Collection flowing from my home in Canada. Most of all, my wife Judith has patiently supported my collecting addiction as we travelled to fairs in Canada, the United States and the UK over almost half a century, to find the type of material that you see in this book.

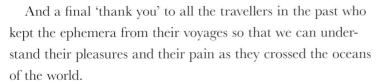

And a final 'thank you' to all the travellers in the past who kept the ephemera from their voyages so that we can understand their pleasures and their pain as they crossed the oceans of the world.

PLANNING THE VOYAGE

Before the advent of commercial jet travel in the early 1950s, an ocean voyage represented a major milestone in one's life. For prospective migrants it meant severing ties with the community and country in which they grew up. It meant selling and converting into cash all of the property, goods and chattels that they did not plan to take to the new country.

For the more experienced traveller, perhaps on a round trip or cruise, it still entailed anticipating the social and financial demands of the voyage (which could last up to three months) and the land-based accommodation that would be needed at the destination. A voyage by sea, whatever its purpose, was not something to be undertaken lightly, even in the golden age of ocean liner travel. By the time that a prospective traveller had decided where and when they wanted to go, the next stage was to book the trip with a shipping agent.

There was no Internet, and early telephone communications were somewhat primitive. The result could be a ponderous and inefficient process, involving communication between the shipping line (which

French Line
PIER 88 NORTH RIVER
NEW YORK

THE SEASICK SERIES

OH. DEAR OH, WISH WE WERE HOME.

1 Comic seasickness postcard printed on the back with the name of the Allan Line, c.1910. Why would this Canadian shipping line want to be associated with seasickness?

maintained the master list of cabin allocations in New York or in the UK) and a local travel agent. The applicant might be asked for a second and third choice of cabin, in the face of the hours that might be required to ascertain first-choice availability. The process may have been frustrating, but it added to the sense of importance that attended ocean liner travel.

There were many reasons to travel by sea. It was of course the only option available for travel outside your continent or island. Emigrants to America, for example, had to be prepared for a voyage across the Atlantic. Fares were cheaper in winter, but passengers could face a frightening, storm-tossed crossing. One of a series of Allan Line postcards from the early 1900s pictures the image most associated with North Atlantic travel (**FIG. 1**). Why the Allan Line would put their name on the back and distribute this as a promotional tool is a mystery, because it surely could deter anyone from selecting the line for their transatlantic voyage.

This postcard may have been inspired by the artist's crossing on a voyage such as the one illustrated on the souvenir log card from the RMS *Virginian* in late November 1913 (FIG. 2). Beginning with Monday's 'gale with high sea', through the 'strong westerly gale, speed reduced' on Tuesday, and the 'moderate gale' on Wednesday with a 'high confused sea', intended immigrants must have been regretting the day when they decided to sail in November. Note the caption that the ship was 'fitted with Marconi's wireless telegraphy'. This would have provided a degree of comfort for fearful passengers a year and a half after the *Titanic* disaster. The document was captioned on the cover as a 'Souvenir Log Card'. One wonders why anyone would retain this record of an utterly unpleasant experience on the North Atlantic.

2 Abstract of log from a November 1913 crossing with gale-force winds on the North Atlantic on board the *Virginian* of the Allan Line.

ABSTRACT OF LOG OF THE
ALLAN LINE ROYAL MAIL T.S.S. " VIRGINIAN."
CAPTAIN A. RENNIE.
LIVERPOOL TO HALIFAX, Nov. 22nd, 1913.

Date, 1913.	Lat.	Long.	Miles	Winds, etc.
	N.	W.		
Sunday, Nov. 23	55.27	9.23	279	From Liverpool
Monday, ,, 24	54.42	19.16	342	Fresh S.W. gale with high sea
Tuesday, ,, 25	53.32	26.58	280	Strong W. gale, speed reduced
Wed., ,, 26	51.23	36.10	360	Mod. gale, high confused sea
Thurs., ,, 27	48.58	43.40	322	Violent squalls, heavy head sea
Friday, ,, 28	45.45	52.05	400	Strong N. wind with snow squalls
Saturday, ,, 29	44.48	61.49	416	Moderate wind and sea
			84	To Halifax
L'pool to Halifax, N.S.	...	...	2483	

ALL ALLAN LINE STEAMERS ARE FITTED WITH MARCONI'S
WIRELESS TELEGRAPHY

WHERE AND WHY TO TRAVEL

All the lines fostered immigration to North America and to Australia. The immigrant service was profitable, but when America imposed restrictions on immigration the flow ended, as when the Immigration Act of 1917 mandated a literacy requirement, and in 1921 the Emergency Quota Act limited annual immigration to 3 per cent of the people from that country already in the United States. An immigration card of March 1911 of the *Corsican*, arriving from Liverpool, carries instructions in English, Bohemian, Russian, Ruthenian, German, French, Hungarian, Swedish, Polish, Italian and Yiddish, underscoring the diversity of the sources of immigration. Trips were made in the return direction, too: some of those who made their fame and fortune in other parts of the globe wanted to return to their homeland for a visit.

It is unusual to find ephemera that specifically point to a business trip; business travellers would be less likely than tourists to preserve souvenirs. If the definition of 'business' is extended to military and government travel, then a non-tourism motive is evident from ship passenger lists. More about those later, but an example from the Henderson Line, travelling from Liverpool to Rangoon on the *Ava* in 1896, gives an insight into the landscape of a passenger list (**FIG. 3**). Guests were likely to survey the contents on boarding the ship, and pick out the passengers whom they would most like to meet.

Mr and Mrs Halliday and their two children may have been headed East for him to assume a post within the British government of Burma. Capt. and Mrs Allenby, Capt. Evans and Surg.-Capt. Entrican were probably part of the military establishment that supported the British rule there. A footnote provided by the original recipient of this list shows that

3 A passenger list from the SS *Ava*, travelling from Liverpool to Rangoon in 1896.

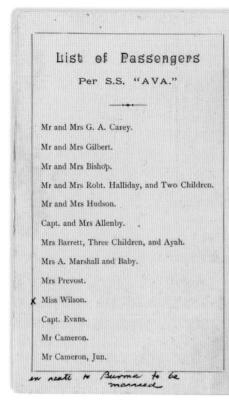

List of Passengers
Per S.S. "AVA."

Mr and Mrs G. A. Carey.

Mr and Mrs Gilbert.

Mr and Mrs Bishop.

Mr and Mrs Robt. Halliday, and Two Children.

Mr and Mrs Hudson.

Capt. and Mrs Allenby.

Mrs Barrett, Three Children, and Ayah.

Mrs A. Marshall and Baby.

Mrs Prevost.

✗ Miss Wilson.

Capt. Evans.

Mr Cameron.

Mr Cameron, Jun.

en route to Burma to be married

List of Passengers
Per S.S. "AVA."

Rev. Mr Finn.

Mr James Dorratt.

Mr D. H. E. Allan.

Mr Conrad M. Mahoney.

Mr A. H. Hurlong.

Mr R. Greenwood.

Mr Bangham.

Surg.-Capt. Entrican (from Port Said).

Mr Kummer.

Mr. Philip Clews.

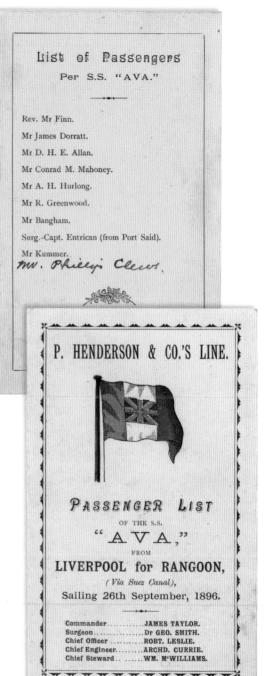

P. HENDERSON & CO.'S LINE.

PASSENGER LIST

OF THE S.S.

"AVA,"

FROM

LIVERPOOL for RANGOON,

(Via Suez Canal),

Sailing 26th September, 1896.

Commander	JAMES TAYLOR.
Surgeon	Dr GEO. SMITH.
Chief Officer	ROBT. LESLIE.
Chief Engineer	ARCHD. CURRIE.
Chief Steward	WM. M'WILLIAMS.

Miss Wilson is 'en route to Burma to be married'. Mr Cameron and Mr Cameron, Jun. may represent a father bringing his son back from a boarding school in the UK. And Rev. Mr Finn is likely to have been a missionary working on assignment for his church.

Finally, the two women travelling with children are in all likelihood returning to their spouses after a visit 'home' to England. Mrs Barrett had clearly been to the Far East before, since she is accompanied by a native servant, who was looked upon as a type of chattel without a name – she is merely an 'Ayah'.

CRUISES

If your trip was not to go from *A* to *B*, but rather from *A* for a cruise that returned to *A*, there were many possibilities. For the traveller in northern climes, the choice of cruises was largest in the colder months, when traffic across the Atlantic dropped off as travellers avoided the winter passage unless they absolutely had to cross. If you were a buyer for a large department store who needed to purchase seasonal merchandise from Europe, for example, you crossed the ocean to preview the manufacturers' offerings as each season approached. The timing was not negotiable.

Passenger lists such as the one in FIG. 4 provide a valuable insight into passenger ship history. The White Star Line's relatively new SS *Arabic* left New York on 6 February 1908. Passenger traffic on the North Atlantic route would have been at its low point of the year, since no one with any options wanted to face the storm-tossed Atlantic in winter.

Two solutions by the shipping companies were to reduce winter-season fares across the Atlantic to entice the very cost-conscious traveller, and to redeploy some ships for periods of time to the task of cruising. Rather than empty cabins and heavily discounted fares for the few brave souls who dared to travel the Atlantic in winter, why not use the ship to take afflu-ent passengers on a cruise to warmer climates? A popular trip was to the Mediterranean and the Holy Land during the winter in the northern hemisphere. For seventy days, participants enjoyed shipboard comforts while ranging across the Medi-terranean as far as Syria and Constantinople (Istanbul), with

4 Passenger list for a White Star Line cruise on the *Arabic*, which included the Holy Land, 1908.

CLARK'S TENTH ANNUAL CRUISE TO THE MEDITERRANEAN AND THE ORIENT INCLUDING SPAIN by the Specially Chartered WHITE STAR S.S. "ARABIC" February 6th to April 16th 1908.

JERUSALEM FROM THE MOUNT OF OLIVES

THE WHITE STAR NEW S.S. ARABIC (15,801 TONS) A SISTER SHIP OF THE BALTIC, CEDRIC AND CELTIC ONE OF THE LARGEST AND STEADIEST SHIPS IN THE WORLD

A TOUR OF 70 DAYS SPENDING 19 DAYS IN PALESTINE AND EGYPT INCLUDING SHORE EXCURSIONS, HOTELS, DRIVES, FEES AND ALL NECESSARY EXPENSES.

PYRAMIDS NEAR CAIRO

visits to Spain and then the UK on the return as spring unfolded there. Then – home to America.

Side trips, at additional cost, were available, just as they are on cruises today. One of the featured aspects of the cruise was 'spending 19 days in Palestine and Egypt'. For many Christian believers at the time, a visit to the Holy Land would have been a highlight of the experience. A close examination of this passenger list shows that the cruise to the Holy Land attracted a number of clergy. To the casual reader this may be unsurprising, but many were not well paid, and would have had difficulty affording this trip. There was a solution.

Even today, someone who recruits enough paying passengers receives a complimentary or heavily discounted trip. In 1908 it was no different. It is possible, for example, that Rev. Howard Duffield of New York had recruited enough members of his congregation and their relatives and friends to receive free or heavily discounted passage. The passenger list contains the names of thirty-one reverends. The number of clerical collars must have been a significant deterrent to inappropriate behaviour on board, and almost a guarantee that 'the power of prayer' could keep the entire ship's company safe from any harm throughout the cruise.

Not all these men of the cloth would have been group organizers. One would probably have been given free passage by the shipping line to minister to the spiritual needs of passengers on board, since there was no certainty on cruises that there would be nearly so many reverends available in time of need. In some cases, an appreciative parishioner or congregation may have given a trip to their minister, particularly on his prospective retirement.

This passenger list also shows the home towns of the passengers. Several were from New York and places in New England. However, the Midwest, including Chicago, was well represented, and some participants journeyed from places such as Tower City, North Dakota; Anaconda, Montana; San Francisco; and New Orleans.

The majority of passengers were women, with mother–daughter pairs in some cases. In an era when many women did not work, those who did not have to do so had the time available to go on educational and informative cruises while the men in their lives pursued business activities. In contrast to many other passenger lists of the era, there is no record here of maids or valets. Either they were deemed unimportant and were not recognized in the passenger list, or the participants who had servants did not bring their maids and valets along. I believe that the former situation is much more likely.

This tiny booklet has many facets. It is a potential treasure trove for genealogists (as it includes names of the ship's officers, and representatives of the Clark tour company), students of social history, and those seeking to map affluent areas of America, who can examine the places of origin of those who could afford to make this trip. For the genealogist, it gives an insight into the life of one's ancestors. Take for example Mr and Mrs W.H. Murch, who feature in this passenger list. There are several postcards picturing the RMS (or SS) *Arabic* during the various stages of her career, produced by a variety of publishers. The chances of finding a card from the Murches in my collection were vanishingly slim; but I *did* find a card, picturing RMS *Arabic* at Constantinople, dated 29 February 1908, which bears the following message:

This is an excellent picture of our ship. We have 650 passengers on board, 350 in the crew. It is like a small town sailing the Blue Mediterranean. We are both making fine sailors and enjoying every minute of the journey. I cannot settle down to write letters. I am just sending cards. Hope you are all as well as we are. W.H. & Auntie Murch.

The Murches are shown as being from St Thomas, Ontario – they were among the few non-Americans on the ship.

Other ships competed in the cruise market in Europe. Summer cruises to Norway's North Cape were popular offerings. The 1930s saw some beautiful art deco images on the covers of cruise booklets produced by British tour providers such as the Orient Line, the Blue Star Line and the Royal Mail Steam Packet Company, to Norway (**FIG. 5**) and other Scandinavian destinations.

Creative minds in shipping-line promotional departments sought reasons for special cruises. An intriguing example is a cruise to Gallipoli and Salonika, site of heavy fighting and grievous loss of life during the First World War, on the twentieth anniversary of the campaign in 1936 (**FIG. 6**). Described in the booklet as a 'wonderful opportunity for re-union', the trip included shore excursions to these places, as well as to Malta and Istanbul. One wonders how the men who fought in that disastrous campaign would have felt about returning to the killing fields that they had survived.

5 This striking art deco image promotes a 1930s' cruise to Norway on an Orient Line ship.

6 (*overleaf*) A brochure for a 1936 tour of Gallipoli and Salonika on Cunard's *Lancastria*.

SHIPPING CHOICES

Considerations by prospective travellers included the country of ownership of the shipping line; the size of the ship; the general style of the ship and its reputation; and the scheduled sailing dates. Choices were constrained to a degree by where

ORIENT LINE CRUISES
BY 20.000 TON STEAMERS

NORWAY
& NORTHERN CAPITALS

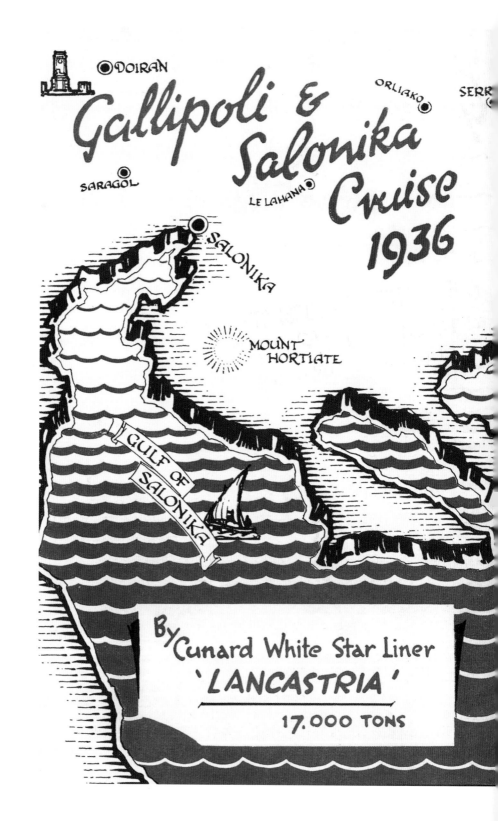

Gallipoli & Salonika Cruise 1936

DOIRAN

ORLIAKO

SERR

SARAGOL

LE LAHANA

SALONIKA

MOUNT HORTIATE

GULF OF SALONIKA

By Cunard White Star Liner 'LANCASTRIA'

17,000 TONS

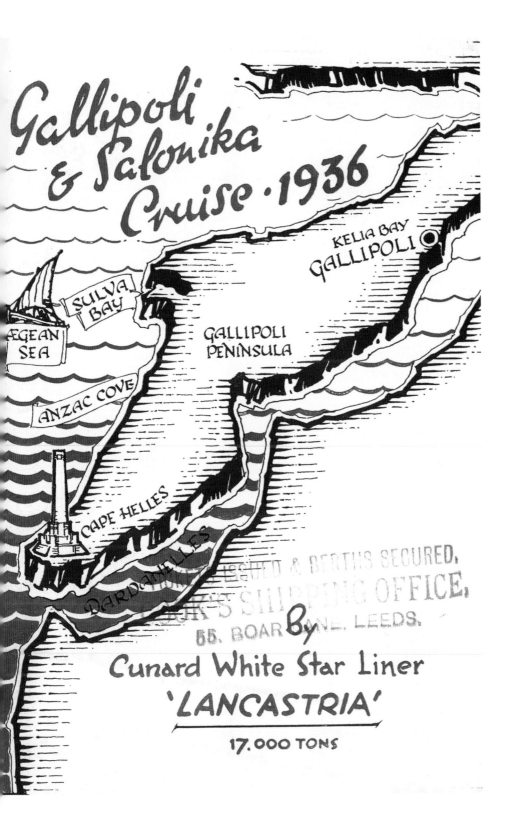

Gallipoli & Salonika Cruise · 1936

KELIA BAY
GALLIPOLI ◉

SULVA BAY

ÆGEAN SEA

GALLIPOLI PENINSULA

ANZAC COVE

CAPE HELLES

DARDANELLES

TICKETS ISSUED & BERTHS SECURED,
COOK'S SHIPPING OFFICE,
55. BOAR LANE, LEEDS.

By

Cunard White Star Liner
'LANCASTRIA'

17,000 TONS

7 The immensity of the superliner *Queen Mary* is measured against a New York landmark in a Cunard–White Star Line promotional booklet, 1937.

one was going and the port of departure. Beyond that, for some travellers relative size mattered. Shipping lines realized this factor early on, and drew comparisons between the dimensions of their vessels and prominent landmarks ashore. In 1906, the Hamburg–American Line issued a postcard comparing its new liner *Amerika* to the City Hall in Hamburg. Prospective passengers from Germany would recognize the building. Thirty years later, a Cunard–White Star Line brochure (FIG. 7) illustrated how the new RMS *Queen Mary* would compare in length to Fifth Avenue, extending from 34th Street almost to 38th Street.

IF THE "QUEEN MARY" WERE PLACED IN FIFTH AVENUE

WITH ITS STERN AGAINST THE SIDE *of the* EMPIRE STATE BUILDING *at* 34th STREET, ITS LENGTH WOULD EXTEND ALMOST TO 38th STREET

It is clear what country's passengers that comparison was courting.

There were other benchmarks for size. An early photograph of the *Lusitania* in dry dock (FIG. 8) featured her propellers. The tiny figures on the dock staring at her provide a measure of their relative immensity. If you contemplated travelling trans-atlantic you would feel little risk of lack of propulsion. Indeed, in the case of *Lusitania* it was not lack of propulsion that destroyed her in 1915, but rather a German submarine's torpedo.

Passengers also sought assurance of their safety by reference to a liner's captain and crew. The German *Imperator*, the largest ship in the world in her time, went into service in 1913 and sailed for only a year before the outbreak of the First World War took her out of action. One of the promotional images

8 'Size is safety' was the mantra of the shipping lines before the *Titanic*. The propellers of Cunard's ill-fated *Lusitania*, which went into service in 1907, dwarf the spectators on the dock.

was of her experienced captain, Commodore Hans Ruser. For her maiden voyage there were reportedly four other prominent Hamburg–American Line captains also appointed to ensure that the *Imperator*'s maiden sailing to New York would go smoothly. One can assume that this rare image is of Commodore Ruser and the other four captains who reported to him (**FIG. 9**). What more assurance could any fearful passenger need?

Imperator had one serious drawback – she was top-heavy and therefore rolled excessively. An American passenger in June 1913 wrote, 'Our steamer is a marvel. Our stateroom very large and everything O.K.' Other Americans who toured her when she was in New York wrote about their very favourable impressions of her size and spaciousness. However, her marble bathrooms and other heavy fixtures in the upper-deck staterooms reportedly accentuated her tendency to roll. The dual action of lightening her upper decks and adding heavy ballast to her hold succeeded in making her more stable, both for stormy days on the Atlantic and for increased directional stability when changing course.

Each of the two Imperial Suites encompassed several rooms and cost 20,000 marks per trip according to a Hamburg–American brochure of 1913. After the First World War, *Imperator* was seized as reparations for the sinking of the *Lusitania* in 1915, and sailed for a year for Cunard as the *Imperator*, followed by a sterling Cunard career as the *Berengaria*.

9 Officers of the Hamburg–American Line's *Imperator* during her maiden year, 1913. If one captain was safe in the immediate post-*Titanic* era, surely five captains would make her even safer.

Many middle-class travellers wanted to travel on a ship of average size – in the 1930s, for example, one of about 20,000 gross registered tons. A 'superliner' the size of the RMS *Queen Mary* (81,000 grt), or the SS *Normandie* of approximately the same size, could be intimidating. Not everybody subscribed to the premiss that the bigger the ship, the safer the ship. After all, people still remembered the *Titanic* disaster.

The country of the line was a further important consideration. For many British travellers (including my parents), for example, the thought of travelling on a French or German ship – or on one of any other 'foreign' country for that matter – would have been repugnant. My parents sailed on Cunard ships and Canadian Pacific ships. No further alternatives. The menus were in English, the stewards spoke English, and the crew whom they encountered were resoundingly British.

Some ships were more prestigious than others. In the late 1930s the French Line's *Normandie* was, along with the *Queen Mary*, the ship to sail on to impress your friends. The *Normandie* was marketed as a distinct 'brand', whereas the *Queen Mary* was positioned as the finest of the Cunard liners. If you travelled on the *Queen Mary*, your baggage label was a Cunard one. If you sailed on the *Normandie*, you had large and distinctive *Normandie* baggage labels (see FIG. 27) to plaster onto your suitcases.

Some ships were glamorous. Others were not. Most emigrants returning to their home town were not returning to a centre of style and elegance. Why dress up on a ship with clothes that would be totally out of place when you arrived at your destination? Unless maybe to show off that you had 'made it' in the USA?

To obtain 'round trip' passage rates you had to travel on ships of the same line. It would cost more, for example, to travel with Canadian Pacific one way and Cunard the other way. With that constraint, the challenge was to find suitable dates that would fit into your available time for the trip. The more ships a line operated, the more likely it was that you would be able to find suitable dates. Larger shipping lines also offered a wider range of destinations, which minimized the amount of overland travel from the port of arrival to the final destination.

CHOOSING A ROUTE

When choosing a route, who could fail to be captivated by advertising brochures such as one for the Italian liner SS *Roma* (FIG. 10)? The *Roma* and other Italian Line ships offered a route to and from America via the Mediterranean and the mid-Atlantic. That was fine for those seeking a Mediterranean destination such as Marseilles or Cannes or Genoa, but of little value for travellers to London, Paris or Bremen.

10 A stylish 1930s' art deco cover of a brochure for First Class travel on the SS *Roma* of the Italian Line.

The North Atlantic route to Europe was highly competitive and the companies produced an array of visual treats to entrance the prospective passenger. The North German Lloyd brochure cover pictured here (FIG. 11) has a charm and simplicity that would have resonated with the passenger who might be easily intimidated by the thought of a large, impersonal shipping line. Just as importantly, it provided a hint of reassurance to the woman travelling alone that there could be other women travelling to Europe by themselves.

The North German Lloyd was one of two major German shipping lines, the other being the Hamburg–American Line (its German name sometimes translated more literally as 'Hamburg America Line'). They offered worldwide services but were particularly active on the North Atlantic routes. Their styles catered for the different tastes of their prospective clients, with Hamburg–American offering traditional grand luxury and North German Lloyd a more up-to-date image embracing the emergent designs of the Deutscher Werkbund movement. After 1905, when the *Amerika* was built in a British shipyard, all German passenger vessels were built in Germany. Given the fragile international diplomatic framework of the time, this government-inspired mandate helped to support the building of German naval as well as commercial shipping. One historian, Matthew Seligmann (2012), has put forward the view that the competition in passenger shipping fostered the Anglo-German rivalry in naval shipbuilding. For the average prospective passenger comparing rates for travel, the costs, comfort and convenient port schedules were probably more important deciding factors than international shipping competition.

Canadian Pacific is a fascinating company – primarily a railroad operator, with shipping and hotel interests besides. With its

11 A beautifully attired woman featured on this brochure by the North German Lloyd line, 1913.

SAILINGS to EUROPE

1913

North German Lloyd

OELRICHS & CO. General Agents
CABIN DEPARTMENT,   5 BROADWAY
BOWLING GREEN OFFICES   NEW YORK, CITY.

H. CLAUSSENIUS & CO.
Gen'l Western Agents
107 N. Dearborn St., Chicago, Ill.

ROBERT CAPELLE
Gen'l Pacific Coast Agent
250 Powell St., San Francisco, Cal.

CENTRAL NATIONAL BANK
Gen'l South Western Agents
St. Louis, Mo.

ALLOWAY & CHAMPION
Gen'l Pass. Agents for N. W. Canada
Winnipeg, Man.

Cuba
Haiti
Jamaica
Panama
Colombia
Dutch West Indies
Venezuela
Trinidad
Barbados
Martinique
Porto Rico
Bahamas
Bermuda

West Indies
Cruises
Canadian Pacific
1926

12 In the 1920s and 1930s, Canadian Pacific employed an array of talented artists; their brochures carried dramatic and alluring artwork such as this booklet promoting cruises to the West Indies, from 1926.

roots in the relatively small (by population) country of Canada, it had to appeal to a much broader audience than the residents of its home country. Its strengths included excellent ports on both Canada's Atlantic and Pacific shores, so it targeted much of its advertising to focus on its destinations rather than its home base. This image suggests that for its trans-Pacific passengers it was appealing to all residents in the western hemisphere who wanted to travel to China and Japan – as well as to Asians heading for North America. Canadian Pacific passenger lists that show the passengers' country and city of origin support this statement. Many Americans sailed on Canadian Pacific rather than on competing lines such as America's Dollar Line and later Matson Line, and Japan's NYK Line.

Canadian Pacific used original artwork throughout many of its brochures and advertising. A wrap-around image on the cover of a 1926 cruise brochure to the West Indies beckons the reader to sail to this exotic destination (FIG. 12). There exist many drawings by Flora and Martin DeMuth, an American couple who sailed on Canadian Pacific cruises over a period of some ten years and produced postcards and prints of their work. Sometimes stereotypical, but nonetheless entertaining, their drawings record sights en route during the trip. Covers and interior artwork on many other Canadian Pacific publications attest loudly to its support of Canadian and other artists.

Finally, it should be noted that there were 'Liner Conference Systems' set up between companies to govern particular routes: agreements to provide similar basic facilities and fares for each class, thereby limiting to an extent the extremes of what was available. This was a clever way of controlling a volatile market – though not one that was necessarily favourable to passengers wanting bargains.

RESEARCHING AND BOOKING THE TRIP

By the time that a prospective traveller had decided where and when they wanted to go, the next stage was to book the trip with a shipping agent. This could be a ponderous and inefficient process, involving communication between the shipping line and a local travel agent, but it added to the sense of ceremony that attended ocean liner travel.

The agent would produce a deck plan, enabling passengers to select their cabin. Most desirable were the cabins amidships – in a head sea, the impact of the pitching would be felt least in the middle of the ship. For the passenger who did not appreciate late-night revellers, distance from staircases and elevator traffic was a consideration.

Booking the ocean travel was only part of the trip. First, one had to get to the port of departure. For a woman from Newcastle sailing on a cruise out of London in 1936, there was first the challenge of getting to the Boat Train's point of departure. There was a distinction and a thrill in being on a 'Boat Train'. You had a special baggage tag. You and your companions were all destined for the ship, so you got a preview of faces that you would next see on board. The woman from Newcastle, who was going on a Canadian Pacific Mediterranean cruise, describes the experience:

> We arrived at St Pancras in good time for the Boat Train and after collecting the luggage we joined the already huge crowd waiting for the train. It was more like a football match and by the time we got into a carriage we were breathless. We left London in a thunderstorm, and finally arrived at Tilbury after 14 stops on the way.

The more expensive the cabin, the more space the traveller enjoyed. A four-berth (two upper and two lower) cabin in

Tourist Third was cheap but not always cheerful, unless you had the luck of three women travelling together and wondering who the 'fourth' would be. Presumably the 'fourth' was not only crowding but also uncongenial. The woman from Newcastle wrote in her diary:

Cunard Line

R.M.S.
"SAXONIA"

THIRD CLASS FOUR-BERTH ROOM

> I may say here that we were lucky in that the fourth cabin mate after two days changed her cabin for one on A Deck; and thus we were left with more space, otherwise I think we'd have been hanging an assortment of dresses, etc. <u>outside the porthole</u>.

Illustrations of a four-berth Tourist Third cabin are hard to find, presumably because for the shipping companies it was akin to showing sardines jammed into a can. In a Cunard brochure of the 1920s, it is called a 'Room' rather than a 'Cabin' (**FIG. 13**). What you saw in the picture was what you got: a double bunk on each side, and a centre aisle which leads from the entry door and ends at a single washstand. This wasn't steerage, but it was close to it.

A world cruise added new dimensions to the extent of planning. Could you plan and finalize your wardrobe for the coming three months, for a variety of settings in a wide range of climates? In the absence of credit cards, could you anticipate the cash and travellers' cheques that you would have to carry with you? These and other issues are part of the next chapter.

13 A four-berth cabin provided little room for anything other than sleeping, but the price was relatively affordable.

SIXTH ANNUAL
ROUND THE WORLD
CRUISE
1928→29

CANADIAN
PACIFIC

WORLD CRUISES

In the nineteenth and early twentieth centuries, taking a world cruise would have entailed going on one ship across the Atlantic from New York, then on another ship for a further leg, and on yet another vessel for a third leg, and so on. These connections would probably not be seamless, so pas-sengers might have to wait in one port for a week to catch the ship for the next port. And if the ship was late arriving because of mechanical or weather problems, they might miss the connection entirely. This all changed with a voyage of the SS *Cleveland*, a Hamburg–American Line ship, in October 1909.

THE FIRST CRUISE AROUND THE WORLD

Ephemera – handwritten and printed letters, documents, and so on – are the key to primary source research on many historical events. In this case, they offer incontrovertible evidence that the *Cleveland* completed the first true around-the-world cruise. This is important documentation because other passenger shipping

CLARK'S CRUISE
OF THE CLEVELAND 18,000 TONS
INDIAN OCEAN
PACIFIC OCEAN
ASIA
EUROPE
AFRICA
AROUND THE WORLD
UNITED STATES
ATLANTIC OCEAN
SOUTH AMERICA
CRUISE No 1 EASTWARD
LEAVING NEW YORK, OCT. 16TH 1909.
FOR FURTHER PARTICULARS APPLY TO
F. C. CLARK, Times Building, Broadway and 42d St., N. Y.

companies have claimed that they had the first such cruise, although at a later date. Not so.

The documents show that the 1909 trip was actually organized by Frank C. Clark Tours of New York rather than by the shipping line itself (FIG. 14). A map of the planned route of the cruise (FIG. 15) is impressive, but it has one significant flaw. The cruise takes the traveller from New York on the East Coast of America, all the way around the globe to the West Coast of America. But to complete the global circumnavigation the world cruise pioneer had to travel by train all the way across America. The reason? As yet, there was no Panama Canal.

Still, this 1909 trip is highly significant. The primary reason is that it was all on one ship. With this cruise, all the organizational challenges had been shifted from the traveller to the Frank C. Clark Company. They made the port arrival and departure arrangements, they handled the food and beverage supplies, and – just as on today's cruises – you didn't have to pack and re-pack your luggage to change to a different carrier. This had already been a feature of shorter cruises, but the idea of covering the entire globe in one cruise on one ship made a major impact.

Promotional material emphasized the challenge of provisioning the ship (FIG. 16). These amounts were just to begin the voyage. Refuelling, docking and provisioning arrangements would have to be pre-planned at each major port of call. One must admire the administrative muscle that was able to accomplish all of this, well before the days of the computer and email. And the quantities would have taxed the resources of some of the ports. Imagine having to schedule for 336,000 pounds of artificial ice – that's 150 tonnes of ice – at a foreign port!

14 A rare promotional booklet for the first round-the-world cruise on the Hamburg-American Line's SS *Cleveland* in 1909. This was the first such cruise on the same ship all the way, with no transfers en route. It was a landmark, even though – without a Panama Canal – the 'circumnavigation' was just from the American East Coast to the West Coast, with a cross-continental rail journey back to New York.

CLARK'S
AROUND THE WORLD CRUISES

By Specially Chartered Hamburg-American Line New S.S. "CLEVELAND" (18,000 tons)

No. 1, Eastward, Leaving New York, Oct. 16, 1909.   No. 2, Westward, Leaving San Francisco, Feb. 5, 1910

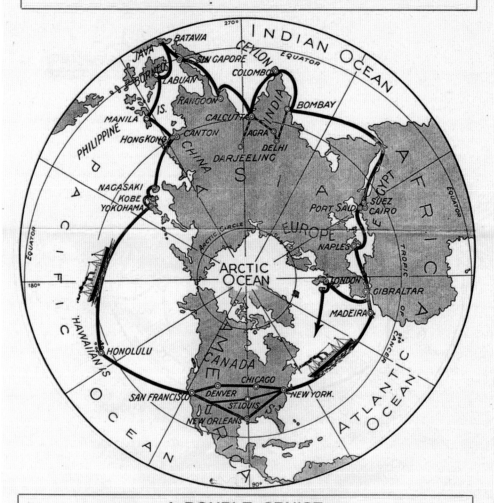

A DOUBLE CRUISE

Leaving New York, Oct. 16, 1909.   Leaving San Francisco, Feb. 5, 1910.

Visiting Out-of-the-Way Places like MADEIRA, BURMA, JAVA, BORNEO and the PHILIPPINE ISLANDS, besides ITALY, EGYPT, INDIA, CEYLON, CHINA, JAPAN and the HAWAIIAN ISLANDS

List of provisions

on board S. S. "Cleveland" the 16th of October 1909 leaving New York.

Fresh meat	88.600 lbs.	Preserved fruit	12.000 tins
Preserved meat	20.000 „	Dried fruit	16.000 lbs.
Ham and bacon	8.200 „	Sugar	18.500 „
Sausages	3.600 „	Spices	1.350 „
Poultries	19.800 „	Sauces	1.800 bottles
Fresh fish	3.800 „	Olive-oil	2.000 quarts
Preserved fish	2.600 tins	Coffee	5.000 lbs.
Smoked and salted fish	1.400 „	Tea	370 „
Oysters, clams crabs	11.500 pieces	Chocolate and cocoa	1.200 „
Lobsters	800 lbs.	Flour	130.000 „
Game	5.400 „	Bread	12.000 „
Cheese	6.500 „	Yeast	1.000 „
Milk and cream	20.000 quarts	Rice, barley. beans, peas,	
Butter	12.000 lbs.	hominy, oatmeal etc.	25.400 „
Eggs	80.000 pieces	Cakes	1.000 tins
Fresh vegetables	25.000 lbs.	Vinegar	3.500 quarts
Preserved vegetables	18.200 tins	Salt	20.000 lbs.
Fresh fruit		Potatoes	80.000 „
Lemons	60.000 pieces	Ice-cream	6.000 bricks
Oranges	63.000 „	Ice, artificial	336.000 lbs.
Grapefruit	20.000 „		
Apples, pears, pine-apples,			
grapes, peaches etc.	26.000 lbs.		

Notice. Fresh meat, poultries, fish, vegetables, fruit, eggs etc. will be taken on board during the trip in every port where obtainable in good condition.

Mineral waters	76.400 bottles	Cigars	65.000 pieces
Wines	22.350 „	Cigarettes	60.000 „
Spirits	4.200 „	Tobacco	150 lbs.
Beer	6.500 gallons		
	Fresh water	3.200 tons	
	Coals	5.500 „	

Why so much ice? In this era, refrigeration was rudimentary. With 6,000 bricks of ice cream to preserve, as well as 80,000 eggs, avoiding spoilage was a real challenge. Students of dietary habits over the years would find this list fascinating in comparison to what might be carried today. For example, in our present low-sodium era, it seems unlikely that any cruise line would want to disclose the amount of salt carried on board – particularly if it were 20,000 pounds.

Detail was minute and painstaking. There were lengthy instructions to those who signed up for the trip, and the shipping line even sent postcards on behalf of its passengers during the cruise, from its office in New York. This became standard

15 Having arrived on the West Coast of America in 1910, the *Cleveland* then embarked on a second world cruise, to return to its point of origin in New York. The logistics involved in fuelling and provisioning the ship around the globe, in an era with primitive communications, would have been daunting.

16 The list of provisions offers an insight into the social history of 1909, with 65,000 cigars and 60,000 cigarettes on board, as well as 22,350 bottles of wine and 6,500 gallons of beer. With refrigeration in a rudimentary state and requiring 336,000 pounds of artificial ice, these supplies – and the ice – would have to be refreshed several times during the voyage.

practice for the Hamburg–American Line for many years afterwards, so that messages could reach everyone on a list of pre-selected American recipients within a relatively short period of time. There are also a few examples mailed from Germany to German addressees. One card corrected with a forwarding address gives a sense of the financial status of the friends of the passengers: a postcard recipient who had relocated to the warmer climate of Daytona, Florida, from Narragansett Pier in Rhode Island, with the advent of winter.

The traveller provided the shipping line with a list of no more than twenty-five names and addresses for postcards, and the recipients would receive a stream of cards as the ship arrived at various highlights among its destinations. This saved a lot of correspondence for the traveller, and avoided the challenge of having to find and send cards from the various locations en route. This was also a brilliant marketing ploy by Frank C. Clark and the shipping line, as friends of the affluent people on board eagerly awaited the card from the next port – and contemplated whether they, too, should go on a world cruise.

This group of travellers was encouraged to think of themselves as a unique and elite group of pioneers. Only the wealthy could afford to pay the fare, and then take three months out of their business and social lives. Nowadays on a Cunarder, it's possible to take just a leg or two of the global voyage and jet back home afterwards. In 1909 the only way to get back home was by ship, so one might as well just stay aboard the *Cleveland*.

In 1934, the Hamburg–American Line held a reception in New York and invited as many of the original 650 passengers as could be found to commemorate the twenty-fifth anniversary of the *Cleveland*'s cruise. A newspaper article listed several passengers as well as the Captain of the *Cleveland* in 1909, Commodore

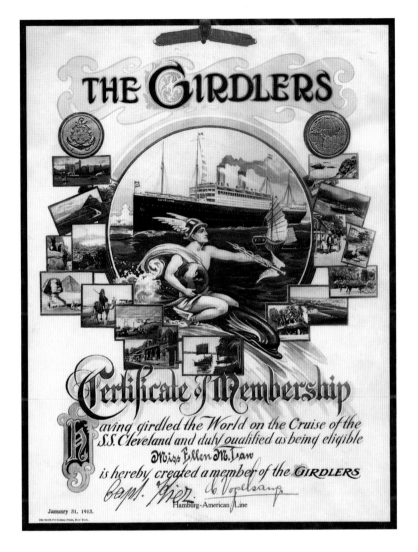

17 At the
completion of
the world cruise,
participants received
a diploma such
as this surviving
example from 1913
attesting to their
membership of 'The
Girdlers'.

Fritz Kruse. The turnout was evidence that the cruise had
created a loyal following for the Line. There had been many
memorable details on the journey, including special baggage
labels and probably a 'Girdler' certificate at the end of the
cruise, such as this example from 1913 (FIG. 17). Even a special

baggage label has been found glued to a vintage steamer trunk that had been purchased by a couple for use as a coffee table, and they would not soak it off for me!

It is logical to ask what sparked the *Cleveland* cruise. It appears to have been a breakthrough in shipping thinking. For the answer, we have to look to the United States Navy. In 1907 the US Navy began a world cruise of a group of its ships in white livery, styled as the Great White Fleet. A small commemorative card from the USS *Minnesota*, one of sixteen American warships in the convoy, shows the ambitious schedule, beginning in Hampton Roads, Virginia, in December 1907, and returning there in February 1909. This appears to have been a true circumnavigation of the globe, including sailing around the tip of South America. The impetus for the trip to 'show the flag' may have been the growing power of Japan's navy and their crushing of the Russian navy at the Battle of Tsushima Strait in May 1905.

The US Navy trip proved that a ship could travel for over a year and be suitably refuelled and revictualled en route. If the Navy could do it, why not a civilian passenger ship? A cruise of more than a year would have been too long for most potential travellers, but if one eliminated the lengthy leg under the tip of South America and instead went from the East Coast of the United States to the West Coast of the United States, the trip could be 'streamlined' to offer a more appealing duration.

Hamburg–American Line's around-the-world cruises ended with the advent of the First World War. It wasn't until 1922, when Cunard's RMS *Laconia* rekindled the world cruise flame, that such cruises resumed – this time as a completely oceanic circumnavigation, in consequence of the opening of the Panama Canal in 1915.

WORLD CRUISES AFTER THE FIRST WORLD WAR

CUNARD

There were many world cruises by various shipping lines after the First World War, though perhaps none carried the lustre or the excitement of the early ones. It was Cunard that reintroduced the concept after both the First World War (with RMS *Laconia* in 1922) and the Second World War (with RMS *Caronia* in 1951).

Are world cruise travellers supposed to be boastful? Perhaps they have the right to be. An unidentified passenger on the *Laconia*'s 1922 voyage began one of her letters with, 'I am on the "Laconia Cruise Around the World" Cunard Line – we are on a calm sea and have had wonderful weather.' This is somewhat redundant since the note is on Cunard stationery with a letter-head which says, 'On board the Cunard R.M.S. Laconia'. The note is addressed to 'Judge Young', who may have been doing some legal work for the passenger.

A letter from the same voyage, signed 'Mother', reported that

> The Get-together Dinner last night was a splendid introduction. The Standard Oil & Pittsburg millionaires wore caps, punched balloons, blew horns, etc. – along with us poor folks. A movie lecture on Magellan by Captain Brown (our captain, only fifty-one years old) & an historic outline of the cruise.

Elsewhere she recounts that there are eighty-five widows on board!

Another letter, written in a different hand by 'Louise' to 'My Dear Laura', gives a different perspective on the Get-together Dinner:

Last night we were all invited to a Get-together Dinner at 7. Most everybody dressed in evening gown. Then they screened off one end of the deck & decorated it with flags and lanterns – informal dancing in the evening – we of course went and such gowns I have never seen. I certainly didn't enjoy it at all. I was bored to death. All the cute men played around with the millionaire girls & didn't even have a show. Some come-down from the attention in N.Y. and home that I have been used to.

I suppose it will take some time before we can all get acquainted. We have met some very interesting people – slow but that is what we desired to do & not get some dumbbells attached to us we couldn't shake.

This was the only letter from 'Louise', and it appears that she is something more of a 'party animal' than her travelling companion.

CANADIAN PACIFIC

World cruising was not exclusive to Cunard. Canadian Pacific offered a similar service by 1925, and the Hamburg–American Line re-established theirs. The cover of a Canadian Pacific brochure for their 1927–28 world cruise (FIG. 18) displays the calibre of artwork that the company sustained all through the period up to 1939; and the line's ongoing relationship with the DeMuth husband-and-wife team (see above) was further evidence of the commitment to support artists and designers.

A passenger list from Canadian Pacific's *Empress of Britain* world cruise of 1935 included Lady Ashbolt, Sir Frederick W.L. Butterfield and Lady Butterfield, Princess L. Donskaia, Vicomtesse E. de Bresson and Major-General S.S. Long. Six of the passengers were accompanied by a maid, and there was a nurse accompanying Master D. Beck. Even in the darkest days of the Great Depression, some people still had money.

18 In 1922 Cunard reintroduced the world cruise, using the Panama Canal to effect a complete oceanic circumnavigation. Other lines soon offered competition, including this seductive brochure from Canadian Pacific.

Fifth Annual
Round the World
Cruise
1927~28
CANADIAN
PACIFIC

Empress of Britain
ROUND THE WORLD CRUISE ITINERARY

Ports	Miles	Arrive	Leave
New York	....	....	Jan. 9
Madeira	2774	Jan. 15	Jan. 16
Gibraltar	616	Jan. 18	Jan. 18
Algiers	419	Jan. 19	Jan. 20
Monaco	461	Jan. 21	Jan. 23
Naples	366	Jan. 24	Jan. 25
Athens	677	Jan. 27	Jan. 27
Haifa	673	Jan. 29	Jan. 29
Port Said	174	Jan. 25	....
Suez	90	....	Feb. 5
Bombay	2963	Feb. 12	Feb. 19
Colombo	890	Feb. 22	Feb. 26
Penang	1287	Mar. 1	Mar. 1
Singapore	394	Mar. 2	Mar. 3
Bangkok	803	Mar. 6	Mar. 6
Batavia	1273	Mar. 9	Mar. 11
Semarang	236	Mar. 12	Mar. 12
Bali	419	Mar. 14	Mar. 15
Manila	1640	Mar. 19	Mar. 20
Hong Kong	633	Mar. 21	Mar. 25
Shanghai	850	Mar. 28	Mar. 29
Chinwangtao	660	Mar. 31	Apr. 4
Beppu	834	Apr. 7	Apr. 8
Kobe	216	Apr. 8	Apr. 12
Yokohama	356	Apr. 13	Apr. 16
Honolulu	3405	Apr. 23	Apr. 24
San Francisco	2100	Apr. 29	Apr. 30
Los Angeles	395	May 1	May 2
Balboa	2937	May 8	May 9
Cristobal	38	May 9	May 9
New York	1972	May 14	....
	30,551		

19 By 1937 Canadian Pacific was using its flagship *Empress of Britain* for an annual world cruise, covering some 30,551 miles. In a recession-ravaged economy, the number of affluent prospective travellers was limited, and there was a challenge to visit new ports each year.

Wealth was a vital ingredient. With some cabins costing as much as $12,300 per person for the suite, including shore excursions, a couple could spend almost $25,000 for the trip, at a time when a teacher earned less than a thousand dollars a year. For the budget traveller, rooms were available for as little as $2,150 per person, and there were also single cabins S1 to S12, for servants' quarters, at $1,750 per person.

There was good reason for the cost – the cruise covered 30,551 miles, visited many ports (as shown in FIG. 19) and carried a large staff to cater to the passengers. Thirteen cruise directors and a social directress came at a price! Note that there was even a press representative and two chaplains. For many years Canadian Pacific even carried two on-board artists, the DeMuths, a married couple who drew images of places visited and sights seen, to sell to passengers on board as postcards. How many designs are there? An American collector of the genre has some 200 different postcards, but there could be more. As well as postcard-sized images, some were available in sets in a larger format suitable for framing: a set from a 1928 cruise is known.

HAMBURG–AMERICAN LINE

German shipping, recovering quickly from the First World War and the depredation of war reparations, soon returned to the world cruise fray. The delightful cover on an SS *Resolute* world cruise brochure of 1928 features drawings of bejewelled elephants and decorated howdahs, oxen pulling elaborate ceremonial carts, and other stereotypical images of exotic foreign lands beckoning to the traveller. The prospect of 140 days on board might have deterred some, but it certainly made the experience more suitable for bragging about.

On the S·S·RELIANCE of the Hamburg-American Line

HAMBURG-AMERICAN LINE · NORTH GERMAN LLOYD

1936 CRUISE AROUND THE WORLD

The brochure makes a great attempt to assure passengers of their comfort in warmer climates:

> A considerable amount of the time is spent in the tropics. The *Resolute* was built especially for service in tropical waters. Unusual spaciousness characterizes her staterooms, public rooms and decks, and a system of forced ventilation, which is in operation throughout the ship, makes for comfort regardless of temperatures on the outside.

While this would have sounded comforting to the traveller who had suffered from excruciating heat and humidity during previous voyages in tropical climates, it still does not provide assurance that air from the outdoors, forced through ventilation pipes, can provide anything other than ongoing blasts of warm, humid air. This was not the era of air conditioning; while there might have been air circulating in the cabins, it would not have been much different from the air outside. Sleeping on deck was a possibility.

The claim that *Resolute* was built 'especially for service in tropical waters' is more a marketing ploy than reality. The context here is Prohibition, the nationwide ban on producing, importing and selling alcohol in the United States that was in force from 1920 to 1933. Ships registered in the USA were covered by the ban but those operating under foreign flags were exempt; *Resolute*'s registration had been transferred to Panama in 1923. For some, 140 days without the constraints of Prohibition would have been the closest thing to a drinker's heaven, whether in tropical waters or elsewhere.

Later brochures were even more dramatic. A cover from 1936 for *Resolute*'s sister ship *Reliance* (FIG. 20) is powerful and seductive for the traveller who can afford the experience.

20 In 1936 the Hamburg-American Line world cruise was on the SS *Reliance*. This dramatic cover on its brochure would have caught the attention of world cruise aspirants.

Hamburg-American Line set the criteria in 1909: one ship for the entire journey; no transfers except for land-based excursions; and a variety of fascinating ports. The Dollar Line of the 1930s is an example of an operator that purported to offer a menu of world cruises, in conjunction with American Express. Although the brochure claims that 'You may make your world-voyage on one ship all the way', it qualifies the statement by completing the sentence with 'confining your adventures ashore to those ports-of-call'.

The ports of call are those regularly serviced by the Dollar Line ships, and do not represent the tailored itinerary of a dedicated world cruise. You might find that you were the only person on board who was not travelling specifically to one of the ports en route. The wording on the cover is clever, in that it doesn't offer a specific world cruise, but rather the prospect of going 'Around the World' on the Dollar Line.

WORLD CRUISES AFTER THE SECOND WORLD WAR

Full credit to Cunard for reintroducing the world cruise in 1951 on the *Caronia*. The liner was built after the Second World War and went into service for the then Cunard–White Star Line in 1949. A significant feature for cruising was the provision of air conditioning in the public rooms. This made her an attractive vessel for cruises, including world cruises. Unfortunately, the air conditioning did not extend to the cabin accommodation, but there would at least be relief from enervating climates for those who spent time in the restaurants, smoking rooms, bars and other public-service facilities.

Cunard continues its programme of world cruises to this day, with offerings on the *Queen Mary 2* and *Queen Victoria*.

For example, one world cruise on the *Queen Mary 2*, advertised more than a year in advance, spans 108 nights and 24 countries, eastbound out of New York, while the *Queen Victoria* heads westbound out of Southampton for a trip spanning 107 days. Each of the trips visits a different set of ports. *Queen Mary 2* arrives in Southampton on the same day as her fleet mate begins her journey in the opposite direction. It is fascinating to note that more than a year before departure that future world cruise on the *Queen Mary 2* was sold out for five of the seven Queen's Grill (First Class) categories, including the most expensive suites.

Cruises of Distinction.

Cunard
Winter & Spring
1930

THE SUPERLINERS

During the 1930s factories were closed around the globe, many people were unemployed, public confidence was eroded, and every government was looking for sparks to boost public morale. There were indeed some signs of hope: in the UK, middle-class salaries were growing due to expansion of 'second-wave' light industries and thus enabling more disposable income, since the cost of living did not rise in relative terms. The modern design styles showcased at the 1925 Paris Exposition were becoming the rage as art deco, and in Europe national design and pride were embodied in a new range of stylish ocean liners. For the very rich everything was cheap, and everyone competed for the business of this demanding elite – including the shipping companies. This was very much a European phenomenon. The European powers had a strong tradition of passenger ships. While Germany was focusing much of its shipbuilding plans and efforts on naval vessels such as the *Bismarck*, Britain and France looked to the stimulus of passenger-ship construction with dramatic 80,000-ton behemoths to foster employment in their shipyards. The bigger the ship, the more jobs she created.

RMS *QUEEN MARY*, A PROUD NATIONAL STIMULUS

In May 1936 the fabled ocean liner *Queen Mary* made her maiden voyage across the Atlantic, at the start of more than thirty years of legendary service. Under construction for many years, she was known only as 'Hull 534' in the John Brown Shipyard in Scotland. Begun in late 1930, her construction was interrupted a year later because of financial difficulties at the Cunard Line. With construction resumed in early 1934, thanks to an infusion of government money and a forced merger between Cunard and its rival White Star, she was the epitome of Britain's rise from the depths of the Great Depression.

A press photo of the era speaks to the immensity of the construction project and the number of related jobs at the shipyard (**FIG. 21**). Not shown is all the supporting work by the off-site suppliers who built the *Queen Mary*'s engines, propellers, equipment and furnishings. Her launch on 26 September 1934 was marked by great fanfare, including a commemorative medallion distributed by the *Daily Record* and a formal brochure prepared by Cunard (**FIG. 22**). Note that the brochure illustrated is marked 'Please return to "Publicity Dept." Cunard White Star Limited.' Obviously, someone didn't!

Following her christening by HM Queen Mary on 26 September 1935, excitement mounted as her opulent interiors were finished and furnished, and the time of her maiden voyage approached. Magazines prepared special issues, such as the 276-page June 1936 Souvenir Number of *The Shipbuilder* (**FIG. 23**) which extolled her technical achievements.

The *Queen Mary*'s maiden voyage, beginning on 27 May 1936, had an impact at the time like that of astronauts reaching the moon decades later. The fashions purportedly worn on board were a springboard for fashion magazines positioning

21 A press photo of the *Queen Mary* under construction, c.1935. This perspective emphasizes her immensity in comparison to the many buildings in the shipyard on the River Clyde.

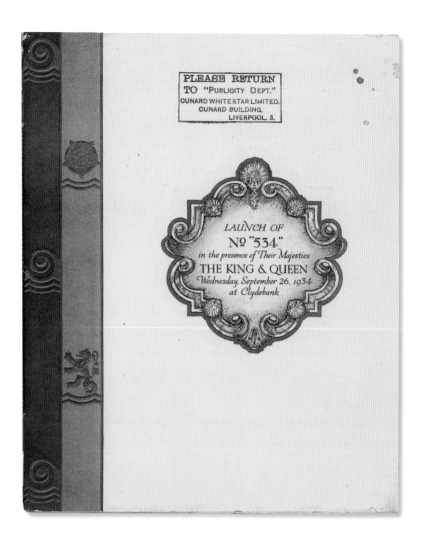

PLEASE RETURN
TO "PUBLICITY DEPT."
CUNARD WHITE STAR LIMITED.
CUNARD BUILDING.
LIVERPOOL. 3.

LAUNCH OF
No "534"
in the presence of Their Majesties
THE KING & QUEEN
*Wednesday, September 26, 1934
at Clydebank*

themselves in association with the *Queen Mary*, as the pinnacle of style and elegance. Advertisers joined in, including the National Hotel Management Co., which operated a chain of top-end US hotels and used the maiden voyage to send promotional messages to Americans.

Imagine yourself coming aboard for this exciting voyage. All your neighbours and friends know that you're travelling on the

22 A formal *Queen Mary* ('Hull 534') launch brochure from 1934 prepared by Cunard.

new 'superliner' RMS *Queen Mary* – because you gave them a copy of a widely distributed Cunard booklet of the same name. As a special memento, when you board you are given an elaborate certificate that exceeds the quality of diplomas from many of the better institutions of higher learning, attesting to the fact that you were on the maiden voyage (FIG. 24). Accompanying the certificate is a large, profusely illustrated booklet crammed

23 The *Queen Mary* was deemed such an engineering feat that an entire issue of *The Shipbuilder* (June 1936) commemorated her completion, with extensive congratulatory advertising by the many companies that participated in her design and building.

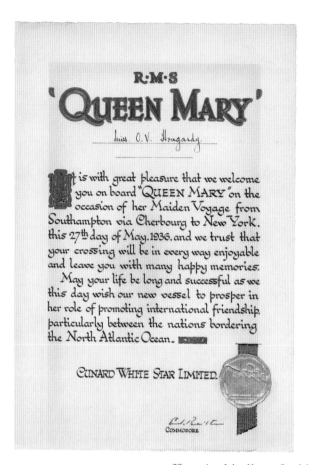

R·M·S
'QUEEN MARY'

Miss. O. V. Hougardy

It is with great pleasure that we welcome you on board "QUEEN MARY" on the occasion of her Maiden Voyage from Southampton via Cherbourg to New York, this 27ᵗʰ day of May. 1936. and we trust that your crossing will be in every way enjoyable and leave you with many happy memories.

May your life be long and successful as we this day wish our new vessel to prosper in her role of promoting international friendship particularly between the nations bordering the North Atlantic Ocean.

CUNARD WHITE STAR LIMITED.

COMMODORE

with images of the art and sculpture which decorate the *Queen Mary*: another trophy to take back to show the neighbours.

During your first full day on board, you stroll the decks and visit the shops in the impressive Shopping Centre. Perhaps you purchase a few souvenirs: a painted china brooch; an enamel lapel pin; and a souvenir spoon for your favourite aunt's collection. A dramatic postcard illustrating how the *Queen Mary*, at some 80,000 tons, would stretch beyond the boundaries of London's Trafalgar Square would be a nice token to send to one of the postcard collectors back at your office. And in lieu of taking your own amateurish photographs you could purchase an envelope of twelve black-and-white glossy views of the ship and her principal rooms.

The next morning, you would read the ship's newspaper, the *Ocean Times*, and absorb its account of the first full day, and then reflect on your good fortune at being on this trip.

If you were a celebrity in one of the better First Class cabins, you might be offered the privilege of signing the ship's autograph book (FIG. 25). Your signature would be joined by those of many famous passengers during the next few years of voyages, including celebrities such as Noël Coward, the American film star Gary Cooper, the silent film darling Mary Pickford, the

24 An impressive diploma (suitable for framing) was presented to passengers on the *Queen Mary*'s maiden voyage in 1936.

publisher William Randolph
Hearst and his companion,
actress Marion Davies,
boxing champion Henry
Armstrong, and names
on numerous other pages
that would warm the heart
of any serious autograph
collector.

The Cunard brochure,
A Book of Comparisons, states
that the 2,075 passengers
would consume an
estimated 10 tons of meat,
5 tons of hams and bacon,
600 pounds of coffee, 25,000
pounds of potatoes, 30,000
eggs and 125 crates of
oranges per voyage. There
are no estimates of alcohol consumption.

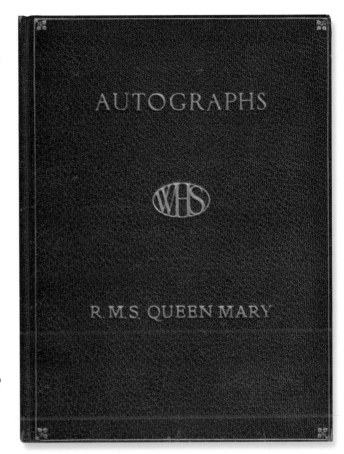

After the Second World War, it was 'business as usual',
and the refurbished *Queen Mary* was paired with her sister
ship, the *Queen Elizabeth*, to provide a regular, dependable,
five-day service across the Atlantic between New York and
Southampton. That pattern continued until the 1960s saw the
decline of ocean liner travel, and the increased popularity of
travel by air. On 31 October 1967 the *Queen Mary* made her
final trip, from Southampton to Long Beach, California, having
been acquired by the City of Long Beach to serve as a tourist
attraction, which now includes restaurants and a museum
alongside a three-star hotel.

25 The presence
of the rich and
famous on board
was captured in this
unique *Queen Mary*
autograph book with
hundreds of celebrity
signatures during
1936–39.

"NORMANDIE"

LE NOUVEAU PAQUEBOT DE LA Cⁱᵉ Gˡᵉ TRANSATLANTIQUE

CHEF-D'ŒUVRE DE LA TECHNIQUE
ET DE L'ART FRANÇAIS

L'ILLUSTRATION

NUMÉRO 4813ᵇⁱˢ
HORS SÉRIE

JUIN 1935
PRIX 10 Fr.

SS *NORMANDIE*, FLAGSHIP OF FRANCE

In late May 1935, the *Normandie*, pride of France and the most stylish ocean liner ever to cross the Atlantic, made her maiden voyage. Like the *Queen Mary*, which set sail the following year, *Normandie* was conceived and constructed during the Great Depression as part of a 'stimulus package' to support workers, artists and artisans – in this case, French workers. In the early 1930s all sectors of the economy were in distress, from steel workers to skilled artisans. A ship was a useful tool to bring all these together and generate a broad range of business activities. As well as the basics of construction and engineering, there was work for firms such as Christofle to provide silverware, for Raymond Subes to design rich metalwork, as well as for the manufacturers of china, glassware, furniture, carpets and all the other elements of a big passenger ship.

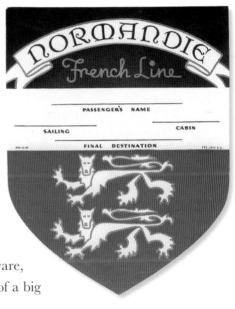

At some 80,000 tons, *Normandie* was the biggest ship afloat. That alone would appeal to some prospective travellers. Full-page advertisements in such elite publications as America's *Town & Country* magazine of April 1935 built a pre-maiden-voyage buzz. A special large-format magazine issue (FIG. 26) extolled the virtues of her construction, her design and her comfort. Overflowing with photographs, this publication, simply titled *Normandie*, positioned her as the prime example of French technology and art. For those from the USA able to afford the life of 'an American in Paris', this was the way to get there.

26 A special issue of the magazine *L'Illustration*, from June 1935, featuring the *Normandie*.

27 *Normandie* had distinctive baggage labels that you would clearly want to keep attached to your luggage as a status symbol.

The marketing expression to sell 'the sizzle not the steak' was redundant in this case, since 'the steak' completely measured up to 'the sizzle'. However, the promotional material included distinctive baggage labels that you would clearly want to keep attached to your luggage as long as they lasted (FIG. 27), so that hotels and other travel professionals could see that you had travelled on the *Normandie*. Enamel souvenir pins and even matchbooks carried through the theme of quality and elegance. During party nights you might receive a festive ribbon with the name *Normandie* and a French flag woven into it. All of this built up what marketers today would call a 'brand'.

The design of brochures, passenger lists and even games booklets all reflected the French *joie de vivre* that the ship represented and said 'Welcome to the high life'. To honour *Normandie*'s maiden voyage, the French government issued a special commemorative postage stamp and collectors eagerly sought covers carried on the maiden voyage (FIG. 28).

28 *Normandie's maiden voyage in 1935 was widely celebrated, with a special French postage stamp, a striking 'poster stamp' and even commemorative envelopes for the ardent stamp and cover collector.*

The *Normandie* brand became so iconic that others used it to add significance to their own products. For example, in 1939 the American car manufacturer Studebaker sent a targeted mass mailing to selected Americans via the *Normandie*, with an elegant card inside on *Normandie* stationery that said:

Mes Amis: Just a line to let you know that we arrive from Paris tomorrow after a marvelous trip on the *Normandie*. While there we attended a very swanky prevue showing of the new 1939 Studebaker. It's so stunning even the voluble French can't find words to describe it.

I picked up a French brochure which I am enclosing. Fred & I think it sets an absolutely new style – be sure to see it.

29 The luxurious First Class dining room on the *Normandie*.

On board the *Normandie*, all the public rooms were dramatic and fashionable. For example, the First Class dining room (FIG. 29) was magnificent, featuring soaring ceilings, a dramatic entranceway, and enormous Lalique chandeliers.

This assessment is a consensus from many sources, but there are other opinions. A woman whose name we know only as 'Georgie' wrote in her diary of a visit to the liner and to the Italian SS *Roma* in New York:

> Saw Clara and Harry who had passes to the Roma and spent afternoon with them going through it and also the Normandie, which happens to be here. We were much disappointed in it. Our conclusion was that the interior decorator designed it either in the throes of the D.T.'s or a nightmare.

The 'regulars', and no doubt some of the crew as well, would have scanned the passenger list at the start of the voyage to see what 'important' people were aboard, and tables would have been assigned accordingly. There would be no such thing as casual dining in this setting, and if you were not formally dressed for the occasion the glances of the other patrons would soon let you know that you didn't belong. For some of the travelling public, it would probably have been intimidating.

In August 1939, on the outbreak of the Second World War, *Normandie* was laid up at her pier in New York. She stayed there until December 1941 when, a few days after the attack on Pearl Harbor, she was seized by the US government, taken over by the Navy and renamed USS *Lafayette*. As a troop transport, she would be invaluable to the American war effort.

During the conversion many of the elaborate furnishings were taken off the ship and put into storage. An Associated

30 This press photo captures the removal of the decorative panels on the *Normandie* in 1942 as part of preparing her for wartime service.

Press release of the time, accompanying a photo of workmen dismantling part of the interior (FIG. 30), reported:

> The former French liner *Normandie*, taken over recently by the U.S. for use as a naval auxiliary and renamed the *U.S.S. Lafayette*, is being stripped of its lavish decorations and furnishings, valued at $2,000,000, and all will be stored. Here workmen remove a bronze casting from a doorway. This picture was released Jan. 8 by the Navy in New York where the dismantling is underway.

Scrambling frantically to meet tight deadlines, Navy workmen were not as careful as they should have been. On 8 February 1942, just a month after the press release, sparks from a welding torch were reportedly the cause of a fire which gutted this magnificent ship. She lay on her side at the French Line pier until after the war. An elderly friend recalls a visit to New York in 1945 with his Scout troop, when one of the sightseeing highlights of New York was this enormous ship looking like a beached whale.

So only seven years after her maiden voyage, including just over four years of service, the former *Normandie* lay ravaged by fire. Was the ship a failure? She reportedly never made money. But as an artistic showpiece she was an outstanding success. As a stimulus project, providing the jobs to build her and afterwards to put her into service and continue operating her, she was equally successful. Above all, as an ambassador for France and the French decorative arts, she was a triumph.

NORMANDIE POSTCARDS AND POSTCARD BOOKLETS

Postcards of the *Normandie* were very popular. A number of publishers produced books of these. If you see a telltale set of perforations on the side of a single card, you can be sure that it's from one of the booklets.

A booklet titled *20 Vues*, published by La Cigogne, contains a sepia-printed image of the ship, and nineteen sepia-printed illustrations of the various rooms within. Similar booklets were produced by Les Éditions Bloc Frères of Bordeaux and Compagnie des Arts Photoméchaniques.

My favourite postcard producer is 'Tito', whose black-and-white Real Photo cards, such as one of the great ship's massive alternators, are crisp and very clear. It is unusual to find photos of ships' engine rooms, presumably because most of the passengers never saw the engines, and probably never even thought about them. Even if they did, it is not exactly the image that you were going to brag about in postcards to your relatives and friends.

The SS *Normandie* was surely the world's most magnificent shipping example of French interwar technology, art and design. Even today her legacy is felt. In June 2017 a set of panels from her Grand Salon, designed by Jean-Théodore Dupas circa 1934, executed in *verre églomisé* by Charles Champigneulle and removed to safety during her 1942 troopship conversion, was auctioned by Sotheby's New York for $1,392,500.

SS *UNITED STATES*: THE WORLD'S FASTEST LINER

The SS *United States*, from her record-setting maiden voyage in 1952 until she was laid up in 1969, was the undisputed greyhound of all the world's passenger liners. Her speed enabled her to sail across the Atlantic and back in under four and a half days each way, compared to the five days needed by her competitors. At some 53,000 tons she was not a superliner by size, but she deserves special mention for her contribution to passenger liner speed and safety. Sadly, the ship today remains a forlorn hulk, which has for many years been the subject of

Name of Vessel: United States	Department: STEWARDS
Design: P6-S4-DS1	Page: 2
M.C. Hull No: 2917	Made By:JWM & WSW
NNS & DD Co. Hull No: 488	Date: 1-7-52
Group Name: BARBER SHOP & BEAUTY SHOP	Rev. No:
	Group No: S36-2

Furn. By	Authority	Cl.	Item No.	Name and Description		Box No.	Unit	Quan.	Inv. Ck.	Diff.
	NN 505-827 & 530-1462			**FIRST CLASS BEAUTY PARLOR MAIN DECK** **FR. 186-194-S**						
x	NNPO 530-69	E	1	Chair, Easy, Arm .	Elev. 47-930		Ea.	3	3	
x	"	E	2	Chair, Side	Elev. 47-935		Ea.	2	2	
x	"	P	3	Mirror & Shelf	Elev. 4-903		Ea.	1	1	
x	NN.530-1462	E	4	Rack, Magazine	Elev. 27-902		Ea.	1	1	
x	NNPO530-69	E	5	Stool	Elev. 47-926		Ea.	1	1	
x	NNPO530-182	E	6	Trash Can			Ea.	2	2	
x	NNPO530-114	E	7	Cash Register #4889941 Model: 126 (4) N gray enamel Maker: National Cash Register Co.			Ea.	1	1	
x	NNPO530-89	P	8	Cabinet, W/Doors,shelves & retainer for Cash Register			Ea.	1	1	
x	"	P	9	Cabinets,Antiseptic Sterilizer W/soiled linen bin under.			Ea.	2	2	
x	"	P	10	Cabinets, W/ Door & Shelves			Ea.	2	2	
x	"	P	11	Cabinets W/Door & Shelves W/Sea rails			Ea.	4	4	
x	"	P	12	Cabinet, Display(over cash register)			Ea.	1	1	
x	NNPO.530-114	E	13	Smoking Stand			Ea.	1	1	
x	NN.505-827	P	14	Mirror			Ea.	2	2	
x	"	P	15	Rack, Hat and Coat			Ea.	1	1	

Operator

U.S.M.C.

Contractor

31 A page of one of the several allowance books of the SS *United States* shows detailed listings of the furnishings and fixtures when she was delivered by her builder in 1951.

various plans to restore what is undoubtedly the greatest liner ever to sail under the American flag.

She was the largest passenger ship ever built entirely in the United States, and the fastest one ever constructed. Her speed records have never been beaten by any passenger liner, and probably never will be. Laid up at her current berth in Philadelphia, the ship is even listed on the USA's National Register of Historic Places.

One of the largest sources of historical and reference material for the SS *United States* was a blockbuster seven-day auction by Guernsey's, held beside the ship in 1984 in Norfolk, Virginia, to sell her entire contents, which had been left *in situ* when she was taken out of service and mothballed in 1969. The intervening fifteen years had confirmed the initial conclusion that the traditional North Atlantic liner passenger service had been superseded by the airlines. As the recipient of government grants, which required that she remain forever in US registry, she could not be moved to a foreign flag with lower labour standards and costs.

The SS *United States* was stripped down to her painted interior, and even the contents of her bridge were auctioned off by Guernsey's. During the auction, for a fee you could go on a guided tour of the barren interior. For $12.50 you could buy an auction catalogue. For another small amount you could purchase a 2½-inch-diameter '1952–1969' souvenir badge. You could also purchase a small cardboard box containing two linen monogrammed napkins, a baggage label, a baggage tag, menu covers and a room key. There were hundreds of these boxes on offer.

RESTORING THE SS *UNITED STATES*

There have been numerous announcements over the years about possible restoration of the SS *United States*. Re-creation would be costly if all the details were followed. Would they re-create the bath mats featuring the eagle logo on a luxurious, toe-caressing grey soft cotton background? Would they re-manufacture the glassware, chinaware and silverware that were the apex of stylish ocean travel? (I could sell them eight dozen highball glasses in their original carton, which I enthusiastically purchased at the liquidation sale in 1984.) And what about fine dining necessities such as caviar servers? With the ubiquitous American eagle on each side, these opulent testimonies to luxurious meals on this fabulous vessel provide the final word on first-class travel.

A set of some twenty books, described as Allowance Books, were included in the 1984 auction. These books provided a detailed listing of the type and quantity of each individual item on board when the ship was handed over to the shipping line. Each item – from ashtrays and silverware to chairs and fixtures – was counted and initialled by representatives of United States Lines. For example, the First Class Beauty Parlour fixtures included three easy chairs, two side chairs, one stool and two trash cans (FIG. 31). Unfortunately, these books were broken up into lots of three or four and sold individually to separate buyers.

A LIVING HISTORY

As well as the design and decor elements, memorabilia of the SS *United States* offer a chance to relive shipping history. Each day passengers were given a copy of the ship's daily newspaper, the *Ocean Press*. The issue for 27 February 1962 has four tabloid-sized pages.

The lead story, 'Glenn Rides in Triumph Down Avenue of Heroes', reports on astronaut John Glenn's triumphant parade past 250,000 cheering spectators in Washington DC prior to ad-dressing a joint meeting of Congress. The article also mentions that the day 'saw Glenn and his family return from Florida aboard President Kennedy's jet plane'.

Advertisements are mostly from cigarette manufacturers, with slogans such as 'the cigarettes that America likes best' and

32 The elegant cover of a menu from a gala dinner on board the SS *United States* in 1957 hints at the luxury of the experience.

33 Some passengers took the key to their stateroom as a memento of their voyage.

the chance to 'Feel new coolness deep in your throat'. Half a century later, we have a more informed perspective.

A booklet of passenger fares for the year 1965 shows the most expensive cabins to be First Class suites for $1,341 per person, each way. Compare this to the current top transatlantic fare on the *Queen Mary 2* – $22,558 per person, one way, for a Grand Suite – and you get a sense of inflation.

AVAILABILITY OF MEMENTOES

Because the SS *United States* was in service until 1969, material collected by those fortunate individuals who sailed on her is still coming fresh to the market from their estates. In the 1950s and 1960s, American advertising and graphic design were world-leading, and the iconic materials created by her designers remain attractive in the light of today's design expectations. For example, her Manhattan-pattern silverware, manufactured by the International Silver Company, is a clean pattern typical of American product design in the early 1950s. A page from the Guernsey's catalogue for the 1984 auction illustrates the many iterations of knives, forks and spoons that were used for formal dining. Each carries the *USL* (United States Lines) identifying mark. These were auctioned in large bulk lots but have since been absorbed into the collecting community and are now relatively scarce.

Fine dining was another feature of the voyage, and the farewell dinner was the zenith of the experience. A menu – with a silken cord – sets out the almost bewildering array of dining options (FIG. 32). With an image of the ship featured on the cover, this was a coveted souvenir for those who sought memories of the SS *United States* experience. Another memento might be the key to your room: a substantial memory of the ship, and especially of your stateroom on board (FIG. 33).

N.Y.K. LINE

M

DESTINATION

M.S." MARU"
S.S.

CLASS

BAGGAGE ROOM

PRINTED IN JAPAN

PICKY, PICKY DETAILS

There was much more to planning a voyage than choosing a ship. Once that was done, there were many more practicalities still to be considered – from selecting a cabin to packing appropriately.

SELECTING THE CABIN

As with airline bookings, some travellers just accept what is assigned to them. In the early days of steerage that didn't make a lot of difference, as we will see later in this chapter. The best known of the conventional criteria was established on the shipping routes from the UK to the East – Port Out, Starboard Home. The premiss was that the left side of the ship would be more shaded from the sun headed east, and the right side on the return voyage. Some readers will already have heard of the acronym – P.O.S.H. – derived from this idea.

The more expensive and larger cabins were on the upper decks. Given the 'wedding cake' profile of ships of the day, there were fewer cabins and fewer people than on the lower decks. The *Titanic* disaster demonstrated that it was easier to escape from cabins on the upper decks than from cabins lower down, from where it was necessary to climb up flights of internal stairs to reach the lifeboats. However, below decks and amidships had the benefit of less exposure to sea motion.

Even among equal cabins, some were more desirable than others. Do you want to be situated near stairs or a bank of elevators so that you can hear the carousers returning from their evening's partying at two in the morning? However, if you were in that community, it wouldn't make any difference, and proximity might even facilitate intoxicated navigation from the elevator to your cabin door.

Proximity to bathrooms and toilets was another consideration. Such facilities en suite were rare, so one had to book a bath in a Bath Room, and travel down the hall at the appointed time, past any fellow travellers who might be in the hallway.

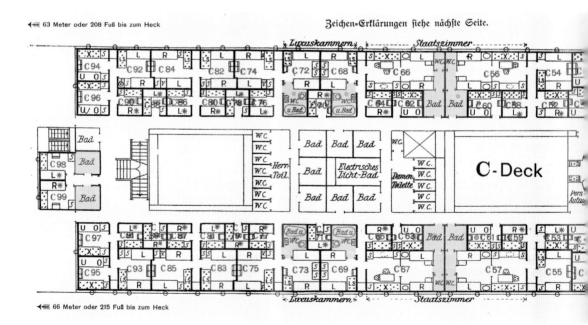

Toilets? Not in your cabin. In the middle of the night – or any other time – an urgent need would require use of a chamber pot or a sprint down the hallway. The Cunard–White Star Line had chamber pots custom-made by Minton.

If this sounds primitive, it is only so compared to today's expectations. At the time, those arrangements were normal on ships and in hotels, and in selecting their cabin the prudent traveller kept these factors in mind. As a prelude to middle-of-the-night sprints down the hall, in a multi-bed cabin one had to select between an upper and a lower bunk. If you were late booking, you might not have a choice, but if both were available one had to weigh up the pluses and the minuses.

Let's look at a concrete example: the *Imperator*, pride of the Hamburg–American Line in 1913. There were two distinctly different categories of passenger on C-Deck (**FIG. 34**). A few of the cabins had their own toilets and baths, accentuated on the plan in bright yellow. If you had the money, you sought a cabin with those wonderful amenities. If you didn't have one of those expensive select cabins, you measured the distance between, for example, C30, back at the stern of the ship, and the *Damen and Herren* WCs and baths (*Bad*) amidships. On further consideration, perhaps you would seek a cabin closer to the facilities.

The smallest cabins had no outside view. Those relatively tiny inside spaces could quickly cause

34 A plan of C-Deck on the magnificent *Imperator* of 1913. Only the most expensive accommodation had en suite toilets.

claustrophobia, even during the short journey across the North Atlantic. For a world cruise they would be agony. And imagine what they would be like in rough weather. This illustration (FIG. 35) from an early series of sketches by Harry Furniss provides a graphic illustration of the perils and problems of a small cabin. Even without a storm, there was very little room to dress or even sit. This lack of space led to considerable usage of the public rooms such as the smoking room, library, and perhaps – if present – the gymnasium. Even huddling on deck could be preferable to a cramped, stuffy cabin. A postcard photograph of a corner of the deck on the Union Steamship Company's SS *Niagara* is captioned on the back, 'This is the way the passengers breathe up here.'

35 Artist Harry Furniss captures life on board during a storm in the early 1900s – dressing for dinner would be a major challenge.

Another aspect that exaggerated the pain of the tiny inside cabin, and probably all cabins, was the likelihood of *mal de mer*. Rude and cruel cartoons showing ill passengers leaning over the rails on deck to disgorge their most recent meal may be hilarious, but only to those not susceptible to seasickness. Why on deck? There was little or no facility in the passenger cabins. They may have had a washbasin, but that would not have been suitable for regurgitating the morning's breakfast, and the equivalent of the airline sickness bag had not yet been invented. Still, chamber pots were available.

WHAT TO PACK

Today's society is relatively casual compared to that during the height of the ocean liner era. Fred Smith, for example, was 'Mr Smith' until you got to know him very well. And if he belonged to a higher social and/or financial stratum than yours, he would always be 'Mr Smith'. Suits and ties were universal attire for men, and women faced the same type of strictures. So, what does one wear on board a ship?

So many factors applied – the time of day, the type of event, the climate, the class of travel you were in, your wardrobe budget – that these decisions would have been intimidating to the infrequent traveller. The experienced sailor would have had to comb their wardrobe to select the most suitable garments, and probably would also have used the occasion as an excuse to purchase several new outfits. Even the Tourist Class traveller would have been sensitive to the need for 'proper' – although less elaborate – attire.

The shipping lines balanced their promotional material between presenting an image of elegance and sophistication – thereby intimidating some of the passengers – and a lower-key appeal to travellers of modest means. A magazine presenting an interpretation of upper-class travel on the *Queen Mary* in her maiden year, 1936, would have been a spur to fashion purchases by intending passengers. In this magazine, a series of fashion photos advertising various American fashion retailers follows the experience of a hypothetical young woman, 'Miriam', as she progresses through the days of her trip on the *Queen Mary* with her parents.

As the story unfolds she meets and gets to know a handsome young man during the voyage. By the end of the five days at sea, she is virtually engaged to him. We trace the young girl in photos from when she has just settled into her cabin after the first evening on board, during which she had been introduced to 'Donald'. We learn that 'Miriam was tired and retired early. Her thoughts were on the evening' (FIG. 36).

A couple of photo panels later, the story has reached the stage that 'Miriam strolled tearoomwards with Donald … finding a secluded table lunch was ordered … or perhaps not … their hands joined.' Then Miriam purrs, 'Oh Donald I can't tell you how glad I am I waited to come with Mother and

36 An illustration from a fashion magazine imagines a pretty young woman's first night on board the new *Queen Mary* after a tiring first day, 1936.

Dad instead of going with the girls from college last year. I am simply having a scrumptious time.'

Further on, we learn that 'Donald' is going to England to compete in the British Golf Championship. Donald reports that this is his last foray into golf and then he will settle down to 'the serious business of the law'. The melodramatic plot of the hypothetical family group's voyage is easy to follow, and the less-than-subtle messages include (i) this is a place to meet your future spouse; (ii) you will meet affluent, influential people; (iii) you will meet well-educated college graduates; and (iv) you must dress for the event (FIG. 37).

In case the story of 'Miriam' doesn't give sufficient fashion advice, consider the guidance provided by Canadian Pacific for cruises on its ships in the 1930s, in the form of lengthy articles by Gladys M. Gowlland as multi-page inserts to *Empress of Britain* cruise brochures.

Gowlland advises that once you have booked your trip, 'Better start gathering that wardrobe right away'. She concedes that 'Every woman has her own particular likes and dislikes. So let's take the average wardrobe.' Synthesizing the advice for

37 Another illustration from the fashion section illustrates the appropriateness of formal attire for dinner on board *Queen Mary*.

around-the-world cruises and for those to the Orient, we come up with the following outline listing, beginning with a basic coat.

First, there's the travelling coat. One of those nice English mixtures is a good choice, or the camel-hair materials that stand any sort of weather and hard usage.

Three-piece suits are treasures for the traveller – with a few blouses.

There are sport clothes … knitted suits … light flannel skirts with twin sweater sets, and very sheer woollens.

For the warmer weather there is a tremendous range in linens, uncrushable cottons, tub silks, and so on.

Evening dresses – as many or as few as you like.

Lace is a great standby for travelling. Even after long packing it always comes up smiling, so include a lace.

A couple of evening wraps are necessary – one medium weight and one very sheer.

Shoes. Check them over carefully. Really comfortable oxford with sensible heels. Sport shoes with composition or rope soles are needed for deck wear. Linen and canvas footgear is the coolest for the tropics. Evening slippers of course.

Stockings. Do buy enough before you leave.

The Orient is the place to pick up underwear, so don't take more than you need. You'll go into raptures about the undies over there.

Bathing suits. Two anyway. A beach robe should be included and a pair of slippers.

The reader may believe that this is the end of the list. Not so. The premiss was that you had to have the correct attire for each occasion, and Gowlland has tried to anticipate all those occasions. The list goes on…

Anything you like in hats. Those new hat boxes have eliminated most of our hat-packing worries.

Take your favourite golf outfit. There are numerous sporty links awaiting you.

A masquerade costume must find a place in your trunks. There's always a jolly masquerade aboard the *Empresses*.

A kimono of course, and bedroom slippers.

A roomy handbag to hold important papers, passports, etc. is a last and worthwhile suggestion.

The list for male travellers is considerably shorter. If you have been mentally packing each of these categories into imaginary suitcases, it will have required more than one. It's not hard to see why steamer trunks (now relegated to serve as coffee tables) were popular, and the baggage room was provided to house trunks and suitcases not needed during certain parts of the voyage.

This refined and exclusive world was far removed from the life of steerage passengers, as we will see later.

WHAT GOES WHERE

Cabin, baggage room or hold? As part of your preparation for the voyage, you would receive a packet of baggage labels and tags. But life wasn't as simple as it is travelling by a good airline today.

Ships, like planes, had more than one class of travel. Their baggage handlers could have thousands of pieces of baggage to process, with incredibly high peak handling demands during the short periods of time for boarding and disembarkation – longer indeed than for the large planes and cruise ships of today, but with less technology to assist. And on a number of ships there was a variety of locations to which a bag might be sent on boarding, depending upon the passenger's needs.

For the individual seeking high-level service, the First Class (also known on some ships as Cabin or Saloon) passenger label was right at the top of their 'want' list. The Red Star Line label was loud and clear as to the status of its owner. Some 4 inches square and sporting a large red star with a white figure *1* in the centre, it proclaimed loudly in a striking black overprint that it was for 'First Cabin Baggage'. It also told the baggage handlers that this piece of luggage was not wanted on the voyage – it was to go in the hold of the ship. Probably a large steamer trunk, it would contain clothing for the land part of the trip, and perhaps gifts for those being visited, or brought back home as mementoes of a grand tour through Europe.

Some ships had a baggage room (with appropriate labels), to which passengers could send suitcases not needed immediately on the voyage. When madam needed a fresh cocktail dress, for example, she could have a steward – or perhaps her maid – retrieve the bag from the baggage room located on their deck, bring it to the cabin, and then return it to the baggage room at the appropriate time. Even large cabins had space limitations – and too much baggage would spoil the look of a beautifully furnished First Class suite.

Other lines – such as White Star – used similar strategies with a colour code and number. For baggage destined to go to the passenger's cabin, colour coding showed which class (First, Tourist, etc.), and a large letter helped to clarify the spelling of the name written on the label (**FIG. 38**). When the ship disgorged all its passengers and baggage at its destination, the large letter and colour also helped the baggage handlers in allocating bags to be picked up by passengers in the arrivals building, at their class of service, under their respective alphabetic section.

Compounding the challenge was the fact that a ship could stop at several ports. An Orient Line passenger list of 1932

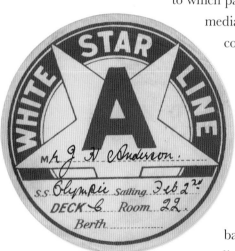

38 This dramatic First Class White Star Line baggage label of the 1920s displayed the first letter of the passenger's surname to facilitate sorting by the stewards at the start and end of the voyage.

shows the RMS *Ormonde* from England to Australia stopping to disembark passengers at Brisbane, Sydney, Melbourne, Adelaide and Fremantle. And if the wrong bag were delivered to the wrong port, it wasn't as easy to recover as errant airline baggage is today. It had to travel by another ship, which was probably no faster than the one it was pursuing. If a bag didn't get to Fremantle because it was inadvertently taken off at Brisbane, it might take a while even to get onto another ship travelling to that port.

As can be imagined, this system required the production, inventorying and distribution of a wide variety of labels. Some shipping lines were cleverer about this than others. NYK Line (Nippon Yusen Kaisha, the Japanese Imperial Mail Line, of which the principal passenger services linked Japan and the USA) produced a dual-purpose label. The passenger could tear off one end, to leave it showing either 'wanted' or 'not wanted' on the voyage (FIG. 39). One wonders how many passengers forgot to tear off one of the alternatives along the perforations provided, and what confusion this would have created for the crew at boarding time.

Whereas rail services had some labels that referred to specific high-profile trains, passenger shipping companies generally produced 'generic' labels, suitable for use on any of the company's ships. The one significant exception was the French Line,

39 This baggage label from Japan's NYK Line carries efficient detachable options for the stowage of the luggage – tear off the end of the label ('Wanted' or 'Not Wanted') that does not apply, and the instruction is left on the other end.

which produced labels for several specific ships, such as the prestigious flagship superliner *Normandie*.

Baggage labels display a wide range of art and design. All the shipping companies gave out vast quantities of them. The labels represented some of their cheapest and most effective advertising, and travellers generally received an envelope with more than they needed. Consequently, many labels have survived, and they are sometimes sold at antique and collectible fairs, ephemera markets and car-boot sales.

Returning to the topic of what goes where, anything in the hold was irretrievable. This option would not apply for cruises because all the baggage was relevant to activities on board, so the hold was not an option; but for all other travel it was necessary to have at least some luggage consigned there.

Picture the hold with tonnes of bags and boxes. There was a reason that steamer trunks were solidly built. Anything sent to the hold should be able to compete with the other luggage in a test of strength and durability. For the wealthy, Louis Vuitton trunks offered a known secure solution for packing items of hold luggage, as they were immensely strong and could withstand heavy loads being dumped on top.

LIFE IN STEERAGE

You may have heard 'steerage' applied as a negative description to the economy section of a plane. It certainly was the economy section of the ship, but one has to put the experience in context. The passengers in steerage certainly had no expectation of twenty-first-century creature comforts.

A passenger ticket of the Allan Line in the 1880s notes that although food will be offered throughout the passage,

Steerage passengers will have to provide themselves with a Plate, Mug, Knife, Fork, Spoon and Water Cup, as also Bedding, all of which can be purchased at Liverpool or Derry for 6s or 7s. Each passenger will be allowed 10 cubic feet of luggage free by Steamer.

The ticket lists the names of twenty ships being operated by the Line, serving five ports in the United Kingdom and five ports in North America. For many of the westbound passengers the prospect of regular meals and a safe place to sleep might have been a positive attribute of the trip compared to their past experiences.

Illustrations of steerage conditions are very difficult to find, but an excellent example is on a postcard issued by North German Lloyd in 1907 and posted in 1908 (FIG. 40). Privacy is

40 An artist's depiction on a North German Lloyd postcard provides a rare image of the crowded life in steerage at the beginning of the last century.

Where the Meals are Eaten in Comfort

650 People Dine at Once in the Third Class
Dining Saloon of the "Empresses"

at a premium, and on a hot summer voyage the conditions, in the absence of forced ventilation, must have been stifling. At the other end of the spectrum, winter passages and North Atlantic storms would have been equally difficult, as the spaces were typically located furthest forward and aft in the hull, where the extremes of sea motion were most felt.

By 1906, Canadian Pacific, competing for many of the same steerage passengers, was providing meals on its own utensils, rather than passengers having to bring their own. This illustration is from a 1906 brochure of the new *Empress of Britain* and *Empress of Ireland* (FIG. 41). The brochure advertises that

Steerage passengers are now provided free of charge with a mattress, bedding, mess tins (plate, mug, knife, fork, spoon and water can). Tables are set for meals and passengers are

41 By 1910 the new Third Class category offered more comfortable (if crowded) dining, menu choices, and company-provided plates and utensils.

waited upon by stewards who take care of eating utensils. A liberal supply of provisions, properly cooked, will be served on the steamers three times a day by the steamers' stewards; breakfast at 9, dinner at 1, supper at 6 o'clock.

For some steerage passengers, three meals a day might have been an unaccustomed treat. The dining facilities in steerage are shown in a rare photograph of the Canadian Pacific's *Ruthenia* (FIG. 42). Handwritten on the back is the note 'New Steerage Dining Saloon to seat 300 passengers. *SS Ruthenia*, Trieste'. This would certainly have been from 1913, when *Ruthenia* went into service between the port of Trieste and Canada. That service ended in 1914 with the advent of the First World War.

The Canadian Pacific 1906 steerage brochure describes typical 'Third Class Bills of Fare' for each of breakfast, dinner and tea, with supper daily and gruel at 8 p.m. Moreover, 'Delicacies are supplied to invalids under the order of the doctor'. Other useful information for the intending immigrant includes:

42 Dining for immigrants aboard Canadian Pacific's SS *Ruthenia* sailing from Trieste in 1913 featured white tablecloths and uniformed stewards.

s/s "RUTHENIA"

Each person over twelve years of age is provided on board with a separate sleeping berth. Married couples with their children under twelve years of age are berthed together in two and four berthed cabins as far as possible.

The Company supplies FREE OF CHARGE the necessary outfit for the sea passage consisting of bedding and all other requisites for the voyage.

Special stewards are assigned to attend to passengers in this class. Meals are served in the GRAND THIRD CLASS DINING SALOON. The seats at the table are revolving arm chairs – upholstered. The white table cloths, china and other table utensils are of fine quality and are washed and kept clean by the stewards in charge.

Each steamer carries an experienced surgeon and stewardess to attend to the women and children.

The provisions supplied are of the very best quality. They are examined and passed by officials detailed for that purpose before being accepted on board.

This was a competitive response to an 1899 steerage advertisement by the Anchor Line, aiming to attract the same passengers from the British Isles, which promised that 'Every comfort and attention is furnished that is possible on an ocean steamer.' All of these were trying to emulate the latest Cunard liners such as *Lusitania* and *Mauretania*, which had all-cabin Third Class to attract a growing tourism market. The migrant trade, by contrast, fluctuated unreliably and was in only one direction.

To put this in context, they were appealing primarily to the residents of the British Isles, in contrast to the contemporary image of steerage in the ships of North German Lloyd, which were more likely to carry immigrants from Russia and Eastern Europe. Their expectations may have been even less than for many of the passengers to which Canadian Pacific was appealing, and their sole objective – like many of today's migrants – was to endure any hardship in the hope of finding a better life elsewhere.

So the days passed for the steerage group, and spontaneous on-deck games helped to pass the time (**FIG. 43**). This photograph gives a delicious insight into the attire of the day, with the few older men wearing hats, and the rest of the group wearing caps. There are seven women, wearing headscarves, with few in the foreground. The competitors are playing an unspecified game on deck to a substantial audience – probably the game called 'Cock Fighting', where two combatants are trussed with sticks within a chalk circle (fractionally visible on the right). Betting on the outcome was a possible sideline to this activity, and to other competitions on board.

Let's put steerage class in a financial context. For the shipping line, the business model was high volume, low prices and low margins. The more amenities that were provided, the greater the costs and the less viable the business. Had any of these prospects for a Canadian Pacific ship ever used – or

43 Deck sports on board the *Royal Edward* c.1912 provided simple entertainment for steerage passengers – and the occasional chance to wager on the outcome.

SECOND CABIN.
RATES OF PASSAGE
SUBJECT TO CHANGE AT ANY TIME FOR ANY SAILING.

NEW YORK TO OR FROM GLASGOW OR LONDONDERRY

	OUTWARD FROM NEW YORK.	PREPAID TO NEW YORK.
CITY OF ROME,	$35.00	$35.00
FURNESSIA,	30.00	32.50
ANCHORIA, }	30.00	30.00
ETHIOPIA, }		

RETURN TICKETS five per cent reduction on combined outward and prepaid rates.
TWO BERTH ROOMS, $5.00 additional each passenger.
CHILDREN over one and under twelve, half fare; infants free.

NEW YORK TO GOTHENBURG AND RETURN
(VIA GRANTON).
Including Board, Lodging and Transfer of Baggage.

CITY OF ROME, - - -	$83.50
FURNESSIA, - - - -	78.75
OTHER STEAMERS, - -	74.00

RATES TO AND FROM GLASGOW
IN ADDITION TO OCEAN FARE
(THIRD-CLASS RAIL).

LIVERPOOL, - -	$3.65	GLOUCESTER, -	$6.70
CARDIFF, - - -	6.95	LEEDS, - - -	4.20
LONDON, - - -	8.00	LEICESTER, - -	6.00
BIRMINGHAM, - -	5.90	MANCHESTER, -	4.40
BLACKBURN, -	3.90	NEWCASTLE, - -	3.15
BRADFORD, -	4.20	NOTTINGHAM, -	5.80
BRISTOL, - - -	7.45	OLDHAM, - - -	5.90
DURHAM, - -	3.40	SHEFFIELD, - -	5.00
YORK, - - -	4.25		

THIRD-CLASS TOURIST TICKETS, GLASGOW TO LONDON AND RETURN, WITH STOP-OVER PRIVILEGES, } $12.50

SECOND CABIN
PASSENGERS are berthed in Staterooms, on the forward Main Deck of all steamers, except "City of Rome," on which they are situated in after part of Spar and Lower Decks. The rooms accommodate from two to six passengers each. Berths are allotted in rotation of purchase, and numbers marked on tickets. Passengers are provided with all necessaries for the voyage, including a liberal supply of well cooked provisions served as per bill of fare in special Dining Room, but do not have access to Main Saloon, and are restricted in their use of the Promenade Deck.

STEERAGES
are large and exceedingly well lighted and ventilated, and fitted up in rooms, each passenger having a separate sleeping berth, married couples, single women and single men being berthed in different compartments, and every comfort and attention is furnished that is possible on an ocean steamer. Steerage passengers are now provided free of charge, with a mattress, bedding, mess tins (plate, mug, knife, fork, spoon and water can). Tables are set for meals and passengers are waited upon by stewards who take care of eating utensils. A liberal supply of provisions, properly cooked, will be served on the steamers three times a day by the steamers' stewards; breakfast at 9, dinner at 1, supper at 6 o'clock.

BAGGAGE.
Second Cabin 20 cubic feet, and Steerage 10 cubic feet, free; any excess will be charged for at rate of One Shilling sterling per cubic foot. All baggage should be sent to Anchor Line Pier should be labeled with name of passenger and steamer on which passage has been engaged. No luggage will be put on board the steamers until it has been claimed by passengers and marked "Wanted" or "Not Wanted," on the voyage, as may be desired by owners. Passengers should be on board with their baggage one hour prior to the time of sailing, as hurry and confusion are thereby avoided, and baggage less liable to be lost. Special Anchor Line labels can be obtained on application at the principal offices and agencies of the line.

BICYCLES $2.50 TO GLASGOW OR LONDONDERRY.

REVENUE TAX ADDITIONAL.
STEERAGE RATES.
INCLUDING BEDDING AND EATING UTENSILS.

These Rates Include Tax.

OUTWARD FROM NEW YORK.				PREPAID TO NEW YORK.	
City of Rome.	Furnessia.	Other Steamers.		By City of Rome or Furnessia.	Other Steamers.
$25.50	$24.50	$23.50	Glasgow or Londonderry,	$25.25	$24.00
25.50	24.50	23.50	Belfast, Rail from Derry,	26.50	25.25
27.30	26.30	25.30	Dublin, Rail from Derry,	27.10	25.85
25.50	24.50	23.50	Liverpool, Rail from Glasgow,		
26.50	25.50	24.50	London, Rail from Glasgow,		
27.00	27.00	27.00	Amsterdam, Antwerp, Rotterdam,	$29.50 from Rotterdam or Antwerp only.	29.50
27.00	27.00	27.00	Bremen,		
27.00	27.00	27.00	Hamburg,		
31.00	31.00	31.00	Oderburg,		
31.15	31.15	31.15	Oswiecin,		
30.50	29.50	28.50	Copenhagen, Christiansand, Christiania, Gothenburg, Malmo, Stavanger, Bergen, Trondhjem, Esbjerg, Frederikshavn, Helsingborg, Laurvig or Skien,	26.00	26.00
33.50	32.50	31.50	Stockholm, -	29.00	29.00
33.50	32.50	31.50	Hango, Abo or Helsingfors,	29.00	29.00

Children between 1 and 12 years of age, Half Fare.

Free	Infants under 1 year, British ports,	$3.00	3.00
$3.00	" Scandinavian ports,	3.00	3.00
2.00	" Continental ports, -	2.00	2.00

NOTICE.
PERSONS wishing to send for friends in the old country can be furnished with certificates of passage on remitting to us the amount of passage money, either by Express or Post Office Order, and giving the full names, ages and addresses of the parties for whom passage is desired. By special arrangement with Railroad and Steamship Companies, Passengers can be booked THROUGH at lowest rates to any Seaport or Railroad Station in America.

DRAFTS
can be purchased from the agents of the Line at lowest current rates, and will be found the safest and most economical way of transmitting money to friends in Great Britain and Ireland.

even seen – a white tablecloth? Had any of them ever used the services of a trained doctor? The Anchor Line of seven years earlier was probably closer to the experiences – but perhaps not the aspirations – of the average steerage passenger. A panel from the 1899 Anchor Line brochure gives an insight into the pricing (FIG. 44).

And a photograph taken on board White Star Line's SS *Ionic* gives another clue to the type of passenger who frequented the steerage quarters (FIG. 45). The image is on a photographic postcard with a divided back, marking this as being from the second *Ionic*, which went into service in 1902, rather than from the earlier ship of the same name, which dated to 1883. So, how do we know they weren't crew? First, the gentleman in the centre looks too old to be a crew member – more likely the patriarch of a group of male immigrants, sailing for prosperity in the distant reaches of the Empire. Second, the crew would have been required to wear White Star Line tops to distinguish

44 Steerage passage rates on the Anchor Line in 1899 varied by ship, and could be prepaid by friends on the other side of the Atlantic.

45 Steerage passengers and a pet dog on board White Star Line's SS *Ionic* were heading west to seek a better life.

them from the passengers. In the absence of other clues, here is a
cluster of steerage passengers.

Steerage was a cheap passage, so in providing incremental
benefits the shipping line management would have had to weigh
those additional costs against the meagre individual revenues from
each steerage passenger. It would have been challenging, because
improving the quality of steerage might make it more attractive to
frugal travellers who would otherwise have sailed in more profitable higher classes. On some ships with very basic steerage, the
dormitories were used for general cargo eastbound. Bigger ships
meant better economies of scale and a more reliable clientele, of
tourists booking passages in both directions. Today there would be
a computer-based model that considered costs, incremental costs
and the prospective customer base, then determined a value for
customer preferences based on surveys and a host of other factors.
In 1906, even without such technology, the shipping companies'
managers and accountants were already smart and sophisticated
in business matters: they knew there was a large base of potentially
profitable customers, and they were competing for them.

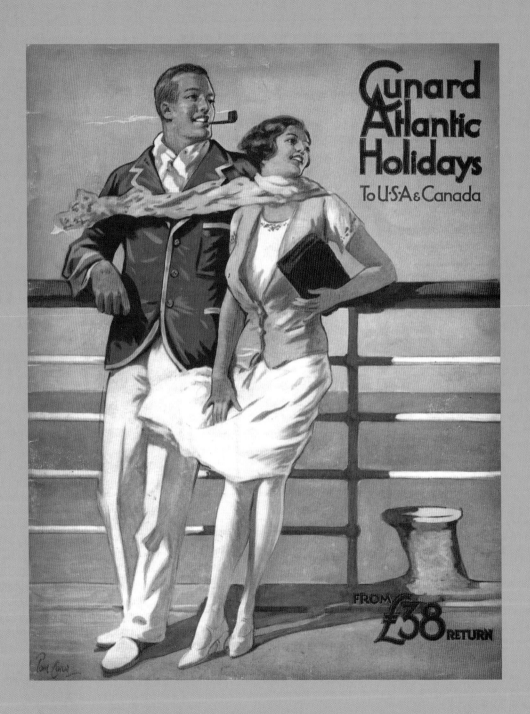

SHIPBOARD DIVERSIONS

A range of diversions were offered to occupy passengers during the long days at sea, which were otherwise interrupted only by meals. For some passengers, *mal de mer* sharply reduced their appetites. For others, the bar was the beacon, particularly during Prohibition in America. Anyone who has been carried across the Atlantic or Pacific Ocean by plane will probably have concluded that it was a long, boring trip by sea. Not so. From embarkation to arrival, there was plenty to distract and entertain the traveller.

CARDS AND FLOWERS

The voyage began before the ship even left the pier. Entering their cabins, travellers might be met with mountains of farewell gifts from family and friends. Before the ship sailed, even more gifts might arrive.

Each one would be accompanied by a card identifying the donor and accompanied by a message of best wishes (FIG. 46). The *President Garfield* sailed trans-Pacific for the Dollar Line in the 1920s and 1930s; for Mr Hardy, who received the card illustrated here, the trip would probably have been a

once-in-a-lifetime experience. Few if any of his peers in the New York Fire Insurance Exchange could even dream of making such a trip.

A traveller on the SS *Paris* of the French Line in 1931, signing her letter only as 'Aunt Emma', wrote about her experience with farewell gifts:

> I mustn't forget to thank you for your letter and the copy of the petit papier, which I read the first day out. Please thank your mother for her letter. And both of you again for the lovely flowers. All our flowers lasted until now & some of those you sent are still nice. Rec'd one box of flowers from Mariam Willard & Howard, & three others. Between us we have 12 or 14 lbs. of candy, salted nuts, candied fruit, etc., which will be taken ashore, together with much of a huge basket of fruit. Should come in handy for roadside pick-nicks in France and Italy.

The quantities of confectionery are surprising, but they would not be out of line for a First Class passenger in the 1920s and 1930s. In an archive of ephemera from a 1935 Dollar Line

46 Flowers were delivered to Mr Hardy in State Room 5 on board the SS *President Garfield*, to express the sender's best wishes for a pleasant voyage.

47 A postcard from a shore excursion in 1911.

48 The design on this NYK Line postcard of 1936 evokes travel to exotic ports.

POST CARD

This Space may be used for Correspondence

This Space is for the Address only

Apr, 14 1911

Have just now reached at Yokohama safely. Will write you from Kyoto or Tokyo later. Hoping you are very well,

I remain
yours sincerely
K. Nakanishi

Miss Lydia Bremer
44 Gunnersbury Lane
20 Windsor St., Acton

Ealing, London, W.

Nippon Yusen Kaisha S.S. "YEIKO MARU."

NIPPON YUSEN KAISHA

voyage ('New York–California; to the Orient and Around the World'), there are five Schrafft's gift tags which would have accompanied a gift of Schrafft's chocolates – and these are only the ones that were saved!

MESSAGES

Prior to sailing, letters and greeting cards were addressed to the prospective traveller with the name of the ship, the shipping line and the city of departure. In the ports visited later, letters were sent to the ship in that port. In all ports, ocean liners and their respective shipping lines were well known and had local offices or agents who handled their post.

The comments written on the backs of postcards may have been formulaic, but the vital detail confirming authenticity was the postal cancellation. This can be seen on the back of a Pacific Mail Steamship Company postcard (**FIG. 47**). The postal cancellation, 'Tokio Japan 2.4.11', provided incontrovertible evidence that the writer really was in Japan. The message, dated 1 April 1911, was bland: 'Have just now reached at Yokohama

safely. Will write you from Kyoto or Tokyo later. Hoping you are very well.' It appears that the card didn't hit the postal system until a day or so later. Another cancellation shows that it reached the London suburb of Ealing on 6 May.

Perhaps even more impressive is a postcard from the Far Eastern shipping line Nippon Yusen Kaisha (FIG. 48). The recipient in 1936 – on this occasion a woman in Cleveland, Ohio – could hardly fail to notice the combined impact of the stylized Mount Fuji, the rising sun, the company's flag, the lifebelt and the image of the SS *Yeiko Maru*. It is all very 'exotic'.

On all ships, some messages came by telegram – a very dramatic touch, greatly enhanced by the envelope in which the telegram was delivered to the cabin (FIG. 49). The basic charge was for ten words, and telegrams rarely exceed this number (they are often precisely ten words), to avoid any additional charge.

49 Telegrams could be sent and received by passengers on board; this Western Union telegram envelope evokes the excitement of the voyage.

50 Before air conditioning, ship travel in hot climates could be enervating; this French Line fan of the 1950s offered exciting artwork and a measure of relief from the heat.

Less dramatic than a telegram was a greeting card with some variety of 'Bon Voyage' sentiment. And possibly moving into the post-war period but undated is a riotously styled French Line fan, provided for the greater comfort of travellers to hot climates (FIG. 50). Even when ships eventually became air-conditioned, that amenity was of no benefit to those who went on shore excursions, though the air conditioning served as a magnet and reward for returning to the ship.

CABIN ✦ PASSENGER ✦ LIST.

RED STAR LINE.

BELGIAN ROYAL AND U. S. MAIL STEAMSHIP

"WESTERNLAND,"

SAILING FROM

NEW YORK for ANTWERP, Wednesday,
April 8th, 1891, 5.00 A. M.

Commander :—J. C. JAMISON.

Chief Officer:—Mr. F. Albrecht. Chief Engineer :—Mr. C. H. Woolley.
Surgeon :—Dr. L. Hormess. Chief Steward :—Mr. Ernest Cointé.
Stewardesses :—Mrs. L. McLean. Mrs. E. Knox.

Miss Edith A. Anning.

Miss Marie Louise Ballou.
Mrs. H. H. Bly.
Mrs. J. N. Borland.
Mr. George Boyd.
Mrs. Cyrus Brewer,
  Child.
  Child.
Miss Katharine D. Burnette.
Miss A. E. Burwash.
Mrs. M. M. Butler.
Miss Butler.

Miss Alice Calvin.
Miss Julia Carroll.
Mr. Carltheime.
Mrs. S. E. B. Channing.
Miss Eva Channing.
Mrs. Edna D. Cheney.
Miss Gertrude Morris Cist.
Miss Bertha Alice Cist.
Prof. Arthur P. Coleman.
Miss Helena J. Coleman.

Mrs. George E. Dean.
Mrs. John Dean.
Rev. H. DeRegge.
Mrs. Charles Seeley Dunning.
Miss May White Dunning.
Miss Lucy B. Dyar.

Miss Caroline S. Eustis.
Miss Ellen L. Everett.

Miss Ruth Farnsworth.
Miss Florence Finch.
Miss Edith A. Fisher.
Miss M. J. Floyd.
Mrs. G. W. Frances.
Miss Alice G. Frances.
Miss Edith Frances.

Miss K. A. Gage.
Mr. John F. Garde.
Mrs. Garde.
Mrs. E. P. Gibson.
Miss Gibson.
Miss Belle Gilcrest.
Miss E. B. Goldthwait.

Mr. Thomas R. Goss.
Miss Susie Goss.

Miss Mabel S. Hall.
Miss Mary L. Hastings.
Miss Elizabeth K. Hastings,
Miss Sarah B. Hastings.
Mr. J. K. Hayward, Jr.
Mr. Wm. Herzog.
Mrs. Herzog.
Miss Julia Herzog.
Miss Tillie Herzog.
Miss Irma Herzog.
Miss Louise Hughes.

Mrs. H. Kabrowsky.
Mr. Edwin C. Kimball.
Mr. G. Clifton Kimball.
Mrs. Kimball.
Miss Martha G. Kimball.

Mr. Nehemiah Lee.
Mrs. Lee.
Miss Georgina Lewis.
Mrs. P. L. Loper.

Capt. R. W. Meade, U. S. N.
Mr. George E. Mills.
Mr. H. Morrell.
Mrs. Morrell.
Miss Paula Morrell.
Miss Edith E. Morris.
Mr. M. B. Mott.
Mrs. Mott.
Miss M. Mott.
Mr. B. Münz.
Mrs. R. P. Myers.
Prof. T. H. McBride.
Mrs. McBride.
Rev. Wm. J. McClure.
Mr. F. C. McLaughlin.
Mrs. McLaughlin.

Dr. Edward Newhall.
Mrs. Newhall.

Mr. Frank W. Oeffinger.

Miss A. C. Palmer.
Mr. A. Pester.
Mrs. A. Pester.
Miss Pester.
Mrs. W. Petzet.

Mrs. Jeremiah Quinn.

Mrs. Howard Richmond.
Miss Caroline Richmond.
Miss Edith Richmond.
Master F. E. Richmond.
Master Lawrence Richmond.
Master Ed. H. Richmond.
  and maid.
Mrs. J. V. Ridgeway.
Miss Helen Ridgeway.
Master Philip Ridgeway.
Master Lawrence Ridgeway.
  and maid.
Mr. G. Theodore Roberts.
Dr. J. A. Rockwell.
Mrs. Charles H. Russell.

Miss Susanna Saunderson.
Miss Minnie Scheitlin.
Mr. Adolph Schaffmeyer.
Baron Leopold von Seldeneck
Baroness Leopold von Seldeneck
Miss Sarah H. Southwick.

Miss Lillian Stevens.
Rev. J. P. Stewart.

Mrs. C. ter Meer.
Master Henry ter Meer.
Miss Emma ter Meer.
Master Edmund ter Meer.
Master Adolph ter Meer.
Mr. Carl Thieme.
Miss Thompson.
Mr. Robert E. Traiser.
Mrs. Robert E. Traiser.

Miss Elise Von Allmen.

Miss Charlotte Welles.
Mrs. George Whiting.
Miss Emma S. Whiting.
Miss Frances Whiting.
Miss Minnie A. Wiggin.
Miss Bertha Williams.
Miss Marion Williams.
Miss Phoebe Wines.
Mr. Wm. F. Wright.

Mrs. Joh Adler.

Mr. Michael Becker.
Dr. E. J. Bernstein.
Mrs. Maria Bucher
  and child.
Miss Amalie Bulster.
Miss Marie Bulster.

Mr. Max Cohnen.

Miss Mary Elsen.

Mrs. Agnes Fels.

Miss Lizzie Habel.
Mrs. Anna Hagen.
Miss Maggie Hagen.
Mr. Chas. Hammond.
Mr. A. Herbst.
Mrs. A. Herbst.
Mr. Jos. Herzfeld.
Mrs. Jos. Herzfeld.
Miss Frances Hoffmann.

Miss Anna H
Mrs. Katie
  and inf
Mrs. C. J.
Miss Flore
Miss Selina
Miss Louis

Mrs. Lizzie
Mr. Ernst
Mrs. Berth

Miss Emma
Mrs. Chris
Mrs. J. Mi

Mr. Fred

Miss Carri
Mrs. Anne

Mrs. Mari
  and in

Mr. Joseph
Mrs. Regi
  and in
Mr. George
Master Wil
Master Jos
Miss Wern
Miss Emm
Mr. Ph. R
Mrs. Ph. R
  and in

Miss Mary
Mr. Henry
Mrs. Anna
Miss Euge
Miss Lina
Mr. Julius
Mr. Ralph

Miss Emili
Mr. F. Tr
Mrs. Julia

Mr. Marg
Mr. Alexa

SECRETS OF PASSENGER LISTS

From the earliest days of ocean travel, the passenger list has embodied the social differentiators and sensitivities of the day. Early lists showed the name of each passenger, title (if any) and city or town of residence. By the time of the first meal, the experienced traveller would have reviewed the passenger list to see whether there were any 'important' people on board. If you were in First Class (also known as Saloon, First Saloon or First Cabin), the quest of the voyage would be to meet celebrities in person and perhaps ask for their autographs.

51 The passenger list served as an aide-memoire about fellow passengers, with names and space for annotations.

Red Star Line

"Steamer
ND 2748 tons
872.

J. Aberle & Cʳ Litho Berlin & London

Latest addition to the fleet
FRIESLAND" 7116 tons
1889.

Members of the aristocracy, barons of business, senior clergy, writers and artists, famous intellectuals, important military men and parliamentarians were all of interest. Beyond that, you would look for other passengers (in the same class) from your own home community, if it were shown on the list.

Equally important for the passenger was remembering the names of the other parties seated at their dinner table. Many passenger lists are annotated with tick marks, under-lining or other symbols as an aide-memoire for the names of table-mates.

The left side of the passenger list from an 1891 voyage of the Red Star Line's *Westernland* is a fine example of this practice (FIG. 51). From the first entry, Miss Anning (from Picton, Ontario), to the last name on the page, Mrs P.L. Loper (from Kansas), we see the process in action. We learn that Rev. H. DeRegge is a bishop. Tick marks may indicate people who have been met and seem congenial. The tiny, precise X beside a few names may be ominous – perhaps they have been categorized as 'the wrong sort' or 'not socially or commercially useful'. Who knows what stigma the cross might represent?

Even more important for some of the elite was the entourage accompanying other travellers in their class. For example, in an RMS *Aquitania* 1920 passenger list one sees 'The Right Hon. The Earl of Craven and Valet', and 'The Countess of Craven and Maid' (FIG. 52). Numerous other passengers were accompanied by maids or valets.

However, some passengers took the competition to a higher level. The same passenger list shows 'Mrs Leatherbee and three maids'. In total there were twenty maids and six valets on that voyage. The list also contains 'Mr C.P. Coleman and Secretary', 'Master John Raiss and Tutor', and 'Master

52 Passenger list covers could be dramatic; in this *Aquitania* First Class passenger list of 1920 there are celebrities, prominent politicians, senior military officers and other potentially 'interesting' people.

R·M·S AQVITANIA

List of Passengers

THE CUNARD STEAM SHIP COMPANY LTD

WHITE STAR LINE

NEW YORK
PLYMOUTH
CHERBOURG
SOUTHAMPTON

MONTREAL
QUEBEC
LIVERPOOL

NEW YORK
QUEENSTOWN
LIVERPOOL

NEW YORK
AZORES
MEDITERRANEAN

BOSTON
QUEENSTOWN
LIVERPOOL

BOSTON
AZORES
MEDITERRANEAN

United States & Royal Mail Steamers

Gallagher and Nurse'. Lists from other ships show chauffeurs, suggesting that the owners also brought their own motor vehicles on the ship.

Note that servants didn't have names. They were merely an anonymous appendage to the names of their masters. This underscores the almost serf-like conditions for staff in many upper-class households. Servants occupied small quarters in close proximity to their masters. Deck plans of the RMS *Mauretania* of the same era show small cabins on the deck below the First Class suites, with nearby stairways. It wasn't just maids and servants who were the equivalent of nameless chattels. A pocket-sized 1879 passenger list of Anchor Line's *Devonia* shows 'Capt. Charles Porter and wife'.

The apex of social competitiveness may well have occurred during a three-day cruise on the RMS *Berengaria* to observe the Royal Naval Review at Spithead in 1935, to commemorate HM King George V's twenty-fifth anniversary on the throne. The passenger list shows celebrities such as Rudyard Kipling and Mrs Kipling ('and Maid'); Lady Brocklebank; Mrs Oswald Mosley; the Hon. Mary, Jean and Sheila Parnell; five members of the Eaton family (owners of Canada's largest department-store chain); and a phalanx of the nobility and members of Parliament. If one were to combine that passenger list with those of the RMS *Lancastria* and the RMS *Majestic*, two other passenger ships providing cruises to witness the Review, a significant portion of the British upper class of the day would be represented.

It would be interesting to track the number of maids, valets and other servants on passenger lists of a given ship over many years, to trace the reduction in the number of servants and other household staff. The best ships to use would probably be

53 This passenger list of the White Star Line's *Cymric* in 1913 carried information about the ship's officers, and listed the company's substantial fleet.

the RMS *Aquitania*, a large, prestigious four-stacker in service (except during the wars) from 1913 until 1949, and/or the RMS *Mauretania* (1907–35), another four-funnelled Cunarder. *Aquitania* was featured on the covers of certain Cunard passenger lists during her early years, even surpassing the SS *Normandie* in such recognition. Incidentally, the *Normandie* merely used a style of passenger list identical to other French Line ships, except that her name was across the foot of the page.

A celebrity sighting could be the highlight of a voyage. A prime example was the presence of 'Mr GRANT, Cary' of 'Beverly Hills, Calif', destined for Cannes, on the 'Prima Classe – First Class' passenger list of the *Andrea Doria*, sailing from New York on 15 May 1954. Everyone on board would be watching for this handsome film star, who would probably have overshadowed another First Class passenger, 'Mr WILLIAMS, Tennessee' of Key West, Florida, who was destined for Gibraltar.

Covers of passenger lists reflected style and design expectations of the day. The 1920s and 1930s marked the peak of dramatic artwork, particularly on Cunard and Canadian Pacific ships. Others, like White Star Line, lagged behind. For example, the turgid design from a White Star Line list from the *Cymric*'s voyage of 9 September 1913 was still being used for passenger lists of 1924, eleven years later (FIG. 53). In contrast, Cunard produced a solid array of creative artwork. For the frequent traveller across the North Atlantic, Cunard's approach would have added at least a small touch of variety to each trip. After the Second World War, this gave way to more prosaic designs.

For private cruises, such as a 1956 occasion where the RMS *Mauretania* was booked for a Caribbean trip carrying General Electric employees and customers, there could be a riot of colour: the General Electric cover even has 'sparkles' in the design.

54 Canadian Pacific used a wide range of contemporary original artwork on its passenger list covers, including this art deco gem from the *Montrose* in 1931.

CANADIAN PACIFIC

Canadian Pacific produced some of the most artistic covers. Some designs pictured a relaxed lifestyle, while others promoted particular classes of ship, the 'Duchesses' or the 'Empresses'. Still others were powerful art deco expressions of CP ships (**FIG. 54**).

Passenger lists of liners crossing the Pacific Ocean could be as artistic as for those voyaging the Atlantic. Dollar Line styled theirs as a 'guest list', while Japan's NYK labelled theirs as a 'souvenir'. It may seem surprising that so many old passenger lists exist. It shouldn't be. Unlike menus and all other ephemera, these provide names of other passengers, which were often easily forgotten even during the trip, never mind afterwards, and were therefore kept by many travellers. Further, they provide empirical evidence of the voyage and of the other passengers on board to display to friends back home.

Unlike the approach taken for dining-room menus, the covers were rarely reflective of special events or seasons. However, they do reflect a sense of time and place and a slice of social, artistic, design, technological and other history. And even an apparently mundane passenger list from an ocean liner can have a valuable story to disclose.

CHANCE ENCOUNTERS

The occasional prestigious chance encounter added special interest to a trip. Imagine meeting the King and Queen! Well, not exactly meeting, but for one traveller it was still an occasion to boast about:

June 21, 1939
Empress of Australia

Since closing my letter to you this afternoon we have had great thrills. The King's Boat came into sight also 2 destroyers Glasgow and Southampton. They passed right side of our ship – crossed in front of the bow – stopped in formation on the left side of our ship while we passed slowly by. Of course <u>everybody</u> was on deck waving, cheering & shouting 'England Forever'. The King & Queen came out on top & waved big white handkerchiefs. We could not see them clearly but could see 2 people and knew it was them. There was a high wind so ships couldn't come too close together but we had <u>wonderful</u> views.

The 'King's Boat' on this occasion was the *Empress of Britain*, and HM King George VI and Queen Elizabeth were returning to Britain after a royal tour of Canada and the United States. The *Empress of Britain*, Canadian Pacific's largest and most glamorous liner, was twice the size of the *Empress of Australia* and probably twice as prestigious. However, the irony was that the royal couple had made their westbound trip some two weeks earlier on the boaster's own ship – the *Empress of Australia*.

The writer probably wasn't aware that the *Empress of Australia* had been specially fitted out to carry the King and Queen and their entourage. One of a series of press photographs accompanying a media release dated 15 May 1939 described the special arrangements:

> The two Royal Suites of the Canadian Pacific liner 'Empress of Australia' which became the largest private yacht in the world when the 21,000-ton vessel was chartered by the Admiralty, for Their Majesties' voyage to Canada, were as luxuriously fitted as Buckingham Palace.
>
> In addition to the comfortable fittings that are part of regular equipment many treasured pieces of furniture from the Royal Yacht 'Victoria and Albert' were placed aboard.
>
> The top deck smoking room of the 'Empress of Australia' was redecorated as a private dining room, democratically equipped for the service of 12 members of the entourage at each meal, and the main lounge where afternoon tea is served was also given added luxury.

The press photo of the Main Lounge shows the degree of
elegance provided for Their Majesties (FIG. 55). It's possible
that those special arrangements were more or less still in place,
since only some four weeks had passed since the royal couple
had been on board the *Empress of Australia* in their private
accommodation.

HUNTING FOR COMPANY

This diary entry by Georgie, a cruise passenger on the *Roma* en route to Italy in 1937, probably reflects the experience of many travellers:

> Have not yet distinguished myself as a good mixer but mustered enough courage to sign up for the deck tennis and ping-pong tournaments. Wonder how they will turn out. Oh yes, I met the hostess, Mrs Farrell, this evening. Perhaps I am progressing after all.

On the other hand, one can get dragged into social events that have no appeal whatsoever, as Georgie discovered on her second day at sea:

> It doesn't pay to spend too much time in one's deck chair; it causes one to be misunderstood. I stayed in mine too long this afternoon and was finally forced by the hostess to be a 'fourth' at bridge with three old ladies, all old enough to be my grandmother.

Ah, yes – the deckchair. One of the many initial tasks on boarding was to book a deckchair. Depending upon the climate, you might want one in either a secluded area or positioned to catch the refreshing benefit of the ocean breezes. If you wanted to be quiet and undisturbed, there were locations to fill your wishes. If you were Georgie, you would probably want a deck location where you could see and be seen. Ironically, her visibility meant that she was singled out by the hostess to partner three old ladies at bridge and thus paid the penalty for her quest to meet people.

Deckchairs were not free. A rare ticket stub from the *Lusitania* tells the story. Four shillings, or a US dollar, secured your chair for the duration of the voyage. The

55 Royalty travelled in style; this press photo shows part of the Royal Suite created on board the *Empress of Australia* when Their Majesties visited North America in 1939.

number on this tiny postage-stamp-sized ticket may relate to a specific deckchair (FIG. 56). It is amazing that it has survived for over a hundred years. Cushions and blankets were available at additional cost.

GAMES AND SPORTS

The shipping companies provided a range of deck games, indoor games, special events and sports as distractions for their passengers. A constant stream of events such as the ones for which Georgie, the previously mentioned passenger on the *Roma*, signed up fostered a sense of community. A 1926 programme from the Cunarder *Caronia* offers shuffleboard, deck tennis, potato race (separate competitions for ladies and gentlemen), shoe hunt (ladies), three-legged race (gentlemen), ladies' tug-of-war (married vs single) and gentlemen's tug-of-war (married vs single). These were all 'subject to weather conditions'.

There are records of individual efforts, including an invitation from (General) Omar Bradley on stationery with the *Caronia* letterhead to 'Come over and enjoy our cribbage board' and a polite undated note with the *Mauretania* letterhead by a Mr Fasting to a Mrs Kravitt, delivered to her cabin:

> Thank you for your nice letter and your kind invitation to join you and your husband for dinner tomorrow. Unfortunately I am unable to accept – but I hope your husband has a Happy Birthday and you can tell him – at least from my experience life certainly begins at 40.

Why the unavailability for dinner (possibly in Mrs Kravitt's suite or in a private dining room)? Perhaps she was one of those passengers beside whose name one marks a pronounced *X* on the passenger list as someone to be avoided!

56 A tiny pre-1915 receipt ticket for the booking of a deckchair on the *Lusitania*.

A *Games* booklet of 1936 from the *Normandie* (FIG. 57) describes and illustrates 'Little Olympics Afloat' on the expansive deck space for tennis, shuffleboard and other sports in what is described as a 'Stadium at Sea; A Work-out on the Waves'. There was also the gymnasium with rowing machine, handball and a shooting gallery; and 'Sun-Deck Sports and Sea Air' including tennis and trap-shooting. Exhausting!

For the twelve days between Honolulu and Yokohama in 1931, the SS *President McKinley* offered a daily schedule of sports capped off with a 'gymkhana' on the final day of the trip. Deck games listed were shuffleboard, deck tennis and golf. The gymkhana appears to have offered something for every passenger in its programme. For women there was a nail-driving contest, a chopstick race, a cracker race and an obstacle race. For men there was a pillow race, a pillow-case race, a suitcase race, a 'cock fight' and 'Are you there, Casey?' – a game in which blindfolded contestants do battle. There was also a group of mixed competitions – a whistling race, a cigarette race, a shoe race, a water-and-spoon race, and needle-threading and cigarette-lighting competitions.

57 Everything about the French Line's *Normandie* was clever and 1930s' 'cool', including the image on this modest fold-over booklet of activities.

Canadian Pacific

EMPRESS OF BRITAIN

———◆———

TO-DAY'S PROGRAMME

DECK SPORTS:- Deck Tennis,
Quoits, Shuffleboard, Golf. Apply
Deck Sailor.

Squash, Lawn Tennis. Apply to
Attendant.

———

Swimming Pool, Gymnasium
"F" Deck Aft.

Turkish Bath & Zotofoam Bath—
Apply Steward, Stewardess, or Swimming
Pool Attendant.

———

11.00 a.m.	**Practice Dancing Class** in the Smoke Room "A" Deck Aft.
4.00 p.m.	**Tea Concert** in the Mayfair Lounge
5.00 p.m.	**Yacht Regatta** on the Promenade Deck Aft.
9.30 p.m.	**"Madeira" Illustrated Talk** in the Empress Room
	Followed by Dancing in Mayfair Lounge

Thursday, January 12, 1939.

Picture yourself on board the *Empress of Britain* during her world cruise in 1939. When not swept up in shore excursions, you faced the daunting choices set out in a programme of daily events. If you went on this cruise for rest and relaxation, the example in **FIG.** 58 suggests that it was not to be found. A vast spectrum of activities confronted you. But if you were trying to meet some of your fellow passengers, these would have been good avenues to do so.

Prizes were offered for competitions on some ships. A passenger on the *Doric* of the White Star Line probably received this tiny trophy (**FIG.** 59) for winning a bridge or other tournament. For those who wanted non-competitive exercise there was a gymnasium on most large ships. Even a relatively modest-sized one like the *Monarch of Bermuda*, which provided a cruise-style liner service in the 1930s between New York and Bermuda, offered a gymnasium with a range of weights, bars and other conventional fitness equipment of the time (**FIG.** 60).

58 The ship's challenge was to keep its passengers entertained during the long days at sea. Sports and more sedentary activities filled up much of each day during this voyage on the *Empress of Britain* in 1939.

59 Prizes such as this small two-handled silver tyg, won on board White Star Line's *Doric*, gave passengers of the 1920s an incentive to compete.

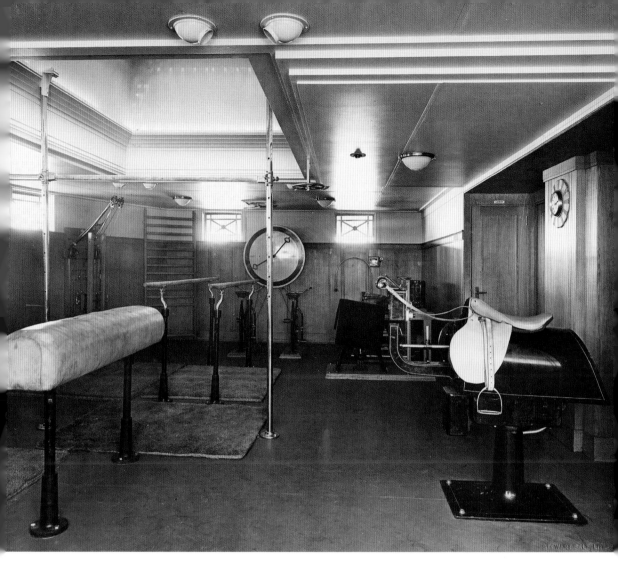

The shipping lines took pride in their diversions. Under the heading 'Pleasures Comforts and Pastimes While at Sea', a Toyo Kisen Kaisha (TKK) brochure of the 1920s describes what the line offers travellers crossing the Pacific Ocean 'From America to Japan, China, Philippines'. TKK provided regularly scheduled trans-Pacific services to both North and South America.

60 A gymnasium on board the *Monarch of Bermuda* in the 1930s.

Out of sight of land, the traveler soon slips into the delightful life aboard ship. Early morning coffee and fruit served in your cabin – pleasant hot or cold salt water baths on arising – a few brisk turns about the deck before the bugle calls for regular breakfast. After that, perhaps a real tramp, for it takes but eight to ten turns about the spacious decks of the Toyo Kisen Kaisha ships to make a mile. Then, social visits or a quiet hour or so in a sheltered nook, in a comfortable deck chair, or games on deck – deck golf, tennis, shuffleboard, bag punching or other exercises in the open air gymnasium. About eleven o'clock refreshments are served on deck, by the ever-solicitous deck stewards, while the welcome bugle call announcing tiffin (luncheon) is heard about 12:30.

The afternoons pass pleasantly, with probably a match game between the two deck baseball teams – a swimming party in the deck forward or cards in the salon.

Tea and cakes are served on deck at four o'clock, which takes the edge off appetite until the call sounds for dinner at seven. After dinner comes the concert or the dance. And a moving picture show in the deck ballroom. As a perfect vacation, nothing can excel this ocean voyage.

INDOOR GAMES

Almost all ships offered bridge and a variety of other card games. Most shipping lines produced their own decks of cards, which could be purchased in the gift shop. For the dedicated bridge enthusiast, there were occasional cruises featuring a specific focus on bridge.

A 1963 brochure by the American President Lines offered a six-week cruise with master bridge player Charles Goren on the SS *President Roosevelt* (FIG. 61). The cruise in the Pacific Ocean promised 'Goren Bridge Lectures', 'Master Point Tournaments', 'Bridge Clinics and Forums' and 'Congenial Playing with Congenial Partners' ('partnerships arranged if desired'). Serious bridge players may question whether playing at this level, with participants prepared to spend the time and money for six weeks honing their competitive skills, could ever be described as 'congenial'.

Other card games also took place, some of them for money. Included in a 1913 White Star Line passenger list of the RMS *Doric* was a slip of paper headed 'Special Notice'. It contains the caution that

> The attention of the Managers has been called to the fact that certain persons believed to be Professional Gamblers are in the habit of travelling to and fro on Atlantic steamships. In bringing this to the knowledge of travellers, the Managers, while not wishing in the slightest degree to interfere with the freedom of action of Patrons of the White Star Line, desire to invite their assistance in discouraging Games of Chance as being likely to afford these individuals special opportunities for taking unfair advantage of others.

The swindlers were very clever. Depending upon your destination and the ship's speed, there were several nights for friendly games. After you retired from dinner to the smoking room or the card room, replete in your tuxedo or dinner suit, there was nothing more satisfying than taking money from that nice chap who seemed a little scatterbrained and played poker badly. A couple of fine brandies on top of the wine at dinner fostered an air of utmost congeniality. It was so pleasant the first few nights for you and the others to win Mr Scatterbrain's money so easily. No big amounts, but worth winning. Then there was the final

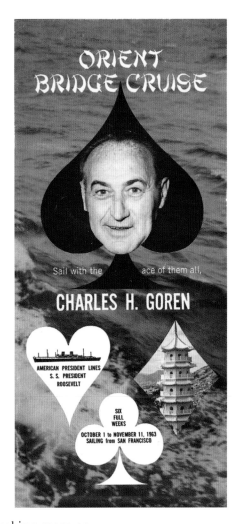

61 A six-week cruise to the Far East in 1963 on board the *President Roosevelt*, led by bridge guru Charles Goren.

night, when nothing went right for you and every pot seemed to fall into the hands of Mr Scatterbrain. With his previous record, you were sure that he couldn't keep winning – but you kept on losing. In fact, you had grabbed the bait, and he was reeling in you and your fellow players. The clever Mr Scatterbrain and his like made a successful living off the passengers on ships. Affluent First Class passengers, of course. The ship's stewards may eventually have recognized him, but there was little they could do formally unless they could discern how he was cheating the other players.

Then there were pickpockets. We tend to think of pickpockets as being a risk on shore, when milling crowds mask the activities of the perpetrators. However, ocean voyages were equally a hazard, from the time that you joined the mob of passengers boarding the ship, through the times that you watched competitions on deck, to the time that you were part of the torrent of passengers streaming from the ship upon its arrival at its destination. For the slick pickpocket, there were plenty of rewards. They could be sure that you were carrying lots of cash in your wallet, and disposal of any incriminating evidence required little more than a deft flip of the empty wallet over the side and into the sea. The risk was so pervasive that the shipping lines even printed formal warnings for passengers.

CROSSING THE EQUATOR

For centuries crossing the equator has been for every ship – mercantile or naval – a time for a ceremony, where those on board who have not previously 'crossed the line' are initiated by an officer costumed as 'King Neptune'. Such events were normal, but each voyage had its own particular take on them. The process no longer included physical attacks on

62 Crossing the equator was a major entertainment for all passengers, as the uninitiated were inducted by King Neptune and his assistants. World cruise passengers on board the *Cleveland* in 1912 received this diploma-sized certificate as a memento of the ceremony.

Around the World Cruise

of the Hamburg-American Line

TWIN-SCREW S.S. "CLEVELAND"

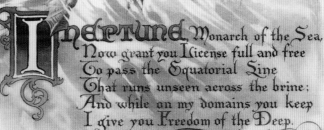

I NEPTUNE, Monarch of the Sea,
Now grant you License full and free
To pass the Equatorial Line
That runs unseen across the brine;
And while on my domains you keep
I give you Freedom of the Deep.

Father Neptune

To _Miss Ellen M. Law._
Dated 14. XII. 1912.

The South Publishing Press, New York.

the participants, as it did among earlier sailors, but instead presented a novel entertainment for both the initiated and the uninitiated. A passenger on the *Belgenland* of the Red Star Line in 1927 wrote about her experience:

> This afternoon everyone gathered around one of the outside swimming pools, where a throne had been erected for Neptune and his staff. The band, dressed like pirates, led the royal procession, the King, Queen and Prince with their attendants followed. Then the Royal Court of Justice and a group of masqueraders appeared. The King greeted us all. Mermaids and sharks were in the pool to properly dunk the victims.... Several people were convicted of hypothetical crimes and duly punished.

And later:

> Another diploma has been awarded to me and I am going to have it framed when I get home. It is my certificate from Father Neptune for crossing the Equator and looks very much like a high school Award of Merit.

A memento from the equatorial crossing of the 1912 cruise of the Hamburg–American Line's SS *Cleveland* was a beautiful certificate, which would have been a wonderful trophy for framing (**FIG. 62**).

FANCY DRESS PARTIES

A number of uncaptioned images of participants in fancy-dress costumes have survived. What was the occasion? It was the fancy-dress ball!

On my boyhood trip, with my parents, on an ocean liner in 1954, on the RMS *Queen Elizabeth*, I noticed many people in Roman togas and Arab robes. I was told that there would be a shortage of bed sheets for a few days, since cutting up bed sheets was the quickest and simplest way to create a costume. There were also more creative costumes, fashioned from anything that might have been available on the ship. I remember Gypsies, a home-made Superman costume, and other innovative ideas. But some costumes were absolutely 'over the top'. There was no way that you could have created them from materials available on board.

My parents explained that a few people, not prepared to be outdone, acquired costumes before they went on board in order to be winners with the best overall costumes (a contemporary advert reveals the type of costume available for purchase: Columbia, Pierrette, Mother Goose and Gypsy for women; Indian Chief, Clown, Devil and Jester for men). In terms of the spirit of the contest, this was cheating – but it still took place. To cope with this strategy, an entertainment programme on the SS *Strathnaver* in 1938, travelling between Europe and India, distinguished between categories for Best Costume Made on Board and Best Costume Bought or Brought on Board.

Even on a minor ship, such as the passenger-cargo SS *Aeneas* of the Blue Funnel Line, they staged fancy dress balls (**FIG. 63**). Inside this booklet there is a dance card; only four dances during the evening have names beside them. During an

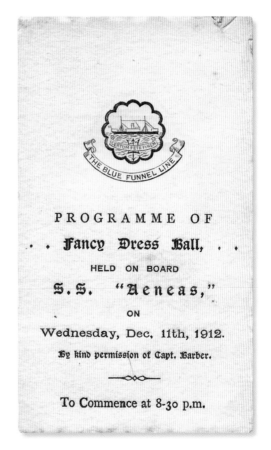

PROGRAMME OF

. . **Fancy Dress Ball,** . .

HELD ON BOARD

S.S. **"Aeneas,"**

ON

Wednesday, Dec. 11th, 1912.

By kind permission of Capt. Barber.

To Commence at 8·30 p.m.

63 A tiny fancy dress ball dance programme from the little-known SS *Aeneas* (1912).

Orient Line cruise on the SS *Orontes*, a fancy-dress dance on 19 July 1932 offered prizes for Ladies' and Men's Best Costume and Most Original Costume, respectively. A competitor would be 'supplied with numbers and requested to wear them in a conspicuous place, and to assemble at the After End of B Deck at 8.50 p.m. The Official Photographer will be in attendance at the After End of B Deck after the Parade.'

Before the advent of digital photography, the official photographer was a critical element of life on board. As well as group photos, such as one showing the costume party participants on board the *Warwick Castle* of the Union-Castle Line (FIG. 64), there were separate photos of groups of friends in costume which they could keep as souvenirs or, alternatively, send gloatingly to friends back home, as in a fascinating, possibly mother-and-daughter, trio of the 1930s on the SS *Themistocles*.

As well as photos taken during scheduled events, the official photographer offered posed photos. On board the SS *München*, a North German Lloyd liner of the 1930s, the ship's photographer used a standard set as the backdrop for passengers, who donned sailor uniforms and stood at an artificial ship's wheel for a souvenir photo.

64 Contestants who competed in fancy-dress competitions occasionally brought elaborate costumes with them. How many had done this for the fancy-dress ball pictured on board the *Warwick Castle* of the Union-Castle Line?

WINING AND DINING

Shipping lines attempted to make meals a highlight of an ocean voyage, helping (along with the various shipboard diversions described above) to distract their passengers from the tedium of long days at sea. In offering their own national cuisines, they could compete with each other in culture, hospitality and sophistication. There was an obvious affinity, sometimes even a direct relationship, with the luxury hotel and restaurant industry ashore. Before the Second World War, ships tied up at New York were often open for the public to dine there. Ritz-style 'hotelier cuisine' evolved so that tasty, fancy-looking dishes could be prepared quickly and served to large numbers.

There are many references to dining and to the quality of the food in passenger correspondence. An enthusiastic one from a postcard from the SS *Normandie* dated 5 June 1937 tells it all:

> What a boat. What a trip. Et What food. We have to fill
> ourselves with Vichy Water and many Pernod Fils in order to
> ward off the indigestion. Frog Legs Poulette and Crepe-suzettes
> are our common dish now. Voila!
> Bill et Hazelle

Some passengers attempted to recoup the cost of their passage through their level of food consumption. For others, the impact of the tossing and rolling of the waves precluded any such recovery. The unknown author of the diary of a cruise on the *Montrose* in 1936 confessed:

> On the Sunday morning I managed a small breakfast in the Dining Saloon – very hurriedly – and then became an early victim to *mal de mer*. It is best to draw a veil but suffice it to say I afterwards discovered 75% of the passengers were fellow sufferers. I did not care whether the ship went down, in fact I'd have welcomed it.
>
> Monday came with the ship still going up, down, over and round, but I struggled up on deck for a few hours and reclined in a deck chair looking very seedy with a yellow – or should I say green – complexion. It matched my coat very well.

MENUS

Menus from ocean liners through the decades titillated the palate while displaying the changing fashions of art and design on the covers, conveying the social and economic framework of the era, and revealing the technological prowess of shipping-line refrigeration systems. Appealing to the palate was always a key consideration, particularly when some passengers displayed the symptoms common to those with delicate constitutions during rolling or stormy seas.

Let's begin with the Cunarder RMS *Mauretania*, relatively new to the fleet but destined to be internationally admired for speed and comfort over almost the next three decades. (In 1909 the *Mauretania* set a transatlantic speed record that she held for the next twenty years.) A single card was used for an April 1908 dinner menu (**FIG. 65**). With embossed symbols for

65 This *Mauretania* menu of 1908, finished in the style of a bronze tablet, offered a range of foods for a traditional Sunday dinner.

R.M.S. "MAURETANIA."

Sunday, April 26th, 1908

MENU.

Hors d'Œuvres — Varies

Oysters—Half Shell

Green Turtle   Creme de Celeri

Codfish—Parsley Sauce   Broiled Shad and Roe

Sweetbreads Grillè   Jugged Hare—Francaise

Roast Sirloin and Ribs of Beef   Roast Spring Lamb—Mint Sauce

Roast Goose   Boiled Chicken—Veloute Sauce

Green Peas   Rice   Grilled Tomatoes

Boiled and Mashed Potatoes

Asparagus — Hollandaise Sauce

Pudding King Charles

Rhubarb Tart   Gelee Clicquot   Millie Fullies

French Ice Cream and Wafers

Pailles au Parmesan

Dessert

Tea   Coffee

Britain and America flanking an engraving of the ship, the list of dishes here is printed, whereas not many years earlier menus were handwritten for each meal, as in the first SS *Normandie* in

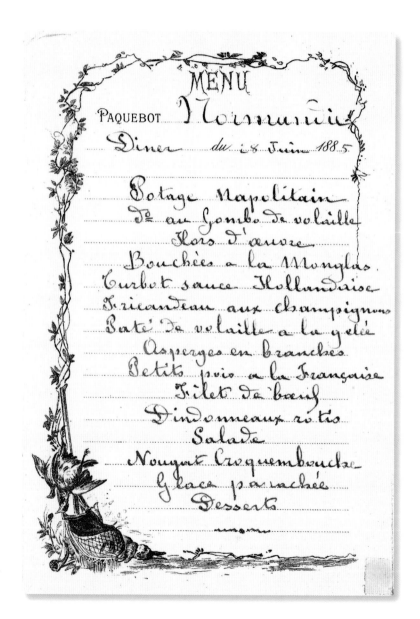

66 Dinner menu from the first *Normandie* in 1885. In the absence of printing equipment, handwritten menus offered the dining choices for the meal. Fortunately, the small size of the ship limited the number of menus required for diners.

1885 (**FIG. 66**). (This was an early passenger ship of the French Line, built in 1881 and less than 10 per cent of the size of her giant 1930s' namesake.)

Consider the amount of work involved in hand-writing a hundred or more menus for such earlier, smaller ships. For the *Mauretania*, with her 563 First Class passengers, 464 Second Class passengers and 1,138 Third Class passengers, hand-writing the number of menus required would clearly have been too much. Fortunately, advances in technology for printing and copying kept pace with the crew's needs.

Loading Simla with ice March/09.

On the earlier liners the refrigeration system consisted of blocks of ice to maintain the temperature. Being able to replenish the ice supplies en route (**FIG. 67**) was almost as vital as maintaining an adequate supply of fuel. Some dishes could be canned or otherwise preserved, but others could not, and fresh fruit and vegetables at sea were always a welcome culinary feature. Refrigerated holds were commonplace by the 1930s.

Other than in the Spartan regime of wartime, ocean liner menus reflected a facet of the ongoing efforts of the shipping companies to create a shipboard climate comparable to the great hotels of the time for First Class passengers, and appropriate equivalents for those in other classes. Even on smaller ships, such as the TSS *Caledonia* of the Anchor Line, whose maiden

67 Loading ice onto the *Simla* in 1909 illustrates what had to be done regularly in the absence of refrigeration systems.

ANCHOR LINE
T.S.S. "CALEDONIA"
MENU

THURSDAY, 30th JANUARY, 1913.

Celery.   Russian Caviare.   Salted Almonds.

Consomme Valetta.   Mulligatawny.

Fillets of Halibut, Salamander.

Lobster Cutlets, Crevettes.

Pigeon en Compote, Rentiers

Ribs of Beef, Horseradish.

Quarters of Lamb, Green Peas.

Boiled Capon, Oyster Sauce.

Cauliflowers.   Rice.   Dressed Cabbage.

Noisette, Baked and Boiled Potatoes.

Braised Irish Ham, Sauce au Vin.

COLD.

Roast Turkey.   Spiced Round of Beef.

Asparagus Mayonaise.

Caramel Pudding.

Baked Apple Dumpling, Hard Sauce.

Boston Cream Cakes.   Sicilienne Meringue.

Vanilla Ices.

Macaroni Calabraise.

Dessert.   Coffee.

Passengers' attention is directed to attached Post Card, which is available for their use.

voyage had been in 1905, the contents of First Class menus in 1913 were extensive and elegant (FIG. 68). Indeed, some smaller lines such as the Scandinavian ones outcompeted on the quality of their cuisine as a way of compensating for having less impressive vessels with fewer other facilities.

A trip for the period 25 January to 1 February 1913 is chronicled in an archive of *Caledonia* menus of the period. Dinner menus were enhanced by having a postcard attached, so that after dinner the passenger could settle back in the smoking room (men only, please) with a comforting glass of brandy and a friendly cigar, and write to friends back home, while his mind was suffused with fond memories of Russian caviar, lobster cutlets and Sicilienne meringue. Similarly in the Ladies' lounge, postcards from the menus would be handy for immediate messages to friends.

Many menu covers were so delightful that they were saved as mementoes of the voyage. Early North German Lloyd menus, such as this luncheon one from the SS *Grosser Kurfürst* of 1 April 1903, reflected the art nouveau influences of the period in Germany's *Jugendstil* (FIG. 69). The Red Star Line's menus of the early 1900s featured a wide range of artwork,

68 Caviar and lobster are on offer for First Class passengers only on Anchor Line's *Caledonia* in 1913.

69 The cover of this menu from the *Grosser Kurfürst* of North German Lloyd in 1903 exuded charm and adventure.

Merry X-mas

X-MAS DINNER 1920

"Sunshine Belt to the Orient"

THOMAS BOYD, COMMANDER

F. PALANDER, 1st Officer   S. L. WELLS, Chief Engineer

E. M. WAGNER, 2nd. Officer   C. B. AHERN, 1st Assist.

WM. M. MATISEN, 3rd. Officer   G. I. COLLINS, 2nd. Assist.

F. T. McBEAN, Radio   H. E. HENDERSON, 3rd. Assist

NED. F. LORENZEN, Purser

WM. K. McGILLIVRAY, Chief Steward

Oyster Cocktail

Celery en Branche   Spring Onions

Manz Olives   Spiced Beets

Potage Castelaine   Consomme Royal

Boiled White Fish Egg Sauce

Boiled Brisket of Beef, Horseradish Sauce

Filet Mignon, a'la Boyd

Peach Fritters au Glace

Roast Young Turkey, Dressing and Cranberry Sauce

Roast Loin of Pork with Apple Sauce

Mashed Potatoes   Sugar Corn

Waldorf Salad

Plum Pudding, Hard and Lemon Sauce

Fresh Apple Pie   Chocolate Ice Cream

Preserved Pears   Bonita Snaps

Assorted Nuts   Fresh Fruits

Cheese—American, Swiss

Cafe Noir

S. S. POINT BONITA.   DECEMBER 25, 1920

70 Trans-Pacific passengers dined as well as their North Atlantic counterparts. This menu for Christmas dinner in 1920 aboard the *Point Bonita* of the Pacific Mail Steamship Company offers traditional turkey, as well as beef or pork, to the pampered passengers.

which frequently also included a postcard. These menu/postcard combinations are difficult to find, and unfortunately each of the components is missing part of the total picture once they are separated. In some cases the image bleeds from the postcard onto the menu, and only when they are together is the charm complete. Even in the 1920s, when the surge of interest in postcard collecting had abated, totally integrated combinations were still being used, such as this beautiful Christmas menu from the SS *Point Bonita* of the Pacific Mail Steamship Company (FIG. 70).

WHITE STAR LINE.
R.M.S. "HOMERIC".

White Star Line special menus of the 1930s expressed a degree of exuberance that was in stark contrast to the economic darkness of the Great Depression (FIG. 71). This Gala Dinner held on the RMS *Homeric* on 10 June 1930 offered Little Neck Clams, Salmon Trout Meunière and Wild Duck à l'Orange among its culinary enticements. Other shipping lines strove for the same level of sparkle.

Cruises raised new challenges to the imagination and creativity of the menu designers. The menu for a Pirate's Dinner during an August 1937 Caribbean cruise of the SS *Haiti* of the Colombian Line was printed on sacking, emulating the coarse clothing of the pirates of centuries before. The dishes were also creative, and the menu offered prospective treats

71 A Gala Night cover from White Star Line's *Homeric* in 1930 hints at an elegant evening – with a Prohibition-era tipple for American passengers.

such as Cartagena melon, potage Port Royal, baked bananas Captain Blood and ice cream from Captain Kidd.

Special occasions also merited recognition, whether it was Abraham Lincoln's birthday on board the Hamburg–American Line's SS *Resolute* in 1925, St Valentine's Day during the Great World Cruise of Cunard's RMS *Caronia* in 1967 (featuring dishes such as lemon sole sauté Antoinette and grilled squab chicken Casanova), or an RMS *Queen Mary* menu to commemorate the coronation of King George VI and Queen Elizabeth in 1937, including oysters Balmoral, croustades Queen Elizabeth, and roast duckling Sandringham (FIG. 72).

Royal commemorative menus did not end in the 1930s. A *Queen Elizabeth 2* dinner menu of 19 July 1981 – well over forty years later – commemorates the royal wedding of Charles and Diana, and that menu also carries allusions to the royal family, such as potage Carnarvon Castle, broiled prime tenderloin steak Lady Diana, and soufflé Bowes-Lyon.

Ocean liner menus are a delicious slice of shipping history.

72 This Cunard-White Star dinner menu aboard RMS *Queen Mary* celebrated the coronation of King George VI in 1937; diners would see appropriately themed offerings such as oysters Balmoral and roast duckling Sandringham.

WINING

Drinking was a key aspect of steamship travel since its earliest days: it made profits for owners and helped fill lengthy hours. The wine list and the drinks menu were important elements of life on board for most passengers. This was particularly true for American travellers during the period of Prohibition (1920–33). Once the ship was outside American territorial waters, the bar opened, and the thirsty traveller could imbibe legally rather than having to patronize a speakeasy or a criminal purveyor of booze whose product quality might not match the brand label pasted on the bottle.

73 This cover of the cocktail menu of Panama Pacific Line was at the apex of the art deco era. The lure of martinis and daiquiris at 25 cents each would have been a dream for booze-deprived American passengers in the early 1930s.

During the Prohibition era, access to any booze at all was a cruise enthusiast's pot of gold at the end of the rainbow. For those who couldn't afford the cost – or the time – of a longer cruise, coastal cities like New York featured weekend 'booze cruises' on ocean liners that went out just beyond American territorial waters and featured well-stocked bars. With martinis and daiquiris at 25 cents and Courvoisier for 35 cents a glass, even the most frugal Panama Pacific Line drinker would have been able to imbibe liberally on this ship (FIG. 73).

During the early 1930s the Depression severely reduced the number of transatlantic passengers, so even very large and famous liners were used instead for three- or four-day booze cruises for thirsty Americans. Booze-cruise material is not easy to find. Who would keep a brochure for a drinking binge when they probably didn't remember much of the voyage in any case? A short cruise on the Cosulich Line's *Vulcania* or the Anchor Line's *Transylvania* was priced from $40, which was a small price to pay for an extended binge. But in none of the cruise material that has come to my attention have I seen an image of a bar.

How bad were the drinking bouts? Recognizing that some of the participants would have been people with what were called 'drinking problems', an insight is provided by the participant in a 1927 cruise on the Red Star liner *Belgenland*. In a letter, she reported that

> There are a number of men of various ages on the boat who formed a Bar Fly Club. The members of this exclusive club are men who frequent the Smoke Room – not for puffing their Lucky Strikes, but for imbibing the forbidden fluid. Last night they had a stag dinner, the motive or express purpose of which was to endeavor to drink more liquor than had been utilized by any other party during the cruise. They accomplished their aim far beyond their expectation.

MID-WEEK CRUISE to NOVA SCOTIA

Revue and Midnight Supper

Thursday, August 25th, 1932

M.V. "BRITANNIC"

WHITE STAR LINE

74 A midweek cruise to Nova Scotia was typical of the party 'booze cruises' of this era. Once the ship was out of American territorial waters, the bars opened and parched drinkers could imbibe freely. These brief cruises helped to offset the serious drop in revenue from transatlantic passenger travel.

I do not mind if older men have no more sense than to get intoxicated, but I think it is a shame for the younger men to. Freedom, idle time, and too much money certainly can cause more destruction than any other combination I know.

A White Star Line folder of August 1932 sets out the programme and menu on board the MV *Britannic* for a revue and midnight supper during a 'mid-week cruise to Nova Scotia' (FIG. 74). To someone who enjoyed a drink, this cruise would be irresistible. When the Eighteenth Amendment establishing Prohibition was repealed in 1933, the temperance movement had come full circle and so had the career of several ocean liners that had been kept in service during the depths of the Great Depression primarily as offshore oases for thirsty Americans.

Looking further back to what might be called more normal times, the spectrum of drink choices was smaller. In 1901, the back of a Cunard First Class dinner menu dated July of that year shows a much greater emphasis on wine than on exotic

75 In 1901, wines were sold by the quart and pint; liqueurs were available by the glass or bottle. Only for wine could you 'run a tab' during the voyage.

The Cunard Steam Ship Company, Limited.

		Per Quart. s. d.	Per Pint. s. d.
Champagnes	POMMERY & GRENO, Extra Sec & Sec	10 0	5 6
	CLICQUOT, Dry	10 0	5 6
	GEORGE GOULET, Extra Dry	9 0	5 0
	„ Extra Brut	9 0	5 0
	PERRIER, JOUET & Co., Ex. Dry Special	9 0	5 0
	G. H. MUMM & Co., Extra Dry	9 0	5 0
	HEIDSIECK & Co., Dry Monopole	9 0	5 0
Clarets	Fine Vintage	6 0	—
	Good Bordeaux	4 0	2 6
	Light	2 0	—
Hocks	Sparkling	5 0	3 0
	Still	5 0	3 0
Moselle	Sparkling	5 0	3 0
	Still	3 6	2 0
Port		4 0	—
Sherries	Pale Dry	5 0	—
	Golden	4 0	—
Burgundy	Nuits	5 0	3 0

		Per Bot. s. d.	Per Glass. s. d.
Liqueurs	CHARTREUSE	5 0	0 6
	MARASCHINO	5 0	0 6
	BENEDICTINE	5 0	0 6
	VERMOUTH	5 0	0 6
	CREME DE MENTHE	5 0	0 6
	KUMMEL	5 0	0 6

July, 1901.

		Per Bot. s. d.	P Liqueur Glass. 0 6 / Per Glass.
Brandy	VERY OLD	7 6	0 9
		5 0	0 6
Whiskies	IRISH	4 0	0 6
	SCOTCH	4 0	0 6
	AMERICAN RYE, Park&Tilfords Y.P.M.	5 0	0 6
	CANADIAN CLUB, WALKER'S		
Hollands		4 0	0 6
Old Tom		3 0	0 6
Rum		4 0	0 6

	Per Bot.
Ale & Porter	0s. 6d.
Soda Water, Lager Beer, Ginger Ale, Lemonade	0s. 6d.
Seltzer, Apollinaris, Johannis & Johannis Lithia Waters	0s. 6d.
Apollinaris & Johannis Water (small)	0s. 4d.
Congress Water	1s. 0d.
Cigars — Havana, No. 1	9d. each.
„ „ 2	6d. „
„ „ 3	3d. „
Manilla	3d. „
Cigarettes — American, Packages of 20	1s. 0d. per Pkge.
„ „ 10	0s. 6d. „
Egyptian— Nestor Gianaclis, or Savory & Co.	1s. 0d. „
Tobacco — CAVENDISH, Light, 4s. per lb.; Dark, 2s. 6d. per lb.	
Do. — CUT, 5s. per lb.	
Apenta Water (medicinal)	6d. per Bottle.

All, except Wines, to be paid for at the Time.

The Steward is directed to present and collect the Wine Bills against Passengers on the day previous to the Ship's Arrival.

cocktails (FIG. 75). Price structures of that distant past suggest that this was only for the affluent, who might think nothing of ordering a bottle of Veuve Clicquot champagne for 10 shillings, which would have been the equivalent of about $2.50, and pricey compared to the drinks of some thirty years later on the Panama Pacific Line.

If the champagne is used as a price barometer, it comes in at $5.25 a bottle on board Cunard's *Caronia* in 1959. For affluent passengers, champagne appears to have been a popular festive drink, to judge from entries in a typed record of a trip on the *Roma* in the late 1930s:

> The dinner included a few extra courses and some wonderful champagne (Gran Spumante) and besides that our own little party celebrated by having champagne cocktails before dinner.

The purist will point out that Spumante is not champagne, but 'Georgie', the scribe of the voyage, doesn't know the difference. Please forgive her.

Alcohol consumed could range from the elegant to locally produced drink purchased during a shore excursion. Quality and alcohol strength could vary widely from more conventionally sourced booze, as the following episode describes. It is recounted in the typed diary of a two-week Mediterranean cruise in 1936 on Canadian Pacific's *Montrose*, quoted earlier:

> Certain gentlemen who had bought Madeira wine onshore were keenly anxious for excuse to sample it so they arranged a bottle party for 8.45 pm. I took a very little drop, but even that must have been too much, for later on when dancing on deck I couldn't follow the steps at all nor control my feet. Said I to my partner, 'Is the ship rolling or is it I?' Said he, 'There's no doubt, it's you.'

M.S. Berlin,

White Star Line. R.M.S. "MAJESTIC."
The Largest Steamer in the World.
PALM COURT.

56,551 Tons.

DINING ROOMS

As well as the main dining saloon for each class of passenger, there were other places to eat your meals. Depending upon the ship and your 'Class', you might dally in the tea room or the Verandah Café (FIG. 76), or the Garden Lounge, or the Palm Court (FIG. 77), or whatever other euphemism might be used for relatively casual on-board dining spots.

For the Cabin Class (First Class) passenger, dining was an impressive experience. Even on the *Montrose*, which was a fairly basic ship, the dining room was impressive, decorated in a style that might be called baronial (FIG. 78). But it lacked one major feature – there was no grand staircase. The ships of the French Line seem to have been more disposed to having a *grand escalier*, perfect for any celebrity or 'wannabe' desiring to make a grand entrance, as on the SS *France* of the 1920s (FIG. 79).

76 The Verandah Café on the *Berlin* offered a simulated garden setting, but note the apparent window covering leaning against the wall in case of stormy weather.

77 The Palm Court on the giant *Majestic* presented a tranquil tropical environment that replicated a large land-based hotel.

78 The Cabin Class dining room on Canadian Pacific's *Montrose* mimicked dining in the hall of a medieval castle, complete with trestle dining tables.

CANADIAN PACIFIC S/S MONTROSE CABIN DINING SALOON

While a grand staircase was a highly visible feature, other, more subtle, elements were of more practical importance. My parents recalled a stormy crossing in the 1930s when, to their initial horror, the dining room stewards poured water onto their tablecloths. It was explained that the water increased the friction between the tablecloth and the table, and between the chinaware and the table cloth. A similar situation was described in a letter of the same era, written on the French Line's *Paris* in 1931:

79 On the 1920s' *France* the grand staircase was designed to showcase 'grand' entrances when descended by stylishly dressed passengers.

> It is very rough on the water today and is hard to walk without hanging on to something. They have chairs nailed to the floor, so people won't fall, and in the dining room they have holders for the plates and glasses, to keep them from falling off the table.

Other precautions included a rim around the dining table perimeter (a metal frame put on top of the tablecloth, to hold all the tableware within); and chairs in the dining room, as well as those in other parts of the ship, being anchored to the floor.

The images here illustrate one of the challenges of the dining room – many of them had long trestle tables, which limit the conversation. Seating was allocated if you had not made a selection. Other than in First Class, the dining room was not large enough to accommodate all the passengers in the class, so one usually had to opt for first or second sitting for meals.

The card illustrated here (FIG. 80) is from the French Line's *Chicago* of the 1920s. It does not show the times of the second sitting, but it does allocate the passenger to a specific table and a designated seat at the table. The napkin rings were numbered at each table, so there was little chance for change. The timing would vary slightly depending upon the ship and the voyage, but information provided to passengers on White Star Line's *Megantic* for a voyage in 1922 is a good example (FIG. 81).

The first sitting requires the traveller to be in for breakfast by 8.00 a.m. and out by 9.00 a.m. Not bad for breakfast, unless one likes to sleep in. The second sitting, at 9.00 a.m., means a very late breakfast, and the risk of a slow-moving group from the first sitting at your assigned table, to make breakfast even later. The timing of departure for shore excursions puts on even more pressure for those on second sitting.

80 Dining times were structured to accommodate multiple sittings. On the *Chicago* of the French Line in the 1920s, this card reminded you that you had the second sitting, and were at Table 10, Seat 55.

81 First-sitting diners on White Star Line's *Megantic* in the 1920s were given an hour for each of breakfast and lunch, and only an hour and a quarter for dinner. Offsetting that was the chance to be early for after-dinner events and shore excursions.

INFORMATION FOR PASSENGERS
(Continued)
☆

		First Sitting		Second Sitting
BREAKFAST	- - -	8.00 A. M.	-	9.00 A. M.
LUNCHEON	- - -	12.30 P. M.	-	1.30 A. M.
DINNER	- - -	6.00 P. M.	-	7.15 P. M.

The Bar is closed at 11.30 p. m.
Lights are extinguished in the Saloon at 11.00 p. m., and in the Lounge and Smoke Room at 12.00 p. m.
Divine Service in the Saloon on Sunday at 10.30 a. m.

Dinner timing can also be a conundrum. Note that one could not select first sitting for one meal such as breakfast and second sitting for other meals. The traveller had to commit to a specific dining track. Second sitting might be valuable on days when you were returning from shore excursions. Not having to appear for dinner until 7.30 would give time to freshen up and have a change of garments before the meal, whereas those who had to appear at 6.00 might have been very rushed. The question was also related to cultural factors and class. Typical Britons and Americans, mainly middle class, preferred to dine early; continental Europeans and the 'smart set' would rather eat late.

Life is filled with risks and rewards. A late dinner would be a nice reward for second sitting after an excursion, but it could be stressful if one planned to attend the evening's entertainments. You couldn't expect to get a good seat in the cinema or a good place in the ballroom if you didn't arrive there until the entertainment was well under way. First or second sitting? There was no perfect answer.

PRIVATE PARTIES

FILM STARS

Among the many social activities on board for the First Class passengers were private parties. Evidence points towards these being intimate gatherings of like-minded passengers who knew each other before the trip and wanted to be able to wine and dine in privacy. When the only way to cross the Atlantic was by ship, menus for private parties and for special events like farewell dinners could offer an insight into the lives of the rich and famous – or infamous. A prime example was a private event held on board Cunard's RMS *Imperator* in August 1920 to honour Jack

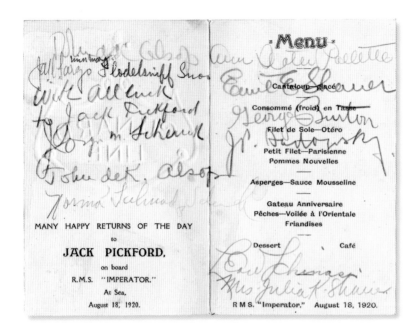

· Menu ·

Cantaloup—glacé

Consommé (froid) en Tasse

Filet de Sole—Otéro

Petit Filet—Parisienne
Pommes Nouvelles

Asperges—Sauce Mousseline

Gateau Anniversaire
Pêches—Voilée à l'Orientale
Friandises

Dessert   Café

R.M.S. "Imperator."   August 18, 1920.

MANY HAPPY RETURNS OF THE DAY
to

JACK PICKFORD,

on board

R.M.S.   "IMPERATOR."

At Sea,

August 18, 1920.

Pickford's birthday. Does the name sound slightly familiar? It should – he was silent-film star Mary Pickford's younger brother.

Jack Pickford had a reputation for wild and dissolute living. He had a number of small film roles but never enjoyed the success of his sister, who was the darling of the silent-film era. In 1920 Jack went to France; en route, on 18 August, he celebrated his twenty-fourth birthday; a tiny (6 × 4½-inch) menu for the event is illustrated here (**FIG. 82**). Signatures of people attending this private shipboard party include those of the silent-film star Norma Talmadge and the actor George Burton, as well as Joseph M. Schenck, who was a business associate of Mary Pickford and the husband of Norma Talmadge. We can see the customized menu, but we can't guess at the amount of alcohol that might have been consumed. Clearly this would have been quite the party – particularly since this was during

82 In 1920, Mary Pickford's reportedly dissolute brother Jack celebrated his twenty-fourth birthday on board Cunard's *Imperator* with film industry greats who included the silent-film star Norma Talmadge.

the era of Prohibition and alcohol was not readily available in the USA.

The menu looks modest, but it was no doubt Jack's own choice of dishes – and it included a birthday cake (Gateau Anniversaire). There may have been other influences, such as limitations to the kitchen facilities, since *Imperator* had been used as an American troopship as recently as one year earlier, having been laid up in Hamburg since 1914. In 1920 she was only on lease to Cunard from the British government; she wasn't refitted until just over a year later, after she had actually been purchased by Cunard, and had been renamed RMS *Berengaria*. The Cunard *Imperator* period during which Pickford travelled was a brief interlude in this liner's career.

Jack Pickford died in Paris in early January 1933 and so had only twelve more birthdays before succumbing, allegedly, to the ravages of drink, drugs and syphilis.

ACADEMICS AND UNIVERSITY ADMINISTRATORS

In September 1920 Lord Beaverbrook hosted a private party on board the Cunarder *Aquitania* to honour the American Rhodes Scholarship recipients travelling to England that year (FIG. 83). The Scholarship, established in 1902, enables postgraduate students from English-speaking countries to study at the University of Oxford. Considerable advance planning would have been necessary to arrange the space for this party, determine the menu, and print the souvenir document with the names of all the participants on the back. Creativity was involved to present menu items with a distinctly American identity – except for the Bollinger 1911 champagne and the Otard Dupuy cognac.

We don't know whether this was a unique event or whether each year's recipients were recognized while sailing to their future academic destination. However, the circumstances suggest that this could have been something special. The graduating classes of 1919 were the first ones after the end of the war. Lord Beaverbrook, wealthy sponsor of the event, had spent part

DINNER

TO THE

CLASS OF 1919.

𝕬merican 𝕽hodes 𝕾cholars

GIVEN BY

Lord Beaverbrook

AND

The Cunard Steam Ship Company Ltd.

GRILL ROOM

R.M.S. "AQUITANIA"

7-30 p.m.   September 26th., 1920.

83 Another private party of 1920 – Rhodes Scholars from America being hosted by Lord Beaverbrook on board Cunard's glamorous *Aquitania*.

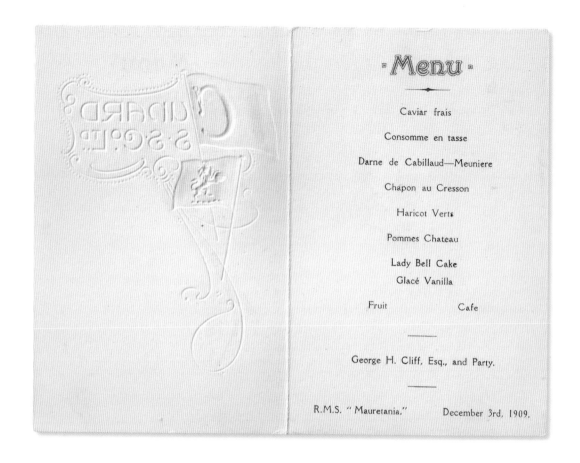

·Menu·

Caviar frais

Consomme en tasse

Darne de Cabillaud—Meuniere

Chapon au Cresson

Haricot Verts

Pommes Chateau

Lady Bell Cake
Glacé Vanilla

Fruit   Cafe

George H. Cliff, Esq., and Party.

R.M.S. " Mauretania."   December 3rd, 1909.

of the war in a cabinet role. A year earlier the *Aquitania*, as a hospital ship, would have been carrying wounded troops home from battle fronts. It was a watershed moment – and a time to celebrate.

Two fascinating menus from 1909 from private parties on board the *Mauretania* reveal the money that university executives and associates could cultivate (FIG. 84). On 3 December a private party for 'George H. Cliff, Esq., and Party' began with caviar and progressed to the choice of Lady Bell cake or vanilla ice cream for dessert. The back cover of the menu carried a

84 This special menu from the *Mauretania* in 1909 was for a private dinner for George H. Cliff.

note of appreciation from 'W.H. Rider'. The following night a private party for 'Three Admirers of Smith College' appears to have been a reciprocal occasion involving Mr Cliff and two others as admirers of Smith, the prestigious women's college in Massachusetts (FIG. 85). Predictably, for a reciprocal event, caviar launched the menu, just like the night before. However, caramel pudding topped off the proceedings.

If First Class passenger lists are sprinkled with the names of the rich and famous, private menus can provide an even better insight into the luxurious side of travel by sea.

85 A private party menu from the following night sheds some light on the George Cliff menu. From the signatures we learn that George Cliff is one of three 'Admirers of Smith College'. There appears to have been a Smith College delegation travelling to (or from) a relevant event in Europe.

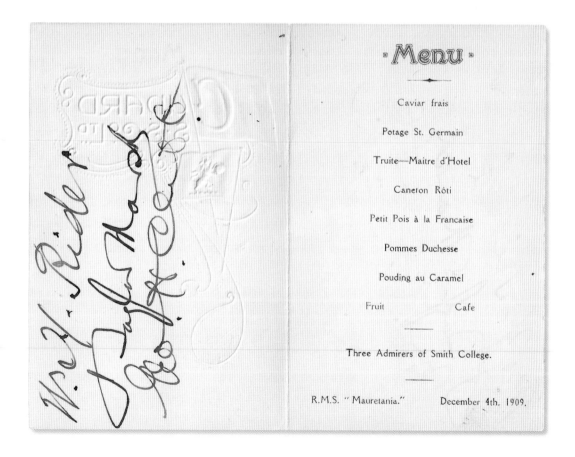

· Menu ·

Caviar frais

Potage St. Germain

Truite—Maître d'Hotel

Caneton Rôti

Petit Pois à la Francaise

Pommes Duchesse

Pouding au Caramel

Fruit   Cafe

Three Admirers of Smith College.

R.M.S. " Mauretania."   December 4th. 1909.

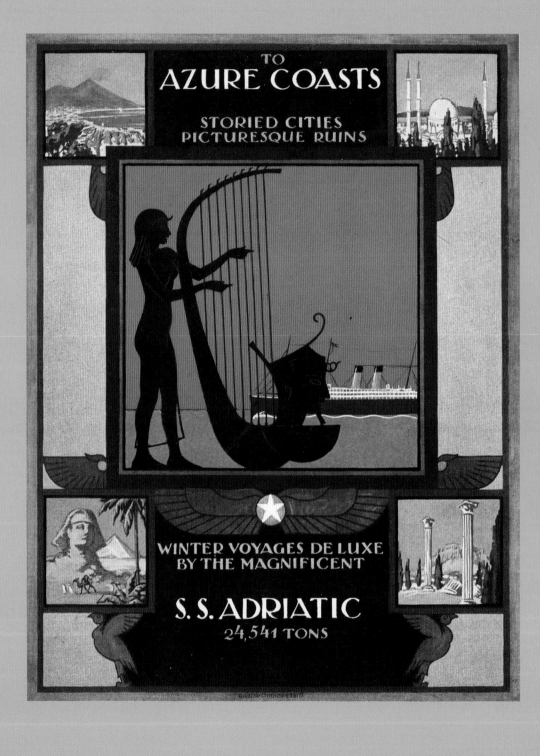

SHORE EXCURSIONS

For the traveller going from Point A (perhaps Liverpool) to Point B (possibly Sydney), the objective was to travel and get there as quickly and directly as possible. In contrast, for the tourist on a cruise the objective was to visit the highlights of distant countries, and the shore excursions were largely the *raison d'être* for travelling on the ship. In the wide sweep from Point A all the way back to Point A, the focus was on land-based excursions. At regular intervals the tourist could look forward to an excursion to see the pyramids, the Wailing Wall or whatever else was planned as part of their cruise – though there were typically more 'sea days' between ports than on cruises today.

DETAILS OF THE DAY

Some of the excursions were of one day's duration but others entailed overnighting for two or more days. An excursion during the Mediterranean cruise of the *Empress of Scotland* in 1928 shows the creativity used to entertain cruise members (FIG. 86). Titled 'A Night in the Desert', the excursion touches upon memories of the handsome and exotic silent-film star

CANADIAN PACIFIC

MEDITERRANEAN CRUISE, 1928

Empress of Scotland

A NIGHT IN THE DESERT.

Arrangements have been made for an excursion to the Desert outside Cairo. This excursion will take place on dates named below, programme as under :

March 19th, 25th, and 26th.

4.30 p.m.   Automobiles will leave Shepheard's Hotel.

5.00 p.m.   Arrive at Mena House Hotel, from whih camels will take members to the Desert Camp, about 3 to 4 miles beyond the Pyramids.

5.30 p.m.   Tea will be served at the Camp.

7.30 p.m.   Dinner will be served at the Camp.

9 to 11 p.m.   Native entertainment.

Next Morning.

7.30 a.m.   Breakfast.

8.30 a.m.   Leave Camp for camels.

9.00 a.m.   Leave Mena House Hotel by automobile.

9.30 a.m.   Arrive Cairo.

Each tent will contain two beds and other necessary equipment.

The excursion on March 19th will be limited to members of Optionals Nos. 12 and 16.

As early advice to Cairo is necessary in order to complete arrangements, Members should take out their tickets at the Cruise Office at once.

Fare $15 each passenger.

(No. 20).

86 Shore excursions included experiences such as a night camping in the Egyptian desert near the pyramids. New experiences were required to attract repeat cruise travellers.

Rudolph Valentino (who had died in August 1926) and his romantic role in *The Sheik*, and it also rekindles the thrill of the discovery of Tutankhamun's tomb six years earlier in 1922.

The trip was available on three separate days, in anticipation that the experience would be very popular. The details as provided are representative of the briefings for shore excursions, and even small information booklets are not unknown. Although there is reference to the camp and to tents, participants would be assured privately that the trip was far from arduous and all the facilities would be of shipboard standards.

EXPERIENCES

Travellers who were accustomed to the comforts of the Western world generally found it difficult to adjust to the lack of those comforts. One traveller of 1927 demonstrated her sense of humour in coping with some of the discomforts of her trip:

> I discovered last night why camels have humps. Their ancestors must have slept or tried to sleep on trains. We arrived this morning with our quota of dirt, had breakfast and like good tourists started out sightseeing.
>
> Six of us with a guide and driver went out to Karnack, a city of ruins two miles from Luxor. We saw the remains of temples, the places where Rameses, Alexander the Great and youthful King Tut himself frisked about. Then we walked down the avenue of Sphinx (or Spinxicus, as our 'Little Guide Esau' called them).
>
> After eating the dust of Karnack, where it has rained only once in the last five years (and then only for fifteen minutes) we pony carted to the hidden city. This was excavated about forty years ago, and has beautiful pillars, sphinx, temples, etc. Before that, there was a town on top of the ruins.

Travel in distant lands was also disturbed by natural factors, which this traveller also described:

Flies. You never swatted so many in your life. One's first purchase is a fly shaker, which you wield lustily in all your waking moments, and perhaps in your slumbers. As yet I do not know but will inform you tomorrow regarding that detail.

87 A Red Star Line passenger in the 1920s would be thrilled to receive a fan, the only defence against hot, humid days during a cruise in the era before air conditioning.

Understanding other cultures could also be a challenge. In another letter the American lady reports the experiences of a previous night while walking on shore. She demonstrates some sensitivity to other cultures, and the perils and inconveniences that were part of fulfilling the requirements of their religion.

Because of the heat last night we did not come over to town but just walked along the docks. Never again will I complain over discomfits. There were five hundred … packed together in one of the warehouses. Some were lying on cots and others on the floor and not an inch of space. Men, women and babies herded in there. One man near the door looked sick and hot so I gave him my fan. He did not know how to use it so the guard showed him how and he was delighted and the center of attention. I regretted that I did not have one for them all. Their boat trip will take about two weeks and then they have to walk forty miles over the desert to reach Mecca.

Heat was always an issue in warmer climes and fans were provided by the shipping companies (FIG. 87). In this illustration of a group of passengers disembarking for a shore excursion, the sensible ones are wearing hats, and all appear to be wearing light-coloured clothing (FIG. 88). In this case, stairs are provided. If the ship were too large for the port facilities, passengers would have had to alight onto tenders to be ferried ashore.

As a counterpoint to the clean, white-clad elegance of the disembarking passengers, there was the inevitable loading of more coal by hand, by a gang of local workers who were probably quite happy to have a paying job despite the rigours

88 Light-coloured outfits were wise for hot, sunny days of cruising – but difficult to keep clean when your cruise ship belched black smoke from its coal-fired engines.

Coaling on the Ship at Nagasaki Harbour　込積炭石ル〃於二港崎長

of the task. This postcard (**FIG. 89**) illustrates the experience in Nagasaki in the early 1900s. One can imagine the passengers returning from their day's excursion to find a fine coating of coal dust on everything on the ship, including their own cabin. Don't lean on the railing until a crew member has washed it off!

By contrast, 'Georgie' recounted the following insight from her Mediterranean trip on the *Roma* in 1936:

89 The damage of dirty smoke from the coal-fired furnaces was exacerbated when the ship had to take on more coal, carried on board by local workers one basket at a time, and generating large amounts of coal dust.

July 12 – Today we took an all-day drive along the French Riviera, during which we passed through seven French towns. From Villefranche we reached Nice first and I was able to pick out the particular spot on the beach where Daddy and I bought the opera glasses when we were there in 1931. Then came Cannes, a city known to us even before the Duke of Windsor and 'Wallis' made it famous because of its importance as a Riviera resort. Our guide assured us that Edward loved Cannes so much that he could not stay away and that he and his bride had been there since their marriage in June.

SHOPPING ASHORE

Tours to the Middle East were always popular, in part because of the biblical connections and also because of the glimpse of ancient cultures and civilizations. Egypt was an important stop along the way. Many travellers wanted a souvenir of the highlights of their trip. A typical example is this photographic postcard in front of the pyramids (**FIG. 90**). The message occupies the entire back of the card, so it was probably mailed in an envelope, possibly using hotel stationery since it was written in Cairo after returning from the excursion.

Cairo Feb 1/28

How do we look? The middle woman is Miss Orr of Toronto, Asst. Hostess of the party – The other one of my old friends – the one for whom the 'stickery' was formed to help her with her trousseau – Strange we should meet on shipboard. She has lived in California for years. We are both very well and hope you are all the same. Love, Edna.

90 A photographic postcard of these five Canadian Pacific adventurers, recording their trip to the Egyptian pyramids in 1928, was empirical evidence of their cruise.

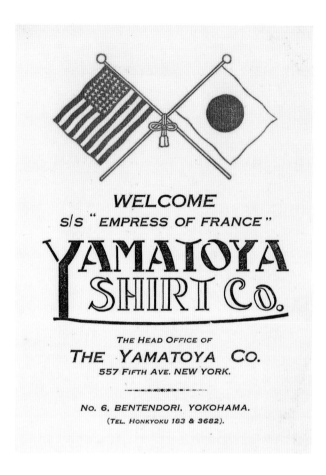

WELCOME
s/s "EMPRESS OF FRANCE"

YAMATOYA
SHIRT Co.

THE HEAD OFFICE OF
THE YAMATOYA CO.
557 FIFTH AVE. NEW YORK.

No. 6. BENTENDORI. YOKOHAMA.
(TEL. HONKYOKU 183 & 3682).

Given the Toronto reference this could have been a group from a cruise on one of the Canadian Pacific liners. Going by camel to the pyramids was very dramatic but the comfort depended upon the tourist's ability to ride on a camel. Other souvenirs were acquired by shopping ashore, probably in a souk.

As with today's cruises, the arrival of a cruise ship in port was an elixir for local businesses. Some of them did not wait for the tourists to walk past their shop. For example, this Yamatoya Shirt Company card is specifically addressed to passengers on Canadian Pacific's *Empress of France* (FIG. 91). Among the locations listed on the back of the card is a branch in Tientsin (now Tianjin) in China. Given that Tientsin fell to invading Japanese troops on 30 July 1937, this card can be dated to a cruise arriving in Japan after that date.

Elsewhere, an advertising flyer from Antonio's in Panama promoted their extensive stock of panama hats. What could be more of a display of social one-upmanship back home than to wear a panama hat that was actually purchased by the wearer in Panama! Even if the price in Panama was no lower than at home, the cachet would make it irresistible.

91 Cruises on Canadian Pacific's *Empress of France* catered to the American trade, as the flags confirm. Vendors in each port competed for the trade of these affluent passengers.

In the pre-credit-card era, a traveller would have to carry a full supply of cash or traveller's cheques. Providing such cheques to the line's travellers was not only a useful service, but also a potential source of revenue. Canadian Pacific offered the service through a subsidiary, Dominion Express. The White Star Line offered the product of the International Mercantile Marine Company, its parent company and also the parent of several other shipping lines. A prospective passenger studying a 1926 White Star Line shipping schedule would learn that for a charge of 0.5 per cent one could purchase cheques in the amounts of $10, $20, $50 and $100. Cunard offered a similar service.

However, when shopping, a passenger would have to face the challenge of finding a local merchant who would accept the cheques, and the equally daunting challenge of negotiating a conversion of them into the local currency. If the purser's office on board could not provide local currency, the shopping trip might have to be preceded by a trip to a local onshore bank – which would charge a fee for cashing, and their own version of the exchange conversion rate from US dollars. Any change travellers had from their shopping in the local currency would not be accepted in the next country that they visited – except through a further conversion into that country's currency. Shopping, in theory easy, would not in practice have been such a simple process.

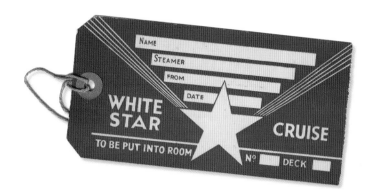

CHILDREN AT SEA

Younger children were never named on passenger lists. They were either an 'infant' or a 'child'. Older children were sometimes listed as 'Master', but there was no way to tell whether a 'Miss Jones' was fifteen or fifty-five. Perhaps unsurprisingly, there is little evidence of them on cruises, which in those days tended to attract almost exclusively an older clientele. When children did travel by sea, it was usually as part of a family trip to revisit a homeland or migrate to a new land.

One of the most interesting but generally ignored aspects of liner travel is children's playrooms. Children in an earlier culture were supposed to be 'seen and not heard', but what did they do during the many days at sea? There were diversions for the parents, but they were 'adult' entertainments such as deck tennis or bridge tournaments. So, what did they do with the children?

Ship interiors of children's playrooms are an intriguing slice of social history. An early *Kaiser Wilhelm II* postcard of the North German Lloyd line with a 1907 US German 'Seapost' cancellation (**FIG. 92**) shows a fairly austere and structured room with a long table down the centre and rows of chairs on each

Nordd Lloydd. „Kaiser Wilhelm II "   Kindersalon.

side of the table. This room almost echoes with authoritarian voices commanding, 'You will sit here. You will be quiet. You will behave. You will enjoy yourself.'

In fairness, the layout is consistent with that of the First Class dining room on the same ship. However, not all images of that era are so rigid, and a contemporary colour postcard of the children's playroom on board the SS *Amerika* of the Hamburg–American Line displays a well-lit and spacious room with toys available (FIG. 93).

There is another telling image in a 1906 brochure promoting travel on the Canadian Pacific sister ships *Empress of Britain* and *Empress of Ireland*. This playroom seems to be inspired by pens that hold animals (FIG. 94). It is noteworthy that this is

92 This postcard of a highly structured children's room on North German Lloyd's prestigious express steamer *Kaiser Wilhelm II* in 1907 dates from a period when children at sea were expected to follow rigid discipline.

Third Class, just above steerage. The facility utilizes deck space, rather than an inside room. There is no decoration or apparent furnishings and it must have been very uncomfortable (although, as is claimed, still 'free from Danger and Harm') during those wintertime crossings when it was bitterly cold and windy on deck.

A postcard from the Cunard liner *Aurania* of the 1920s pictures a warmer, less structured world, where children could move around in the Peter Pan Nursery and play with a generous number of toys. These include a rocking horse, a 'rocking boat' (as if a stormy crossing of the Atlantic Ocean might not provide enough rocking!), dolls, books and even a toy train.

On to the 1930s, and an Orient Line Tourist Class brochure shows a sparse room captioned 'Children's Playroom' on the

93 In contrast to her contemporary German competitor, the children's playroom on Hamburg–American Line's *Amerika* appears much more welcoming and child-friendly.

"The Mothers' Delight"

The Children's Playground—in the center of the Third Class Enclosed Promenade—free from Danger and Harm

94 The image of a children's playground in a 1906 Third Class promotional booklet for Canadian Pacific's twin *Empress of England* and *Empress of Ireland* shows what looks like a cattle pen for children. There is little doubt that they would be 'free from Danger and Harm'.

Orion with three desks, four chairs, four stuffed animals, an open book on one of the desks and nothing else. The photo is captioned 'All of the Orient Liners have special playrooms for children, both in the first and tourist class. A children's hostess and nursery stewardess are carried and every effort is made to keep children occupied and amused.' Given that the ship sailed between England and Australia, it would be a real challenge to keep any child amused with the minimal resources in evidence. However, *Orion* was well known for its clean-lined interiors in which all clutter was hidden from view: so, here, more toys and games might have been put away in drawers and cupboards.

The children's playroom pictured here (FIG. 95) is provided for Cabin Class passengers on the RMS *Queen Mary*, probably in the late 1940s. This is Cabin Class – a notch above Tourist Class, and a level below First Class. This photograph has attractions to appeal to both boys and girls, from a truck and a construction crane to dolls, including an iconic 'sailor boy' doll that is probably by the renowned British toymaker Norah Wellings, as widely available for purchase on liners (see FIG. 109). If this room looks larger than some of the others

95 This pre-1950 illustration of the Cabin Class children's playroom on the *Queen Mary* features many toys, including a Norah Wellings 'Sailor Boy' doll, with the name of the ship on his hatband.

1266 C. R. Hoffmann, Southampton.

CUNARD WHITE STAR LINER "QUEEN MARY."
The World's Largest and Fastest Liner.
CABIN CHILDRENS' PLAYROOM

80,773 Tons.

pictured, one must recognize that the *Queen Mary* had a capacity of some 776 passengers in Cabin Class alone, so could have more children aboard.

Some of the images show empty playrooms – the tendency of the shipping illustrations was to show rooms without people, to emphasize their architecture and design. The dramatic furniture and furnishings on the *Normandie* distinguish her playroom from any other (FIG. 96) – note, for example, the seats in front of the Punch and Judy show screen, designed to look like horses grazing.

The children would have had their own nurse or supervisor in attendance, as is shown in a photograph from the *Montrose* of the Canadian Pacific Line. The illustration shows two apparent supervisors, with one barely discernible in the background. If either of these was a nanny accompanying the family during the trip, sending her charges to this facility would have provided her with a brief respite from her twenty-four-hour duties. It is difficult to see how a child could skip rope in this room without hitting something, but that emphasizes the smaller size of the *Montrose* (about a quarter of the *Queen Mary*'s) and her proportionately smaller number of Cabin Class passengers' children.

Nowhere have I found a reference to the hours of operation of the children's playroom. The assumption is that it was open in the daytime. When the parents were involved with evening activities, there were likely to be lucrative opportunities for the nurse/supervisor and other members of the crew to provide after-hours child-sitting services.

Some shipping lines produced separate brochures highlighting their services for children. In the 1950s, the Italian Line created a delightful booklet illustrating the many activities available. These included deck games; masquerade parties (although the

Cie Cie Transatlantique . Paquebot « NORMANDIE » La Salle de Jeux des Enfants .
(photo Desbout)

Tito

illustration shows just a young child with a party hat and a
'noisemaker'); parties on deck with more party hats and apparently empty cups (of coffee, tea or perhaps hot chocolate – but
why would one want any hot beverages on the southern route
through the Mediterranean and mid-Atlantic?); and playing
what appears to be a game of dodgeball on deck in swimming
attire. This typifies the era when extended exposure to the sun,
and a resulting deep tan, were deemed to be 'healthy'.

Finally, let's leap ahead to just sixty years ago. The transatlantic voyage may have been long and boring enough, but
it was a quick hop compared to travel by ship to India, South
Africa and the Far East. A First Class playroom on the P&O
liner *Iberia* might keep children entertained for a day or two
(including ongoing competition for the right to drive one of the

96 The dramatic
and stylish children's
playroom on board
the *Normandie* of
the 1930s included
cleverly designed
'grazing horse' seats,
which coincided with
the ship's overall
dramatic flair and
style.

two model racing cars) but I would hate to have to be the crew member assigned to supervising this facility for the many, many days of travel at sea.

CHILDREN'S MEALS

Part of the entertainment to keep people amused and gratified while at sea was the meals. This was equally true for children. The oldest children's menu that I have found is from the *Royal George* dated 8 May 1911 (FIG. 97). Surprisingly, if it wasn't headed 'Children' it could have passed for a Third Class adult menu.

There are oats, fish (brill) and a variety of meats. The high-light for many children would probably be the cake or pastry. This array of choices suggests that it is similar to an adult menu, but examination of an adult breakfast menu of the same date provides a puzzling result. There are far more choices on the adult menu than on the one for children. Why aren't the children offered fresh fruit? Or Grape Nuts or Shredded Wheat in addition to Quaker Oats and Force? Equally, why aren't adults given the opportunity to order cake or pastry? Other menus described as being for children seem to fall into two categories: party-type fare, and what appear to be adult dishes but probably with smaller portions.

In 1922, it was only four years after the end of the First World War. I have never seen an adult Memorial Menu, so imagine the surprise in coming upon a menu from a tea party for children (FIG. 98). This menu does not appear to be a standard-ized Cunard issue, or I would have seen copies from other ships. An afternoon tea party to recognize the end of the war and the massive losses of life seems to be rather incongruous. I have never seen a menu from any other year for an Armistice Day children's tea party, whether from Cunard or any other line. Although it would help the children to recognize a milestone of the past history of the world, surely a more sombre event would have been preferable. The decision to hold this one may reflect the personal experience during the war of the captain, the head chef or even the pastry chef. Probably the parents and other passengers would have taken part in a service of remembrance; and just as today's schoolchildren are encouraged to do projects to remember past conflicts, so it might have seemed appropriate for the children on the liner to have done at least something, whatever it may have meant to them.

A Cunard children's menu from the *Aurania* in 1929 has a charming cover (FIG. 99); the menu of cakes, jelly and tarts for this afternoon tea would have gladdened the hearts of all the children, if not their dentists (FIG. 100). More typical, from much later on, is a *Dunnottar Castle* menu of 1957 during a Union-Castle Line voyage. It looks as if the artwork is for children, featuring a colour cartoon drawing of a hippopotamus playing with two equally 'cute' lions, and it is labelled as a children's menu, but the offerings look like adult dishes.

A 1965 menu of the *Uganda* of the British India Line underscores the *Dunnottar Castle* approach. The strategy

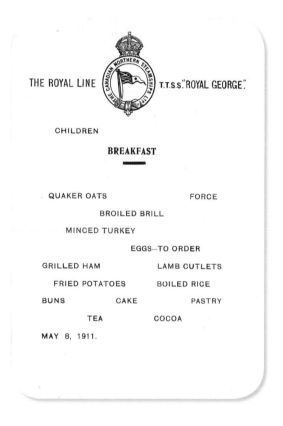

THE ROYAL LINE — THE CANADIAN NORTHERN STEAMSHIPS 1911 — T.T.S.S."ROYAL GEORGE".

CHILDREN

BREAKFAST

QUAKER OATS		FORCE
BROILED BRILL		
MINCED TURKEY		
	EGGS—TO ORDER	
GRILLED HAM		LAMB CUTLETS
FRIED POTATOES		BOILED RICE
BUNS	CAKE	PASTRY
TEA	COCOA	

MAY 8, 1911.

97 Breakfast for children on the *Royal George* in 1911 was little different from an adult menu – but perhaps the portions were smaller.

CUNARD LINE.

"Lest we forget."
—*Kipling.*

Armistice

Day : : :

SATURDAY,
NOVEMBER 11th,
. . . 1922 . . .

R.M.S. ANDANIA.

98 This cover for a children's tea on board Cunard's *Andania* to celebrate Armistice Day in 1922 seems disconnected from the seriousness of the day, given that it was only four years after the war's end.

99 A charming menu cover for a children's tea party on board Cunard's *Aurania* in 1929.

seemed to be to make it look like a children's menu visually, call it a children's menu, but populate it with choices that could come from the same kitchen as the one that prepared dishes for adults. Would cream of turtle soup or fried lamb cutlets tease the taste buds of a young traveller? The menu looks festive, but the festivity begins below the threshold of 'Sweets'. Iced party cake, cream ices and assorted pastries were most likely to help a child forget long afternoons cooped up in a playroom

Cunard Line

for yet another day in a row, while the ship pitched in ocean storms.

Finally, a few ships even had a children's dining room. Supervising this, with children of affluent and influential businesspeople and politicians, would probably make supervising a school cafeteria seem like a simple chore. But the wall decorations of the example on the MV *Ruahine*, built for the New Zealand Shipping Company, are delightful and this Real Photo card shows them well (FIG. 101).

100 The *Aurania* menu from 1929 featured an array of sweet treats to gladden the palate of every child.

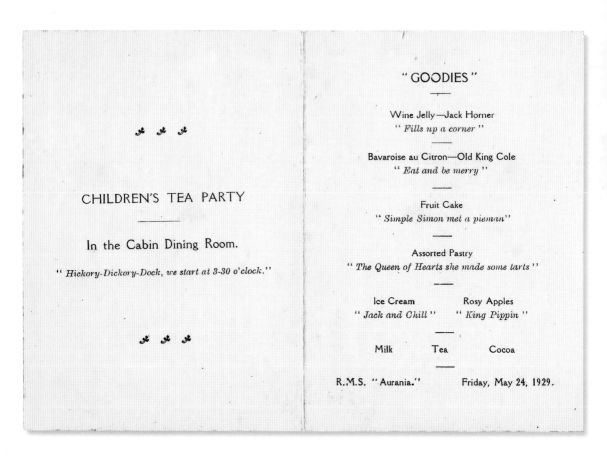

CHILDREN'S TEA PARTY

In the Cabin Dining Room.

" *Hickory-Dickory-Dock, we start at 3-30 o'clock.*"

"GOODIES"

Wine Jelly—Jack Horner
" *Fills up a corner* "

Bavaroise au Citron—Old King Cole
" *Eat and be merry* "

Fruit Cake
" *Simple Simon met a pieman* "

Assorted Pastry
" *The Queen of Hearts she made some tarts* "

Ice Cream   Rosy Apples
" *Jack and Chill* "   " *King Pippin* "

Milk   Tea   Cocoa

R.M.S. " *Aurania.* "   Friday, May 24, 1929.

'RUAHINE'   CHILDRENS DINING ROOM

These images, like children's menus, are not easy to find. But tracking down such ephemera helps us to appreciate what it would be like to be a child on board an ocean liner: the playthings that would be available to us, and how we would have dined. These images may be purely two-dimensional, but when examined as a group they tell a three-dimensional story.

101 The decoration of the children's dining room on the New Zealand Shipping Company's *Ruahine* displays a conscious effort to make the room 'child-friendly'.

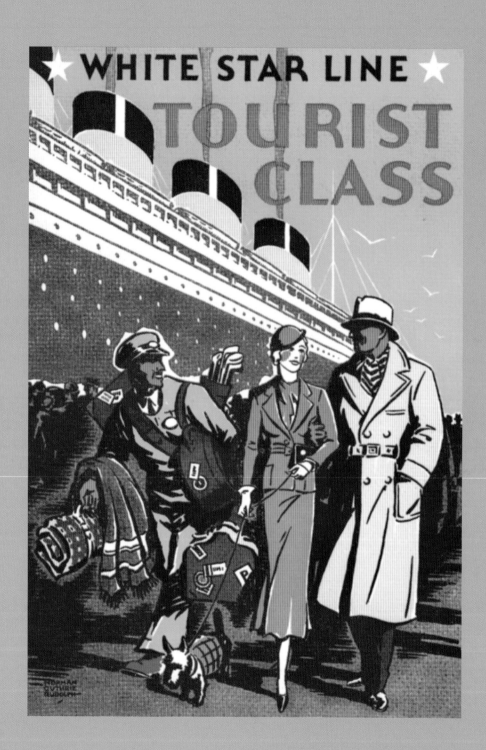

SOCIAL ISSUES AT SEA

Many aspects of sea travel reflected the rigid class hierarchy that was an unremarkable feature of life in the nineteenth and early twentieth centuries – especially in Britain and western Europe. It was emulated too in the USA, where greater social mobility ironically often led to a heightened consciousness of hierarchy. Distinctions among the various classes of traveller – and between travellers and crew – were often strictly observed. But ocean liners also gave an opportunity to make unexpected connections and friendships, and even to strike up a romantic relationship, with the people a passenger encountered on board. Some countries and liners were more or less class-conscious than others – for example, from 1962 the French Line (CGT) had some spaces on the SS *France* open to all.

CLASS DISTINCTION

The framework of the ship defined the social structure of the voyage. First Class passengers did not mingle with other classes: First Class deck areas were off-limits to other passengers and were rigidly policed by the crew. A sign on the wall behind a group of women on board White Star Line's *Homeric*

warns 'Notice – 2nd class passengers not allowed forward of this' (fig. 102). Forward would have been a First Class area.

For British passengers, distinctions of class among fellow passengers were very clear, based on the evidence of educational, cultural and/or economic capital. Having the proper accent was important, but so was the range of outfits one wore on board. On the back of an Austin Reed brochure marked as from *Queen Mary*'s maiden voyage in 1936 a woman has inked in her schedule of outfits: 'First night – No change; Second night – Blue frock; Third night – White frock; Fourth night – Pink frock; Fifth night – Pink frock'. It is not difficult to tell that this woman is not in First Class accommodation. Wearing the same frock two nights in a row would have been seen as distinctly plebeian.

Even within the First Class framework there were distinctions. A suite was of higher status than a mere cabin. Having servants placed the individual in an even higher social echelon

102 A photo of a group of women on board White Star Line's *Homeric* in the 1920s shows the restriction on their movement. The sign in the background emphasizes that they are not permitted to enter the adjoining First Class area.

(at least in their own eyes). Related to this was wealth. There were many nouveaux riches travelling in First Class too. Elsewhere in this book a passenger refers specifically to the wealthy Americans on board. Cultural differences abounded – and, to a degree, they still do.

Then there were the servants, who were expected to know their place in the outer fringe of the social firmament. A 1921 fare schedule for the French Line, under 'Rates for Servants', shows the rates for those accompanying passengers, and notes that 'If booked in Second Class they will not be allowed access to First Cabin'. What good is a servant who cannot serve you? Booking them into a small First Class cabin would be necessary. A couple of lines below is the fare category for 'Transportation of Dogs, Birds, etc. (belonging to passengers)'.

By 1948, a list of First Class fares on the French Line's SS *De Grasse* still anticipates that some passengers will have servants and notes that 'Servants accompanying passengers in First Class will be allowed a 20% reduction from the Minimum First Class rate.'

SHIPBOARD ROMANCES: PREDATORY CREW

Women generally sailed in pairs or as part of a larger group. One poignant image pictures a single woman alone on deck while the couple on a nearby bench are wrapped up in each other, and the others are also paired up except for the woman with children (FIG. 103).

A woman in a party of three on a Mediterranean cruise on the SS *Montrose* in 1936 commented in her diary:

> The Second Steward, who appeared to be quite a general favourite, introduced me to the Chief Steward (who was big, burly and jolly) as the 'Dining Room Vamp' –

I wonder why??? Some of the Stewards certainly were interested if the mysterious note handed to me by the bell-boy one lunch time was any indication.

Given that the male crew were at sea for extended periods of time it's not surprising that they might be on the hunt for female companionship, even though fraternizing with the passengers was not permitted. And it wasn't just the two weeks of the cruise that kept the crew away from home – they might do a succession of cruises without a break. And those officers in their uniforms could look very handsome (FIG. 104, with handwritten note 'Take your Choice?').

Even more difficult was the world cruise – glamorous for the passengers but strenuous in many ways for the crew. A group

103 Everyone in this picture of life on deck on board a Dollar Line vessel is accompanied except for the forlorn woman in the right foreground. Long voyages could lead to lonely moments for the single traveller.

of notes written by an officer on board the SS *President Van Buren* of the Dollar Line to one of the passengers over several days during a world cruise in 1935 gives a fascinating insight to officer–passenger relationships.

The ship left New York in mid-January 1935. An undated note at 6.20 p.m. – probably in early February – from a crew member called Ralph reports:

> My Dear; I was disappointed last night. I went over on the 8:00 tender. Went straight to the Palace Hotel. Was sitting in the saloon and every few minutes I would walk through the lounge until 9:15 then went over to the Cathay then to the Bodega where I met Captain Anderson. We stopped again at the Palace at 9:25 on our way out to Captain Anderson's place, where I stayed all night, came back 11:45 in private Launch.

104 Officers, such as this group on the *Aorangi* of the Union Steam Ship Company which served the Far East, looked very handsome and professional in their full uniform.

I wonder whether he is trying to assure the recipient, Lillian, that he did not spend the night with another woman. But, more importantly, how would she have known that he did not return to the ship until morning? The relationship carried on:

4:30 AM Good Morning, 'Sweet Heart'. I tried to make a date with you yesterday after noon. While you were in the deck chair on the port side, remember when I held up five fingers and pointed to the Boat Deck. I meant to ask you to meet me at the same place we met before at 5 pm, but I guess you didn't understand me. I waited up there until 5:15. When I came down you were playing that table tennis or whatever it is called.

I don't think I shall go ashore at Manila this time. Possibly I may go over for a swim & wonder if you would care to come along, say about 7:30 or 8 pm 'i.e.' if you are not engaged.

While all this conspiracy is swirling around one wonders what Lillian's fellow cabin passenger, a Mrs Yauch, would have thought about it. We know that they were travelling together because some of the ship's 'Bon Voyage' material was addressed to them jointly. The serious gap for the twenty-first-century voyeur is that we don't have Lillian's notes to Ralph, but this reply hints at what might have been mentioned in one of them:

Sat. AM Feb 16th – My dear L.M.C., Thanks for the sweet Valentine letter. I had completely forgotten Valentine Day until you mentioned it, sorry. I wouldn't have written you such a mean letter had I known it was to be a Valentine note. I think we would both miss each other if we couldn't see each other at least once each day. Yes, I am sorry I can't enjoy some of the good times on board with you.

Anticipating the stop at Kyoto, Ralph suggests joining her for 'a little sight seeing trip as soon as we arrive' by meeting Lillian in the lobby of the Oriental Hotel. Reading this interaction, one gets the feeling that Ralph has made this type of arrangement with other women on previous trips. He tops off the day's activities with the suggestion that

> I know a place where we could meet tomorrow. say between 4:30 & 5:00 pm, in the Chief Radio Operator's Room. He will be on watch at the time. I asked him for permission to use his room at that time so it is at my disposal. I will be waiting and watching for you to pass. It is the first door on that side that you come to. If you do not show up by 5:00 pm then I will know that you couldn't get away or considered it un-safe.
>
> O.K.; Yes, the other best thing is two nights' rest. Of course there are many other things that I like better. See you tomorrow.
>
> Your Ralph

Ralph's note includes a hand-drawn map of the layout of the boat deck showing the location of the radio room operator (FIG. 105). Ralph may have been taking a calculated risk. He

105 This map was drawn for a woman passenger showing how to get to an assignation with an amorous ship's officer in the radio room of the Dollar Line's *President Van Buren* in 1935.

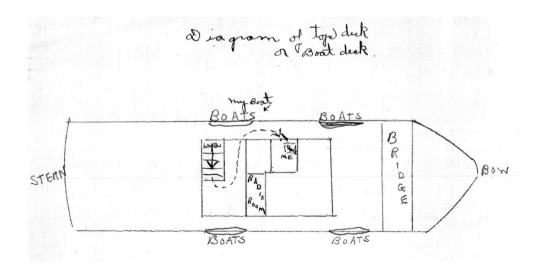

was likely to be working at sea for many years to come, in the middle of the Great Depression. Women such as Lillian – and for that matter any other cruise passenger – must have had the financial resources to pay for a very expensive travel experience. If Ralph could make a connection with Lillian, his financial future might be greatly improved.

Ralph was apparently more than just a serial lothario. On 22 February he counsels, 'Take your choice of the sweaters or if you don't like any of them O.K. I will turn them over to the Barber or keep them'. Note that the barber also operated the equivalent of the ship's gift shop.

Have things cooled down? On 8 March, Ralph is now signing himself 'R.G.' and he addresses his letter to 'My Dear Lilly-Ann'. The letter includes the observation, 'Haven't seen much of you of late'.

A day later, at 7.35 p.m., the greeting has reverted to 'My Dear Lillian', and the message suggests that the relationship is flourishing:

> I think I should stay aboard tonight and rest as I had just three hours broken sleep during the last thirty-six, however we may change my plans if I see you before you receive this or we may go some place, if we see each other about 8AM in the morning, but I feel that I should be very uninteresting to any young lady this evening. Will try to see you about 8 this evening if not will see you some time tomorrow.

Between servicing his responsibilities to his ship and his shipboard romance, poor Ralph may have been teetering on the brink of exhaustion. By this stage many of the passengers would probably have become aware of the relationship, but it might not have been the only one flourishing during the months at sea.

I wish that I could recount the outcome of this romantic episode. The experience with these letters is like reading a mystery novel and finding the last few pages missing. However, it provides a picture of a specific woman's life, the constraints and the risks on board ship during a cruise. A final brief letter, dated 10 March, says:

> My Dear
>
> When you get this come on deck for a minute. Hope you have enjoyed Singapore, and tomorrow (tonight) also.
>
> Your Ralph

There is a final puzzling message, but not on ship's stationery. Included in the archive of the trip is a tiny scrap of plain paper, which has been folded over many times and possibly carried in a wallet, and advises:

> I will meet you up on the 4th floor down near the back. You go up on Pat's elevator. I shall have this date with you on June 1st.

No address. No phone number. No name. Was this for a later assignation with Ralph, who had risked his job with the shipping line to spend time with Lillian? Or was Lillian the instigator and Ralph just one of a string of male conquests?

SHIPBOARD ROMANCES: FELLOW PASSENGERS

Probably more common than wooing by crew members was the attention paid to women by some of the male passengers. Georgie, whom we met earlier, travelling with her parents on the SS *Roma* in 1936, wrote in her diary of her experience with an inebriated male passenger:

> July 2 – Met a Mr. Murphy from Los Angeles at breakfast who promised to dance with me this evening and kept his

word. Seemed to be a sociable fellow, but a member of the older generation – 'fortyish'.

July 3 – My evening was – shall I say – spoiled by fear that Mr Murphy, who had a few too many cocktails, would find me and ask me to dance, since he had mentioned it earlier in the day. However, I managed to escape him. Georgie, you must do better than this!

Quoting from a diary of one woman's experience with male admirers gives but a hint of what happened at sea, and such written records are rare, so one has to read between the lines of Georgie's entry for a later evening:

In one of the Paul Joneses I danced with a tall, dark, mysterious gentleman who turned out to be a Portuguese and the brother of the present ambassador to the US. He was the flattering kind, but not sincere I think. Anyhow, it was a pleasant evening.

SMOKING ROOMS

There was a time when smoking was part of the image of being in sophisticated high society, and that was mirrored in the recognition given to smokers on board ship. Shipping line advertising and postcards depict this wonderfully, and the extent of smoking-related ephemera shows just how widely this image was promoted.

One of my favourite depictions of smoking rooms on ocean liners is a picture of formally dressed gentlemen puffing away on their cigars and cigarettes on board the RMS *Royal George* around 1912, in what they believe to be the most sophisticated poses (FIG. 106). Women were not allowed into this exclusively male domain. (There was in fact more than one domain. Each class of passenger had its own smoking room, in the same way that they had their own restaurant.)

R.M.S. "ROYAL EDWARD." SMOKE ROOM. R.M.S. "ROYAL GEORGE."

While the men were puffing away and quaffing their post-prandial brandies, the women were in a different room designated as the Palm Court or with some similar name. Were the women smoking and drinking? Not likely. They were expected to fulfil that stereotype of the period, and do their reading and needlework, or perhaps even discuss the challenges of running a household such as finding and retaining good servants. As we have seen, some First Class passengers would have brought some of their servants along with them – maids, valets, governesses for the children, and even chauffeurs. None of them would have been permitted to enter the halls of the smoking room or the Palm Court since they would not have been needed by their masters.

106 A drawing of the exclusively male smoking room on the *Royal George* emphasizes the formality of the postprandial cigar and brandy experience, c.1912.

Hamburg-Amerika Linie

„Amerika"

Rauchzimmer.

107 The smoking room on Hamburg–American Line's *Amerika* underscores the masculine appearance of the decor, replicating the panelled exclusivity of a private gentleman's club.

Back to smoking. The *Rauchzimmer* (smoking room) on board the SS *Amerika* of the Hamburg–American Line shows that the smoking room in a German ocean liner could be just as stuffy and formal as in a British ship of the era (**FIG. 107**). Imagine being in one of those rooms after the cigar smokers had been puffing away for a couple of hours! You would probably want to send your clothes for cleaning and freshening after the evening was over. Of course, your servant could look after that; and, later, forced ventilation might help.

Cigar smokers generate other forms of complementary ephemera. Cigar bands designated the type and source of the cigar. Other smokers would be watching to see what quality of cigar you were smoking. If it was a high-quality smoke, you were clearly a discerning – and affluent – fellow.

And the cigars had to be lit. A hundred years ago a finely crafted match case (known as Vesta cases on account of the original brand of safety matches) would have been de rigueur. Match cases exist with hunting, classical and even erotic artwork on the back of the case. If you produced a 'plain' box of matches, you were clearly a less sophisticated type and your social acceptability among the elite on board would go down faster than the *Titanic*.

With the advent of book matches, the 'right' matches might give you some social cachet among your friends when you got back home. Imagine pulling out a matchbook from the iconic *Normandie* when you lit a cigarette, cigar or pipe. Of course you would have to flourish it so that everyone nearby could see it; the name spoke for itself.

108 Jackets and ties were de rigueur, but in this less formal drawing of one of Cunard's middle-tier ships before the First World War we might guess that this was midday rather than after dinner. The upholstery is quite striking!

Smoke Room, CUNARD R.M.S. "CARMANIA" — "CARONIA."

A postcard showing the smoking room on board the RMS *Carmania* or its sister ship RMS *Caronia*, contemporary with the *Royal George* and the *Amerika*, breaks the stereotype in the other cards (FIG. 108). It appears that one of the gentlemen is having a beer, and another appears to be smoking a pipe. And where are the dinner jackets? Perhaps this is during the afternoon. Is this really the image that the Cunard Steamship Company wanted to convey to prospective First Class passengers? Perhaps Cunard was sufficiently confident of its reputation that it felt that a more relaxed image would not harm it.

The design of these smoking rooms was overtly masculine. Dark wood in mahogany or oak predominates, carved in a variety of ponderous styles, and the general atmosphere is a heavy one. Compare that to smoking rooms of the 1950s. In the smoking room of the Canadian Pacific liner *Empress of England* of 1956–7 clean and modern prevailed, with artificial leather (rexine) and plastic laminate.

By the 1930s women were actually being allowed into smoking rooms. A Canadian Pacific postcard of the late 1930s carries a message from a woman who feels pleased that women are allowed to sit at the mezzanine tables in the smoking room (but not at tables in the main level, which were for men only). In this period of social change, promotion of tobacco might be seen in terms of female emancipation: after the Second World War smoking rooms were open to both sexes. But thereafter smoking gradually fell out of popularity because of reported health risks, and the smoking room lost its allure. A 1952 Canadian Pacific image of the smoking room on the *Empress of Scotland* has a very 'institutional' look, and by the 1970s the few remaining ships in service had made the smoking room sterile and boring, if they had one at all. There were still many smokers in the 1970s, but air conditioning meant it was possible for them to light up wherever they wished.

Smoking rooms provide an insight into the history of architecture and design, and also of social customs and trends. They also reveal details about the distinction between the various classes in the shipboard social order. Blended with other forms of ephemera, they are a lens through which scholars, researchers and collectors can study social history more broadly.

Who's
Who
on the
High Seas

Aquitania
Berengaria
Mauretania

Who's
Who
on the
High Seas

Aquitania
Berengaria
Mauretania

ARRIVING AT THE DESTINATION

After days or weeks at sea, the time inevitably came to disembark. Arriving at the destination wasn't just a matter of stepping off the ship, however. There were a number of preludes and formalities to be attended to first.

GETTING READY TO LAND

The night before, there would have been a farewell dinner at which the food was of far higher quality than at other meals during the voyage – and for those in First Class it would have been very lavish indeed. There was a tradition of signing menus and promising to keep in touch after the voyage. There are numerous surviving examples of menus signed in the wine-fuelled exuberance of the moment, but one has to question the long-term sincerity of the gesture. A signatory leaving no contact information, or one that merely adds 'San Francisco' or some other city name to the entry, surely doesn't really intend to have a reunion with any of their tablemates.

Landing arrangements were complex. A pre-1950s booklet from the *Queen Mary* includes topics such as landing cards

('Obtained at the Purser's Office. Passports will be required'); customs declarations ('should be completed and returned to the Bedroom Steward as soon as possible. The slip at the bottom is to be detached and retained by the passenger'); immigration inspection ('Officials usually board the Steamer at Quarantine. Passports and Landing Cards are required'); baggage ('special facilities can be arranged on board through the Baggage

109 'A Sailor boy' doll by British doll-maker Norah Wellings, from Canadian Pacific's *Duchess of York*, 1930s.

Master'); and banking ('A branch of the Midland Bank Limited, London is located on A Deck Square amidships').

Particularly for the first-time traveller, the paperwork must have felt overwhelming. Immigrants to North America faced the need for a two-part clearance: first was the medical examination, and then the immigration clearance. Only after their inspection card had both elements filled in could they leave the ship.

The customs declaration would force passengers to review all of their personal and souvenir purchases (FIGS 109 & 110). The experienced traveller tried to hold off souvenir purchases until towards the end of the trip, to avoid having to cart them along during land travel. The simplest approach was to confine most purchases to the return voyage. Those purchases would be

110 This 'life preserver' with an image of a White Star Line ship, the first *Majestic*, would have made an attractive souvenir of the voyage when found in the gift shop, c.1910.

R.M.S. " QUEEN ELIZABETH "

Notice to Eastbound Passengers

New Monetary Regulations have been imposed by the British Treasury, and passengers are advised that the limit of Sterling Notes which may be taken into or out of Great Britain has been reduced to £5 per person.

There is no limit to the amount of Sterling which may have been obtained from the Midland Bank on board, in exchange for dollars, being taken into Great Britain.

All passengers are warned to declare to the Immigration Officer at the time of Passport Inspection the amount of Dollar Currency or Travellers' Cheques they are carrying, and have an endorsement made in their Passport, as no more than this amount may be taken out of Britain.

easy to value for customs purposes since the receipts were close at hand; and if the customs agents wished to examine them, they were packed at the top of the case, and easy to pull out for examination.

When Prohibition was in effect in America, there was zero tolerance for the importation of alcohol, so purchases had to be consumed on board or left there.

During the period of exchange controls after the Second World War, international travellers were cautioned about the limits of the movement of sterling, and reminded to review their situation with the branch of the Midland Bank on board. Restrictions were very detailed (FIG. III).

III In the period immediately following the Second World War there were stringent exchange controls over the outflow of sterling, and travellers by ship were not exempt, as shown on this *Queen Elizabeth* warning to passengers travelling to the United Kingdom.

RECOVERING YOUR BAGGAGE

Once the pre-disembarking process was completed, you left the ship via a gangplank. The next task was to go to the arrivals shed and find your luggage. If you had appended to each of your bags a label, as provided, bearing the first initial of your last name, you would find them in the part of the room where bags with your letter were held.

First Class passengers were disembarked first, and their bags were in a separate section of the arrivals shed. An image from a postcard of the early 1900s provides an impression of the crowds and disarray, but First Class passengers with servants would have them performing this chore, and where there were no servants the men would probably have been applying the muscle (FIG. 112). Hovering over this scene were the porters, scanning for the opportunity to help a lady or family in distress, for a fee.

Retrieval of personal automobiles was a further step. Shipping lines encouraged affluent passengers to bring their personal cars across the Atlantic. A 1937 Cunard brochure describes the experience and shows the price of a transatlantic round trip for a personal vehicle as $255 for the largest car on one of the express steamers (FIG. 113). This was a clever way of generating

112 Large, cumbersome steamer trunks added to the general crowding on the dock as passengers scrambled to retrieve their luggage and clear customs. First Class passengers expected and received priority.

Custom-House Inspection

113 This Cunard brochure encouraged passengers to bring their own cars to Europe, and set out the rates for carrying them on the ship.

114 Your car was treated as another piece of baggage, as illustrated by a baggage tag from the *St. Louis* of the Hamburg–American Line, 1937. There is a slot for the car's weight, since the cost was based on that factor.

additional revenue; apart from requiring more room for stowage in the
hold, a car was just another piece of
baggage. On most ships, cars were lifted
on board by derrick, in harnesses; on the
Normandie they could be driven directly
into the hold, via side hatches. Recovering
the car at either end of the journey meant
looking for the car and a door tag, such as this
Hamburg–American Line tag from the *St. Louis*
(FIG. 114). If you had your chauffeur along with
you, everything to do with the vehicle, including
checking and retrieval, would be done by them.

A traveller on the SS *Paris* in 1931 – 'Aunt Emma',
whose letter envisaging 'roadside pick-nicks' was quoted
in an earlier chapter – wrote to relatives in anticipation of
her arrival in France:

> At about 6 pm we expect to reach Le Havre; probably too
> late to get to Paris by auto tomorrow night. Have had two
> stormy days & feel proud that I've not been sea-sick. But
> last night I decided it wouldn't be so much fun to sit at the
> dinner table for two hours. Shall write you next from Paris.

These comments lead to a number of interesting questions. Was
this a business-related trip? Why were they able to 'pick-nick'?
This latter comment suggests that they were not part of a tour
group, but rather making their own way to Paris in a rental
car, or a rental car and driver, or they had their own car and
chauffeur that they had shipped from America, as described
above. Any of these were possibilities, which illustrates the
post-voyage options available to travellers depending upon their
financial resources.

"HOMERIC"
35,000 TONS

THE CRUISING SHIP OF SPLENDOUR
WHITE STAR LINE

LINERS AT WAR

In both world wars, the only way to transport large numbers of men and women (the latter generally as nurses) across the Atlantic or from Britain to far-flung parts of the British Empire was by sea.

FIRST WORLD WAR

The British passenger fleet was extensive, and the Admiralty could call upon passenger ships of the British Empire and press them into service. That included many ships from Canadian and Australian lines, which were in any case mostly registered in British ports. It was fortuitous that the ships had been offering a steerage service that provided substantial amounts of open accommodation on the lower decks. An examination of the steerage section of the North German Lloyd liner illustrated earlier (see FIG. 40) hints at how easy it would have been to use a steerage area to pack in many soldiers – perhaps even more than in the dense accommodation pictured for civilian passengers.

Several German passenger ships had been requisitioned by the United States at the outbreak of the war. Chief among them

View of one of the troop decks on the giant transport *Leviathan*
Copyright from F. W. Moser, N.Y.

115 In the First World War it was a relatively easy task to convert the vast open steerage accommodation, as pictured in fig. 40, to equally vast and even more crammed bunks for troops as on the USS *Leviathan*, formerly the German *Vaterland*.

was the *Vaterland* of the Hamburg–American Line, the largest ship in the world at the time, which sailed to the USA on her maiden voyage in May 1914 and was requisitioned at New York on the outbreak of war just three months later. Like the other seized German liners, she remained in port until the United States entered the war in 1917. Her steerage accommodation was almost perfect for troop accommodation, as shown in this illustration of the men's sleeping quarters on the *Leviathan* (née *Vaterland*) in 1917 (FIG. 115).

The crews were also interned; some remained with their ships in the interim. A photograph from a postcard sent in 1915 shows the senior officers of the SS *Kronprinzessin Cecilie*, looking less than happy at their enforced stay in the United States (FIG. 116). With the advent of war, the men were incarcerated. The *Kronprinzessin Cecilie*, which had been requisitioned in

Boston at the time, was renamed the *Mount Vernon*. Most other ex-German ships were renamed; for example, the *Kronprinz Wilhelm* became the *Von Steuben*, the *Kaiser Wilhelm II* became the *Agamemnon*, the *Prinzess Irene* became the *Pocahontas*, and the *Prinzess Alice* became the *Princess Matoika*. These examples give an idea of the magnitude of the trooping accommodation already held in detainment.

Ships travelled in convoys, accompanied by destroyers for safety. There was more than one enemy to contend with. Most of the soldiers would not have had a previous ocean voyage, and storms on the North Atlantic can be uncomfortable. An unsigned message on the back of a postcard picturing the Anchor Line's *Cameronia* describes the experience:

116 The officers of the requisitioned German liner *Kronprinzessin Cecilie* of the North German Lloyd line, 1915. When the United States joined the war in 1917 she subsequently sailed as the American troopship *Mount Vernon*.

This picture shows the floating (and rolling) home of the 157th Batt'n on its trek across the Atlantic. Speed 20 knots ahead and 40 sideways, mostly all sideways.

The large numbers of men in cramped quarters necessitated a high level of discipline and control. A lengthy document presented to all as part of their boarding information included strictures that they

> Follow specific mess directions posted in your berthing compartment and use only the ladders directed to your mess space. When mess gear is sounded every man will go to his assigned bunk and stand by with his mess kit.
>
> Consult Bulletin Board for your station at Abandon Ship. When the General Alarm gong is sounded go to your Abandon Ship Station.
>
> Sea-sick men must use lee rail (side away from direction of wind) and vomit overboard. Fresh air is best cure. No smoking in bunk spaces, washrooms, latrines or urinals at any time.
>
> Smoking lamps are provided instead of matches. Matches are not allowed. Turn in same to your Captain. The use of tobacco, either smoking or chewing, will be prohibited at all times in the berthing spaces and during the serving of food in the mess spaces of the troops. No food will be permitted in the troop berthing spaces. Sleeping and lying upon the decks is prohibited. Don't enter Officers' quarters. When going to hospital use outside ladders.

An interesting element of the First World War was the use of 'dazzle paint' on ships, a type of camouflage that was designed to confuse a submarine captain looking through his periscope. The broken lines were supposed to blend with the waves to make it difficult to aim at a particular part of the ship. The illustration of the White Star Line's *Olympic* shows the potential of the effect (FIG. 117). The concept was reportedly suggested by the artist Norman Wilkinson, famous as a marine painter in the realist mode, and other artists were involved in coming up with the wide range of possible designs.

According to photographs of the period some ships were not camouflaged. Did dazzle paint help to avoid lethal attacks by German submarines? Opinion is divided, and the statistics inconclusive; but in the Second World War dazzle paint was less used, and ships such as the *Queen Mary* were just painted grey – leading to her being described as the 'Grey Ghost' on account of her speed.

R.M.S. 'OLYMPIC' CAMOUFLAGED

SECOND WORLD WAR

The impact of the Depression of the 1930s was to accelerate the retirement of older ocean liners, and as a result there was probably not the same number of liners by 1939 as had been in service at the outset of the First World War. From the Allies' point of view, there were three trump cards in the presence of the largest ships of the time, the *Queen Mary*, the *Queen Elizabeth* and the *Normandie* – but, as we have seen, this last was all too soon destroyed by fire while undergoing conversion

117 White Star Line's *Olympic* in dazzle paint, designed to confuse enemy submarines about her dimensions during the war.

to a troopship in New York Harbour. They could each carry as many as an entire 15,000-man division of troops in one crossing.

TABLE 147
BERTHING CARD

Deck___E___   STARBOARD
Room___SECTION E-4
Berth___HAMMOCK

PLEASE RETAIN THIS CARD

The immense size of the ships must have been confusing to the contingents on board, and a berthing card from the *Queen Elizabeth* in 1944 illustrates the complexity (FIG. 118). The recipient was told to go to Deck E – on the starboard side. As long as he didn't get confused going down the stairwell as to which was the starboard side, he then had to search out Section E-4 where he would find his hammock. Then he would have to find the dining area and look for Table 147. Only then would he have time to be seasick!

LIFE WHILE TROOPING

If it was a challenge to keep peacetime passengers on the ship occupied, it must have been even more of a challenge to entertain the thousands of military personnel who were jammed into close quarters on board.

Above all, there was the continuing threat of attack from German submarines. An American doctor from Wyandotte, Michigan, writing 'At Sea, Aug 22, 1917' on paper with the letterhead of the Anchor Line ship *Tuscania*, captures the frustrations of a trip, but it is worth noting that he would have been an officer and therefore one of the more privileged people on board. His references to the pleasure of the trip may have

118 This card carried detailed instructions for the soldier sailing on the *Queen Elizabeth* in 1944. The directions for the massive ship showed the deck and side, the section number of his sleeping hammock, and his table in the mess hall.

been sarcastic – only his recipient would have known him and been able to tell.

> We are now within about 24 hours of land, so when we land I am going to mail you this to let you know that our trip has been a delightful one; at least, so far it has. If we are torpedoed or mined before we land, of course I will have to revise this letter.
>
> We were shipwrecked off the Nova Scotia coast; ran aground on a reef in a fog. This delayed us over a week, but the damage was only slight and did not interfere with the pleasure of the trip in the least.

He closes with a request typical of such a situation: he would appreciate receiving letters from home.

119 During wartime dining on the *Queen Elizabeth*, officers were able to choose from a menu, but enlisted men had to accept what they were given.

> If you or any of the folks have time to write, I would appreciate any news of the old town; and I assure that I will reply with as much news from the front as may be likely to get by the censor.

There appears to be more written information about the First World War than the Second. However, a menu from the *Queen Elizabeth*, serving as a troopship in 1944, is informative. It was obtained from a resident of Niagara Falls, who sailed to Europe on her. It covers the entire day and looks very attractive (FIG. 119). The donor pointed out that this had not been his own menu,

OFFICERS' MENUS

Monday, 24th January, 1944

BREAKFAST

Stewed Apples   Quaker Oats

Kippered Herrings

OR

Grilled Lamb's Kidneys   Scrambled Eggs

Rolls   Scones   Preserves   Tea   Coffee

LUNCHEON

Potage Bretonne

Stewed Beefsteak and Onions

OR

Cold : Boiled Ham   Raised Pie

Salade : Mexicaine

Creamed Spinach

French Fried and Baked Potatoes

Rice and Raisin Pudding

OR

Tea   Cheese   Coffee

DINNER

Cream of Celery

Poached Cod, Parsley Sauce

OR

Roast Quarters of Lamb, Mint Sauce

Green Peas

Roast and Boiled Potatoes

Vanilla Creams, Apricot Sauce

Tea   Coffee

though – it was an officers' menu that he had picked up on the ship as a reminder to himself of the difference between them and his own status. There was no menu choice for the enlisted men like himself; you just accepted what was dumped onto your mess tin.

In both wars, the life of an officer was much more tolerable than that of an enlisted man. A diary from an anonymous American private begins with a brief summary for Thursday and Friday 25 and 26 April 1918, on the experience of getting to France.

> Left Camp Upton at 2:30 AM; electric rail to Long Island City; ferried to Hoboken Pier; boarded transport 'U.S.S. Northern Pacific' by noon; and left from an unknown port the following day, April 26th at 5:30 PM. Just getting dark when the transport *Von Stuben* joined us to make the trip. The most important event aboard was finding the mess hall for the first time and getting there ever after. The trip abroad was filled with a combination of all the discomforts of life.

Another insight into life on board for the regular soldier is on the back of a postcard posted by an unknown Canadian from Quebec City at the beginning of his transatlantic trip in June 1915.

> I am on this boat sailing along at the rate of 2½ miles per hour. There are about 2000 men aboard. Passed a submarine a few moments ago. Some of our boys are sea sick all ready and we are only about 100 miles at sea. Don't write till I write again. So good bye.

This note reminds us of the uncertainty these people faced. They didn't know where they were going and were not even certain that they would get there alive, given the risk of torpedoes.

During the First World War, concerts had the dual purpose of keeping the men occupied and raising funds for seamen's charities. This illustration is from the HMT *Olympic*, referred to on this programme only as HMT 2810 (FIG. 120). This designation may have been for security purposes, in case the

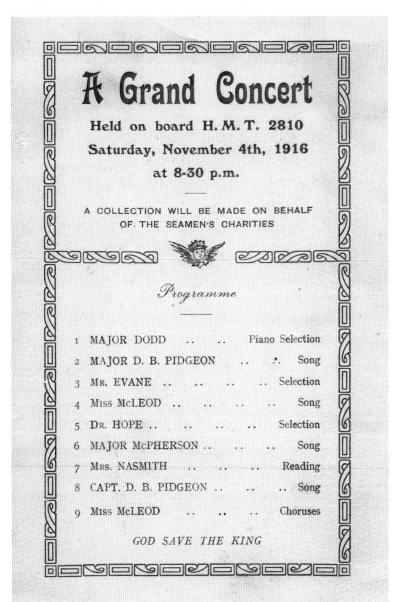

A Grand Concert

Held on board H. M. T. 2810
Saturday, November 4th, 1916
at 8-30 p.m.

A COLLECTION WILL BE MADE ON BEHALF
OF. THE SEAMEN'S CHARITIES

Programme

1	MAJOR DODD	Piano Selection
2	MAJOR D. B. PIDGEON	Song
3	MR. EVANE	Selection
4	MISS McLEOD	Song
5	DR. HOPE	Selection
6	MAJOR McPHERSON	Song
7	MRS. NASMITH	Reading
8	CAPT. D. B. PIDGEON	Song
9	MISS McLEOD	Choruses

GOD SAVE THE KING

120 During the First World War, White Star Line's *Olympic* was retitled HMT (His Majesty's Transport) 2810. The military passengers needed as many distractions as possible, and this rare Grand Concert programme from 1916 helped to fill those needs.

paper somehow ended up in German hands, or it may have merely been to fit into the Navy's nomenclature. In 1940, there were apparently no such security concerns. Although documents relating to a boxing match (FIG. 121) are unidentified, an accompanying concert programme (FIG. 122) clearly mentions

P. & O. CRUISES   Venice

SOUVENIR PROGRAMME

OF A BOXING MATCH BETWEEN THE
R. A. F. AND THE 15th L.A.A. REGT. R.A.

AIR FORCE		ARMY
CAPTAIN:- A.C. *Head.*		
Cpl. DUCKER.	V	Gnr. ROBSON
A.C. HALL.	V	Gnr. BENTLEY.
L.A.C. PATHER.	V	Gnr. LANGFORD.
A.C. BROUGH.	V	Gnr. DAVIES.
A.C. BALDWIN.	V	Gnr. ELLIS.
L.A.C. POTTS.	V	Gnr. ARMSTRONG.
A.C. HANCOCK	V	Gnr. DAWSON

During the interval the Ship's Commander will present Prizes to the winners of the R. A. F. — 15th L.A.A. Regt. Boxing Contest.

Prizes will also be presented to the winning R. A. F. teams in the Tug-of-War matches against the Army.

121 A rare programme of boxing matches featuring Royal Air Force versus Army representatives on board the *Viceroy of India* of the P&O Line, 1940. Boxing was another entertainment to pass the time.

No.................. **125**   PRICE TWO PENCE.

R.A.F.S' AFTERNOON FROLICS.

A Concert Party

ABOARD

H. M. T. "VICEROY OF INDIA."

SATURDAY, DECEMBER 21st 1940.

AT 5 P.M.

ARTISTES

Gnr. *W. Sizer.*	... ...	PIANIST
Gnr. *G. Jacobson.*	... ...	DRUMMER
L. A. C. *H. C. Morton.* ... BAND ...		SAXOPHONIST
Bdr. *Lanagan*	... ...	VIOLINIST
Steward *Ansell.*	...	TRUMPETER
A. C. *G. E. Chapman*	... ...	CROONER
A. C. *R. Muir.*	... ...	TENOR
A. C. *R. Bassnett.*	... ...	TENOR
A. C. *G. Ridpath.*	... ...	PROFESSORS
A. C. *A. Fletcher.*	... ...	OF HUMOUR
A. C. *L. V. Cole*	... ...	HANDS IN
A. C. *I. J. Griffiths*	... ...	HARMONY
A. C. *W. H. Pigg*	... ...	LAUGH'S SALESMAN
Jock Duncan	... ...	GUEST ARTIST
A. C. *J. Nellis*	... ...	ONE VOICE
A. C. *R. Gilchrist*	... ...	& A GUITAR
A. C. *J. C. Lee.*	... ...	ACCORDIONIST
A. C. *J. C. Beer.*	...	STRANGER THAN FICTION

COMPERE - L.A.C. *L. T. M. Morris.*

**4 FAUTEILS & 2 CANTEEN PRIZES FOR THE
LUCKY NUMBERS.**

ALL PROCEEDS TO SEAMEN'S CHARITIES.

the *Viceroy of India*, of the P&O Line, which was torpedoed and sunk two years later. These are printed on pre-war forms from the ship, which were presumably not removed when she was taken over for trooping service.

122 A concert party, also on the *Viceroy of India*, was another approach to distract the thoughts of troops heading into combat.

THE EMPRESS NEWS

At Sea   Friday, July 10, 1942   No. 16

BIGGEST TANK BATTLE RAGES FOR THE DON

One of the biggest tanks battles in history is now raging along the River Don, where the Germans have begun a new drive 100 miles east of Kharkov. There are more than 2,000 tanks in battle in front of Voronesh.

Crossings of the River Don are being made under heavy Soviet artillery fire and aerial bombardment, and German losses are described as tremendous. The Moscow-Rostov railway is now virtually useless in this sector, as it is under German artillery fire.

Following Russia's attack on the Tirpitz, a Soviet submarine has sunk an enemy convoy of one transport and three escort ships.

Today's Cairo communique states that operations in the southern sector of the El Alamain front has resulted in our armoured columns forcing enemy troops, including tanks, to head north.

U.S. heavy bombers operating in the Middle East shot down two enemy fighters over the Mediterranean.

GEORGE CROSS FOR AIRMAN

The award of the George Cross to Aircraftsman Albert Matthew Osborne is announced today. Osborne was killed after he had poured water over torpedoes in imminent danger of exploding during an aerial attack on Malta.

BRITAIN TAKES OVER AN ISLAND

British forces have occupied the island of La Mayotte, Portuguese East Africa, situated in the Mozambique Channel, the stretch of water that separates Madagascar from the mainland of Africa.

There was no resistence to the occupation and no casualties, according to an official statement issued last night. The occupation took place last Saturday.

Japanese submarines have been operating recently in the Mozambique Channel.

FIFI BACK AGAIN TOMORROW

"The Empress News" will, (we hope) resume its normal size and features tomorrow.

Ships' newspapers from wartime are very difficult to find. First, they were as transitory as today's newspapers. Second, when men were going to war they would be unlikely to save a newspaper and carry it into battle with them. A Second World War example is *The Empress News*, published on board Canadian Pacific's 'Empress' ships (FIG. 123). A copy from Friday 10 July 1942 is headlined 'Biggest Tank Battle Rages for the Don' and describes the battle involving more than 2,000 tanks in a German drive along the River Don in Russia. Newspapers published on board the *Queen Elizabeth* while she was trooping are headed *The Elizabethan*. Again, few of these papers were saved by the men whose lives were going to be put in jeopardy when they arrived to join their comrades-in-arms.

Even more rare are those from the First World War. An American example, *The Hatchet*, performs the same type of morale building as what would today be called 'managed news'. The good news is emphasized, and the bad news is glossed over.

On-board newspapers provided internal news, but families back home were always hoping for communications from the men and women heading to conflict zones. A clever example is the greeting card illustrated here (FIG. 124). With a picture of an unnamed Cunard 'two-stacker' on one side, the other carries a very basic Christmas message to the folks back home. This small card, tinier than a

123 *The Empress News*, from an unknown Canadian Pacific liner serving as a Second World War troopship, provided positive perspectives on the war, although success hung in the balance during July 1942.

124 The censors permitted little information, as this sparse Christmas greeting from the difficult fighting in Gallipoli and Salonika in 1916 illustrates.

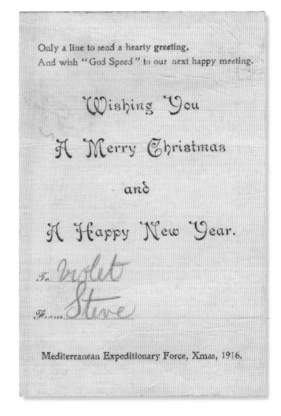

Only a line to send a hearty greeting,
And wish "God Speed" to our next happy meeting.

Wishing You

A Merry Christmas

and

A Happy New Year.

To *Violet*

From *Steve*

Mediterranean Expeditionary Force, Xmas, 1916.

postcard, disclosed to 'Violet' only that it was sent from 'Steve' and that he is with the Mediterranean Expeditionary Force at Christmas 1916. This card would not entail any review by the censor because it controlled the information provided.

AFTER THE WAR

Soldiers do not appear instantly on the battlefield. They have to be trained and then shipped. At the end of a war, ocean liners also played a major role in bringing soldiers home. A new genre of postcard was devised: it depicted 'the ship that brought me home' and could be sent to friends and relatives on safe arrival at the port.

Several years ago, I received an email from a woman in Iowa, who had come across an article I had written for the Ephemera Society of America on 'ship that brought me home' postcards produced by the Jewish Welfare Board after the First World War. In an old rented house, my correspondent had come across a bag of what appeared to be rags. However, one of the rags was actually a handkerchief printed with the caption 'The Ship that Brought Me Home' and displaying the troopship USS *Imperator* as well as specifications of this very large (for its day) passenger liner (FIG. 125).

Having been laid up in Germany during the war, the *Imperator* sailed from Hamburg on 27 April 1919 to New York to be handed over to the USA. Records show that she began service as a US Navy transport on 5 May 1919 and was laid up at New York in August of the same year. This handkerchief is a rare bird, having been printed on a very flimsy silken fabric during only

125 In 1919 millions of servicemen from the United States and Canada were repatriated, some on the same ships that had previously delivered them to Europe. This rare souvenir handkerchief from the massive *Imperator* would have been brought back for a loved one.

WOVEN IN SILK.

H.M.S. OLYMPIC.

Length 883 ft. Breadth 92½ ft. Tonnage 46359. Speed 22½ Knots.

a three-month period. Beginning in 1920 *Imperator* sailed under her original name for the Cunard Line, and a year later was renamed RMS *Berengaria*.

I have several 'the ship that brought me home' postcards, and some similar handkerchiefs. The two aspects show the spectrum of mementoes of the return from the First World War. If you're coming home to a wife or girlfriend, an illustrative ship postcard isn't very romantic. But a sweet, delicate, delightful handkerchief is feminine and relevant – and a poignant reminder of the distance that a loved one has travelled.

A postcard that could, exceptionally, serve as a romantic reminder of a homecoming is the Stevengraph postcard of the *Olympic*, which is explicit as to the time frame of the ship's life (**FIG.** 126). Normally a Stevengraph would show a caption of RMS *Olympic* – Royal Mail Ship. This one refers to HMS

126 A silk Stevengraph postcard of the *Olympic*, beautiful but relatively expensive.

Olympic – His Majesty's Ship – a term normally applied to warships; but the publisher apparently did not know the difference, and probably created this as a deluxe souvenir for those travelling back to their homes in Canada at the end of the First World War.

A delicate purse mirror, picturing the RMS *Queen Mary* in her Second World War livery, seems to be a comparable souvenir from the Second World War (**FIG. 127**). The style of image and the ship in her wartime grey paint confirm her period. Whether purchased on board by a returning member of the military or by a war bride, the mirror is a reminder to any party that war has ended, and civilian life now awaits the personnel being demobilized.

Cunard White Star Liner "QUEEN MARY"

Most items of the genre 'the ship that brought me home' are American, and to a lesser degree Canadian, because those countries had the greatest number of men travelling the greatest distance by ship. For most British and European combatants, the trip was just across the English Channel, or a train ride from their training camp, with the exception of those fighting in the Gallipoli Peninsula and in the Middle East. There was not the drama of a trip across the Atlantic Ocean, so no special emphasis on the form of transportation that brought them home.

However, there is some British Second World War material from those who served in India and the Far East. One card records the trip on the Union–Castle liner *Capetown Castle*,

127 Mementoes for the home front also exist from the Second World War, as in this compact purse mirror with an image of the *Queen Mary* in her grey wartime livery.

after war service, from Africa to England in November 1945. Pencilled on the back is the curious note 'This is the ship Dad and I came back to England on.' Two generations of army men would have been ecstatic to have survived the war and returned home together, and their family back in the UK would have been just as pleased.

These cards help us to remember the risks taken by armed forces personnel, and their relief at having survived those risks. 'Here I am, back home', they enthuse. 'Alive. And this is the ship that brought me home.' Some had had to wait for years to be brought home.

WAR BRIDES

On Independence Day, Americans set off their fireworks, enjoy their steaks from the barbecue, and celebrate a popular holiday to mark their independence from British rule in 1776. But a piece of poignant ephemera reminds us that the fight for independence and freedom is ongoing, and highly treasured by those who attain it.

Some years ago, at a local flea market, I came across a rather undistinguished-looking set of ship menus. Unlike the normally expressive large-format menus with powerful graphics, these were printed on buff-coloured postcard-sized cards – not the kind of product that would bring you back for another voyage. Even if you had opted for a cheap cruise today, this would have been far worse than the fare you expected.

The ship was the iconic RMS *Queen Mary*. The date on each menu – breakfast, lunch and dinner – was 4 July 1946. The menu offerings were unspectacular and verged on boring (FIG. 128). Research confirmed that the RMS *Queen Mary*, having served as a troopship during the war ferrying American

R.M.S. "QUEEN MARY"   Thursday, July 4, 1946

Breakfast

Oranges   Compote of Prunes

Rolled Oats
Grape Nuts   Wheat Cereal   Corn Flakes

Fried Kingfish, Tomato Sauce
Smoked Fillet of Codling, Melted Butter

or

Broiled Breakfast Bacon
Eggs : Fried, Turned and Boiled

or

Minced Collops

Rolls   Toast   Scones
Preserves
Coffee   Tea   Cocoa

"QUEEN MARY"

I send you my best wishes for your happiness and good fortune in your new life in the great Dominion, the country of your adoption.

Captain

CUNARD BUILDING,   230, HOSPITAL STREET,
PIER HEAD, LIVERPOOL   *July, 1946*   MONTREAL

128 A rare war-bride breakfast menu from 4 July 1946 from the *Queen Mary* appears very basic, but would have been a breakfast feast for the bride coming from wartime rationing and shortages in the UK.

129 Adding ceremony to the *Queen Mary* war-bride voyage, this 'welcome' from the captain of the ship rounded out the set of three menus for the day.

troops to the battlefields of Europe, and then having brought many of them back home again, was at this time shuttling war brides from England and Europe to North America, before a major refit in 1946–7 enabled it to go back into regular transatlantic service.

A war bride, on board the ship, coming to join her soldier husband for a new life in North America, had saved these to mark her first Independence Day from life 'back home'. This wonderful souvenir probably came to market after the demise of the owner, who had proudly saved this memento of her trip to a new life in Canada. Although dull by today's cruise standards, the food would have been a fabulous treat after years of rationing and scarcity. The oranges and cocoa for breakfast, coming from climates far from northern Europe, would have been a treat beyond measure. Even having a choice among rolls, scones and toast – with preserves to spread liberally on them – would have been, after years of rationing, sheer luxury.

Furthermore, the set of menus was accompanied by an equal-sized card from the captain of the ship welcoming the recipient to 'the country of your adoption' (FIG. 129).

At one stage this was a two-way traffic. A note on the back of a pass dated March 1946 relating to a crew member of the time, Stewardess Miss B. Bellamy, records 'First S'ton [Southampton] pass on return with brides. Brides left in Canada. Returned with German prisoners.'

DEMOBILIZED

A crudely produced mimeographed newsletter from the American troop transport *William Mulholland* dated 3 August 1945, returning from Europe when war was still taking place in the Pacific theatre, is headlined with the reminder, 'American

Paratroopers Ready to Enter Japan' and ends with 'What to Expect Upon Reaching Port'. (They had no idea that just three days later the first atomic bomb would be dropped on Hiroshima and those American paratroopers would be able to stand down.) Here is what to expect:

> After reaching shore you will immediately go to Camp Kilmer or Camp Shanks.
> You will remain in either of those camps for 24 to 48 hours.
> You will receive one set of Khakis at this camp.
> You will find telephone and telegraph services available here.
> You will dine like a civilian, eating from plates.
> There will be no passes issued at this camp.
> You will be divided into Reception Center groups.
> At the Reception Center you will be paid, receive additional clothing, and then given leave or furlough.

The last paragraph of the paper, their last link with the war and their trooping experience, asks them:

> Remember the faces you saw when you made that ocean crossing a couple of years ago? Many of them are not with us now – some will never be … Let's give a thought to those not so fortunate and silently wish them well.

LINERS AS HOSPITAL SHIPS

Wars inevitably create casualties, and in the First World War some liners were commandeered as hospital ships. The *Aquitania* served first as a troopship and then as a hospital ship in the Mediterranean. The public rooms were converted to hospital wards and no effort was made to institutionalize the decor (FIG. 130). As with the *Aquitania*, the other hospital ships were visibly marked, with large red crosses painted prominently on their sides. In order to comfort and assure the families and friends back home that the wounded were being well cared for, even publications such as *The Times* provided reports on 'the Care of the Wounded in Modern War', picturing recuperating men enjoying time in the sun on deck.

A soldier receiving a wound was not a topic that government or the military wanted to advertise, but the care element had to be addressed. Patients were given toe tags identifying their ailment and rank (FIG. 131). This example (which could easily be mistaken for a luggage tag, given the similar format) is from the Australian hospital ship *Karoola*. She reportedly served in that capacity from 1915. It was for C. Morris, a driver with B Battery of the HAC (Honourable Artillery Company). He was

130 Major ocean liners such as Cunard's *Aquitania* were commandeered for hospital-ship service. *Aquitania* was the only major liner to serve in both world wars – this image is from First World War material.

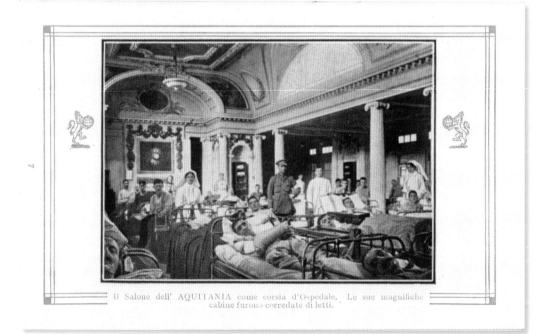

Il Salone dell' AQUITANIA come corsia d'Ospedale. Le sue magnifiche cabine furono corredate di letti.

On His Majesty's Service.

625 125   Driver

MORRIS. C.,

"B" Bty. H, A. C.

Diarrhoea.

Dysentery

From
Beirut   2 days
to
Alexandria
21st Gen Hospital

Australian Imperial Force.

originally invalided with diarrhoea when the tag was typed, but that apparently deteriorated into dysentery during his trip from Beirut to Alexandria of two days' duration (the prognosis was written in the same hand as the one that recorded his trip). There is a further notation that I believe reads '21st General Hospital'. Did Mr Morris survive his affliction and the war itself? A blog by the Ephemera Society elicited the information from an Australian source that Mr Morris recovered from his wounds and went on to lead a full life.

131 A 'toe tag' from an Australian soldier carried on the hospital ship *Karoola* in the Middle East (he survived his afflictions).

The White Star

Triple-Screw Liners

"Olympic" & "Titanic"

Souvenir Number

of

"The Shipbuilder"

NOTEWORTHY DISASTERS

Although the majority of ocean voyages
passed smoothly, a number of disasters at
sea loom large in the popular imagination.
In wartime these were largely the result of enemy action;
in peacetime, weather conditions, engineering flaws and human
error led on occasion to spectacular loss of life.

A *TITANIC* INSIGHT

Much has been written about the tragic sinking of the *Titanic* in
1912. Formal inquiries have come to their conclusions. Writers have
advanced a range of theories. Films have created hypothetical
stories on board. Is there anything more to say? Yes, there is.

RMS *Titanic* sank during the golden age of the postcard.
Whenever there was a newsworthy event – from the FA Cup
Final to the sinking of the *Titanic* – one or more commemorative
postcards appeared in the display racks of shops around the
world. Postcards were big business, with billions produced in
the era by a wide range of publishers to appeal to the tastes of
the day. Today we might expect to see T-shirts or baseball caps
created to sell to the public. Then, it was postcards.

The Largest and Finest Steamers in the world
WHITE STAR LINE
"OLYMPIC" ☆ "TITANIC"
882½ FEET LONG   45,000 TONS REGISTER   92½ FEET BROAD

Postcards of the *Titanic* fall into two categories: those issued before the disaster, and those published afterwards to chronicle it. Both types are well represented and those examples give us a further insight into the story. Pre-disaster cards remind us that *Titanic* was not unique. A year earlier her virtually identical sister ship *Olympic* had begun a very successful regular service across the Atlantic.

I have two examples of the card shown here, each one important because of its message (FIG. 132). A card dated 27 July 1911 reports 'Saw the *Olympic* steam out of New York harbor today.' This was just a month after she had made her maiden voyage, capturing worldwide attention as the largest passenger ship in the world. Her comings and goings were noteworthy.

The other copy of that same card, sent in September 1911, reports from New York, 'We sail Saturday at noon. The loveliest

132 *Titanic's* more or less identical sister ship *Olympic* was in service well before *Titanic's* fatal maiden voyage, as this postcard from 1911 reminds us.

ship. Floating palace. The only S.S. in the world that the dining chairs are not screwed down. Crosses in six days.' Another card, with a message dated 2 October, reports to the recipient that 'Henry Cornwell came over on her First Trip'. *Olympic* had a stellar reputation and a long-lasting career; why didn't the *Titanic*?

Some suggest that Captain Smith was to blame. It is worth observing that Smith was certainly accident-prone. Other images depict the serious collision between the *Olympic*, with Captain Smith at the helm, and the Royal Navy destroyer HMS *Hawke* on 20 September 1911 (FIG. 133). More common than pre-disaster cards are those produced in massive quantities after the disaster. Opportunistic publishers produced and sold even poorly done cards, printed at an angle and not cropped properly. One example, seen occasionally, is attributed to 'Debenham', and could have been made hurriedly for the London department store.

133 *Titanic*'s captain, Edward J. Smith, commanded the *Olympic* before his *Titanic* appointment, and had displayed his propensities by colliding with the destroyer HMS *Hawke* seven months earlier.

R.M.S. TITANIC.

134 Opportunism flourished – this *Titanic* memorial postcard produced by Salmon of Sevenoaks after the tragedy carried the identical image to one produced a year earlier by them and labelled as the *Olympic*.

Or consider the ingenuity of this card, published by the British firm Roy Salmon (**FIG. 134**). The front is unadorned with narrative and the back makes only a slight reference to the disaster. The reason? An identical image had already been published, being labelled and described previously as RMS *Olympic*. We are sure that the *Olympic* version was the original image because a message on the back of an example of that one, dated 8 July 1911, reports 'We have just got off the boat.'

Surprisingly, 'disaster' version cards that were posted in April 1912 make no reference to the disaster, but rather carry reports of local and family activities. Does this mean that they didn't care about the disaster? It is more likely, in an era when a large part of the population collected postcards, that they were trying to add hot current material to the recipient's collection while sending news that today we would convey in an email. In the absence of radar and other electronic navigation aids, ship collisions and the resultant loss of life were not rare. But adding one or more new postcards to your collection was an important moment.

White Star Line's bad luck carried on with the loss of *Titanic*'s younger sister *Britannic*, which never went into the three-ship transatlantic service that had been visualized by the company. *Olympic* sailed on to a successful career for White Star Line until 1935, just after the merger with Cunard. But the member of the brilliant trio that will always be remembered is *Titanic*. Associated ephemera are highly collectable: in recent years a postcard, written on board the ship and posted before she went to sea, was sold at auction by Henry Aldridge & Son auctioneers of Devizes, England, who provided this scan of the menu side of the postcard (FIG. 135). Including buyer's premium the postcard sold for the staggering amount of £89,000.

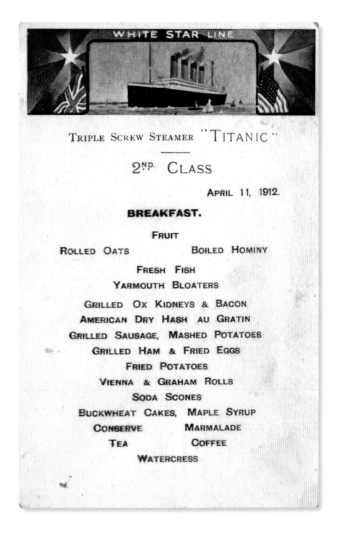

WHITE STAR LINE

TRIPLE SCREW STEAMER "TITANIC"

2ND. CLASS

APRIL 11, 1912.

BREAKFAST.

FRUIT
ROLLED OATS   BOILED HOMINY
FRESH FISH
YARMOUTH BLOATERS
GRILLED OX KIDNEYS & BACON
AMERICAN DRY HASH AU GRATIN
GRILLED SAUSAGE, MASHED POTATOES
GRILLED HAM & FRIED EGGS
FRIED POTATOES
VIENNA & GRAHAM ROLLS
SODA SCONES
BUCKWHEAT CAKES, MAPLE SYRUP
CONSERVE   MARMALADE
TEA   COFFEE
WATERCRESS

135 This Second Class 'postcard menu' of the *Titanic* from the first leg of her voyage survived to come to auction in 2014 and realize £89,000 (over $120,000). *Image courtesy of Aldridge & Son.*

LUSITANIA

When RMS *Lusitania* went into service in 1907 she was, at some 31,550 gross registered tons, the largest ship in the world. *Lusitania* was a large, high-profile liner which Cunard compared in size, in one of their brochures, to the Marshall Field building in Chicago. Her furnishings were luxurious and her seaworthiness without question (**FIG. 136**). Planned by Cunard to be a running mate to the *Mauretania*, she remained in civilian passenger service after the outbreak of the First World War, even though the *Mauretania* was requisitioned for wartime service as a troopship.

How would you feel as a wartime passenger on the *Lusitania*? Since the menu in September 1914 – dressed lobster, potted shrimps, soused salmon (**FIG. 137**) – looked like business as usual, you would probably be relatively unconcerned, as were the

The Lounge. s.s. LUSITANIA.

CUNARDER ARRIVING AT LIVERPOOL

R. M. S. "LUSITANIA"   FRIDAY, SEPTEMBER 25, 1914

- - LUNCHEON - -

Dressed Lobster   Norwegian Anchovies   Potted Shrimps   Queen Olives
Hazelnut Sausage   Celery   Œufs—Romanoff   Amieux Sardines
Soused Salmon   Filleted Herrings   Salad—Mexicaine
Salambos de Foie Gras   Cornets of York Ham

- - HOT - -

Consommé Flamarion   Pea Soup
Broiled Pickerel—Hongroise   Bouillaibaise—Provençale
Œufs—Monaco   Omelettes—Espagnole
Welsh Rarebits

OX TAIL—JARDINIERE   **CHICKEN POT PIE**
Ribs of Beef—Browned Potatoes
Dressed Cabbage   Puree of Parsnips
Plain Baked, Mashed & Chipped Potatoes

TO ORDER FROM THE GRILL—15 Minutes
Mutton Chops—Macaire Potatoes

- - COLD BUFFET - -

Roast Beef   Devonshire Ham   Ox Tongue   London Pressed Beef   Boar's Head
Melton Mowbray Pie   Boiled Capon   Oxford Brawn   Braised Duckling
Selle d'Agneau—MacAlpin   Caneton—Mirabeau   Cailles aux Cerises
Galantine of Veal—Pistaches   Cotelettes en Chaudfroid—Russe
Grouse   Partridge
Lettuce & Tomatoes—French Dressing   Sliced Beetroot
Salads—Britannia & Bontoux
Sago Pudding
Pears & Custard   Rhubarb & Creamed Rice
French Pastry
Ice Cream—Wafers
Cheese :—Cheshire, Wiltshire, Port du-Salut, Camembert, Cream,
Gorgonzola & St. Ivel
Apples   Oranges   Bananas   Pineapple   Assorted Nuts
Ceylon, China & Blended Teas   .   Coffee   Cocoa

passengers who boarded this same ship some six months later for her last fateful voyage, when she was torpedoed and sunk.

On 4 February 1915 the German government declared the waters around Great Britain to be a war zone. *Lusitania* continued to make her regular transatlantic crossings despite warnings from the enemy that the blockade of Britain included passenger ships capable of carrying troops and war materials in addition to her civilian passengers. On 7 May 1915, *Lusitania* was torpedoed by the German submarine U-20 and reportedly sank in twenty minutes, with the loss of 1,198 people of the 1,959 on board. The public on the Allied side were outraged, although the German government claimed that the ship was carrying war materials and therefore a justifiable target in wartime.

The controversy has been explored in many books, with a surge of publications on the centenary of the sinking in 2015. I don't propose to revisit any of the positions presented on the matter, but rather to introduce a new aspect. An Allan Line ship, the RMS *Hesperian*, also remained in passenger service between Canada and Britain. In August 1915 she sailed from Montreal, up the St Lawrence. A passenger who had boarded her in Montreal wrote a postcard as she headed towards Quebec City, with the following message:

> Just a few lines to let you know I am on board this ship traveling up the St. Lawrence.... We reached Montreal about 9 o'clock last night.... I thought that you would like to see the ship that we are sailing on. It's a slow boat. It is all soldiers on board but we stop at Quebec to take a few passengers.

The card was postmarked at Quebec City on 26 August 1915. On 4 September 1915 (nine days later) the *Hesperian* was torpedoed and sunk off the coast of Ireland with the loss of thirty-two lives by the submarine U-20 – the same one that had torpedoed the *Lusitania* in the same general area four months earlier. The *Hesperian* was returning to Canada to pick up another consignment of passengers. One of the German allegations was that the *Lusitania* was being used in part as a troopship. Based on the message on this postcard, it is clear that the liner *Hesperian* was certainly being used as a troopship, just a few months later.

A programme for a charitable concert on board another Allan liner, the RMS *Grampian*, on 13 July 1916 shows the chairman of the evening as Lieutenant D.T. Appleton. The programme includes several non-military performers, but also Sergeant Harris, Private Horn, Lieutenant Appleton and Private Stockdale. Any of the participants who were nurses, Red Cross personnel or doctors might not show a military rank.

So, let's revisit the *Lusitania* question with this new insight. Troops were travelling in ships with civilian passengers. Wouldn't the German navy feel pressed to peel off the facade and treat these ships as though they were primarily troopships? And has anyone ever attempted to do a demographic study of the *Lusitania*'s passengers? How many were male, under twenty-five, and British, Canadian or even American? There certainly would have been a disproportionately high number among the *Hesperian*'s passengers.

Another insight: in fifty years of collecting and searching in three countries I have never found a passenger list from any ocean liner between the beginning and end of the First World War. If all the passengers were civilians it would be the usual tool for fostering passenger interaction, and of no military consequence. On the other hand, if the liner were ferrying any military personnel, it would be a bad idea, from the point of view of security, to publish a list of their names and ranks.

Sinking of the Lusitania

The last plunge. 6.

This helps us to understand why the German supreme command would be suspicious of the innocence of any Allied passenger ship. The sinking of *Lusitania* helped to tip America towards entering the war, a decision encouraged by emotional presentations of the incident such as the illustration in FIG. 138.

EMPRESS OF IRELAND

The *Empress of Ireland* disaster on 29 May 1914 has continued to be relatively overlooked by marine historians, although her loss of life was close to that of *Lusitania* and more than two-thirds that of the *Titanic*. Perhaps part of the reason is that there was not the emotion of wartime, as with the *Lusitania*, and the *Empress* was a considerably smaller and less prominent ship than either of the other two.

The *Empress of Ireland* was one of a pair of Canadian Pacific sister liners which each went into service in 1906. She had a

138 Dramatic propaganda images such as this one from a set of six postcards helped to further stoke the outrage at the *Lusitania* sinking.

service life of just under eight years, while her sister, the first *Empress of Britain*, served for twenty-three years, including a period of time as a First World War troop transport, and was renamed the *Montroyal* for her last five years. Each ship was of some 14,000 tons, which put them in the 'intermediate' size category.

Booklets describe and picture Second Class and Third Class (steerage) accommodation. One of the illustrations is captioned 'Third Class Two-Berth Room on the "Empresses"', and underneath it there is the statement 'Third Class Passengers may now Secure their Rooms and Berths on the "Empresses" and have the numbers written on their tickets.' Apparently Third Class passengers had become accustomed to a mad scramble to claim a cabin when they came aboard.

The Third Class passengers perhaps felt comfortable and secure in their berths that fateful night, enjoying the luxury of free mattresses and bedding, and reflecting on their relatively bountiful supper. Then came the crash. The *Storstad* was a collier (coal-carrying ship) which had sailed fully loaded from Sydney, Nova Scotia, and was heading to Montreal when she collided with the *Empress of Ireland* in dense fog, with the loss of 1,012 of the *Empress*'s passengers and crew out of a complement of 1,477 persons. The bow of the *Storstad* ripped into the starboard side of the *Empress*, similar to the effect of the iceberg on the *Titanic*.

139 The loss of the *Empress of Ireland* in late May 1914 is covered in the three images of this multi-panel postcard. Its loss, and that of the 1,012 souls who perished in her, did not make the global headlines.

140 A black-bordered postcard hymn to mourn the loss of the *Empress of Ireland* in 1914 is an interesting insight into the mourning process of the times.

SALVATION ARMY STAFF BAND WITH COMM. REES AND COL. MAIDMENT
AS EMBARKED ON THE ILL-FATED S.S. "EMPRESS OF IRELAND"
THOSE MARKED X WERE RESCUED

Of the 87 First Class passengers, 36 were saved. Only 133 of the 717 Third Class survived. Memorial tributes poured off the postcard presses. A black-bordered mourning card with compound images of the ill-fated liner, the damaged *Storstad* and the dead being taken off a ship in Quebec was no doubt a popular commodity (FIG. 139). Showing a little more imagination, another publisher provided a black-bordered card with an image of the ship and the words and music to the hymn 'God be with You!', perhaps reflecting the significant part that the Salvation Army suffered in the losses (FIG. 140).

One of the most telling photographs is an image of the Salvation Army band, which was part of a contingent of 167 members of the Salvation Army sailing to participate in a conference in England (FIG. 141). The image, taken in Toronto before the band set out, was later edited to show the few surviving

141 This poignant photograph of the Salvation Army Band was taken before they departed on the *Empress of Ireland*, and was later marked by the photographer with *X*s for the few survivors. Image courtesy of Ray Ruddy.

members of the group. It is a poignant benchmark of the extent of the casualties.

Fewer than 20 per cent of the Second and Third Class passengers survived, in comparison to more than 40 per cent in First Class. These relative survival rates are not much different from those of other shipping accidents. It probably has little to do with the actual class of travel, except in so far as First Class tended to have cabins in the upper decks of the ship, and therefore easier access to the decks on which the lifeboats were located. The location of the actual strike, amidships on her starboard side, would also have affected the outcome.

The *Storstad*, the Norwegian coal freighter that rammed the *Empress of Ireland*, remained afloat, although badly damaged (**FIG. 142**). Not a small ship, she was slightly less than half the

142 The *Empress of Ireland*'s assailant, the collier *Storstad*, survived, but with extensive damage, testifying to the force of the collision.

tonnage of the *Empress*, but with a load of coal she would have had considerable momentum.

Blame is always an issue in accidents. It doesn't change the casualty numbers, and it doesn't recover lost shipping, but it does provide a platform for litigation and insurance claims. In this case, *Storstad* was found to be at fault and Canadian Pacific, which owned the *Empress of Ireland*, lodged a $2 million lawsuit against *Storstad*'s owners. Whether the deceased members of the Salvation Army band's heirs received any of that is not disclosed.

Why is the significant loss of life on the *Empress* relatively underrepresented internationally? She was neither a premier ship on a maiden voyage, nor a casualty of enemy action in time of war. A further possibility is that, compared to *Titanic* and *Lusitania*, there were no American (or British) millionaires on board, and therefore fewer headline losses. A cynic might suggest that a Salvation Army band would not trump a multi-millionaire industrialist or financier in competing for the global media spotlight.

WILHELM GUSTLOFF

If you work for a large corporation – particularly in a sales capacity – you will probably be familiar with incentive pro-grammes. They are not unique to the corporate world, and an interesting historical example is the *Strength Through Joy* travel programmes offered in Nazi Germany during the 1930s.

Global tourism was in recession, and in order to maintain German tourist resources – and jobs – a series of travel in-centives was offered through the *Strength Through Joy* movement. Low-priced domestic tourism was available to the Nazi Party faithful as a reward for their support and contributions. The

level of tourism was related to the amount of that support, and ship cruises were at the apex of possible rewards.

A ship named the *Wilhelm Gustloff* was built and launched in 1938 specifically to cater to this travel trade. This was the first large liner built specifically and solely for cruising. There was no air conditioning, but note her slab sides rather than a stepped 'wedding cake' profile (FIG. 143). At over 25,000 tons, she was larger than many of the liners used by Cunard for Tourist Class transatlantic service, and represented a significant development in ocean liner cruises for the 'mass market'.

When *Gustloff* went into service in April 1938, she represented the highest travel reward for a Party member or supporter. A postcard, written on the first day of her maiden voyage and postmarked with a *Wilhelm Gustloff* cancellation two days later,

143 Germany's *Wilhelm Gustloff,* the first large ship designed exclusively for cruising, was built for the Nazi *Strength Through Joy* movement. It had a similar profile to today's full-time cruise ships.

would make a significant statement to the recipient about the sender's elevated stature in the eyes of the Nazi administration. The message may be mundane but the postmark tells it all (FIG. 144). The bill of fare was comparable to a Third Class tourist offering on a commercial liner, but for the chosen worker or party supporter the trip was probably less about the food and more about recognition in the eyes of the Nazi Party.

Wilhelm Gustloff was in cruising service for only a short period of time. In September 1939 she was requisitioned by the military and used primarily as an accommodation ship during the war. In January 1945, carrying a flood of refugees and wounded fleeing the oncoming Russian army, she was torpedoed and sunk by a Russian submarine in the icy waters of the Baltic. Estimates of the passengers crammed on board range from 6,000 to 9,000 – in the chaos there were no formal records kept. Almost all of those passengers perished in the frigid waters, leading to the greatest loss of life in maritime history.

These disasters are the exception to the general rule. Even in the tragic losses of the SS *Andrea Doria* in 1956 and the MV *Costa Concordia* in 2012, the great majority of passengers and crew survived. For almost all ocean travellers in peacetime, the voyage was the most exciting, memorable and positive experience of their lives.

144 A message sent from the maiden voyage of the *Gustloff* would have conveyed to the recipient the knowledge that the sender had a position of influence in the Nazi regime. There are no postmarks from her final fatal voyage in January 1945 when some 9,000 people died.

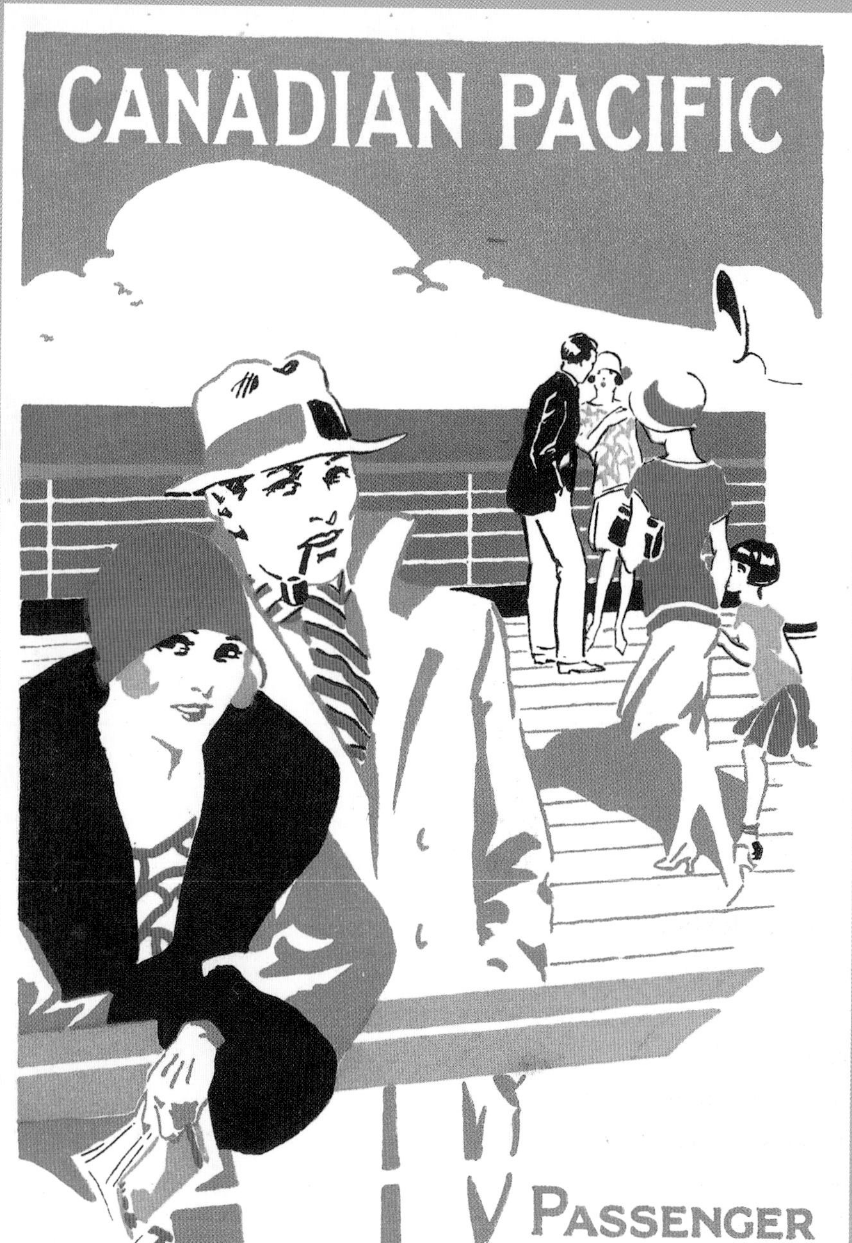
CANADIAN PACIFIC
PASSENGER
LIST

TICKING THE
COLLECTOR BOXES

The question has been asked many times, 'Why did you collect
all these thousands of items of ocean liner material, and where
did you find them?' There is more than one answer. To assess
all the factors, one needs to look at a set of hypothetical collector
boxes. The final array of ticked boxes may help to explain why all
collectors collect.

For me personally, ocean liners are a fond recollection of a
transatlantic journey many decades ago with my parents, one
way on the elderly RMS *Franconia*, and the return voyage on
the fabulous RMS *Queen Elizabeth*. So one element is personal
memories, and mementoes of those ships
have been the genesis of my collecting
adventure. Tick the first collector box.

Every migrant during the lifetime of
my parents crossed the Atlantic (or any
of the oceans) by ship to seek a better
life in a new land. Air travel was in its
infancy. Genealogists revel in information about the ships that their ancestors
took to travel from Europe to North

America and other immigration destinations. My parents left England in 1926, in the midst of labour unrest and the General Strike. It was a good time to leave. Tick collector box number two, the desire for personal family history.

Periodically, I receive requests from people for information about the ships that carried their ancestors across the Atlantic – anything that enhances their understanding of the challenges that 'their' migrants experienced long ago. Pictures of the ships, information about their capacity, menus, fares and a host of other aspects all help to bring the past into focus for their present.

Even the most basic menu can evoke strong positive memories. My barber came from Italy as a young child on either the *Vulcania* or the *Saturnia*. He cannot remember which one, but he does remember vividly the food in Third Class. After wartime in impoverished and war-torn Sicily, the quantity and quality of food (probably any food) was an overwhelming experience. Tick collector box number three, genealogy.

At university I majored in History. Readers will understand the passion of a historian for primary source material about their topics of interest. Shipping ephemera can be a fabulous source of primary information, including letters, shipping line booklets and schedules, deck plans, menus, postcards, and even tiny pieces such as a deckchair ticket for the ill-fated *Lusitania*.

Collecting reflects more than just 'names and dates' history. The picture is on the broader palette of social, economic, artistic and business history. Travel differentiated the affluent from the less so, and underscored the social difference by menu selections, cabin size and amenities, and the presence of maids, valets, chauffeurs, nurses and governesses. Chauffeurs? Yes – if one was shipping an automobile to Europe, then one needed a reliable person to drive it! Can there be such fascination with primary source material? Definitely so. Check collector box number four.

Promotional material from the shipping companies featured contemporary artwork, some of it signed by the artist, some not. For the student seeking fine examples of art nouveau or art deco design, shipping material is a pot of gold at the end of the proverbial artistic rainbow. Place a large – and artistic – 'tick' in collector box number five.

As a chartered accountant, I have been accused of harbouring compulsive instincts. Probably so. There is a correct place for everything, and every piece of ephemera belongs in a specific binder or set of binders for the related shipping line. All binders are white, with clear sleeves on the front and spine to show the shipping line and the number of the volume for that line. Perhaps it's a demonstration of the 'debits on the left and credits on the right' mentality for which accountants are renowned. But if all collectors have a tendency to reflect varying degrees of compulsive behaviour, are all compulsives collectors?

Collecting is a community which subsumes the individual collector as the years progress. When my wife Judith and I attend postcard and ephemera fairs we see other collectors whom we have come to know and the vendors whom we have made prosperous over the years. As an active member and present council member of the Ephemera Society in the UK and for many years a board member of the Ephemera Society of America, over the past decades I have benefited from being pointed towards desirable material by all those who know us well.

Recently I read an article which visited the old question of whether collecting is a manifestation of man's long-ago hunter–gatherer instincts. It's an interesting thesis except that the hunter–gatherer sought food for the table while the predatory collector is searching for something beyond mere survival. Studying Maslow's premise of the *Hierarchy of Needs*, the hunter–gatherer is fulfilling one of the lowest levels of human needs – food. On the other hand, the collector setting out to hunt for insights to his or her understanding of history is targeting Maslow's highest level of human need – self-actualization. When I find a modest postcard on which a passenger enthuses about the fine quality of food aboard the SS *Normandie*, I have attained an insight that no one else possesses. What a feeling of accomplishment, and perhaps even power! Another perspective, and a heavy broad-tipped felt marker tick to collector box number six.

These comments are derived from the stealth of sneaking up on one's ephemera prey and pouncing on it at a dealer's stall. None of this involves the Internet. Buying on the Internet is akin to ordering your prey from the nearby butcher's shop online and having it delivered to your home. They know what they are selling, and you think you know what you are buying. But is that sausage really all-beef?

If you believe that 'knowledge is power' you have the greatest chance of exercising it when you see a target close at hand and realize that the document in your hand from the RMS *Britannic* is from the ship that was a sister to the ill-fated *Titanic*, not a later, much more common namesake that sailed in the 1930s. Pull the trigger and shoot a hole in collector box number seven.

So here's a toast to Dr Maslow, who may have helped both you and me to understand how this very large collection came to be. And a further toast to the John Johnson Collection at the Bodleian Libraries, where the Sayers Collection will shine as a beacon for ocean liner researchers for centuries to come.

FURTHER READING

Donzel, C., *Luxury Liners: Life on Board*, Vendome Press, New York, 2006. Good illustrations but light on text.

Drechsel, E., *Norddeutscher Lloyd Bremen 1857–1970*, vols 1–2, Cordillera, Vancouver, 1994.

Finamore, D., and G. Wood (eds), *Ocean Liners: Speed and Style*, V&A Publishing, London, 2018. Focuses on fashion and design.

Gardiner, R., *The History of the White Star Line*, Ian Allan, Hersham, 2001.

Harding, S., *Great Liners at War*, Tempus, Stroud, 2007.

Howarth, D., and S. Howarth, *The Story of P&O*, Weidenfeld & Nicolson, London, 1986.

Hyde, F.E., *Cunard and the North Atlantic*, Humanities Press, Atlantic Highlands NJ, 1975.

Kludas, A., *Great Passenger Ships of the World*, Volume 1: *1858–1912*; Volume 2: *1913–1923*; Volume 3: *1924–1935*; Volume 4: *1936–1950*; Volume 5: *1951–1976*; Volume 6: *1977–1986*, Patrick Stephens, Wellingborough, 1975. The single best reference source for specific liners, well indexed and cross-referenced – much better than the Internet.

McCluskie, T., et al., *Titanic and Her Sisters Olympic and Britannic*, PRC, London, 1998. A massive volume, but the only book to put *Titanic* in context with her White Star Line sisters, which were intended to compete with *Mauretania*, *Lusitania* and *Aquitania* on the North Atlantic.

McCann, T., *An American Company: The Tragedy of United Fruit*, Crown, New York, 1976.

Musk, G., *Canadian Pacific*, Holt, Rinehart & Winston, Toronto, 1981.

Niven, J., *The American President Lines and Its Forebears 1848–1984*, University of Delaware Press, Newark DE, 1987.

Steele, J., *Queen Mary*, Phaidon, London, 1995. An excellent, comprehensive book.

Streater, L., *Imperator 1913–1921/Berengaria 1921–1938*, Marine Publishing Concepts, Southampton, 2003.

Wall, R., *Ocean Liners*, Dutton, New York, 1977.

Zeni, D., *Forgotten Empress: The Empress of Ireland Story*, Goose Lane Editions, Fredericton, New Brunswick, 1998.

PICTURE CREDITS

All images are in the Sayers Collection of Ocean Liner Ephemera at the Bodleian Library, unless otherwise indicated. Finding aids are at www.bodleian.ox.ac.uk/johnson/search/indexes/named-collections. Any enquiries about the collection should be addressed to the John Johnson Collection: jjcoll@bodleian.ox.ac.uk.

FIGS. 1–3 Secrets of the Great Ocean Liners binder. FIG. 4 Sayers box 1. FIGS 5–6 Secrets of the Great Ocean Liners binder. FIG. 7 Sayers box 4: Queen Mary. FIG. 8 Secrets of the Great Ocean Liners binder. FIG. 9 Misc Glossies (2). FIG. 10 Italian Lines: Promotional Materials (9). FIG. 11 North German Lloyd: Rates and Schedules pre-1914 (16). FIG. 12 Canadian Pacific: Cruise Booklets (51). FIG. 13 Cunard Line: General Ephemera vol. 3. FIG. 14 Sayers box 1 (3/RS18). FIG. 15 Sayers box 1 (3/RS24). FIG. 16 Sayers box 9 (3/RS23). FIG. 17 Sayers Outsize box 1 (3/RS33a). FIG. 18 Canadian Pacific: Cruise Booklets (12). FIG. 19 Canadian Pacific: Cruise Booklets (30). FIG. 20 Sayers box 9: Hamburg-American/North German Lloyd. FIG. 21 Cunard: Glossies (10). FIG. 22 Sayers box 4 (2/RS2). FIG. 23 Sayers box 5 (2/RS7). FIG. 24 Sayers box 4 (2/RS3). FIG. 25 Sayers Albums 1. FIG. 26 Sayers box 7 (2/RS17). FIG. 27 Baggage Labels 3. FIG. 28 French Line: SS Normandie (5). FIG. 29 Sayers box 7 (2/RS17). FIG. 30 Misc Glossies (10). FIG. 31 SS United States Allowance books. FIG. 32 United States Line: Menus (10). FIG. 33 Private collection. FIG. 34 Sayers box 4. FIG. 35 P&O: Furniss sketches. FIG. 36 Sayers box 4: Queen Mary. FIG. 37 Sayers box 4: Queen Mary. FIG. 38 Baggage Labels 3. FIG. 39 Baggage Labels 2. FIG. 40 Secrets of the Great Ocean Liners binder. FIG. 41 Addenda 2017. FIGS 42–9 Secrets of the Great Ocean Liners binder. FIG. 50 Fans (3). FIG. 51 Secrets of the Great Ocean Liners binder. FIG. 52 Cunard: Passenger Lists 1. FIG. 53 White Star: Passenger Lists (6). FIG. 54 Canadian Pacific: Passenger Lists (28). FIG. 55

Misc Glossies (7). FIG. 56 Cunard: pre–1920 (17). FIG. 57 French Lines: SS Normandie (14). FIG. 58 Canadian Pacific: Cruise Booklets (38). FIG. 59 Private collection. FIG. 60 Furness Bermuda Line (15). FIG. 61 Secrets of the Great Ocean Liners binder. FIG. 62 Sayers Outsize box 1. FIGS 63–4 Secrets of the Great Ocean Liners binder. FIG. 65 Cunard Line: Vintage Menus (10). FIG. 66 French Line: SS Normandie (24). FIG. 67 Secrets of the Great Ocean Liners binder. FIG. 68 Anchor Line: Menus. FIG. 69 North German Lloyd: Menus Pre First War (6). FIG. 70 Postcard & Menu Combinations (80c). FIG. 71 White Star Menus (27). FIG. 72 Cunard: Menus 6 (18). FIG. 73 Panama Pacific Line (19). FIG. 74 White Star Menus (12). FIG. 75 Cunard Line: Vintage Menus (1) verso. FIGS 76–9 Secrets of the Great Ocean Liners binder. FIG. 80 French Line: Misc (8). FIG. 81 White Star Line: Cruises (22). FIG. 82 Cunard Line: Vintage Menus (32). FIG. 83 Sayers Outsize Menus (1). FIG. 84 Cunard Line: Vintage Menus (14). FIG. 85 Cunard Line: Vintage Menus (16). FIG. 86 Canadian Pacific: Postcards 1. FIG. 87 Fans (2). FIG. 88 Postcards: Miscellaneous. FIGS 89–90 Secrets of the Great Ocean Liners binder. FIG. 91 Canadian Pacific Cruises. FIGS 92–3 Secrets of the Great Ocean Liners binder. FIG. 94 Addenda 2017. FIGS 95–7 Secrets of the Great Ocean Liners binder. FIG. 98 Sayers Cunard Line: Vintage Menus (35). FIGS 99–100 Sayers Cunard Line: Vintage Menus (50). FIG. 101 Secrets of the Great Ocean Liners binder. FIG. 102 Unshelfmarked. FIG. 103–4 Secrets of the Great Ocean Liners binder. FIG. 105 World Cruise 1935. FIG. 106–8 Secrets of the Great Ocean Liners binder. FIGS 109–10 Private collections. FIG. 111 Queen Mary & Queen Elizabeth Early (13). FIG. 112–15 Secrets of the Great Ocean Liners binder. FIG. 116 North German Lloyd: Postcards. FIG. 117–24 Secrets of the Great Ocean Liners binder. FIG. 125 Handkerchiefs (1). FIG. 126 Secrets of the Great Ocean Liners binder. FIG. 127 Pinbacks and Mirrors (7). FIGS 128–31 Secrets of the Great Ocean Liners binder. FIG. 132 Titanic Postcards (14). FIG. 133 Secrets of the Great Ocean Liners binder. FIG. 134 Titanic Postcards (16). FIG. 135 Image courtesy of Aldridge & Son. FIG. 136 Secrets of the Great Ocean Liners binder. FIG. 137 Sayers Cunard Line: Vintage Menus (30). FIGS 138–40 Secrets of the Great Ocean Liners binder. FIG. 141 Image courtesy of Ray Ruddy. FIG. 142 Secrets of the Great Ocean Liners binder. FIG. 143–4 Strength Through Joy addenda.

INDEX OF SHIPS

Page numbers in italics refer to illustrations

HMHS = His/Her Majesty's Hospital Ship; HMS = His/Her Majesty's Ship; HMT = His Majesty's Transport; HMY = His/Her Majesty's Yacht; MS = Motor Ship; MV = Motor Vessel; RMMV = Royal Mail Motor Vessel; RMS = Royal Mail Ship; SS = Steamship; TSS = Twin-Screw Steamship; USS = United States Ship.

GENERAL INDEX

Page numbers in italics refer to illustrations